Legal Education and Professional Development —An Educational Continuum

Report of
The Task Force on Law Schools
and the Profession: Narrowing the Gap

American Bar Association
Section of Legal Education and Admissions
to the Bar

JULY 1992

©1992 American Bar Association. All
rights reserved. American Bar
Association, 750 North Lake Shore Drive,
Chicago, Illinois 60611, (312) 988-5000.

ISBN: 0-89707-774-1

Dedication

To our departed colleagues,

Dean Robert B. McKay,

Honorable Alvin B. Rubin, and

Dean Albert M. Sacks,

in appreciation of their lasting
contributions to legal education and
the professional development of lawyers.

AMERICAN BAR ASSOCIATION SECTION OF LEGAL EDUCATION AND ADMISSIONS TO THE BAR

Task Force on Law Schools and the Profession: Narrowing the Gap

Robert MacCrate, Esq., *Chairperson*
Professor Peter W. Martin, *Vice Chairperson*
Associate Dean Peter A. Winograd, *Vice Chairperson*
Professor J. Michael Norwood, *Reporter*

Members

Cory M. Amron, Esq.
Professor Anthony G. Amsterdam
Honorable Dennis W. Archer (to December 1990)
Professor Curtis J. Berger (to December 1991;
    thereafter AALS Liaison)
Talbot D'Alemberte, Esq. (to December 1990)
Dean Joseph D. Harbaugh
Professor Richard G. Huber
Dean Maximilian W. Kempner
Dean John R. Kramer
Dean Robert B. McKay (deceased, 1990)
Honorable Robert R. Merhige, Jr.
John O. Mudd, Esq.
Dean Susan Westerberg Prager
Norman Redlich, Esq.
Harold L. Rock, Esq.
Honorable Alvin B. Rubin (deceased, 1991)
Dean Albert M. Sacks (deceased, 1991)
Professor Roy T. Stuckey
Michael Traynor, Esq.
Honorable Sol Wachtler
Honorable Rosalie E. Wahl
Dean Marilyn Yarbrough

Association of American Law Schools Liaisons

Dean Betsy Levin
Professor Thomas D. Morgan

American Bar Foundation Liaisons

Bryant G. Garth, Esq.
Joanne Martin, Esq.

Task Force Consultants

Professor Bruce A. Green
Professor Randy Hertz
Richard Diebold Lee, Esq.
Professor Marjorie A. McDiarmid

Special Consultants

Dean James P. White
Kathleen S. Grove, Esq.

Staff Directors

Frederick R. Franklin, Esq. (to December 1991)
Rachel Patrick, Esq. (as of January 1992)

Contents

PROCESS AND PROCEDURES OF
THE TASK FORCE

The Council of the Section of Legal Education and Admissions to the Bar established the Task Force at the beginning of 1989. Justice Rosalie Wahl, chairperson of the Section, appointed the initial members. Over the ensuing three years the Council of the Section has lent strong support to the Task Force and the successive chairpersons of the Section (Philip S. Anderson, Esq., Dean Norman Redlich, Jose Garcia-Pedrosa, Esq. and Dean Henry Ramsey) have worked closely with it. Justice Wahl and Dean Redlich were appointed members of the Task Force following their terms as chairperson of the Section.

From the outset the Office of the ABA Consultant on Legal Education has been an indispensable resource for the Task Force both in collecting the data from the Task Force's survey and by providing information from its unique store of historical materials relating to legal education. Both Dean James White and Assistant Consultant Kathleen Grove have been active participants in the work of the Task Force.

The Task Force met for the first time on May 19, 1989 in Washington, D.C., surveyed earlier studies, identified sources of data and information potentially useful in its work and began assembling a comprehensive bibliography (Appendix A to the Report is the bibliography of material utilized by the Task Force).

As part of its effort to describe the breadth and complexities of the legal profession (see Part I of this Report), the Task Force decided, at its initial meeting, that it would be useful to update the empirical data about the profession contained in earlier studies such as that of Zemans and Rosenblum, *The Making of a Public Profession*. To that end, the Task Force enlisted the assistance of the American Bar Foundation, which conducted a study of recent law school graduates and their employers that has informed the deliberations of the Task Force. This project was supported by a generous grant from the Charles E. Culpepper Foundation. The findings of the Foundation study "Learning Lawyering: Where Do Lawyers Acquire Practice Skills?" are summarized in Appendix B to the Report. B.G. Garth, Director, and Joanne Martin, Assistant Director, have acted as liaisons to the Task Force and greatly assisted in the development of this Report.

As described in Part II of the Report, the Task Force conducted an in-depth study of the full range of skills and values necessary for a lawyer to assume professional responsibility for handling a legal matter. A subcommittee of the Task Force enlisted Professor Randy

Hertz of the New York University Law School as a volunteer Consultant to conduct the study and to assist in the development of the Statement of Skills and Values. A tentative draft of the Statement was completed in June 1991 and widely circulated for comment on its content and the uses to which it might be put. This circulation was generously undertaken by West Publishing Company and by ALI-ABA through its CLE Journal and Register. The Statement of Fundamental Lawyering Skills and Professional Values in Part II of the Report is the product. It will also be published in a free standing edition available to all who wish to make use of it.

To broaden the perspective on the issue of the preparation of lawyers for practice, a subcommittee of the Task Force conducted four public hearings between February 1990 and June 1991. Participants in the hearings were asked their opinion: on whether newly admitted lawyers were prepared to practice law without supervision; as to what should be taught to improve graduates for practice; on how any additional training, if desirable, should be accomplished; and whether they favored a skills training requirement and/or performance testing for bar admissions. The subcommittee responsible for the conduct of the hearings prepared a report which is appended as Appendix C. The information obtained through the hearings was extensively supplemented by informal submissions made to the Task Force over the entire period of its deliberations.

Impressed by the lack of any authoritative appraisal of the state of skills and values instruction in the law schools, the Task Force in 1990 undertook a comprehensive survey of ABA-approved law schools regarding the extent of curriculum development in the skills training area and the availability of such programs to students. The questionnaire sent to the law schools is Appendix D to the Report. The data gathered through this survey, together with that from other surveys to which the Task Force was given access, are the principal bases for the assessment in Chapter 7.B. of the Report "Current Instruction in Lawyering Skills and Professional Values." The University of New Mexico donated substantial computer support to this project. Professor Marjorie A. McDiarmid of the West Virginia University College of Law was initially enlisted in 1990 as a volunteer Consultant to help design the computer program for the storage of the collected data. In 1992 she returned to the project generously giving of her time and experience to provide special support for bringing other survey materials together with that gathered by the Task Force.

To develop a comprehensive picture of post-admission legal education the Task Force was fortunate to enlist as a volunteer

Consultant, Richard Diebold Lee, Esq. of the California bar, a former law professor at Temple University, director of in-house training for the law firm of Morrison & Foerster and chair of the California State Bar's Committee on MCLE. He made a principal contribution to Chapters 8, 9 and 10 of the Report regarding the role of continuing legal education in professional development after law school and the need for a national institute to enhance the continuum of professional development.

Professor Bruce Green of the faculty of the Fordham University School of Law joined the Task Force as a further volunteer Consultant and gathered the material for the portions of Chapter 8 of the Report that relate to the licensing process and programs for bar applicants and new lawyers, including the material in Appendix E on practical skills training programs in Commonwealth countries.

In developing the material with respect to the proposed national institute for the practice of law, the Task Force had the benefit of consultations with Paul Wolkin, the Director of ALI-ABA; Richard Carter, the Director of the ABA Division for Professional Education; and Victor Rubino, the Executive Director of the Practising Law Institute.

The Task Force functioned during its early stages through seven active subcommittees responsible for developing separate phases of the project. In the final stages of the project consecutive drafts of segments of this Report were circulated among Task Force members. It is conservatively estimated that in excess of 12,000 hours of volunteer time and substantial supporting services provided without charge were given directly to the project over its three year span. The ABA Business Law Section made grants to support the work of the Task Force during 1991 and 1992 and the Sections of Legal Education and Admissions to the Bar and of Tort and Insurance Practice are helping to defray the Task Force's costs of publication.

The Task Force held seven plenary meetings:

May 19, 1989	Washington, D.C.
December 4, 1989	New York City
April 22, 1990	New York City
November 2-3, 1990	St. Louis, Missouri
April 26-27, 1991	New York City
November 22-23, 1991	New York City
March 27-28, 1992	New York City

The St. Louis meeting in November 1990 was held in conjunction with a conference conducted by the ABA Standing Committee on Lawyer Competence. The five plenary sessions of the Task Force in

New York City were hosted by the law firm of Sullivan & Cromwell which over the more than three years of the project provided extensive logistical and staff support without charge.

Over the life of the project the Task Force has greatly benefited from its liaison with the Association of American Law Schools provided by Dean Betsy Levin, Executive Director of AALS, Professor Thomas Morgan, the President of AALS in 1990, and, during 1992, Professor Curtis Berger, who became President-elect of AALS while serving as an appointed member of the Task Force.

Introduction
to the Report

Introduction

The Common Enterprise

At its birth this Task Force acquired a name that projects a distorted image of a legal education community separated from the "profession" by a "gap" that requires narrowing. As the Task Force proceeded to fulfill the mission suggested by its name and to narrow the "gap," it recognized that the image was false. Thus, the title of this Report attempts to correct the distortion, and suggests a different and more accurate vision of the relationship between legal education and the practicing bar. Both communities are part of one profession. The skills and values of the competent lawyer are developed along a continuum that starts before law school, reaches its most formative and intensive stage during the law school experience, and continues throughout a lawyer's professional career. Legal educators and practicing lawyers should stop viewing themselves as separated by a "gap" and recognize that they are engaged in a common enterprise—the education and professional development of the members of a great profession.

Law schools and the practicing bar have different missions to perform, and they function in different experiential worlds with different cultures. These differences are pronounced and result from a system of legal education that relies on university-based professional schools for the formal education of the country's lawyers.[1] The transition during this century from a clerkship/mentoring system of educating lawyers to reliance on professional schools in a university setting has been traced by many observers to the acceptance of the Langdellian appellate case-method, which views the study of law as an academic science. Other observers have pointed to the dissatisfaction of the profession with the exploitative aspects of law-office training and the poor quality of the product. Other, more skeptical, observers have claimed that the requirement of a professional degree, and the additional requirement of an undergraduate degree before admission to law school, was devised by the profession as an unnecessary and artificial barrier to entry.

---

1. In terms of their structure, curriculum, and academic emphasis, the 15 freestanding ABA-approved law schools are virtually indistinguishable from their university-based counterparts.

3

Whatever may have been the genesis, the in-house clerkship form of legal education was increasingly incompatible with the needs of the emerging corporate law firms created to meet the complex needs of institutional clients. This may account for the parallel development in this century of three interrelated entities—the modern American industrial and financial corporation functioning within the complex administrative state, the multi-service corporate law firm structured to service its corporate clients, and the university-based law school that emphasizes analytical skills and the ability to deal with complex legal issues.

Thus, in contrast to virtually every other country, prospective lawyers in the United States commence their study of law in a professional school, after receiving an undergraduate degree. Students in other countries experience their first academic contact with the law as undergraduates, similar to students studying history, literature or philosophy. In other countries, the practicing bar assumes the major responsibility for accomplishing the transition of these students into practicing lawyers. Here, the bar's role is ill-defined.

The Gap Between Expectation and Reality

It has long been apparent that American law schools cannot reasonably be expected to shoulder the task of converting even very able students into full-fledged lawyers licensed to handle legal matters. Thus, a gap develops between the expectation and the reality, resulting in complaints and recriminations from legal educators and practicing lawyers. The lament of the practicing bar is a steady refrain: "They can't draft a contract, they can't write, they've never seen a summons, the professors have never been inside a courtroom." Law schools offer the traditional responses: "We teach them how to think, we're not trade schools, we're centers of scholarship and learning, practice is best taught by practitioners."

Too often these responses are thoughtless reactions to unfair criticism, and reflect an unwillingness of the academy and the practicing bar fully to understand the cultures, needs, aspirations, value systems, and accomplishments of each community. The community of over 6,000 full-time law professors does not consist of ivory-tower scholars removed from the problems of the profession and concerned only with their academic pursuits. Conversely, lawyers are not oblivious to the contributions of law schools to the quality of the profession or to a broad-based legal education system that extends beyond technical skills and the knowledge of certain substantive areas of law.

Nevertheless, the criticisms that the law schools and the practicing bar level at each other have a strong base in reality. From the perspective of law schools, the practicing bar may not fully appreciate the benefits, and the limitations, that flow from a system of academically strong university-based law schools. Law teachers are university professors with academic responsibilities and aspirations that extend both to teaching and to scholarship. While law schools vary in the emphasis placed on scholarship, there are few, if any, ABA-approved law schools that do not incorporate a scholarship component into the requirement for tenure. A strong academic cultural commitment to research and scholarship arises from the university's academic requirements, the law school's self-imposed academic standards, ABA accreditation standards and AALS membership requirements, and the intellectual aspirations of individual professors. Law schools achieve national status in large part because of the scholarly reputations of their faculties. Such reputations help attract the best students who, in return, have the best job opportunities upon graduation. Inevitably, law schools tend to seek out, as new faculty members, those who show promise of high-level scholarship.

While practicing lawyers undoubtedly appreciate the value of the law school experience to their own careers, surveys understandably indicate that practicing lawyers believe that their law school training left them deficient in skills that they were forced to acquire after graduation. Practitioners tend to view much academic scholarship as increasingly irrelevant to their day-to-day concerns, particularly when compared with the great treatises of an earlier era. It is not surprising that many practicing lawyers believe law professors are more interested in pursuing their own intellectual interests than in helping the legal profession address matters of important current concern.

The gap between the teaching and practice segments of the profession is further accentuated by the apparent lack of participation by law professors in the activities of the organized bar. Whether this results from a lack of interest on the part of law teachers, or the cost of such participation which must, in most cases, be borne by the individual faculty member, or whether law professors perceive (probably incorrectly) that their involvement in the work of the organized bar is not particularly welcomed, both the organized bar and the law schools suffer from this apparent failure of the two cultures to work in the areas of common interests.

Actually, law teachers are more actively involved in the work of the profession than is commonly recognized. They serve as members of bar association committees, are frequent participants on continuing legal education panels, and are actively involved as reporters for the various projects of the American Law Institute. The recent group membership program of the American Bar Association enables full-time faculty members of law schools that joined the program to become members of the American Bar Association without paying the membership dues.

Development of the Skills Training Curriculum

It is, of course, in the area of curriculum that the practicing bar has traditionally been most critical of law schools. Paradoxically, it is precisely in the area of curriculum development where law schools have made changes that are most responsive to criticism from the bar. For that reason there is often widespread resentment at the failure of the practicing bar to appreciate and recognize legal education's response to the concerns of the bar.

Unquestionably, the most significant development in legal education in the post-World War II era has been the growth of the skills training curriculum. As recently as twenty years ago, the typical skills training component of a law school curriculum consisted of a first-year moot court program, and perhaps a trial advocacy course. Today, clinical courses, both in a simulated and live-client setting, occupy an important place in the curriculum of virtually all ABA-approved law schools. Many are taught by full-time faculty members who, pursuant to an ABA accreditation standard, are eligible for tenure or some form of equivalent job security. A clinician is present on virtually every ABA site inspection team to help the team evaluate the quality of the law school's skills-training program, with particular emphasis placed on the commitment of resources and the availability of full-time faculty supervision when students are involved in externship forms of clinical programs.

A major aspect of the work of the Task Force has been to conduct an in-depth survey to document the full extent of curriculum development in the skills training area, and the availability of such programs to students. The survey demonstrates the major commitment of resources that law schools have made to the development of skills training programs. Despite this commitment there is a widespread belief in the legal education community that the practicing bar has taken little notice of these important developments in legal education while decrying, at the same time, the "gap" between legal education and the needs of the profession. Most importantly, few employers appear interested in whether students have enrolled in such courses or how they perform in them.[2] To legal educators, this reaction reveals an inexcusable indifference to legal education's commitment to skills training and calls into question the legitimacy of the practicing bar's incessant criticisms and constant demands that law schools should do more.

For What Must Lawyers Prepare?

At its first meeting the Task Force considered a threshold question: For what kind of a profession are we trying to educate lawyers? The law teaching profession has advanced considerably beyond the point where, fifty years ago, Karl Llewellyn could confidently state: "No faculty, and, I believe, not one percent of instructors, knows what it or they are really trying to educate for." Nevertheless, the Task Force was aware that even law teachers with a strong interest in developments in the profession have been unable to keep pace with the rapid changes. It was important, therefore, to gather an all-inclusive overview of the profession today, its great growth, change, diversity in practice settings and differentiation in lawyers' work, as well as its organization and regulation. Information was gathered from a wide array of sources both within and outside the ABA. Part I of this Report: "The Profession for Which Lawyers Must Prepare" is the result of that project.

The Skills and Values to Be Acquired

Early in its deliberations this Task Force concluded that it was not possible to consider how to "bridge" or "narrow" the alleged "gap" between law schools and the practicing bar without first identifying the fundamental skills and values that every lawyer should acquire before assuming responsibility for the handling of a legal matter. Surprisingly, throughout the course of extensive decades-long debates about what law schools should do to educate students for the practice of law, there has been no in-depth study of the full range of skills and values that are necessary in order for a lawyer to assume the professional responsibility of handling a legal matter. Recognizing that such a study is the necessary predicate for determining the extent to which law schools and the practicing bar should assume responsibility for the development of these skills and values, the Task Force prepared a Statement of Fundamental Lawyering Skills and Professional Values. In Part II of the Report, the Task Force sets forth its view of the skills and values new lawyers should seek to acquire.

---

2. The American Bar Foundation survey of hiring partners found, for example, that this selection of particular courses has little or no impact on hiring decisions.

The Continuing Process of Professional Development

The Task Force's collective effort has resulted in the recognition that the task of educating students to assume the full responsibilities of a lawyer is a continuing process that neither begins nor ends with three years of law school study. Having reached this conclusion, the Task Force, in Part III of the Report, has identified the roles of law schools and the practicing bar in assisting prospective lawyers as they move along the continuum from applicant to student to qualified lawyer.

Thus, we have concluded that there is no "gap." There is only an arduous road of professional development along which all prospective lawyers should travel. It is the responsibility of law schools and the practicing bar to assist students and lawyers to develop the skills and values required to complete the journey. To identify those skills and values, to describe what law schools and the practicing bar are now doing to advance the professional development of lawyers, and to recommend how the legal education community and the practicing bar can join together to fulfill their respective responsibilities to the profession and the consuming public has been the central mission of this Task Force.

Part I
The Profession for Which
Lawyers Must Prepare

An Overview of the Profession

The legal profession for which law students prepare today is larger and more diverse than ever before and yet is more organized and unified as a profession than at anytime in its history. It is also a vastly changed profession not only in its demography, but in how lawyers practice, the variety of services they provide, the multiplying of areas of law, the differentiation of practice settings and the different methods for delivering legal services now employed. But at the same time, the organization of the Bar has grown and the law has remained a single profession identified with a perceived common body of learning, skills and values.

We have attempted to piece together an overview of the profession as a whole, providing a picture of the extraordinary growth in both the number of lawyers and in the demand for lawyers' services, the change in the profession's gender makeup and its belated opening to racial minorities. Against a background of great growth in law and its complexity, profound social, economic and technological change, and a societal movement toward greater specialization, we note how in virtually every practice setting the individual lawyer is compelled to concentrate in one or several areas of law, while clinging to the traditional image of being a "generalist."

We have gathered available data on lawyers in the different practice settings of private practice, as well as on in-house counsel for private organizations and for local, state and federal government. In addition, we sketch the rise of the "new providers" of legal services for the poor and for persons of moderate means and the growth in lawyer advocacy for group legal rights under the rubric of "public interest law."

Finally, we examine how the legal profession organized itself in its quest for identity and professional status; transferred legal education and the place where a lawyer's professional development begins from the law office to the law school; and, with the support of the Judiciary, successfully preserved, to this time, the vision of a single profession with a common notion of what it means to be a lawyer.

11

Chapter One
Lawyers and Legal Services: Growth, Change and Multicultural Diversity

A. Explosion in Numbers and Use of Legal Services
B. The Change in Gender Make-up
C. The Belated Opening to Minorities and Diversity

A. Explosion in Numbers and Use of Legal Services

The phenomenal growth in the number of lawyers since World War II has been accompanied by an unprecedented increase in demand for legal work, both from business clients and on behalf of previously unrepresented individuals. One result has been that by 1990 the profession had become a $91 billion-a-year service industry, employing more than 940,000 people, and surpassing the medical profession in the number of licensed professionals, with one lawyer for every 320 persons in the United States.[1]

The growth has affected the manner in which law is practiced and how law firms are structured and organize their work. It has permitted greater specialization in law practice and an increased division of labor among lawyers.

The exceptional growth in the profession has permitted many changes, and stimulated the call for others. Some observers have pointed to the paradox in having a burgeoning number of lawyers at the same time that increasing numbers of ordinary citizens are unable to obtain effective and affordable representation for their personal legal problems.[2] At least a partial explanation for this apparent contradiction lies in the substantially increased use of legal services by those who are able to pay and have been willing to pay for lawyers' services.

The explosive growth in the number of lawyers began in the law schools. It was possible only because the law schools first attracted, then enrolled and taught record numbers of students. In the years

---

1. U.S. INDUSTRIAL OUTLOOK 1991, PROFESSIONAL SERVICES: LEGAL SERVICES (SIC81), at 52-4; *see also* R.L. ABEL, AMERICAN LAWYERS, Table 23, at 281 (1989).
2. *See* Hickerson, *Structural Change in Nebraska's Legal Profession and the Implications for Broad Based Efficacy in Representation*, 15 CREIGHTON LAW REV. 1 (1981); Galanter, *Why the 'Haves' Come Out Ahead: Speculation on the Limits of Legal Change*, 9 LAW & SOC'Y REV. 95, 114-19 (1974).

immediately after World War II, when the then-existing law schools accommodated record numbers of students by doubling-up and offering accelerated programs for returning veterans, admissions to law school temporarily soared and a surge in new admissions to the bar followed. However, enrollments fell back by the middle-1950s to their pre-World War II level and the number of new entrants to the bar similarly declined and remained at lower levels until the early 1960s.

By 1963-64, however, enrollments matched the post-World War II bulge and there began a yearly increase in the number of law school enrollments that fueled the profession's remarkable expansion between 1965 and 1991.[3] New law schools were established to accommodate the rising tide of applicants. The number of ABA-approved schools grew from 112 in 1948 to 176 in 1991. The following table shows for selected years the climb in LSAT test-takers, number of law schools, JD enrollments and new entrants to the bar.[4]

Academic Year	LSAT Test-Takers[5]	ABA-Approved Law Schools	J.D. Enrollments	First Admissions to the Bar
1965–66	39,406	136	56,510	13,109
1970–71	74,092	146	78,018	17,922
1975–76	133,546	163	111,047	34,930
1980–81	112,750	171	119,501	41,997
1985–86	95,129[6]	175	124,092	42,450
1991–92	152,685[7]	176	129,580	43,286

The resulting growth in the profession during this period was unprecedented. In the 60 years preceding World War II, the number of lawyers grew at approximately the same rate as the total population of the United States. In 1880 the total U.S. population was approximately 50 million and included some 64,000 "lawyers" (which in the 19th century census included notaries, title abstractors and justices of the peace). This meant that there was one "lawperson" for every 780 persons. Over the next 60 years while the population grew three-fold to around 150 million, the number of

---

3. In one four-year period, 1980 to 1984, the profession grew by 107,000.

4. *Source*: AMERICAN BAR ASSOCIATION 1991 REVIEW OF LEGAL EDUCATION and ANNUAL REPORTS OF LAW SCHOOL ADMISSION SERVICES.

5. The test-taker volume for the test year ending in the first year stated.

6. Between 1974 and 1986 there was a 32% decrease in the number of LSAT test-takers (from 135,397 to 91,921).

7. This figure, provided by Law School Admission Services, includes 839 test-takers who were Saturday Sabbath Observers not included in the 1991 test year total reported in the 1991 REVIEW OF LEGAL EDUCATION.

lawyers (with a few temporary aberrations) grew at approximately the same rate. The overall ratio of population to lawyers in 1940 was very much as it had been in 1880.

Since 1950 there have been radical changes in this ratio, as the following table reflects:[8]

7/1–6/30 Year	Lawyers	Ratio of Population/Lawyers
1947–48	169,489	790/1
1950–51	221,605	695/1
1960–61	285,933	627/1
1970–71	355,242	572/1
1980–81	542,205	418/1
1990–91	777,119	320/1

This ratio of population to lawyers varies considerably from state to state. The geographical spread and the uneven distribution of the estimated 777,000 lawyers, state by state, is reflected in the following table of the estimated number of attorneys resident and active in each jurisdiction as of December 1990-January 1991 and showing the ratio for each jurisdiction of total population to lawyers:[9]

	Resident and Active Attorneys	Ratio of Population/ Lawyers
Dist. of Columbia	29,397	21/1
Rhode Island	3,600	179/1
New York	95,005	189/1
Massachusetts	27,387	220/1
Colorado	14,596	226/1
Connecticut	13,400	245/1
Illinois	43,908	260/1
Alaska	2,062	267/1
New Jersey	27,820	278/1
California	99,631	299/1
Minnesota	14,301	306/1
Vermont	1,814	310/1
Virgin Islands	326	312/1
Hawaii	3,516	315/1
Maryland	14,943	320/1
Louisiana	12,573	336/1
Washington	14,375	339/1
Oklahoma	9,132	345/1

8. *Sources*: AMERICAN BAR FOUNDATION, 1985 SUPPLEMENT TO THE LAWYER STATISTICAL REPORT; R.L. ABEL, *supra* note 1, Table 22, at 280; ABA Membership Department.
9. *Source*: ABA Membership Department and 1990 U.S. Census figures.

	Resident and Active Attorneys	Ratio of Population/ Lawyers
Texas	48,474	350/1
Oregon	7,995	355/1
Georgia	17,880	362/1
Kansas	6,667	372/1
Nebraska	4,205	375/1
Pennsylvania	31,457	378/1
Maine	3,199	384/1
Florida	33,245	389/1
New Mexico	3,883	390/1
Ohio	27,309	397/1
Michigan	23,168	401/1
Missouri	12,752	401/1
Montana	1,989	402/1
Tennessee	11,805	413/1
Virginia	14,464	428/1
New Hampshire	2,565	432/1
Arizona	8,456	433/1
Idaho	2,260	446/1
Delaware	1,468	454/1
Kentucky	7,794	473/1
Iowa	5,834	476/1
Nevada	2,515	478/1
Puerto Rico	7,208	489/1
Wisconsin	10,000	489/1
North Dakota	1,285	497/1
Wyoming	898	506/1
Alabama	7,886	512/1
Utah	3,212	536/1
Mississippi	4,790	537/1
Indiana	10,296	538/1
South Dakota	1,293	538/1
West Virginia	3,296	544/1
Arkansas	4,095	574/1
South Carolina	5,616	621/1
North Carolina	10,074	658/1
	777,119	320/1

It will be noted that by far the greatest concentration of lawyers in relation to population in any jurisdiction is in the District of Columbia, where the ratio drops to one lawyer for every 21 residents.[10]

---

10. *See* C.A. HORSKY, THE WASHINGTON LAWYER, (1952); *cf.* T. Susman, *A Perspective on the Washington Lawyer Today and Charles Horsky's Washington Lawyer of 1952*, 44 ADMINISTRATIVE LAW REV. 1 (1992).

A further effect of adding so many new lawyers to the profession has been to alter materially its composition with respect to age and experience in practice. The median age of lawyers dropped between 1960 and 1980 from 46 years to 39 years, with lawyers under age 36 making up almost 40 percent of the lawyer population.[11]

A striking feature of the changes since World War II has been that the great growth in the number of lawyers has been matched by the growth in demand for all kinds of legal services, particularly from the business community. The economic base that supports legal services greatly expanded. For much of the past 40 years, there have been steadily increasing numbers of clients willing and able to pay for lawyers' services.

New areas of law and regulation, largely designed by lawyers, have created whole new fields for legal services: the environment, occupational health and safety, nuclear energy, discrimination and individual rights, health and mental health care, biotechnology, the development and use of computers. At the same time, economic activity vastly expanded, new business enterprises multiplied and the number of transactions in every segment of the economy proliferated.[12]

---

11. It is possible that one consequence of this decline in the proportion of senior and experienced lawyers was a reduction in mentoring by senior lawyers which some observers have noted. By 1988, the median age had risen slightly to 40 years as new entrants of the previous decade moved into their middle years, the number of bar admissions stabilized and the average age of new admittees rose. *See* AMERICAN BAR FOUNDATION 1988 SUPPLEMENT TO THE LAWYER STATISTICAL REPORT, at 3. The total number of lawyers under age 35 rose only from 191,500 in 1980 to 198,400 in 1988. Id. at 5.

12. Professor Thomas C. Fischer surveyed these developments in this way:

Much of the growth in demand for legal services has occurred in sharply expanding or entirely new fields of practice, e.g., new business formation, mergers and acquisitions, international trade and finance, malpractice, consumer protection, environmental concerns, tax reforms and litigation.

[Lawyers] have become "transactional engineers," whose contributions make business ventures more certain or less risky. Whatever their cost, they are viewed as indispensable. . . .

Economic growth has been accompanied by an increase in the number of statutes and regulations governing business and private transactions. States and local governments are entering regulatory fields once chiefly federal. . . .

The increase in legalism and regulation is most evident when several individuals or groups compete for scarce resources (e.g., the fishing and oil industries over George's Bank) or over social policy (e.g, toxic waste and zoning). . . .

. . . . many legal risks are not highly complex, and have for years been handled efficiently and economically by solo or small firm practitioners. . . . it remains a solid, predictable base of legal activity. Indeed, such transactions probably comprise well over one-half of all legal transactions in the United States today.

T.C. FISCHER, LEGAL EDUCATION, LAW PRACTICE AND THE ECONOMY: A NEW ENGLAND STUDY, 77 (1990).

Significantly, individuals who had never before sought legal assistance began seeking help from lawyers, while the courts declared the rights of persons charged with serious crime to have counsel and of groups of people collectively to seek legal redress in the courts.

In sum, while the number of ABA-approved law schools increased from 136 in 1965 to 175 in 1990, J.D. enrollments rose from 56,510 in 1965-66 to 129,580 in 1990-91.[13] Over the same period, the practice of law grew from a service activity estimated at $4.2 billion-a-year in 1965[14] to an estimated $91 billion-a-year in 1990.[15] The parallel growth of law schools and law practice underscores the great interdependence of those who teach law and those who practice law.

B. The Change in Gender Make-up

Perhaps the most significant change during the 1970s and 1980s, first among law students and thereafter in the legal profession as a whole, was the growth in the number of women choosing the law as a career vocation. The number of women applicants and students in ABA-approved law schools increased from 4 percent in the mid-1960s to more than 40 percent in the 1990s.[16]

The following table vividly illustrates this phenomenon:[17]

Academic Year	Women J.D. Enrollments	Percent of Total Enrollments
1965–66	2,374	4.2%
1970–71	6,682	8.6%
1980–81	40,834	34.2%
1991–92	55,110	42.5%

We noted in the preceding section the decrease between 1974 and 1986 in the number of LSAT test-takers,[18] but it was almost entirely a male phenomenon as the accompanying chart of LSAT tests

---

13. AMERICAN BAR ASSOCIATION 1991 REVIEW OF LEGAL EDUCATION.
14. 1981 STATISTICAL ABSTRACT OF THE UNITED STATES, at 444.
15. U.S. INDUSTRIAL OUTLOOK 1991, *supra* note 1, at 52-4.
16. In 1964 there were three law schools that did not admit women; in 1974 the last one of the 3 dropped its ban on the enrollment of women. (Information provided by the ABA Consultant on Legal Education)
17. *Source*: AMERICAN BAR ASSOCIATION 1991 ANNUAL REVIEW OF LEGAL EDUCATION.
18. See *supra* note 6.

administered, provided by the Law School Admission Services, makes apparent.

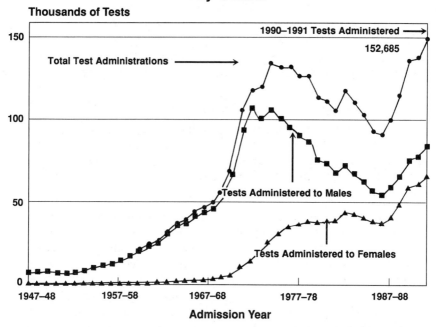

LSAT TESTS ADMINISTERED
by Gender

Thousands of Tests

1990–1991 Tests Administered ⟶

152,685

Total Test Administrations ⟶

•Tests Administered to Males

Tests Administered to Females

150

100

50

0

1947–48   1957–58   1967–68   1977–78   1987–88

Admission Year

The first significant increase in the admission of women to the Bar occurred in the 1968-69 court year. From 1951 to 1967, the percentage of new admittees to the Bar who were women had hovered around 3 percent, but in the 1968-69 year it increased by one-third to 4 percent. Further increases in women admittees to the Bar followed year-by-year, with women comprising 34 percent of new admittees by 1982-83 and more than 40 percent by 1990-91.[19]

With this rising tide of women admittees, the percentage of all lawyers who are women has risen sharply in the past two decades as the following table reflects:[20]

---

19. See *supra* note 17.
20. These figures were provided by the ABA Commission on Women in the Profession (June 1991).

Year	Women lawyers as a percentage of total lawyer population
1950–51	2.5%
1960–61	2.6%
1970–71	2.8%
1980–81	8.1%
1990–91	22.0%

Among lawyers under 36 years, women in 1985 comprised approximately 24 percent and by 1988 almost 30 percent.[21]

Since the rate of growth of the number of women in the profession substantially exceeded that of men, by 1988 women lawyers were, as a group, substantially younger than men, with a median age for women of 34, contrasted to a median age for men of 42. Three-quarters (74%) of female lawyers were less than 40 years of age and almost 90% were under 45. In contrast, the majority (59%) of male lawyers were 40 or older.[22]

In what segments of the profession has this growing number of women lawyers found employment? Data comparing the employment of women and men in the legal workplace suggest contrasting patterns. A smaller percentage of women lawyers (66.4%) than of men (73%) are in private practice. On the other hand, a higher percentage of women than men have legal employment in government, in private associations and in legal aid and public defender offices. Women lawyers in 1988 while comprising only 14.9 percent of the lawyers in private practice, were estimated to be 24.4 percent of federal government lawyers, 27.3 percent of state and local government lawyers, 33.3 percent of private association lawyers and 36.5 percent of the lawyers working in legal aid offices and as public defenders.[23]

The annual Employment Reports and Salary Surveys of the National Association for Law Placement (NALP) for the period 1978 to 1990 indicate, however, that the legal employment patterns of women and men graduates are now tending to converge with less and less distinction between them in their first legal employment, but that in judicial clerkships, government and public interest positions, the percentages of women consistently exceed those of men,

---

21. These figures were derived from the AMERICAN BAR FOUNDATION, 1985 and 1988 SUPPLEMENTS TO THE LAWYER STATISTICAL REPORT.
22. AMERICAN BAR FOUNDATION, 1988 SUPPLEMENT TO THE LAWYER STATISTICAL REPORT, at 3.
23. Id. at 4.

while the percentage of men entering law firms exceeds that of women.[24]

The Gender and Law Project of Stanford Law School found a number of distinguishing features between the careers of the women and men in the law whom it surveyed:[25] that more female graduates (but not students) than male graduates expressed the desire to serve society;[26] that female graduates remained a shorter time in their first job than males;[27] that significantly more men (64.8%) than women (45.2%) reported that they were practicing corporate law;[28] and that more men (43.1%) than women (27.4%) found the adversarial part of their work important to their satisfaction with legal work.[29] The survey found that the women (29.4%) were much more likely than the men (8.6%) to have interrupted career paths (76.8% for maternity) and to work part-time at some point in their careers (women: 31.3%; men: 9.5%).[30]

Women who were older than traditional law students appear to have blazed a path for older men as well to enroll in law school. Law is, increasingly, a second career and law firms' recruiting patterns are changing to give older graduates of both sexes equal opportunity with the traditional graduates in their mid-twenties.

While most barriers for women entrants to initial employment in the law appear to be falling, bias and sexual stereotyping continue to confront women in various practice settings. In addition, various commentators have written of the "glass ceiling" in the legal profession, which forecloses women from its higher echelons, whether in law firms, corporate law departments, the law schools, the judiciary, public sector employment or bar associations.[31]

Despite the problems women lawyers continue to encounter, it is clear that their substantial presence and growing role in the

---

24. *See* NATIONAL ASSOCIATION FOR LAW PLACEMENT, CLASS OF 1988 EMPLOYMENT REPORT AND SALARY SURVEY (ERSS) (1990) at 118-121, CLASS OF 1989 ERSS (1991) at 68-75, and CLASS OF 1990 ERSS (1991) at 62-70; *see also* AMERICAN BAR ASSOCIATION YOUNG LAWYERS DIVISION, THE STATE OF THE LEGAL PROFESSION 1990, Chapter 14, "The Status of Women in the Profession," at 63-70.

25. 40 STAN. L. REV. 1209 (1988).

26. Id. at 1241.

27. Id. at 1243.

28. Id. at 1245.

29. Id. at 1246.

30. Id.

31. *E.g.*, L.A. La Mothe, J.M. Snyder, R.P. West, *Women as Rainmakers*, 7 AMERICAN BAR ASSOCIATION LITIG. J. no. 3 (1991) at 29; Florence K. Murray, *Women and the Law, Have We Really Come a Long Way?*, AMERICAN BAR ASSOCIATION JUDGES JOURNAL (Winter 1990), at 19–23, 48; REPORT OF AMERICAN BAR ASSOCIATION COMMISSION ON WOMEN IN THE PROFESSION, "Women and the ABA" (August 1989); *Women in Law*, 74 A.B.A.J. (June 1988), at 49.

profession have placed on the agenda, in the law schools and in the profession at large, matters of particular concern to women which previously were ignored and have provoked serious reexamination of the legal workplace.

The interpersonal issues brought to the fore by women lawyers have included matters relating to pregnancy; rape; sexual harassment in the workplace; judicial treatment of domestic violence; sexual relations between attorney and client; sexual stereotyping and other forms of bias and discrimination in both the courts and the other practice settings which are part of a lawyer's professional life.[32]

The expressed concerns of women lawyers have also raised consciousness on a broad range of issues pertaining to the established structure of the practice of law. These structural issues include the work/family conflict, the rigidity of the established practice-model, pregnancy and parenting leaves, day-care, flexible work schedules, including working part-time, temporary hiring of lawyers and alternative tracks for career advancement.[33]

Legal scholars debate the issues as to women's "different voice" and the "sameness" and "difference" between women and men,[34] as well as the reality of a "feminist jurisprudence," advanced by a gender who, because of their own life's experience, may be better able to identify with the disenfranchised than those who have traditionally created and interpreted the law.[35]

At the center of this discourse lies the practical imperative of how legal education and the legal profession will adapt to the gender change.[36] Having begun in the law schools in the late 1960s, it has now spread in varying degrees into every segment of the profession, but with mixed results. Equal opportunity for women and freedom from gender bias are goals toward which the profession as a whole continues to struggle.

---

32. *See* Judith S. Kaye, *Women Lawyers in Big Firms: A Study in Progress Toward Gender Equality*, 57 FORDHAM L. REV. 111 (1988).

33. For examples of this discourse, *see Symposium on Women in the Lawyering Workplace: Feminists Considerations and Practical Solutions*, Karen Gross, J. Williams, S. Caplow, S.A. Scheindlin, C. Fuchs Epstein, 35 N.Y. LAW SCH. L. REV. 293 (1990)

34. *Compare* C. GILLIGAN, IN A DIFFERENT VOICE: PSYCHOLOGICAL THEORY AND WOMEN'S DEVELOPMENT, (1982) with C. MACKINNON, FEMINISM UNMODIFIED, (1987).

35. *See* L.H. Schafran, *Lawyers' Lives, Clients' Lives: Can Women Liberate the Profession?*, 34 VILL. L. REV. 1105 (1989); C. Weiss & Louise Melling, *The Legal Education of Twenty Women*, 40 STAN L. REV. 1299 (1988): "Powerful men made American law and American law schools by and for themselves." at 1299.

36. D.L. Rhode, *Prospectives on Professional Women*, 40 STAN. L. REV. 1163 (1988).

C. The Belated Opening to Minorities and Diversity

Another significant change in the legal profession during the decades of the 1970s and '80s has been its gradual and belated opening to minority lawyers and multicultural diversity. Symptomatic of the historic plight of minority lawyers in America was the formal exclusion of black lawyers from membership in the American Bar Association until 1943. Despite the formal lifting of the racial barrier in 1943, it was not until 1950 that the first African American lawyer was knowingly admitted to the Association.

Legal education was equally exclusionary. Although Howard University Law School in Washington, D.C. received its charter from the Federal Government as early as 1869, it remained the only substantial source of legal education for blacks in the entire country from 1877 to 1939. In 1939 North Carolina Central University Law School was established and, in 1947, two other predominately black law schools were founded, Texas Southern University Law School in Houston and Southern University Law School in Baton Rouge. Thereafter, and as late as 1983, Howard and these three other predominately black law schools had trained the majority of black lawyers in the nation.[37]

However, beginning in the middle 1930s black advocates brought suit to gain admission for African Americans to all-white law schools.[38] Nevertheless, not until the Supreme Court's decision in *Brown* v. *Board of Education*[39] overruling the "separate but equal" doctrine, and the later passage of civil rights legislation in the early 1960s, did the academic legal community begin to give serious attention to the problem of the exclusion of blacks and other racial minorities from law schools.

It was not until 1964 that the Association of American Law Schools' Committee on Racial Discrimination could state for the first time that no member school reported denying admission to any applicant on grounds of race or color.[40] Notwithstanding this AALS report, there were only 433 African American students of the more

---

37. *See* GERALDINE SEGAL, BLACKS IN THE LAW, PHILADELPHIA AND THE NATION, 27 et seq. (1983).

38. *See Pearson* v. *Murray,* 168 Md. 478, 187 A. 590 (1936); *Cf. Missouri ex rel. Gaines* v. *Canada,* 305 U.S. 337 (1938).

39. 347 U.S. 483 (1954).

40. ASSOCIATION OF AMERICAN LAW SCHOOLS PROCEEDINGS, PART ONE: REPORTS OF COMMITTEES, at 159 (1964).

than 50,000 law students enrolled during the 1964–65 academic year in the nation's predominately white law schools.[41]

Ultimately, with the coordinated efforts and support of the law schools and the organized bar, the federal Office of Economic Opportunity initiated programs of increased financial aid and remedial study in the late 1960s which soon began to show results. The number of black law students in accredited law schools rose from 700, or approximately one percent, in 1965; to 4,423, or 4.3%, in 1972; and to 8,149, or 6.3% of JD enrollments in 1991-92.

For racial minorities other than African Americans, there is little historical data, either on their enrollment in law school or on their participation in the profession. However, since the early 1970s, the office of the ABA Consultant on Legal Education[42] has included in the Annual Review of Legal Education a survey of minority group students enrolled in JD programs in approved law schools. In addition to "Black Americans," the groups included have been "Mexican Americans," "Puerto Ricans," "other Hispano-Americans," "American Indians or Alaskan Natives," and "Asian or Pacific Islanders." Over that period, the total minority enrollment grew from 5,568 in 1971-72 to 19,410 in 1991-92. Of the total minority enrollment, black law students were 59.7% in 1974-75 but only 42% in 1991-92, reflecting the substantial increases during that period in the enrollment of Asian and Hispanic students. Mexican American law students grew in number at approximately the same rate as blacks and accordingly their number as a percentage of total minority enroll-

---

41. Report of the Philadelphia Bar Association's Special Committee on Pennsylvania Bar Admissions Procedures, *Racial Discrimination of Pennsylvania Bar Examinations*, 44 TEMPLE L. Q. 141 (1971), at 182.

42. Professor Millard H. Ruud, who became the ABA Consultant on Legal Education in the fall of 1968, has provided, in summary, these insights regarding the early gathering of data on minority enrollments:

The first national legal education organization to gather minority law school enrollment data was the Law School Admissions Council (LSAC). The Association of American law Schools (AALS), and Council on Legal Education Opportunity (CLEO) endorsed and supported the effort. Professor William G. Hall, Jr. of the University of Maryland chaired LSAC's Background Factors Committee and directed the effort. (Professor Ruud was at the time the chair of LSAC.)

Hall's first survey sought minority enrollment data on the fall 1969's entering class. To encourage full participation by the schools confidentiality was promised with respect to each school's information.

Reasonable participation was obtained for fall 1969 enrollment, but not for fall 1970 enrollment. Upon becoming the ABA Consultant in the fall of 1968, Professor Ruud added minority enrollment questions to the 1971 ABA fall questionnaire. Believing that it was necessary to promise confidentiality to obtain maximum participation, this was done by the Consultant with respect to the questionnaire in the fall of 1971 and 1972, but was abandoned with respect to the fall 1973 questionnaire. Individual school enrollment is now published for individual schools each year in the annual Review of Legal Education.

ments also dropped over the 1974-1991 period from 16.3% to 10.4%.

These figures confirm that significant progress has been made during the last two decades in enrolling increased numbers of minority law students, but there remains substantial under-representation of minority groups in the legal profession when compared with total minority populations.

Since its founding in 1925, the National Bar Association has been continuously concerned with the dearth of black lawyers in proportion to the African American population.[43] By 1960, the total number of black lawyers and judges was only 2,012, out of a total of 205,515 lawyers and judges in the country (0.98%). In the next ten years the number grew a scant one-half percent to 3,728 or 1.4% of a total of 272,401. But, during the 1970s and 1980s, along with increased political activity and the dismantling of racial segregation in American public schools, there was a rising number of black law students and the number of black lawyers and judges jumped to 14,839 in 1980 and 25,704 in 1990. The following table summarizes this growth:[44]

	1960	1970	1980	1990
Total lawyers	285,933	355,242	542,205	777,119
African American lawyers	2,012	3,728	14,839	25,704
Percent of total	0.7%	1.0%	2.7%	3.3%

From a different perspective, the 1990 census estimated the total population of the United States to be 248,709,873, with African Americans numbering approximately 30 million or 12.1%. This compares to the 3.3% of all lawyers who are African Americans. On another scale, all lawyers make up .3% of the total U.S. population, while African American lawyers make up only .086% of the African American population.

The National Bar Association Magazine, in its April 1991 issue, analyzed the current distribution of African American lawyers, geographically and by practice setting. The tabulation showed 80 percent of all black lawyers to be in ten states, and a distribution

---

43. *See* J.C. Smith, *Black Bar Associations in Civil Rights*, 15 CREIGHTON L. REV. 3, 651 (1982), at 655.
44. The figures for total lawyers are from the AMERICAN BAR FOUNDATION LAWYER STATISTICAL REPORTS and the ABA Membership Department; the figures for African American lawyers are from the 1990 U.S. Census figures.

among practice settings at marked variance with the distribution of majority lawyers: 31 percent were in law firms (less than half the percentage of majority lawyers in law firms); 24 percent were in solo practice; 22 percent were government employees (twice the percentage of majority lawyers); 11 percent were employees of corporations; nine percent were judges and three percent were law professors. The NALP employment reports on law graduates show similar disparities between minority and majority lawyers who are entering the profession.[45]

Today the organized bar at the national, state and local level is working to achieve equality of opportunity within the profession. Since 1986 the ABA Commission on Minorities, in cooperation with the National Bar Association, the Hispanic National Bar Association and an ever-widening circle of local and regional ethnic associations, has led the effort to bring minorities into the mainstream of the profession.[46]

The advances of the past two decades and current actions hold promise for the future. As recently as the 1960s, there were comparatively few blacks or other racial minorities trained in law or admitted to the bar. Today, a growing number of minority lawyers are engaged in virtually every field of legal endeavor—in private practice in a variety of specialties; as attorneys in corporations and government offices; as prosecutors and defense attorneys; in the judiciary, as federal, state and local judges; in law schools as teach-

---

45. Surveying the law school graduates of the class of 1990, NALP reported that of the 873 African Americans with full-time employment who responded to the survey, 27 percent had accepted full-time employment with government (more than twice the rate for non-minorities (13%)), and that there was also a slightly higher rate of employment in business (8% vs. 7%) and twice as high in public interest work than for non-minorities (4% vs. 2%). However, in judicial clerkships there was a solid 14 percent generally comparable to non-minority clerkships.

On the other hand, NALP further reported that the differences in government, business and public interest employment were reflected in a correspondingly lower rate of employment within private practice, which comprised only 45 percent of the jobs taken by blacks as contrasted with the non-minority rate of 66%.

NALP reported that the national profile of the 644 Hispanic graduates with full-time employment who responded was generally similar to that for African Americans, although their percentages in judicial clerkships (11%) and business (6%) were somewhat smaller and their acceptances of private practice jobs (57%) and public interest jobs (5%) were somewhat higher.

The information provided NALP regarding 499 Asian and Pacific Islanders indicated the following profile of job types: government (17%), clerkships (11%), business (6%), public interest (3%), academic (1%) and law firms (62%). NALP, 1990 ERSS (1991) at 57-59.

46. Recently in San Francisco and in New York City, law firms and corporate law departments, under the auspices of the local bar associations, have signed statements of goals for the hiring, retention and promotion of minority lawyers and calling for equivalent work opportunities for minority and non-minority lawyers. *See* N.Y. LAW JOURNAL (Nov. 1, 1991), at 1-2.

ers, administrators and deans and as leaders of the organized bar.[47]

It is a promising beginning, but only a beginning. The law schools and the organized bar were slow to recognize their essential role and responsibility for promoting equal justice for racial minorities. In recent decades, barriers have been lowered and exclusionary policies have been renounced, but racial minorities continue to be seriously underrepresented in the legal profession. The goal of equal opportunity within the profession is still a long way from realization.

---

47. *See* SEGAL, *supra* note 37, at 207 et seq.

Chapter Two
The Diverse Practice Settings

The great variety in practice settings and the highly differentiated work in which lawyers are engaged present today the greatest challenge to law schools and the profession in maintaining the unitary concept of being a lawyer.

Historically the lawyer in America was an independent professional who was neither employed by another nor dependent on others to help the lawyer provide legal services. The lawyer was also a generalist, personally ready to render whatever legal service a private client might require. The vast majority of lawyers were sole practitioners, either as a full-time or a part-time occupation. Many supplemented their income and filled out their time in other activities—real estate, banking or political office—but employment of lawyers by public agencies and private organizations was virtually non-existent until the late 19th century.

Nor were law firms the usual practice setting. In urban centers some lawyers shared office space or entered into loose partnership arrangements, but this was not common. A study found that as late as 1872, only 14 law firms in the entire country had even four lawyers; three had as many as five lawyers; and only one had six.[1] The gradual emergence of the law firm as a common mode of private practice began only in the last quarter of the 19th century to provide the legal services which were required by those leading the great expansion of industry, commerce and finance.[2]

In the early years of the 20th century, businesses and other organizations employed increasing numbers of lawyers to be in-house counsel, and during the so-called progressive era, with public attention focused upon law and social issues, a growing number of lawyers entered government service in a variety of law-related positions. The depression years of the early 1930s saw once again an increase in the percentage of lawyers joining government agencies.

The makeup of the legal profession at the end of World War II was summarized in a U.S. Department of Commerce Survey of Current Business. It reported that in 1947 three-fourths of the lawyers in the United States were in private law practice and that the remaining one-quarter was employed on a salaried basis by industrial firms, banks, labor organizations and other private agencies, and by government. The latter quarter was disproportionately concentrated in the larger population centers. The concentration of the bar in urban centers is a natural consequence of the direct relationship of legal activity to economic activity.[3]

The Commerce Department report estimated that about 74% of those in private practice in 1947 were sole practitioners and more than 98% either were in solo practice or were lawyers in firms of less than nine lawyers. Lawyers in firms of nine or more practitioners were less than 2% of those in private practice.[4]

In the mid-1950s, a later Commerce Department survey reported

---

1. *See* W.K. Hobson, *Symbol of the New Profession: Emergence of the Large Law Firm 1870-1915* reprinted in THE NEW HIGH PRIESTS: LAWYERS IN POST-CIVIL WAR AMERICA, at 5-7 (Gawalt ed., 1984); J.W. HURST, THE GROWTH OF AMERICAN LAW: THE LAW MAKERS, Chapter 13: "The Uses of the Bar" (1950).
2. By 1898, 67 firms had five lawyers or more and by 1915 there were 240, with the firms predominately in New York City, Chicago and Boston. The pattern of law firm growth continued and by 1924 there were 101 firms of seven lawyers or more in the five largest American cities, with a total lawyer complement of 1,303 (id.) out of approximately 137,500 lawyers in the United States at the time. *See* R.L. ABEL, AMERICAN LAWYERS, Table 32, at 290 (1989).
3. *See* F. ZEMANS & V. ROSENBLUM, MAKING OF A PUBLIC PROFESSION, at 65-66 (1981).
4. W. Weinfeld, *Income of Lawyers, 1929-48* in U.S. DEPARTMENT OF COMMERCE, SURVEY OF CURRENT BUSINESS (August 1949).

a marked shift in the organizational pattern, with more lawyers moving into law firms and a substantial drop in the percentage of lawyers who were sole practitioners (65% in 1954, against 74% in 1947). However, when sole practitioners were combined with lawyers in firms of less than nine lawyers, together they still accounted for just under 98% of the lawyers in private practice.[5] The major growth in the size of law firms did not come until the 1970s.

Since 1970 there has been a steady movement of law firms of all sizes from smaller practice units into larger. Private practice has become a spectrum of different practice units, differentiated not only by size but by clients, by the kind of legal work performed, by the amount of specialization, by the extent of employment of salaried associates and other support staff, and by the degree of bureaucratization of the practice.

To a significant extent, firm size and practice setting have had a direct relationship to the kind of clients served, the type of law practiced and the financial rewards of practice. Community-oriented solo and small firm practitioners of the traditional model work predominately for individuals.[6] Lawyers in larger firms in urban centers work predominately for business clients.[7]

The financial rewards of legal work for individuals (except for personal injury claims) have in general been less than the rewards for representing business.[8] Various studies of law practice show a clear relationship between the size of a firm and the source of its income: as firm size increases the percentage of fees from business clients rises and the percentage of fees from individuals drops. The larger the firm, the greater is the concentration of work for business

---

5. *See* M. Liebenberg, *Income of Lawyers in the Post-War Period*, U.S. DEPARTMENT OF COMMERCE, SURVEY OF CURRENT BUSINESS (December 1956).

6. *See* D.D. LANDON, COUNTRY LAWYERS—THE IMPACT OF CONTEXT ON PROFESSIONAL PRACTICE, 9-10 (1990).

7. *See* ZEMANS & ROSENBLUM, *supra* note 3, at 65-90. Heinz & Laumann estimated that somewhat more than half (53 percent) of the total effort of Chicago's bar at the time of their study was devoted to the corporate client sector. J.P. HEINZ & E.O. LAUMANN, CHICAGO LAWYERS, at 42 (1982).

8. According to Commerce Department surveys, although seven of every ten lawyers in private practice in 1947 depended on individuals rather than business for a major part of their income, about 48% of the income of practicing lawyers came from business, and by 1954, more than half. Lawyers who concentrated on legal work for individuals earned substantially less as a group than those whose work was predominately for business clients. Sole practitioners with the greatest proportion of work for individuals had the lowest level of income. Weinfeld, *supra* note 4 and Liebenberg, *supra* note 5.

clients and the larger the average income of a firm's lawyers.[9]

Economic analysts of lawyers' work have found little relationship between the demand for legal services and total population, but they do find a positive relation between demand for legal services and per capita income, noting, for example, the strong demand for legal services in urban areas of high business and financial concentration.[10]

No sharp line demarks "small" from "large" among law firms; moreover, what is "large" has changed with place and time.[11] However, to provide a comprehensible overview of the profession we have marked off several segments of private practice for separate analysis: sole practitioners and small firms of up to 10 lawyers; medium firms of 11 to 50 lawyers; and large firms of 51 or more lawyers.[12]

The accompanying table tracks the movement in firm size from smaller practice units to larger, reflects the drop in the percentage of lawyers who are sole practitioners and the growth during the 1980s in the size of large law firms, with the greatest growth in the percentage of lawyers in law firms of 51 lawyers or more.[13]

The table reflects the steady movement toward larger and larger law firms in which a greater percentage of lawyers' time is devoted to business law and less to the representation of individuals.

At the same time, new forms of organization have been developed for providing legal services to individuals of modest means and new methods for financing such services. A sector of "new providers" of legal services for individual clients and client groups has emerged. Increasing numbers of sole and small-firm practitioners are participating in these new delivery systems which together are estimated today to provide potential access to legal services for more than 70 million middle-income Americans.[14]

---

9. *See* S.R. Hickerson, *Structural Change in Nebraska's Legal Profession*, 15 CREIGHTON L. REV. 1, 21 (1981); Weinfeld id.; and R.H. Sander & E.D. Williams, *Why Are There So Many Lawyers? Perspectives on a Turbulent Market*, 14 LAW & SOC. INQUIRY 478 (1989).

10. *See* R.L. ABEL, *supra* note 2, at 179.

11. *See* Hobson, *supra* note 1.

12. This segmenting of private practice generally follows that found in ZEMANS & ROSENBLUM, *supra* note 3, at 67, and resembles that employed in HEINZ & LAUMANN, *supra* note 7, at 13.

13. Sources: B.A. Curran, *The Legal Profession in the 1980s: A Profession in Transition*, 20 LAW & SOCIETY REV. 19 (1986); AMERICAN BAR FOUNDATION 1988 SUPPLEMENT TO THE LAWYER STATISTICAL REPORT.

14. *See* National Resource Center for Consumers of Legal Services, *Legal Plan Letter* (Special Census Issue, August 30, 1991).

	1960		1970		1980		1985		1988	
	Private Practitioners N = 206,000	All Lawyers N = 285,933	Private Practitioners N = 240,000	All Lawyers N = 355,242	Private Practitioners N = 370,111	All Lawyers N = 542,205	Private Practitioners N = 460,206	All Lawyers N = 655,191	Private Practitioners N = 519,941	All Lawyers N = 723,189
Sole Practitioners	64%*	46%**	52%	35%	48%	33.2%	47%	33%	46.2%	33.2%
2 to 10 Lawyer firms	N/A	N/A	N/A	N/A	32%	21.5%	28.3%	19.9%	25.1%	18.0%
11 to 50 lawyer firms	N/A	N/A	N/A	N/A	12.6%	8.7%	13.6%	9.6%	14.1%	10.2%
51 or more lawyer firms	N/A	N/A	N/A	N/A	7.3%	5%	11.2%	7.9%	14.6%	10.5%
	Percentage of all lawyers in private practice: 72%		Percentage of all lawyers in private practice: 67.6%		Percentage of all lawyers in private practice: 68.3%		Percentage of all lawyers in private practice: 70.2%		Percentage of all lawyers in private practice: 71.9%	

N/A—not available from existing data base.
*percent of private practitioners.
**percent of all lawyers.

In addition, substantial new provision has been made of services for the poor. Although some legal services have always been provided by various members of the bar to those unable to pay for them, during the past 25 years organized legal services to the poor have been greatly expanded by increased numbers of legal aid attorneys, now funded both publicly and privately, and by public defenders employed by government. Such services have been supplemented by a great many new programs of organized pro bono services furnished by lawyers in private practice.

There are two other major segments of law practice today in which legal services are provided outside the traditional setting of private practice. One is comprised of those providing in-house legal services to corporations and other private organizations, and the second is made up of the lawyers employed by government in all of its functions. The private bar historically has provided legal services both to corporate clients and to governments, but since the late 19th century there has been a steady trend toward bringing law work "in-house," both for corporations and for governmental departments and agencies, and toward employing salaried lawyers instead of retaining individual lawyers and law firms on a fee basis, to handle at least part of the client's legal matters.[15]

The 1988 Supplement to the Lawyer Statistical Report of the American Bar Foundation provided the following distribution of lawyer population by generic divisions of practice settings:

	(1988 Lawyers)	(N = 723,189)
Private practice	519,941	71.9%
Legal aid/public defender	7,369	1.0%
Private industry and association	70,727	9.8%
Federal/state/local government	57,742	8.0%
Federal/state/local judiciary	19,071	2.6%
Education	7,575	1.0%
Retired/inactive	40,762	5.6%

In the following sections detailing the sectors of practice, we seek to provide an overview of each of the settings in which lawyers practice in the 1990s. We first look at the sector of sole and small-firm practitioners who are the principal providers of legal services to individual citizens and small business, in which the traditional model of general practice, while altered, is sometimes still evident. Next we examine the new methods for delivering civil and criminal

---

15. *See* EVE SPANGLER, LAWYERS FOR HIRE, SALARIED PROFESSIONALS AT WORK (1986).

legal services to the poor and persons of moderate means, as well as to client groups, which today significantly augment the representation of individuals and of their legal interests.

We next turn to the sector of medium and large law firms principally serving the business community, which firms have experienced exponential growth in the 1970s and 1980s. Finally, we review the movement in-house of legal services for corporations and other organizations and the many legal roles of lawyers in the public sector.

Greater knowledge of what lawyers do in the various sectors of practice can be useful to legal educators in better preparing students for the realities of practice. It can be equally useful to the law graduate in helping him or her to seek employment compatible with the lawyer's interests and aptitude.[16] Zemans and Rosenblum in their seminal study, *The Making of a Public Profession,*[17] concluded that the nature of the first law job generally determines the field of substantive law in which a lawyer will specialize. This phenomenon emphasizes the importance to the law student of informed choice upon entering practice.

The great diversity in practice settings and in what lawyers do challenges law schools to identify the skills and values which are common to lawyering in all its settings, to provide a rational and effective beginning for their students' professional development, and to impart to their students the legal knowledge which each will need to have upon entering practice.

A. Sole Practitioners and Small Firms

The most numerous segment of the legal profession continues to be the sole and small firm practitioners for whom the traditional community-based, general practitioner was the prototype. Such lawyers generally served a large number of individual clients for whom they handled a variety of discrete matters.[18] The work of the community-oriented lawyer commonly included real estate transactions, intergenerational transfers of property (wills and trusts), personal injuries, matrimonial and family matters, some corporate and commercial law for small businesses, as well as occasional crim-

---

16. In 1975 Thomas Ehrlich and Geoffrey Hazard, recognizing the dearth at that time of material on different careers in the law, published a collection of "readings on a legal career" under the title: *Going to Law School?.*

17. *Supra* note 3.

18. *See* LANDON, *supra* note 6, at 123.

inal cases.[19] They have been traditionally the true general practitioners representing both plaintiffs and defendants, borrowers and lenders, buyers and sellers, public agencies and private parties.

Although there has been a continuing decline in the proportion of lawyers in sole and small-firm practice, in 1988 more than half of the nation's lawyers remained in sole-to-ten-lawyer units in private practice.[20] Moreover, following a decline during the 1960s in the total number of sole practitioners (from 131,840 to 124,800), the record growth of the profession during the 1970s and 1980s included a significant increase in the number of sole practitioners (from 124,800 to 240,141).[21]

Between 1985 and 1988 (the latest years for which complete statistical data are available), the number of lawyers in solo practice increased in every state except Iowa and Utah (in which there were modest declines). In 1988 there were four states in which the percentage of private practitioners who were solos was more than 50%: Massachusetts (54.1%), Maryland (53.4%), New Jersey (53.4%) and California (52.3%). Nationwide 46.2% of the lawyers in private practice were in solo practice: one out of every three lawyers in the United States.[22]

For a decade there was a marked decline in law graduates going into either solo or small firm practice. The National Association for Law Placement (NALP) reported that the percentage of new lawyers beginning practice alone dropped between 1979 and 1988 from 4.5% to 1.7% of those entering private practice, and between 1985 and 1988 that the percentage of new lawyers joining small law firms (2 to 10 members) fell from 21.3% to 17.8%.[23] More recently, however, NALP reports that there have been increases in both solo and small firm

---

19. *See* ABEL, *supra* note 2, at 181; *see* also EHRLICH & HAZARD, *supra* note 16, at 3: "The Small Town Lawyer"; at 20: "The Individual Practitioner"; Thomas R. Bell, *Law Practice in a Small Town (in a rural Alabama county)*, (J.S.D. diss. Howard Univ., 1969); JOEL F. HANDLER, THE LAWYER AND HIS COMMUNITY: THE PRACTICING BAR IN A MIDDLE-SIZED CITY (1967); Richard S. Wells, *The Legal Profession and Political Ideology: The Case of the Carr Law Firm of Manchester, Iowa* (a detailed record of one small law firm's practice in the 1960s), (Ph.D. diss. State University of Iowa, 1963); J.E. CARLIN, LAWYERS ON THEIR OWN: A STUDY OF INDIVIDUAL PRACTITIONERS IN CHICAGO (1962).

20. Solo practice: 33.2%; small firms 18%; combined 51.2%. AMERICAN BAR FOUNDATION 1988 SUPPLEMENT TO THE LAWYER STATISTICAL REPORT.

21. Id. at 5.

22. *See* AMERICAN BAR FOUNDATION 1985 and 1988 SUPPLEMENTS TO THE LAWYER STATISTICAL REPORT. The September 1991 Survey Report of the California State Bar Association projected a substantially smaller percentage for sole practitioners. This discrepancy may reflect the difficulty in surveying this segment of practitioners, who particularly prize their independence.

23. *See* NALP, *Private Practice—Ten Year Comparison* (1990).

entrants (solo: 1989 2.7%, 1990 3.3%; 2-10 lawyers: 1989 24%, 1990 26.6%).

Moreover, among the law schools there is considerable variation in the percentage of graduates entering solo practice. NALP reports that more than 10% of the graduates entering private practice from 25 law schools entered solo practice, with two schools having between 20% and 24% going into solo practice.[24]

It remains to be seen just how many of the latest group of new attorneys will follow the pattern of many of their predecessors who turned to practicing alone (or with a small firm) only after first gaining experience in practice with more senior lawyers, acquiring particular expertise and having had the opportunity to develop a network of colleagues in their local professional communities upon whom they could call.[25]

The ABF's survey of the profession in 1988 reported that 370,608 lawyers were engaged in private practice with ten or fewer colleagues

---

24. National Association for Law Placement, unpublished data from the 1990 Employment Report and Salary Survey Data Base. The following tables from the NALP data base reflect the variation among law schools:

Table 1
Percent, by School, of
Graduates in Solo Practice out of
Those in Private Practice

Solo %	# of Schools	% of Schools
0 to 4% Solo	91	57.6%
5 to 9% Solo	42	26.6%
10 to 14% Solo	16	10.1%
15 to 19% Solo	7	4.4%
20 to 24% Solo	2	1.3%
Total	158	100.0%

Table 2
Percent, by School, of
Graduates in Solo Practice out of
Employed Graduates with Known Job Type

Solo %	# of Schools	% of Schools
0 to 4% Solo	130	82.3%
5 to 9% Solo	22	13.9%
10 to 14% Solo	6	3.8%
Total	158	100.0%

25. *See* L. M. VOGT, FROM LAW SCHOOL TO CAREER: WHERE DO GRADUATES GO AND WHAT DO THEY DO? Harvard Law School Program on the Legal Profession (May 1986); Cf. ZEMANS & ROSENBLUM, *supra* note 3, at 82-84, finding a statistically significant relationship between lawyers' first practice setting after law school and that later in their careers; HEINZ & LAUMANN, *supra* note 7, at 193-198, reporting job stability (i.e., remaining in the same practice setting) most pronounced among those in large firms and those in solo practice.

and were distributed among practice settings as follows:[26]

Firm Size	Number of Firms	Number of Practitioners
Solo	240,141	240,141
2 lawyers	17,501	34,680
3 lawyers	8,028	23,890
4 lawyers	4,460	17,687
5 lawyers	2,740	13,598
6–10 lawyers	5,497	40,612
		370,608

This segment accounted for 71 percent of the 519,914 lawyers in private practice, and 51 percent of the national lawyer population of 723,189 in 1988.[27]

Sole and small-firm practitioners are found in a great diversity of practice settings: rural counties, small cities, seaports, riverports, border towns, state capitals, suburban shopping malls, inner-city storefronts and center-city high-rises, with a diversity of clientele and legal problems to match. Many adhere to the modern day version of the general practitioner, particularly in rural settings, deeply involved in their local communities and serving as friendly counselors and advisers to a variety of persons and organizations in their locales.[28] However, the opportunities for traditional community-oriented sole and small-firm practitioners have dwindled with the evolution of the social context in which lawyers function. The increasing anonymity of urbanization and the enormous sprawl in recent decades of suburbanization mean that legal transactions and services are mainly with strangers, in marked contrast with the social context of the small town where so many transactions and services are between persons known to each other.

Without established relationship to a local community or ethnic circle and faced with the anonymity of metropolitan life, many sole and small firm practitioners seeking to develop new clients have enrolled as members of lawyer panels sponsored by the recently developed prepaid and group legal services plans.[29]

Solo practice takes many forms. It includes those working at home as well as those sharing office space with one or more other lawyers. Sole practitioners include neophyte lawyers who have not

---

26. AMERICAN BAR FOUNDATION 1988 SUPPLEMENT TO THE LAWYER STATISTICAL REPORT, at 5.
27. *Id.*, at 21.
28. *See* D.D. LANDON, *supra* note 6, at 96.
29. *See* discussion in Chapter 2.B, *infra*, regarding these new delivery systems.

yet found the association in practice which they seek, as well as veteran lawyers who have established clienteles and networks of linkage within the profession and who prize the independence of practicing alone. For the former, it may be the practice of last resort as they seek other employment; for the latter, the fulfillment of a professional life's ambition.[30]

Small firms of 2 to 10 lawyers have typically been formed by several lawyers, after some initial experience in practice, who decided to pool their efforts and resources and brought with them into the firm different practice skills and areas of concentration which permit the firm to provide a broader range of legal services for a larger clientele. Firms that remain small have no regular recruitment program and no continuing link to law school placement offices, but simply seek to add a lawyer as their practice warrants. Nevertheless, about one of every 5 or 6 law graduates who entered private practice in recent years has been hired by a small firm of 2 to 10 lawyers.

A principal function of most sole and small-firm practitioners is handling the resolution of disputes for individual clients over different things in a variety of circumstances. The Justice Department's Civil Litigation Research Project in the early 1980s provided empirical insights as to the nature and extent of lawyers' activities in resolving their clients' disputes.[31] Surveying 5,000 households and more than 1,000 lawyers in five federal judicial districts in Wisconsin, Pennsylvania, California, South Carolina and New Mexico, the study sought to determine the incidence of "disputes" in eight selected general areas (tort, consumer, debt, discrimination, property, government, post-divorce and landlord-tenant) and compared the number of disputes with the number of complaints filed in the courts by disputants. The researchers offered the study as a rough estimate of the frequency of litigation involving individuals in the United States,[32] but in so doing they provided a unique insight into lawyers' work.

Seventeen percent of the lawyers in the survey were sole practitioners; the typical lawyer in the survey who handled individual clients' disputes was in a small firm of 5 to 9 lawyers. The study

---

30. Eve Spangler, in Appendix A to her book on salaried lawyers, surveys the scholarly literature on "Solo Practitioners" and summarizes the findings to be compared with her findings regarding the work life of salaried lawyers who are in large law firms, corporate staff counsel, civil service attorneys and legal services advocates. (EVE SPANGLER, *supra* note 15, Appendix A at 199-212).

31. *See* Trubek, Sarat, Felstiner, Kritzer & Grossman, *The Costs of Ordinary Litigation*, 31 UCLA LAW REV. 72 (1983).

32. *Id.*, at 86.

reported the following incidence of litigation in the various areas:

Consumer	3.0%
Discrimination	3.9%
Landlord-tenant	7.3%
Debt	7.6%
Government	11.9%
Property	13.4%
Tort	18.7% and
Post-divorce	59.0%[33]

In just over 10 percent of the disputes, lawsuits were filed, but only 8 percent of the cases commenced actually went to trial.[34]

The study found that lawyers' time in handling the disputes for individual clients was divided as follows:[35]

Conferring with client	16.0%
Factual investigation	12.8%
Legal research	10.1%
Pleadings	14.3%
Discovery	16.7%
Settlement discussions	15.1%
Trial and hearings	8.6%
Appeals and enforcement	.9%
Other	5.5%

Such an allocation of lawyer time, which the researchers regarded as typical of the deployment of lawyers in representation of individual clients in their disputes, is suggestive of what lawyering skills are important to many sole and small firm practitioners.

Specialization

However, changing law and new complexities have put an increasing premium on specialization to maintain competence and to keep abreast of subject matter. The process of professional differentiation has accelerated in clients served and kinds of legal work performed. Although solo and small-firm practice continues predominately to serve individual clients, the lawyers in these practice settings, like in all other practice settings, are increasingly becoming "specialists." When asked, the great majority of lawyers now describe themselves as specializing by legal doctrine, lawyering skill

---

33. *Id.*, at 87; for an appraisal of the distinctive character of a matrimonial law practice, *see* Sarat & Felstiner, *Law and Strategy in the Divorce Lawyers Office*, 20 LAW & SOC'Y REV. 93-134 (1986).

34. *Id.*, at 86.

35. *Id.*, at 91.

or type of client.[36] A 1991 survey of the State Bar of California found that three-quarters of the lawyers spent at least 50 percent of their time in one area of concentration, and more than half the lawyers limited their practice to three or fewer areas of law.[37]

A 1990 national survey made by the ABA Young Lawyers Division reached similar conclusions, finding that 55 percent of the sole practitioners who responded spent 50 percent or more of their time in one substantive area. For solos who spent three-fourths of their time in one area of practice, the most common specialties were real estate, probate and trust, family law, torts and insurance, patent/trademark/copyright, criminal law, and taxation.[38] A 1989 study made for the Commission on the Legal Profession and the Economy of New England reported that the most frequently identified specialties by small firms in New England (excluding sole practitioners) were the following:[39]

General Practice
Real Estate Law
Civil Litigation
Corporate Law
Probate Law
Negligence Law
Family Law
Trusts and Estates
Tax Law
Criminal Law

The prosecution and defense of serious criminal matters have become a discrete specialty in most large urban and metropolitan suburban areas. Full-time prosecutors commence all proceedings and most of the privately-retained defense counsel are sole and small-firm practitioners who limit their practice to criminal law. Frequently members of the defense bar have gained their initial experience in their specialty through service as an assistant district attorney or an assistant United States Attorney.

---

36. *See Economics of Legal Services in Illinois—A 1975 Special Bar Survey*, 64 ILL. BAR JOUR. 73-102 (1975); *Preliminary Report: Results of Survey on Certification of Specialists*, 44 CAL. ST. BAR JOUR. 140, 142-44 (1969).

37. CALIFORNIA STATE BAR ASSOCIATION, SURVEY RESULTS (September 1991), at 26 and 27.

38. *See* AMERICAN BAR ASSOCIATION YOUNG LAWYERS DIVISION, THE STATE OF THE LEGAL PROFESSION 1990, at 14.

39. T.C. FISCHER, LEGAL EDUCATION, LAW PRACTICE AND THE ECONOMY: A NEW ENGLAND STUDY, at 80 (1990). The California 1991 Survey, *supra* note 37, at 25, reported that the areas practiced in by the greatest number of individual attorneys were Business Law, Real Estate, Plaintiffs' Personal Injury, Domestic Relations, Landlord-Tenant and Bankruptcy.

The work of lawyers in the criminal justice system has been elucidated by a detailed analysis of the work tasks of a sample of prosecutors and public defenders.[40] The subspecialty of defending persons accused of white-collar crime today is frequently included in the areas of law practiced by larger firms as well as by small boutique firms. The work and activities of lawyers engaged in this subspecialty have been detailed by Kenneth Mann in *Defending White-Collar Crime: A Portrait of Attorneys at Work* (1985). He describes the strongly adversarial stance of defense counsel who assume that the government does not have sufficient evidence to convict, or even to charge, and who view counsel's task as being to find out what the government knows and to prevent the gathering of additional information.

The growth of specialization has presented the legal profession with a dilemma. Until very recently the profession's ethical rules forbade lawyers to hold themselves out as specialists except in patent, trademark or admiralty law. Yet it has become increasingly clear that every lawyer is obliged as a practical matter to limit the subjects on which he or she will keep abreast and develop particular competence.[41] Consumer surveys confirm that the public feels the need to look for lawyers with specific competencies and wants more information on lawyers' qualifications and the special services lawyers provide. To facilitate client referral and intra-professional communication, ways for identifying capable specialists are needed, but there is a dearth of reliable information. Self-selection by a lawyer of an announced specialty is no assurance of any special competence in the chosen area of law or type of work. Some choices of specialty are not so much a conscious division of labor as they are an identification of the clientele whom the lawyer seeks to serve.[42]

Specialization presents other problems as well. From the individual lawyer's point of view there is the difficulty that when one lawyer refers a client to another lawyer because of some presumed expertise on the other's part, absent some ethical restraint there is no assurance that the client will ever return to the referring lawyer. Specialization also favors larger firms who can cultivate a variety

---

40. J.D. HARBAUGH AND H.G. MCDONALD, TASK ANALYSIS OF THE CRIMINAL JUSTICE ATTORNEY: IMPLICATION FOR THE USE OF PARALEGALS (1977).

41. *See* I.F. Reichert, *The Future of Continuing Legal Education"* in LAW IN A CHANGING SOCIETY, 167-182, at 177 (Geoffrey Hazard, ed. (1968)).

42. HEINZ & LAUMANN, *supra* note 7, at 56, found that lawyers in their study tended to practice more than one specialty, reflecting the needs of the lawyer's clients and not any logic of the law.

of specialists among the firm's members; smaller firms see the result as a competitive disadvantage.

Moreover, specialization is inextricably bound to lawyer advertising, which is frequently the basis for distinguishing one lawyer from another. The most common type of advertising by sole practitioners and small firms is in the telephone Yellow Pages[43] and specification of practice area is the principal feature of such advertising.[44] It was a small firm, in fact a legal clinic, that won the right to advertise in the *Bates* case.[45] Nevertheless, proposals to regulate special-

---

43. Surveys suggest that 10% to 30% of lawyers in urban areas advertise in the Yellow Pages; primarily they are solo attorneys or in small firms. *See* AMERICAN BAR ASSOCIATION COMMISSION ON ADVERTISING, *Yellow Pages Lawyer Advertising: An Analysis of Effective Elements* reported in *The Compleat Lawyer* (April 1992).

44. The NYNEX YELLOW PAGES FOR MANHATTAN, 1990-1991, contains a *Guide of Lawyers Arranged By Practice*. It bears the legend: "Lawyers in this guide have chosen to list themselves by the Field of Law to which they limit their practice. This guide may not include all lawyers." The following Fields of Law are listed:

Accidents—Personal Injury/Property Damage
Administrative & Governmental Law
Appellate Practice
Aviation Law
Bankruptcy
Civil Rights Law
Civil Service Law
Copyright Law
Corporation Partnership & Business Law
Criminal Law
Debt Collection
Entertainment Law
Estate Planning and Administration
Franchise Law
General Practice
Health Care and Hospital Law
Immigration & Naturalization
Insurance Law
International Law
Labor Law
Landlord and Tenant
Malpractice Law - Legal & Medical
Marital & Family Law
Patent Law
Pension & Profit Sharing Law
Product Liability
Real Property Law
Securities Law
Social Security Law
Taxation
Trademark Law
Trial Practice
Vehicle & Traffic Law
Wills Trust and Probate Estates
Workers' Compensation

45. *Bates & O'Steen* v. *State Bar of Arizona*, 433 U.S. 350 (1977).

ization have generally been opposed by sole and small-firm practitioners.

Proponents of regulation of specialties maintain that it provides greater access by the public to appropriate legal services, that it helps identify and improve the quality and competence of legal services, and that it leads to the rendering of appropriate services at a reasonable cost. They argue that the public's lack of knowledge and sophistication about legal services magnifies the harm of inherently or potentially misleading advertising and that regulation establishes a uniform definition of what is a specialty and who is a specialist. They further urge that the "certifying" of specialists educates the public on the qualifications and competency level it should seek and that enforcement agencies have a standard against which to judge advertisements and a standard of care against which to judge performance.[46]

As of August 1990, the ABA Standing Committee on Specialization had promulgated Model Standards for Specialization in 24 specialties (in stunning contrast to the 2 or 3 specialties that the profession traditionally sanctioned—patents, trademarks and admiralty).[47] As of April 1991, 15 States had specialization plans in

---

46. *See* REPORT OF AMERICAN BAR ASSOCIATION STANDING COMMITTEE ON SPECIALIZATION (August 1990).

47. ABA *Model Standards for Specialty Areas* (August 1990), cover the following subject areas:

    Admiralty
    Appellate Practice
    Bankruptcy Law
    Business and Corporate Law
    Civil Rights Law
    Civil Trial Practice
    Collection Practice
    Commercial Law
    Criminal Law
    Estate Planning and Probate
    Family Law
    Franchise Law
    Governmental Contracts and Claims
    Immigration Law
    Insurance Law
    International Law
    Labor and Employment Law
    Military Administration Law
    Patent, Trademark and Copyright Law
    Personal Injury and Property Damage
    Real Property Law
    Securities Law
    Taxation Law
    Workers' Compensation

effect for the certification of from one to 25 specialties.[48]

The plans in a few States provide for a State board of legal specialization and strict regulation. In Texas, for example, lawyers who are *not* "board certified" and are practicing in one of 13 specified "specialty fields," must include a disclaimer of board certification in their advertisements. Other States, have approached regulation indirectly by regulating outside organizations which seek to act as certifying bodies. Still others, following an ABA Model Plan, permit self-identification of specialty but prescribe minimum standards, peer review and mandatory continuing legal education and may or may not require examinations for certification.

Lawyers in larger firms, which firms have essentially been built upon the efficiencies and cost-effectiveness of *de facto* specialization, generally see nothing to be gained by having specialization regulated. Lawyers practicing solo and in small firms look upon regulation of specialties as just more red tape, increasing costs of practice and further deprecating the "general practitioner," and erecting an additional hurdle for the beginning lawyer. Given this resistance, it is not surprising that regulation of specialization, since it was first adopted in California in 1972, has been adopted in only 14 other states.

However, in 1990 in *Peel* v. *Illinois Attorney Registration and Disciplinary Commission*, 496 U.S. 91, a plurality of the Supreme Court held that States may not bar a lawyer's truthful advertisement that he is certified a specialist by the NBTA, i.e., the National

---

48. States with specialization plans:
   Alabama
      (outside agency certification)
   Arizona
   Arkansas
   California
   Connecticut
      (outside agency certification)
   Florida
   (two-tier)
   Georgia
      (outside agency certification)
   Louisiana
   Minnesota
      (outside agency certification)
   New Jersey
   New Mexico
   North California
   South Carolina
   Texas
   Utah
      (not implemented)

Board of Trial Advocates, without regard to the merit of such certification. This decision further lessened the controls over lawyer advertising and has stimulated new interest in the regulation of specialization. In the light of *Peel*, the ABA Committee on Specialization has recently declared:

> The question is no longer whether or not to have specialization. The *Peel* decision answered that. . . . The question is how best to regulate certification.[49]

Meanwhile, modern technology and improved practice management are making small practice units more cost effective than in the past. More and more lawyers are focusing on one or several practice specialties which they announce and publicize, further departing from the traditional general practitioner model. "Legal boutique" has been added to the lawyers' lexicon and the referral practice developed by such specialty firms has actively grown alongside the larger law firms.

On the other hand, some see the role of the general practitioner in an age of specialization as evolving into that of the diagnostician who identifies and defines the client's problem and then refers the client to the appropriate specialist. No doubt such referrals will increase with further specialization and many general advisers will play an important role in seeing that their clients get the legal services appropriate to their needs.

Networks of Firms

One growing technique for leveraging the practice of small firms is to join in formal and informal networks of firms in different parts of the country engaged in the same lines of practice. Some arrangements provide for no more than mutual referrals of clients who seek representation in another jurisdiction, while others seek some of the advantages of large firms by agreeing to share clients, training facilities, management know-how, practice-development strategies, support services and even experts for litigation.[50]

Special Needs in Preparing for Practice

The continued growth in the number of lawyers in solo and small-firm practice is an indication of continued vitality in this segment of the profession in its latest roles. The absence of an established

---

49. For a summary of the status of regulation of specialization after the *Peel* discussion, *see* Randall Sanborn, *Post-'Peel' Battles*, NAT'L LAW JOUR. (Dec. 30, 1991 - Jan. 6, 1992), at 1, 10-11.

50. See discussion of "Networks and Affiliation Groups" in GALANTER & PALAY, TOURNAMENT OF LAWYERS, at 130 (1991).

structure is both the attraction and the drawback of such practice. The ABA Task Force on Solo and Small Firm Practitioners adopted the statement of one of its witnesses: "The biggest problem that solos and smalls have is isolation."[51] Graduates entering such practice seldom have an experienced attorney to whom they may go for advice, nor do they have access to training programs in which to learn on the job. Without mentor, collegial support or on-the-job training, the lawyer needs to reach out for assistance while attempting to establish a professional network on whom to call.

It is not surprising that successive assessments of the profession have found that the smaller the setting in which beginning lawyers practice, the more they rely on their legal education for learning practice competencies.[52] However, one frequently heard plaint is that law schools in preparing students for practice give greater attention to the needs of those lawyers entering practices in which they will serve the business community than to the needs of those entering practices in which they will provide legal services to individual clients.[53] The transition from law school into individual practice or relatively unsupervised positions in small offices, both public and private, presents special problems which the law schools and the organized bar must address.

B. New Providers of Legal Services

During the past 30 years traditional private practice serving individuals has been significantly supplemented by new organizations and methods for providing legal services to the poor and to persons of modest means and for generally facilitating the public's access to legal services. These organizations and methods have increased both the demand for and the supply of legal services, which are provided both by staff attorneys employed by the new organizations and by private practitioners who participate in the new delivery systems.

The new organizations and methods include greatly expanded legal services to the poor, including publicly-funded civil legal assistance identified with the emergence of a new field of poverty law,

---

51. AMERICAN BAR ASSOCIATION TASK FORCE REPORT, at 39 (November 1991).

52. *See* ZEMANS & ROSENBLUM, *supra* note 3, at 123-64; AMERICAN BAR ASSOCIATION FOULIS COMMITTEE, LAW SCHOOLS AND PROFESSIONAL EDUCATION, at 83-4 (1980); Mudd & La Trielle, *Professional Competence: A Study of New Lawyers*, 49 MONT. L. REV. 11, at 27 (1988).

53. See, e.g., *Symposium: The Growth of Large Law Firms and Its Effect on the Legal Profession and Legal Education*, 64 IND. LAW J. 423 (1989).

and greatly expanded legal assistance in criminal proceedings furnished by legal aid, public defenders and programs of court-appointed defense counsel; bar-sponsored and privately operated lawyer referral and information services; law clinics or what have been referred to as "advertised" law offices; group legal service plans, free plans, prepaid plans, employee assistance plans and individual enrollment plans; as well as local, state and nationally organized programs of *pro bono* services by lawyer volunteers.

The Historical Antecedents

Public access to lawyers and the ready availability of legal services to all who need them have concerned thoughtful members of the profession for more than a century. It is a "basic tenet of the professional responsibility of lawyers . . . that every person in our society should have ready access to the independent professional services of a lawyer of integrity and competence." (Code of Professional Responsibility, EC1-1.)

The first organized effort to provide legal assistance to the poor was the formation in 1876 in New York City of what became The Legal Aid Society formed by an organization of German-American immigrants. Other legal aid organizations thereafter were formed by bar associations and civic groups in other cities. By the turn of the century, six cities had legal aid organizations and by 1917 thirty-seven cities had a total of forty-one functioning legal aid organizations. Reginald Heber Smith in his study for the Carnegie Foundation reported that the forty-one organizations in 1916 handled a total of 117,201 cases. However, Smith found this in no way commensurate with the need and wrote a scathing indictment of the American legal system for its inaccessibility to the poor.[54]

Following the model of the New York Legal Aid Society,[55] the early focus of the legal aid organizations was predominantly upon civil legal services. Criminal defendants for many years received scant organized assistance other than from groups of private attorney volunteers.[56]

---

54. REGINALD H. SMITH, JUSTICE AND THE POOR (1919).

55. The original intention of the Legal Aid Society had been to assist indigent defendants. However, a lack of money and personnel led to the Society refusing most criminal business until public monies became available in the 1960s, except for the work under Society auspices carried on by volunteer lawyers. *See* HARRISON TWEED, THE CHANGING PRACTICE OF LAW, (1955).

56. It was not until the *Scottsboro* case in 1932 that the right to legal representation in state courts even in capital cases was recognized. *Powell* v. *Alabama*, 287 U.S. 45. *See* JOHN M. MAGUIRE, THE LANCE OF JUSTICE, 238-45 (1928), for a history of legal aid 1876 to 1926.

The public defender movement, seeking to have government provide counsel to indigent defendants, was initiated in 1893 by Clara Shortridge Foltz, the first woman to be admitted to practice in California. For many years she advocated with great persistence a countrywide system of defense for the indigent, but the number grew slowly. There were five public defender offices in 1917 and only 28 by 1949.[57] Significant implementation awaited the Supreme Court's grant of the constitutional right to counsel to criminal defendants in federal courts in 1938,[58] its extension to felony defendants in state courts in 1963[59] and to all those at risk of imprisonment in 1972.[60]

During the 1920s and 1930s the twin problems confronted by many members of the public, of knowing when to seek legal assistance and of finding a lawyer competent to assist them, grew with the anonymity of urbanization and the pervasiveness of law in everyday life. The legal realists[61] and others picked up on Reginald Heber Smith's criticism of the maldistribution of legal services and urged various reforms to make law more accessible to the ordinary citizen.

One response during the late 1930s was the organization in Philadelphia of bar-sponsored neighborhood law offices operated by private practitioners.[62] It was not until the 1960s, however, that other neighborhood law offices were opened with a new mission of providing legal services to the poor, funded first by private foundations as social experiments and later funded by the federal Office of Economic Opportunity as part of the War on Poverty.[63]

Another initiative to make lawyers more accessible to the ordinary citizen was the establishment in 1937 of the first lawyer referral service by the Los Angeles County Bar Association. This marked the beginning of what has become in the post-war period a nationwide program of bar-sponsored referral services to inform potential individual consumers of legal services about local lawyers.

---

57. *See* R.L. ABEL, *supra* note 2, at 131.
58. *Johnson* v. *Zerbst*, 304 U.S. 458 (1938).
59. *Gideon* v. *Wainwright*, 372 U.S. 355 (1963).
60. *Argersinger* v. *Hamlin*, 407 U.S. 25 (1972).
61. *See* K.N. Llewellyn, *The Bar Specializes—With What Results?* The Annals of the Academy of Political Science (May 1933); Llewellyn, *The Bar's Troubles, and Poultices—and Cures?*, 5 LAW & CONTEMP. PROB. 104 (1938); Reginald H. Smith, *Legal Services Offices for Persons of Moderate Means*, 31 AM. JUD. SOC'Y JOUR. 37 (1947).
62. The experiment in neighbor law offices is described in R.D. Abrahams, *Twenty-five Years of Service: Philadelphia's Neighborhood Law Office Plan*, 50 ABA JOUR. 728 (1964); R.D. Abrahams, *The Neighborhood Law Office Experiment*, 9 U. CHI. L. REV. 406 (1942); R.D. Abrahams, *Law Offices to Serve Householders in the Lower Income Groups*, 42 DICK L. REV. 13 (1938).
63. *See* E. JOHNSON JR., *The Neighborhood Lawyer Experiments and the Goal(s) of Social Reform* in JUSTICE AND REFORM, (1974, new edition 1978), at 21-35.

Legal services of a different character are needed, and frequently not available from the private bar, when individuals find themselves in situations where they share with others substantially the same legal interest as against some third person or the government, and they seek as a group to invoke their legal rights. Advocacy to advance and enforce "group legal rights" has been a part of the American scene for many years, but it has been commonly looked upon by the law with suspicion and restrained by rules such as those regulating class actions and standing to sue.

From the early decades of this century organizations have been formed by lawyers and political activists, such as those advocating women's suffrage, the American Civil Liberties Union and the NAACP Legal Defense and Education Fund, but the development of a special segment of the legal profession, engaged in what has come to be called "public interest" law, did not materialize until the activist decade of the 1960s.

The 1960s was the seminal period for today's legal profession and particularly with respect to legal services for the poor. It was the time that important court decisions and legislative enactments made way for the great expansion in the delivery systems for civil and criminal legal services. It was also the time when the concept of legal education for professional responsibility was brought forcefully to the law schools by the Ford Foundation's institution of its CLEPR program.[64]

In the following subdivisions of this section, while recognizing the serious problem of unmet legal needs which continues, we look at today's expanded practice settings for lawyers in non-traditional delivery systems which now provide legal services for the poor, legal services for those of modest means and advocacy for group legal rights in the "public interest."

Lawyers for the Poor

Civil legal assistance for indigents. By the 1960s, civil legal assistance, financed privately by community chests, bar associations, individual lawyers and special fund-raising campaigns, provided such organized legal assistance to the poor as was available.[65] The earliest canons of ethics had recognized the professional

---

64. The Ford Foundation supported the Council on Legal Education for Professional Responsibility for a period of ten years commencing in 1968. See The President's Report in the Proceedings of CLEPR for 1979 in which the project is reviewed at 7-43.

65. *See* E. JOHNSON, *supra* note 63, at 5-10: *A Brief History of the Legal Aid Movement*; see also R.L. ABEL, *Law Without Politics: Legal Aid Under Advanced Capitalism*, 32 UCLA L. Rev. 474, 502 (1985).

obligation of individual lawyers to assist the poor[66] and in traditional practice settings lawyers in their local communities had always handled many legal matters for which they were not paid. Any organized programs were almost exclusively in large urban areas.

However, in the decade of the 1960s there was increasing public scrutiny of the legal profession and the adequacy of its performance in distributing legal services, including legal services to those unable to afford a lawyer.[67] This was at a time when national policy was focused on the poor who were unable to break the cycle of poverty. It was advanced that legal advocacy for the poor should be an integral part of any comprehensive "War on Poverty."[68]

Thus in 1965, the Office of Legal Services was established within the federal Office of Economic Opportunity and the federal funding of local legal services programs began.[69] It marked the beginning of the emergence of poverty advocacy and of the development of what is today known as poverty law, greatly supplementing and broadening the mission of legal assistance for the poor as previously provided by traditional, privately financed legal aid.

During the years 1965 to 1973 the federal Legal Services Program, with the strong support of the organized bar, created a presence of lawyers in poor urban neighborhoods and began the representation of organized groups of the poor. Earl Johnson reported in his history of these formative years that by 1973 the Program comprised 250 community-based agencies staffed by more than 2,600 full-time lawyers manning 900 separate law offices. Program lawyers had served over five million low income clients and argued a hundred appeals in the United States Supreme Court.[70]

Following the establishment of the Legal Services Corporation ("LSC") in 1975 with the organized bar again playing a leading role, federal funding for civil legal services rose rapidly to its peak in 1981 with a budget of $321 million which supported programs

---

66. *See,* for example, The Alabama Code of Ethics of 1887 setting forth a code of duties for attorneys and concluding with the duty to be a friend to the defenseless and the oppressed.

67. *See* M.L. Schwartz *Changing Patterns of Legal Services* in LAW IN A CHANGING SOCIETY, 109-124, (Geoffrey Hazard, ed. (1968)).

68. *See* E. JOHNSON, *supra* note 63, at 39-70: *Birth of the Federal Program.*

69. *Id.,* at 71-102: *Development of Local Legal Services Organizations.*

70. *Id.,* at xxix. See also A.W. Houseman, *A Short Review of Past Poverty Law Advocacy,* CLEARINGHOUSE REV. 1514 (April 1990).

employing some 6,000 staff lawyers.[71] The following year the budget was cut by 25% and throughout the 1980s the challenge for proponents of publicly-supported legal services, including the American Bar Association, was to maintain at least the 1982 level of funding.[72]

During the formative years of the Legal Services Corporation between 1974 and 1981, it brought civil legal services to all parts of the country through its "minimum access" plan, which was calculated to provide two lawyers for every 10,000 poor people. It broadened the issues receiving attention through expanded national support and the development of state support. It greatly expanded the training available to local staffs. Specialized components and programs for farm workers and Native Americans were established and functioned in all areas that had significant farm worker and Native American populations. In addition, funds from other federal programs supported legal services for older persons and for the developmentally disabled.[73] While the financial cutbacks during the 1980s substantially reduced many of these programs, the general pattern of publicly financed legal services for the poor was firmly established by these early initiatives of the Legal Services Corporation and a distinct body of poverty law created.

It has been said that during the 1980s legal services became the last resort for many poor people because of the severe reduction in public benefits grants, restrictions on eligibility for benefit programs and the increasing lack of affordable housing and of access to health care.[74] At the same time, the legal framework for poverty advocacy changed. In prior years, a large part of the work of legal services centered on federal protections and benefits for the poor.[75] Beginning with the Omnibus Budget Reconciliation Act of 1981[76] many federal programs were redesigned to shift program design, operation and control from the federal government to state governments, and

---

71. R.L. ABEL, *supra* note 2, Tables 5 and 6 at 254-255. In 1990 the federal appropriation for the LSC was $316,525,0 00. Another $182,711,515 of non-LSC funding was provided to local offices and support centers, including $51 million from 35 state programs of Interest on Lawyer Trust Accounts ("IOLTA") and $48 million of state and local government grants.

72. A striking example of what happened following the 1982 budget cut was the closing in 1983 of the Southeast Legal Aid Center in Compton, California, obliging the State Bar to take responsibility for some 36,000 case files abandoned by the Legal Aid Center. R.L. ABEL, *supra* note 2, at 133.

73. This summary is taken from a paper of Justice John A. Dooley III presented in May 1989 at the ABA Conference on Access to Justice in the 1990s. See REPORT OF THE AMERICAN BAR ASSOCIATION NATIONAL CONFERENCE ON ACCESS TO JUSTICE IN THE 1990s, New Orleans, Louisiana (June 9-11, 1989).

74. A.W. Houseman, *supra* note 70, at 1519.

75. *Id.*

76. Pub. L. No. 97-35 (Aug. 1981).

efforts were made to deregulate the federal protections earlier enacted. The result of these and other policy changes was to shift reliance in poverty law advocacy from major federal court litigation and federal regulatory practice, to the states and to rely on state agencies, state legislative bodies and state court systems for expanding and protecting existing entitlements and rights.

In addition, litigation during the 1980s required much greater reliance on proof of facts and far less reliance on legal arguments and motion practice. At the same time, the Legal Services Corporation imposed restrictions on certain kinds of policy advocacy by legal services offices. Nevertheless, new issues did arise such as those relating to the homeless and AIDS victims, and some additional poverty law specialties were developed.[77]

Under the umbrella of the Legal Services Corporation, poverty law today has become a complex collection of specialties with various sub-specialties.[78] NLADA's 1991/92 Directory lists a total of 2,369 main and branch offices in the United States and Territories which today provide civil legal assistance to persons unable to retain private counsel. This listing includes programs funded wholly or in part by the Legal Services Corporation as well as those funded by other sources.[79] The offices range in size from offices with one or two staff attorneys to offices of a hundred or more attorneys, paralegals and investigators. The Legal Services Corporation reports that programs for civil legal services to the poor which it supports employ approximately 4,800 full-time staff attorneys and 2,000 paralegals working in local legal aid and legal services offices as well as in the Corporation's state support and regional training centers and its computer assisted legal research programs.[80]

In recent years, the work of staff attorneys in legal services offices has been supplemented by the work of more than 100,000 private attorneys, working with staff attorneys and accepting referrals on a pro bono or reduced fee basis.[81]

---

77. A.W. Houseman, *supra* note 70, at 1521.
78. *See* lists of *Programs for Special Needs* in NLADA 1991/92 DIRECTORY, at 147-171.
79. *See* NATIONAL LEGAL AID AND DEFENDER ASSOCIATION, 1991/1992 DIRECTORY, 1-85 (1991).
80. LEGAL SERVICES CORPORATION 1990 ANNUAL REPORT, at 15.
81. The "referral program" to private attorneys is the result of initiatives by the Legal Services Corporation in recent years to "privatize " civil legal services. The so-called "compensated model" covers the private lawyer's overhead and offers particularly to beginning lawyers an opportunity to gain experience in practice.
    Private bar involvement in organized pro bono programs of civil legal assistance is substantially broader than that falling under the umbrella of the Legal Services Corporation. Sixty percent of the funding for pro bono legal projects comes from non-

The work and careers of legal services and legal aid lawyers were reported upon by various authors writing in the late 1970s and early 1980s. They underscored the difficulties encountered in representations that are usually summary, with the volume allowing only cursory preparation, involving personal problems at a crisis stage and frequently not "legal" problems in the customary sense.[82] Several of these authors also surveyed lawyers who had left legal services offices and reported that the frequent explanation for leaving, despite the challenges, was that the work became intellectually boring and routine.[83] However, for many new lawyers civil legal services offices have proven to be excellent training grounds in lawyering skills and values and such offices continue to attract more graduating law students than they can hire on their curtailed budgets, notwithstanding the demand for the services continuing to outstrip the capacity of legal services offices.[84]

The role of the law schools in legal services to the poor is of a special character. While law schools could never be major providers of services to low income clients and fulfill their basic educational mission, their contribution today is highly significant. Principally developed in the past twenty years, the law schools' clinical programs provide not only training and experience with poverty law issues, but they have given birth to valuable research centers at the schools which contribute on a continuing basis to the improvement in the delivery of legal services to the poor.

Both the law schools and the organized bar during the 1960s and 1970s greatly increased the profession's commitment to providing civil legal services to the poor. A significant element in this increased commitment was the promotion at the law schools of clinical legal education with its focus on translating the needs of society for the profession's services and skills into their educational equivalents.

Criminal defense for indigents. Thirty years elapsed between

LSC sources. In the more than 600 pro bono programs tracked by the ABA's Private Bar Involvement project, 123,808 individual lawyers participated during 1990 and an additional 11,882 participated in partially compensated programs. Participation in pro bono programs reached 59% of Idaho's 2260 lawyers and almost 56% of Maine's 3199 lawyers. See *1990 Statistical Analysis for the 1991 Directory of Private Bar Involvement Programs*, (April 1991).

82. J. KATZ, POOR PEOPLE'S LAWYERS IN TRANSITION (1982); HANDLER, HOLLINGSWORTH & BERLANGER, LAWYERS AND THE PURSUIT OF LEGAL RIGHTS (1978); see also E. SPANGLER, *supra* note 15, at 144-174: "Generally Contentious People - Legal Services Advocates"; J. Katz, *Routine and Reform: A Study of Personal and Collective Careers in Legal Aid* (Ph.D. diss. Northwestern University 1976).

83. Handler et al. *Id.*

84. See, for example, N.Y. Times (December 11, 1991) at A24, reporting that due to a shortage of lawyers only about half of the nation's Legal Services offices handle bankruptcies.

the *Scottsboro* case in 1932 and the sounding of Gideon's Trumpet in 1963.[85] During that period modest advances were made in providing representation for indigent defendants,[86] but it was only in the wake of *Gideon* and the passage of the Criminal Justice Act of 1964, with its provisions for the compensation of defense counsel, that legal assistance for persons accused of crime became a publicly-acknowledged responsibility.

Thereafter, the traditional role of ad hoc court-assigned defense counsel greatly diminished and most jurisdictions created government-supported public defender offices staffed by salaried employees to satisfy the new constitutional requirements. In 1967, state governments spent $17 million and the federal government $3 million to provide legal representation for indigents charged with felonies.[87] By 1977, the combined total reached $403 million[88] and by 1988 expenditures for criminal defense services reached $1.4 billion.[89]

Public defender programs grew from 28 in 1949 to 163 in 1973, by which time state-subsidized counsel under programs for indigent defendants were representing 65% of all felony defendants (leading one commentator, with a measure of hyperbole, to characterize private defense counsel as a "dying breed").[90] The 1991/92 Directory of Legal Aid and Defender Offices in the United States and Territories now lists a total of 1,529 main and branch offices providing criminal representation to persons unable to retain private counsel operated by public defender programs and by legal services programs which contain a public defender component.[91] The largest publicly-supported program is the Criminal Defense Division of the New York City Legal Aid Society with an average complement of 675 supervising and staff attorneys who handled 170,000 cases in the

---

85. Anthony Lewis, Gideon's Trumpet, (1964)

86. *See* Report of the National Legal Services Policy Committee to Board of Directors (January 4, 1965), at 4-8, cited in E. Johnson, *supra* note 63, at 9.

87. R.L. Abel, *supra* note 2, at 131, citing D.J. Scari, "The Financial Impacts of the Right to Counsel for Criminal Defense of the Poor," Law & Society annual meeting, San Francisco (May 1979).

88. *Id.*

89. 1988 is the latest year for which there is data available from the National Criminal Justice Reference Service, U.S. Department of Justice, Bureau of Justice Statistics (July 1990 Bulletin).

90. National Legal Aid and Defender Association, the Other Face of Justice, at 83 (1973); P.B. Wise, the Endangered Species: America's Private Criminal Lawyers (1973).

91. National Legal Aid and Defender Association, 1991/92 Directory (1991), at 87-143; Maine and North Dakota are the only states for which no offices are listed, but coverage varies widely: three offices each in Utah and South Dakota, only 16 offices in all of Texas (compared with 88 civil legal services offices), and 273 offices in California.

most recent year.[92] In addition, special programs in a number of urban centers, both publicly and privately funded, now provide lawyers for juveniles in both criminal and family court proceedings, as well as for prisoners and other institutionalized persons.[93]

Although state-subsidized public defenders predominate in the representation of felony defendants today, private practitioners in every jurisdiction continue to play a significant role in representing defendants on both a retainer and publicly-subsidized basis. White-collar crime has emerged in recent years as a significant specialty for retained private defense attorneys.[94]

It was estimated in 1982 that 6% of the counties in the United States had experimented with the contracting out of defense services to private law firms, but with mixed results.[95] Substantial representation continues to be on a pro bono basis, both court-appointed and volunteer (including post-conviction death-penalty representation).[96] NLADA reported in the summer of 1991 that increasing numbers of private practitioners were joining NLADA specifically to take advantage of the Association's insurance program for lawyers engaged in the representation of criminal defendants.

Today the criminal justice system is confronted with record numbers of prosecutions. The principal burden of representing the defendants is upon the federal, state and locally-supported public defender programs across the country. These providers of indigent defense services have in some jurisdictions been overwhelmed by the ravages of the drug epidemic and the federal "war on drugs." The National Center for State Courts in 1991 reported that 70-90% of defendants charged with drug and drug-related offenses were indigent and required appointed counsel. In various jurisdictions, any semblance of balance has been destroyed between resources made available for police and prosecution and for defense. Many public defender offices are today overburdened and underpaid, with high

---

92. Information provided by Robert Baum, Esq., Chief of the Criminal Defense Division, New York City Legal Aid Society, April 16, 1992.

93. *See* NLADA, *supra* note 90, at 150, 157, 162.

94. *See* NATIONAL DIRECTORY OF CRIMINAL LAWYERS (B. Tarlow ed. 3rd Ed. 1991): a directory of lawyers who the editor represents have been evaluated for demonstrated ability and commitment to conscientious representation.

95. *See* R. Spangenberg, A.D. Davis, P.A. Smith, *Contract Defense Systems under Attack: Balancing Cost and Quality*, 39(1) NLADA BRIEFCASE 5 (Fall 1982).

96. The Programs for Special Needs section of the NLADA 1991/92 Directory lists 41 offices which provide direct representation for death penalty defendants, although there are none in some states that have a large number of death-row inmates. NLADA, *supra* note 90, at 148-49.

turnover, and unprepared to handle their massive caseloads.[97]

Services for Persons of Moderate Means

Following World War II it became increasingly apparent with respect to the delivery of legal services that supply and demand in the legal services marketplace as traditionally structured operated no more effectively to provide equal access to legal assistance for persons of moderate means than for the poor.

In 1951 the ABA Standing Committee on Lawyer Referral Services prophetically reported:

> . . . . the requirements of the public for legal services at moderate fees is greatly in excess of its requirements for free legal aid.[98]

Experience in later years confirmed the magnitude of this potential demand after the Supreme Court had lifted the ban on advertising[99] and had struck down minimum fee schedules[100] and legal services came to be more or less freely marketed to middle income persons.

One leader in the legal services movement in the 1970s recently wrote:

> Service creates demand. Some of that demand widens the understanding of what service should be given. New notions of legal need emerge. Thus, as service increases, perceived need increases.[101]

Another student of the delivery of legal services concluded that the availability of legal services for people of moderate means is "essentially a marketing problem," reflecting the fact that the more legally savvy clients become, the more likely they are to utilize the legal services available to them—before signing a contract to buy a house, or becoming mired in debt, or trusting to dumb luck that the

---

97. *See* T.R. Murphy, *Indigent Defense and the War on Drugs*, 6 CRIMINAL JUSTICE, No. 3 (Fall 1991), at 14-20.

The National Law Journal (February 24, 1992, at 18) reported that the Attorneys at the Public Defenders Office in Knoxville, Tennessee became so overwhelmed by the number of cases which they were required to handle (average case load: 435) that the courts appointed every member of the bar in the county, including the mayor and other local leaders, to represent the indigent accused few of whom had any criminal defense experience.

See also State of Louisiana v. *Peart,* reported in Nat. Law Jour. (February 24, 1992), at 3-4.

98. AMERICAN BAR SSSOCIATION REPORTS, STANDING COMMITTEE ON LAWYER REFERRAL SERVICES.

99. *Bates & O'Steen* v. *State Bar of Arizona,* 433 U.S. 350 (1977).

100. *Goldfarb* v. *Virginia State Bar,* 421 U.S. 773 (1975).

101. J.A. Dooley, paper presented at the ABA Conference on Access to Justice in the 1990s, Tulane Law School (1989).

intestacy laws will provide for their families and estate what they would themselves.[102]

The years between 1960 and 1980 not only brought new delivery systems for civil and criminal legal services for the poor, but also substantial market innovations in providing lawyers' services to the middle class.[103] These innovations included experimentation with a new kind of law office which were at first called "legal clinics," as well as greatly expanded lawyer referral services and prepaid legal service plans.

As the consumer movement gained momentum during the late 1950s, the need of middle-income consumers for improved access to legal representation received increasing attention. Some consumer groups, primarily those associated with organized labor, concluded that a way should be found to surmount the obstacles faced by the rank and file in accessing the justice system and obtaining legal assistance at a price they could afford.

The labor movement was experienced in the role of lawyers, both in the protection of rights before the courts and in legislative and administrative bodies, and recognized the utility to individual union members of having legal representation readily available to them. In response to this perceived need, lawyers—many with experience in delivering legal services to the poor—developed financing and delivery mechanisms aimed at middle-class working people.

Some approaches were initiated by individual lawyers and were entrepreneurial in nature; others were sponsored by the organized bar and conceived as a means for fulfilling the bar's responsibilities to the public; while still others, inspired by experience in delivering legal services to the poor, were developed in furtherance of public policy objectives and adapted to the needs of particular groups of consumers.

Basically, each of the mechanisms was aimed at the same three things:

- helping people to know when to seek legal assistance;
- letting them know that lawyers were available; and

---

102. B.F. Christensen, Lawyers for People of Moderate Means, Some Problems of Availability of Legal Services, (1970) at 39.

103. *See* Carroll Seron, *Managing Entrepreneurial Legal Services: The Transformation of Small Firm Practice*, in Lawyers' Ideals/Lawyers' Practices: Transformations in the American Legal Profession (Nelson, Trubek & Solomon eds., 1992), at 63-92.

- making legal services affordable for persons of moderate income.[104]

Advertised legal services and clinics. The approach of enterprising individual lawyers, taking their cue from the medical profession, was to organize "legal clinics." A "legal clinic" has been defined as ". . . a law firm that offers legal assistance at below-market rates for relatively routine types of . . . legal services [to individuals rather than to business] and that uses advertising, fixed-amount fees and standardized operating procedures and forms to increase volume and reduce costs."[105]

Although a few adventurous lawyers started clinic-type operations in the early 1970s, the movement to organize clinics did not take hold until after the Supreme Court's decision in the *Bates* case in 1977, holding that lawyers might advertise prices at which services are performed.[106] The basic idea behind the legal clinic approach was that consumers would be attracted to low, fixed and advertised prices, convenient storefront locations and an informal atmosphere.

Lawyers who organized their practice on the clinic model sought to reduce the cost of providing legal services by reducing the amount of lawyer time involved in rendering individualized legal assistance.[107] It required high volume to justify setting up standard procedures. Standardization was more readily accomplished in highly specialized offices such as those for conveyancing, personal bankruptcies or workers' compensation. It also required intensive use of paraprofessionals under a lawyer's direction, as interviewers, investigators and technical assistants. It called for word processors and computer software to generate standard forms and checklists, and to maintain practice controls and accounts, so that fees could be lower than those charged by traditional law firms.

A 1980 national survey of legal clinics indicated some difficulty in identifying true clinics which by then had become a diverse group, not generally high-volume nor streamlined in operations, but all advertising, at least in the Yellow Pages, and providing routine legal services for set fees.[108] In 1980, it was estimated that there were

---

104. *See* CHRISTENSEN, *supra* note 102, at 1-39; *see also* REPORT OF THE STAFF TO THE FEDERAL TRADE COMMISSION, *Improving Consumer Access to Legal Services* (1984).
105. G. Singsen, *Report on the Survey of Legal Clinics and Advertising Law Firms,* ABA Special Committee on Delivery of Legal Services (August 1990), at 1.
106. *Bates & O'Steen* v. *State Bar of Arizona,* 433 U.S. 350 (1977).
107. *See* L. Brickman, *Expansion of the Lawyering Process Through a New Delivery System: The Emergence and State of Legal Paraprofessionalism,* 71 COLUM. L. REV. 1153 (1971).
108. Carol Richards, *Legal Clinics: Merely Advertising Law Firms?,* (ABA Special Committee on the Delivery of Legal Services, November 1981), at 86.

between 475 and 583 private clinics across the country, mainly in metropolitan areas, run predominately by sole practitioners.[109]

Eight years later, a 1988 follow-up study reported that legal clinics were not booming but the report went on to acknowledge that many law firms had adopted the efficient, high-volume practice techniques developed by the clinics.[110] While it appears that the name "clinic" may be disappearing as connoting "poor people only" to many prospective clients,[111] large numbers of firms are in fact using a "clinic" approach. The 1988 study reported that there were at least 15,000 to 16,000 lawyers nationally in law offices that had adopted the techniques of the clinic, advertised civil legal services for individuals on a basis other than contingent fees and addressed their marketing primarily to middle income consumers.[112]

National legal services firms. The recent experience of both Hyatt Legal Services and The Law Offices of Jacoby and Meyers may suggest limits upon the effectiveness of national organizations operating local law offices which use the "clinic" approach. Both Jacoby and Meyers and Hyatt grew into interstate chains of small law offices supported by heavy television advertising. They generally avoided head-to-head competition with each other by locating their offices primarily in different media markets.[113] However, both organizations have contracted in recent years.

Hyatt, which was the larger, began contracting in 1987, while Jacoby and Meyers did not begin to contract for another two years.[114] Both firms remain unique, continuing to build on similar foundations, relying on the techniques of business and marketing to provide legal services for lower-income Americans who have limited resources and time for legal matters. Both continue to draw on the

109. *Id.*, at 6-7.

110. Singsen, *supra* note 105, at 29-30.

111. *Id.*, at 127. It is instructive to note that Hyatt Legal Services began as "Hyatt Legal Clinics," but then changed its name when market research determined that "Clinic" carried a connotation of "poor people" as clients. Similarly, Jacoby and Meyers began as the "Legal Clinic of Jacoby and Meyers," but also changed its firm name and now prefers the designation of "a retail law firm." Singsen, *supra* note 105, at vii.

112. *Id.*, at 132-133.

113. Seron, *supra* note 103, at 126-27.

114. Between 1987 and 1991, Hyatt Legal Services reduced the number of cities in which it maintained offices from 31 to 23, its offices from 187 to 112 and its lawyer staff from 674 in 1986 to 302 in 1991. It currently has offices in nine states and the District of Columbia. (Hyatt initiated during 1990 a program to offer partnerships to managing attorneys in local offices as part of transferring more control from headquarters to local offices.)

The Law Offices of Jacoby and Meyers since 1987 report a generally stable number of 150 offices in six states. In 1989 it had a lawyer complement of 329 which dropped to a complement of 305 lawyers in 1991.

National Law Journal's Annual Surveys of Large Firms, 1987 to 1991.

imagery of the legal services movement of the 1960s and 70s claiming the goal of filling a void for those in the middle.[115] No comparable multistate chains of law offices have emerged to this time.[116]

Hyatt Legal Services (HLS) state that their objective continues to be "to make quality legal service affordable and accessible to middle income Americans." To this end, they locate their offices in regional shopping centers, have the offices open in the evenings and on Saturdays and for most cases charge standard fees. Their standardized systems include an integrated client accounting and document generation software package and an operations manual covering topics from telephone protocol to professional ethics. Hyatt maintains that close to two million people have patronized the firm's local offices since 1977. Now, in a separate affiliate, Hyatt Legal Plans, Inc. (HLP) is providing plans for prepaid legal services to corporate and union sponsors, as described later in this section.[117]

Van O'Steen, of *Bates* case fame, now practices as "Van O'Steen and Partners." In 1989 he wrote:

> . . . my three lawyer legal clinic has grown into a law firm with four offices in metropolitan Phoenix and one in Tucson. We have a staff of 14 lawyers, 22 paralegals and 12 clerical and administrative employees.[118]

Various small firms around the country have followed the O'Steen model and, while frequently not describing themselves as legal clinics, also target their practice toward persons of moderate means. These are the firms in which the 1988 study estimated that at least 15,000 to 16,000 lawyers were practicing law.[119]

From the perspective of the individual lawyers engaged in these new methods of delivering legal service, there are marked differences between working in a "clinical" storefront law firm of the "O'Steen variety" and in a local unit of either of the two "national" legal service firms. In the small, entrepreneurial setting of the locally advertised, clinic-like operation, many of the aspects of traditional solo and small firm practice survive, but are altered by the adver-

---

115. Seron, *supra* note 103, at 68-9.

116. In June 1991, James Mattox, a former Attorney General of Texas, began advertising the opening of a chain of storefront law offices within Texas to serve middle income clients, six locations in Houston and three in San Antonio with additional sites under consideration in three other Texas cities. National Law Journal (June 10, 1991), at 2.

117. The information on Hyatt Legal Services and Hyatt Legal Plans was provided in a letter dated September 26, 1991 from William H. Brooks, Senior Partner. See also Seron, *supra* note 103, at 68-75.

118. Singsen, *supra* note 105, at vii.

119. Singsen, *supra* note 105, at 132-33.

tising which frequently draws a different clientele of single-matter drop-ins for whom the lawyer performs a standardized service at a fixed fee with little opportunity for developing a client base.

As for the attorney working in one of the chains, the lawyer must adapt to working in a large organization which emphasizes managing the work of its lawyers and their fitting into the management scheme focused on the efficient, productive and cost-effective delivery of service. Within an otherwise structured context, Professor Seron found in her study, that staff attorneys were expected to give special attention to self-promotion and the development of social skills among attorneys and staff alike. Moreover, quality service was equated with how consumers rated their treatment by an attorney on criteria deemed important by consumers: tidiness, returning telephone calls and politeness. However, the managers and the individual attorneys agreed that each attorney retained control over his or her own cases and clients, and that the relationships were private and personal between attorney and client without interference from management.[120]

Professor Seron found a consensus as to what is required to be a successful attorney in a national legal service firm: One must be able to carry a high-volume practice of individual-client cases—wills, bankruptcies, divorces—while acting in an entrepreneurial fashion, bringing in new business, complying with a managed reporting system, working very long hours and with a determination to build on the advertising provided by headquarters.[121]

Lawyer referral services. In parallel with the private entrepreneurial efforts directed to middle income clients, the organized bar has sought to strengthen its traditional lawyer referral services as a way of facilitating public access to legal assistance. The first lawyer referral services in the late 1930s were established in major metropolitan areas where bar associations frequently receive inquiries by middle income people looking for legal help. Many times these people can afford lawyers' fees, but are in search of information on how to find a lawyer best suited to handle their specific problem.

Bar-sponsored lawyer referral services today are operated by state and local bar associations providing coverage for virtually every county in the United States; however, the services they provide vary considerably. In a basic system, a caller is simply given the name of the next lawyer on a rotating list who handles the kind of matter involved; an appointment is made, and the caller can then go to the

---

120. Seron, *supra* note 103, at 68-73.
121. *Ibid.*, at 129-30.

lawyer's office and receive a half-hour consultation at a fixed fee of $15 or $20.

However, among the more than 350 lawyer referral programs nationwide, a great variety of additional services are offered.[122] Many programs are directed by staff attorneys with in-house staff available to furnish basic legal advice as well as suggestions as to where prospective clients may obtain help. Some programs have added "and information" to their title and conduct consumer education regarding lawyers and the law, and publish "legal check-up" materials and lists of community resources. A small number charge no fee for initial consultation.

Many referral services operate in conjunction with legal aid offices or have "no-fee" pro bono panels of lawyers. Bilingual staffs are common and a few accept credit cards for legal service.

To help ensure the competency of members of referral panels, a number of the services have screening procedures for would-be panelists or have CLE requirements or peer review as a condition of continued membership on panels. In some jurisdictions panels of specialists are available, for which qualifying education and experience are a prerequisite to membership.

According to the ABA Standing Committee on Lawyer Referral and Information Services, in 1978 there were 294 bar-sponsored lawyer referral services which received about 1.5 million inquiries annually. Today, five to six million requests are handled each year by more than 350 referral services nationwide.

Membership on a lawyer referral panel is seldom, if ever, the principal source of a lawyer's practice, but tens of thousands of sole and small firm practitioners are today members of bar-sponsored panels which provide a useful channel of introduction to prospective clients, while aiding members of the public to locate lawyers who can serve their needs. Nonetheless, a 1989 survey conducted by the American Bar Foundation on the public's use of legal services, found that only 1% of the persons surveyed who had used a lawyer during a three-year period reported that they had actually found the lawyer through a lawyer referral service.[123] It has been found that

---

122. The information on lawyer referral services is drawn from the *Reference Handbook* published in 1988 by the ABA Lawyer Referral and Information Service Committee and from *Characteristics of Lawyer Referral Programs* published by the Committee in 1991.

123. Barbara A. Curran, *1989 Survey of the Public's Use of Legal Services*, in AMERICAN BAR ASSOCIATION CONSORTIUM ON LEGAL SERVICES AND THE PUBLIC, TWO NATIONAL SURVEYS: 1989 PILOT ASSESSMENTS OF THE UNMET LEGAL NEEDS OF THE POOR AND THE PUBLIC GENERALLY (September 1989).

for lawyer referral programs to succeed they must receive substantial publicity.

Recently, privately sponsored lawyer referral services have sprung up. These are operated and funded primarily by groups of law firms specializing in handling personal injury and professional and product liability claims on a contingent fee basis. These services are frequently more visible than bar-sponsored services because of the television and other advertising which they employ.

Prepaid and group legal service plans. If legal clinics can be seen as arising from the entrepreneurial efforts of individual lawyers, and lawyer referral services as the bar's program for increasing public access to legal services, then prepaid and group legal service plans may be looked upon, at least initially, as a consumer group response to the problem of legal assistance for persons of moderate means.

Following a series of Supreme Court decisions between 1963 and 1971 holding that private associations may advise members on legal claims and recognizing the right of people to associate to obtain legal assistance, legal service plans of a variety of types proliferated.[124] Some of these arrangements were very simple: an agreement between a group of consumers and a law firm under which members of the group could receive a certain amount of free advice and receive predetermined fee-discounts on routine legal services. Information about the arrangement would be provided by the group to its members. The endorsement of the firm by the group's leadership assured the group's members that the law firm involved had been specially selected by the group's leaders. It seemed to provide a ready answer to the common question: "Where can I find a good lawyer?"

This type of legal service arrangement exists today between literally thousands of groups of consumers and individual lawyers and law firms. The largest and most elaborate of these plans is the Union Privilege Legal Services Plan sponsored by the AFL-CIO. Theoretically, some 17 million union members are eligible to receive free and discounted service under this plan from a nationwide panel of attorneys selected by the plan's administrators. The panel members are primarily drawn from among solo practitioners and 2-3 three lawyer firms.

Such "group discount" plans address consumer concerns as to

---

124. See *NAACP* v. *Button*, 371 U.S. 415 (1963); *Brotherhood of Railroad Trainmen* v. *Virginia*, 377 U.S. 1 (1964); *United Mine Workers of America* v. *Illinois State Bar Association*, 389 U.S. 217 (1967); *United Transportation Union* v. *State Bar of Michigan*, 401 U.S. 576 (1971).

the availability and price of legal services, by extending the existing framework for financing and delivering legal services. The group member is still on his or her own to determine whether a legal problem is present and is substantial enough to warrant getting a lawyer and coming up with the money to pay the fee.

One commentator in the late 1960s described the problem in this way:

> . . . the underlying question is whether the existing patterns are adequate to enable the average person to recognize that a lawyer can help . . . with a problem and to make an informed decision about the value of those services as against their cost; to provide . . . financial resources to pay those costs; and to lead . . . [that person] to a lawyer competent to handle the problem.[125]

Group discount plans were not enough. It was recognized that a more comprehensive approach was needed.

In the early 1970s consumer groups and the organized bar, with the cooperation of the insurance industry, jointly developed the prepaid legal service plan. In one sense, a prepaid legal service plan is simply a way of financing the cost of legal services. In Europe, legal expense insurance, as it is called, has been performing this financing function for over 80 years. However, from the basic idea of an "insurance policy" which pays lawyers' fees for a specified service, prepaid legal service plans in the United States evolved into a variety of options. One of the most popular prepaid legal plan systems is a direct derivative of the "group discount" plan of the kind sponsored by the AFL-CIO. This type of plan—termed the "access plan"—is designed to provide a member with easy access to legal advice and other non-complicated preventive legal services.

Under an access plan the basic service is unlimited legal advice and consultation by telephone during normal business hours directly to a lawyer's office using a toll-free number. Under the pure access plan, benefits are limited to this service only. In addition, service may include brief in-office consultations, the preparation and review of simple legal documents, such as a will, and short letters to be written or phone calls to be made to adverse parties. If more complex legal work is necessary, the plan member is referred to an attorney who has agreed in advance to furnish such services at a discount. The fees for these additional services are paid directly by the group member to the attorney.

---

125. Murray L. Schwartz, *Changing Patterns of Legal Services*, in Law in a Changing Society (Geoffrey Hazard, Ed. (1968), at 109-124.

This type of prepaid legal service plan is currently marketed directly to millions of American households by major credit card issuers at a cost of between $7 and $12 per month. For the consumer, it provides a low-cost, convenient and unstressful way of getting legal advice and information. With telephone access, the usual barriers to seeking legal assistance—fear of high costs, having to make an appointment, taking time off from work and anxiety about what the lawyer may do—are virtually eliminated.

The established comprehensive form of prepaid legal service is typically arranged in connection with employment. Either a labor union has negotiated a legal service benefit plan for all employees as an employer-paid fringe benefit, or an employer offers such a benefit to employees on a voluntary basis as part of a flexible benefits plan.

Comprehensive prepaid legal service plans are commonly designed to cover 80-90% of the average person's legal needs in a given year. Specific benefits of the plan may include direct telephone access to services, as under an access plan, but in addition coverage for both in-office and court work in most areas of the law. Such plans cover the types of problems most often brought by individuals to lawyers: wills and estates, consumer problems, landlord-tenant, real estate transactions, domestic relations, bankruptcy, representation before administrative agencies, civil disputes, and certain limited types of criminal matters.

Hyatt Legal Plans, Inc. (HLP), the affiliate of Hyatt Legal Services (HLS), claims to be the nation's largest provider of prepaid legal plans. It reports serving more than fifty corporate and union sponsors with a variety of benefit packages. Plan participants call toll-free the HLP service center which directs the callers to the nearest service providers. To support the plans HLP maintains a network of law offices which provide services to plan participants. This network is comprised of 110 local offices of Hyatt Legal Services as well as 1,400 private law firms in areas where HLS does not have an office.[126]

---

126. See *supra* note 117; *Free Lawyering for Employees*, Fortune (March 13, 1992), at 18. Three plans are summarized:
1. Introductory (cost per month $3):
   - any consultation
   - living trusts
   - mortgage preparation
   - wills
2. Basic Plan (cost per month $6): adds
   - adoption
   - defense against creditors
   - divorce
   - name change

The largest individual prepaid legal plan in the country is the UAW Legal Service Plan which covers all hourly workers of Ford, Chrysler and GM and provides access to a comprehensive list of legal services to over 2 million people, counting employees and family members. The second- largest employer-funded plan involves the over 275,000 employees of AT&T, followed by the Municipal Employees Legal Services plan covering 130,000 public employees of New York City.[127]

For any of the prepaid legal service plans arrangements must be made by plan administrators with attorneys in the areas where group members reside to provide services in accordance with the terms of each plan. The size and distribution of the network of lawyers and law firms recruited is dependent upon the scope of the plans and the location of plan members. The network supporting some plans number as many as 12,000 lawyers, predominately sole and small-firm practitioners.

Prepaid legal service plans evolved beyond the original notion of a simple financing mechanism, in part because of consumer interest in better legal services and in part because of the commercial interest in marketing the plans. Many plans have developed today into full-fledged legal service delivery systems with computerized referral systems, complaint mechanisms, quality control protocols, nationwide attorney networks, client information newsletters and cost-conscious administrative controls. Administration of plans by insurance companies and other service organizations has added the element of mass marketing designed to get consumers to enroll.

The type of arrangements entered into with lawyers under these plans has also evolved. Originally, arrangements with lawyers were of two types: under one type the member's choice of attorney was open, under the other the selection was limited to lawyers chosen by the plan. Today, there are plans where staff attorneys service all

---

3. Comprehensive (cost per month $12): adds
- consumer complaints
- defense of civil law suit
- personal bankruptcy
- traffic violations

The Wall Street Journal (August 6, 1991) at B1 provided a list of the "eight largest" marketers of prepaid legal service plans: Lawphone, Lanhan, Md.; Caldwell Legal USA, Sacramento, Calif.; Signature Group, Schaumburg, Ill.; Hyatt Legal Plans, Cleveland, Ohio; Midwest Legal Services, Des Moines, Iowa; Pre-Paid Legal Services, Ada, Okla.; Prudential Group Legal Services, Louisville, Ky. and National Legal Shield, Lakewood, Colo.

127. The MELS program is based on a pilot project funded in the 1970s by the Ford Foundation for District Counsel 37 of the American Federation of State, County, Municipal Employees to learn how social workers and lawyers might work together in the delivery of legal services. Letter of Curtis R. Berger, December 10, 1991.

members; others have a network of law firms under contract; while still others have a loose panel of general practitioners who have agreed with the plan's administrator to accept cases under the plan; sole practitioners continue to serve as exclusive plan attorneys for small groups, as well as participating in any of the other arrangements.

The American Prepaid Legal Services Institute (APLSI), an ABA-related clearinghouse organization, estimates that in mid-1991, approximately 17 million Americans were covered by some type of prepaid legal service plan, compared to less than 1.5 million prior to 1978.[128]

The total number of persons potentially covered by legal service plans of all kinds, including group discount arrangements, is substantially larger. The 1989 American Bar Foundation study indicated that 18% of U.S. households, representing some 43 million people, reported at least one person as a member of a prepaid or group legal service plan.[129] The National Resource Center for Consumers of Legal Services in August 1991 estimated that there were 71 million people eligible to use at least one legal service plan (including the armed services' legal assistance plans), or 28.6% of the population.[130]

From the perspective of sole and small-firm practitioners, the spread of legal services plans has presented new business opportunities for lawyers, most typically as legal service providers for plan members. To provide lawyers with an introduction to this new and growing field of practice the ABA Section of Economics of Law Practice (now the Section of Law Practice Management) published in 1988 "A Lawyer's Guide to Prepaid Legal Service." The guide is directed to permitting sole and small-firm practitioners to evaluate whether and how they might be involved in prepaid legal services.[131]

Since legal service plans involve elements of insurance, market-

---

128. Alec M. Schwartz, executive director of the APLSI, greatly assisted the Task Force in the development of material on legal service plans for this section of the Report.

129. *NewsBriefs*, "Bar Foundation Study Yields Prepaid - Lawyer Use Data," American Prepaid Legal Services Institute, Chicago (June, 1989).

130. National Resource Center for Consumers of Legal Services, *Legal Plan Letter* (Special Census Issue, August 30, 1991). Professor Thomas C. Fischer provides the following record of growth in the number of Americans covered by legal services plans (in millions):

1981	1983	1985	1987	1988
5.5	10	13	30	42.3

T.C. FISCHER, *supra* note 39, at 97.

131. See also *Who's Who in Prepaid Legal Services*, published by the American Prepaid Legal Services Institute (1991).

ing and employee benefits, their emergence has brought new forms of regulation into the legal-service-delivery equation. Initially, provisions of state codes of professional responsibility severely limited the extent to which lawyers could participate in prepaid legal service plans. The decade of the 1970s saw serious debates between the bar and sponsors of legal service plans regarding ethical rules prohibiting plans which limited the choice of lawyers that could be used by plan members. During the 1980s these ethical restraints were eliminated and most states during the 1980s revised their professional codes to accord with the optional provisions in this respect of the ABA Model Rules of Professional Conduct.

Although the debate over legal ethics impeded the growth of prepaid legal services for a time, many of the regulatory developments were in fact helpful in increasing the availability of these programs to the public. The insurance codes of many states were amended to allow insurance companies and other commercial firms to market, underwrite and administer legal insurance plans. Both the Taft-Hartley Act and the Employee Retirement Income Security Act of 1974 (ERISA) were modified to contain provisions recognizing legal services as a legitimate employee benefit. Finally, the Internal Revenue Code was amended in 1976 to exempt the value of employer payments to legal service plans from employee taxable income, thereby enabling major labor unions to successfully bargain for legal-service benefits.

Considering the premise that improving the delivery of legal services requires letting people know that legal services are available, making them affordable and expediting access, prepaid and group legal service plans have taken the most comprehensive approach. The experiments with legal clinics led to many practitioners adopting the "clinic" approach in more conventional practice settings. Bar-sponsored lawyer referral services, though highly developed and providing diverse services in some large metropolitan areas, may not be as effective in reaching out to the public as have some of the privately sponsored referral services and the prepaid legal service plans.

However, there is evidence that all of these mechanisms, together with the spread of lawyer advertising and increased public awareness of the need for and availability of legal services, have significantly stimulated the use of legal services. We are now told that the percentage of adults who have ever used legal services increased from 64% to 72% between 1974 and 1989. The proportion of adults having used legal services within three years of the 1989 survey was 39%, up from 27% during the same period prior to the 1974 survey.

While the use of legal services increased for all income groups, it grew at the highest rate among the moderate income segment of the population.[132]

Advocates for Group Legal Rights

Private lawyers are frequently retained by groups of individual citizens who have a similar legal interest. Taxpayers, members of a profession, residents of a community, consumers of a particular product or service, members of a labor organization and stockholders of a corporation routinely employ private counsel to press their group legal rights.[133] For the disadvantaged members of the community their access to redress has been more problematic, but following the Supreme Court's decision in *NAACP Legal Defense Fund, Inc.* v. *Button*[134] in 1963 litigation to vindicate group legal rights became a favored avenue by which "public interest" advocates sought to redress what were perceived to be social and economic injustice.

In the *Button* case Mr. Justice Brennan declared:

... litigation may well be the sole practicable avenue open for a minority to petition for redress of grievances.[135]

While the public interest bar established its separate identity and enjoyed its broadest support during the ten years, 1965–1975,[136] it remains today an active and significant segment of the practicing profession working in three interrelated practice settings.[137] The first setting is the so-called public interest law firm, a private entity funded by individuals, frequently by foundations, and, when successful and recoverable, by attorneys' fees awarded in litigation. In 1988 there were reported to be 200 such firms employing 1000 lawyers and financed to the extent of $130 million a year to help their clients.[138]

Some public interest law firms are identified by the client group they represent: children, the disabled, industrial workers, women,

---

132. Curran, *supra* note 123, at 57.
133. ABA Consortium on Legal Services and the Public, *Legal Services for the Average Citizen*, (Discussion paper 1977, reprinted 1978).
134. 371 U.S. 415.
135. 371 U.S. at 430.
136. *See Symposium-The Practice of Law in the Public Interest*, 13 ARIZ L. REV. 797 (1971); Brickman, *Legal Delivery Systems - A Bibliography* 4 TOLEDO L. REV. 465 (1973); Hanburger, *Private Suits in the Public Interest in the United States of America*, 33 BUFF. L. REV. 343 (1974); *Warth* v. *Seldin*, 422 U.S. 490 (1975).
137. See N. Aron, Liberty & JUSTICE FOR ALL (1988); see also EHRLICH & HAZARD, *supra* notes 16 and 19, at 81: "The Public Interest Lawyer".
138. N. Aron, *Non Traditional Models for Legal Services Delivery*, presented at the ABA Conference on Access to Justice in the 1990s (May 1989).

the elderly, gays and lesbians, minorities or the poverty stricken.[139] Other firms are known by the causes they advocate: the environment, natural resources, civil liberties, human rights or issues pertaining to the communication media. Still other firms take the names of organizations which support them: Pacific Legal Foundation, National Legal Center for the Public Interest, Mountain States Legal Foundation, Washington Legal Foundation or Moral Majority Legal Defense Fund. Public interest firms which comply with IRS regulations enjoy tax exempt status and today span the ideological spectrum from liberal to conservative.

The work of the public interest law firms is significantly augmented by a large number of private public interest lawyers and law firms who devote a substantial segment of their practices to representing community groups, environmentalists and civil rights plaintiffs. A recent study found in Louisiana, thirty-four private public interest law firms employing over 300 attorneys, and the report pointed to California, New York and Washington, D.C., as jurisdictions where large numbers of firms handle a wide variety of public interest litigation.[140]

A recent project co-sponsored by the National Legal Aid and Defender Association and the ABA Litigation Section, with additional funding provided by the Ford Foundation, joins private law firms with legal aid offices in individual matters of significance to large groups. Called the Litigation Assistance Partnership Project (LAPP), it provides legal aid programs with a capacity to handle complex poverty litigation, through training programs and mentors from large firms, financial expertise in low-income housing developments, support for antitrust litigation and other types of litigation with an impact on the poor but not traditionally handled by legal aid offices.[141]

The third practice setting for public interest lawyers is in government. The agencies in which they work are frequently the product of prior successes by public interest advocates and have been established to serve disadvantaged groups. The most extensive public interest service of this nature is said to be provided by the New

---

139. See the twenty-five pages of listings of legal services programs for special needs in the NLADA 1991/92 DIRECTORY, *supra* note 91, at 147-71.

140. *Id.*, p. 16.

141. The Summer 1991 issue of NLADA's *Cornerstone* includes a description by the Executive Director of Legal Services of Northern California ("LSNC") of two recent matters for which LSNC called on LAPP for assistance. One involved alleged violations of federal and state civil rights laws by a Sacramento federally subsidized housing cooperative and the other involved the litigation of a series of issues pertaining to California's Child Support Enforcement System.

Jersey Department of the Public Advocate who has been described as a "combination public defender, ombudsman and trouble-shooter—'a triple threat champion for citizens beset by arrogant bureaucratic and self-aggrandizing private interests.' "[142]

In an apparent effort to rein in the use by legal services offices of litigation to pursue policy-oriented objectives, the Nixon administration prohibited grantees of the Legal Services Corporation from representing undocumented workers and draft resisters, or from handling cases concerning abortion, school desegregation and voter registration.[143] Notwithstanding these and later restraints on LSC-funded legal services (some introduced by amendments to the authorizing legislation), the advocacy of public interest law in support of group legal rights continues to thrive and to engage a significant number of attorneys in each of the three practice settings.

Justice Thurgood Marshall has summarized the contribution of public interest law in these words:

> Public interest law seeks to fill some of the gaps in our legal system. Today's public interest lawyers have built upon the earlier successes of civil rights, civil liberties, and legal aid lawyers, but have moved into new areas. Before courts, administrative agencies and legislatures, they provide representation for a broad range of relatively powerless minorities . . .

> They also represent neglected interests that are widely shared by most of us as consumers, as workers, and as individuals in need of privacy and a healthy environment. These lawyers have, I believe, made an important contribution. They do not (nor should they) always prevail, but they have won many important victories for their clients. More fundamentally, perhaps, they have made our legal process work better. They have broadened the flow of information to decision makers. They have made it possible for administrators, legislators, and judges to assess the impact of their decisions in terms of all affected interests. And, by helping open doors to our legal system, they have moved us a little closer to the ideal of equal justice for all.[144]

---

142. Bierbaum, *On the Frontiers of Public Interest Law: The New Jersey State Department of the Public Advocate—The Public Advocacy Division*, 13 SETON HALL L. REV. 475, 481 (1983).

143. See R.L. Abel, *Socializing the Legal Profession: Can Redistributing Lawyers' Services Achieve Social Justice?* 1 LAW & POLICY QUARTERLY 1, 30 (1979); see also E. JOHNSON, *supra* note 63, at ix-xxiii (forward 1978 ed.)

144. Justice Thurgood Marshall, "Financing Public Interest Law: The Role of the Organized Bar." Address to the Award of Merit Luncheon of the Bar Activities Section of the American Bar Association (August 10, 1975). (Quoted by N. ARON, *supra* note 137, at 2.)

C. Large and Middle-Sized Firms

We turn from the segments of practice predominately involved with the representation of individuals to the segment in which the representation of business predominates. The American Bar Foundation's survey of the profession in 1988 identified 4,423 law firms having eleven lawyers or more, a somewhat arbitrary line to demark "small" from "large," but empirical studies indicate that it is a line which tends to identify the practice settings in which business law comes to predominate. For purposes of analysis, based on that survey we have arrayed the firms into the following four segments, divided between "medium" and "large":

Firm Size	Number of Firms	Number of Practitioners
Medium:		
11-20 lawyers	2,583	36,859
21-50 lawyers	1,201	36,563
Large:		
51-100 lawyers	381	26,273
101 or more lawyers	258	49,639
	4,423 firms	149,334 lawyers

It is important to a balanced and inclusive view of the private practice of law that this entire array of medium and large law firms be considered and not only the very largest firms on which the legal press as well as scholars and pundits tend to focus their attention. When considering these more than 4,400 medium and large firms it would be seriously mistaken to look upon them either as a "monolith"[145] or as sharing all the characteristics of the very largest firms.

Middle-Sized Firms

One out of every four lawyers in private practice in 1988 worked in one of the approximately 3,800 medium-sized law firms (11 to 50 lawyers). Collectively, they represent a cross-section of current law firm practice in all its diversity of substantive areas of practice, of clients and of firm organization and structure. They provide legal representation both for individuals and for business; some have a mixed practice, others stress legal problems of individuals and still others focus almost entirely on business law issues.

The medium-sized firms are large enough for some to offer what they describe as a "full line" of legal services, while other firms limit

---

145. *See* ZEMANS & ROSENBLUM, *supra* note 3, at 66.

their practice to one or several specialties. They fully reflect in their organization and structure the extent to which modern law practice of the more complex type forces upon the individual lawyer a measure of specialization in order to remain abreast of the expanded knowledge and skills increasingly required for competent service.[146]

Professor Fischer, reflecting on the current problems faced by medium-sized firms, observed that the "cycle of growth and development feeds on itself," which gives these firms a choice either to grow larger "to compete with larger firms (and accept the tremendous overhead consequences), or . . . focus their practice on limited clients and legal fields, remaining competitive, although small."[147]

Many medium-sized firms, following the design of the small specialty boutiques, have directed their practice and developed their expertise to serve clients in one of the burgeoning areas such as the entertainment industry, media communications or the publishing industry. Some firms specialize in representing performers, authors, radio and television personalities, movie actors, recording artists or musicians on concert tours. Others have directed their practice to working for professional athletes in tennis, golf or boxing, or members of basketball, baseball or football teams, counseling on player contracts and product endorsements. Other law firms focus their practice on serving the business organizations which provide this high visibility entertainment and sports employment.

Also common among middle-sized firms is specialization in aviation accidents, product liability, toxic torts, taxation or corporate behavior; while others have specialized in the rapidly developing field of intellectual property (which today embraces long-recognized specialties of patent, copyright and trademark law), of health and hospital law, of waste disposal and of environmental law.

In one sense the middle-sized firm stands at the center of the profession today. Many have resisted the institutionalization of practice and the bureaucratic model. While now acknowledging the importance of effective law office management, they have continued to lend emphasis to the idea that law is first a profession, and only secondarily a business. As a consequence, lawyers from this segment of practice have frequently been the backbone of activities within the organized bar stressing "professionalism" and providing leadership for professional organizations. In some ways, the medium-

---

146. See discussion "Networks or Affiliation Groups" and "Subcontracting" in M. Galanter & T. Palay, *Why the Big Get Bigger: The Promotion-to-Partner Tournament and the Growth of Large Law Firms*, 76 VA. L. REV. 747 (1990).

147. T.C. FISCHER, *supra* note 39, at 79.

sized law firm appears to have mitigated the effects upon the profession as a whole of the transformation of the large law firm, to which we next turn.[148]

The "Large Firm" Phenomenon

The more than 75,000 lawyers in the 600 largest law firms are the most prominent sector of the profession today. They trace their origins to Wall Street, not to Main Street. It is clear that the emergence of what came to be referred to as the "Wall Street law firms" has profoundly affected both the structure and the operations of many law firms of both large and of lesser size. In addition, it has had a significant effect upon the profession generally, as well as upon recruitment and placement policies at many law schools, if not upon curricula.[149] One recent study concludes that the elite large firms have been the "critical catalysts" of recent changes in the legal profession.[150]

The largest law firms of today are the professional progeny of "the Wall Street lawyer," who rose to prominence in the early years of this century as servant and adviser to big business and architect of its financial structure. Legal historian Lawrence Friedman writes:

> There is no question that the rise of the Wall Street lawyer was the most important event in the life of the profession during [the 1890s to 1930s] period.[151]

Friedman and others[152] have recounted the revolution in the structure and operation of large law firms led by Paul D. Cravath, which began in New York City early in this century. He instituted a system of firm operation that was adopted by other firms serving the business community. It included hiring outstanding graduates straight out of law school, each with the prospect of a partnership after an extended probationary period. They were required to work only for the firm, were paid a salary and were provided training and a graduated increase in responsibility.[153] The system developed by

---

148. *See* J.S. Studley, *Building on the Assets of Midsize Firms*, Manhattan Lawyer (November 1991), at 45.

149. *See* R.L. NELSON, PARTNERS WITH POWER: SOCIAL TRANSFORMATION OF THE LARGE LAW FIRM, (1988), at 1.

150. Sander & Williams, *supra* note 9, at 478.

151. L. W. FRIEDMAN, A HISTORY OF AMERICAN LAW (1985) at 636.

152. *Id.*; GALANTER & PALAY, *supra* note 50, at 9-10; W.K. HOBSON, THE AMERICAN LEGAL PROFESSION AND THE ORGANIZATION SOCIETY 1870-1930 (1986) at 108, 195-203; W.K. HOBSON, *supra* note 1; R. Nelson, *Practice and Privilege: Social Change and the Structure of Large Law Firms* 1981 AM. BAR FOUND. RES. J. 95; P. HOFFMAN, LIONS IN THE STREET (1973); J.W. HURST, THE GROWTH OF AMERICAN LAW (1950) at 303-05; R.T. SWAINE, THE CRAVATH FIRM AND ITS PREDECESSORS, Vol. 1 (1946).

153. R.T. SWAINE, *supra* note 152, Vol. 2 (1948), at 2-12.

Cravath and by other corporate lawyers of his day further included turnover and outplacement of lawyers who were not promoted to partner and the concept that only the firm had clients and not the individual lawyers.[154]

Wayne Hobson has chronicled the spread of this system of law firm operations among firms in New York and to other large cities and the related growth in the size of law firms with growing ranks of salaried lawyers (who came generally to be called "associates" in the 1920s to distinguish them from the partners of a law firm).[155] After 50 years of steady but gradual growth by law firms adopting the Wall Street model of hired associates, the Census Bureau reported in 1947 that there were 77 law firms having 50 or more employees, still concentrated, however, in New York, Chicago and Washington, D.C.[156]

By 1950 these larger firms had well-established law practices providing the high-quality and sophisticated legal services sought by major corporations and other large institutions. Their relations with their clients were stable and commonly reenforced by retainer agreements under which they provided continuing counsel, while standing ready to handle any special matters for their clients that might arise. The consumer and civil rights movements were heating up, and with spirited enforcement of the antitrust laws as well as a high level of business scrutiny by the federal regulatory agencies that had been established during the 1930s, the corporate law firms were in heavy demand by their clients.

Moreover, it was a period of heightened general economic activity. The federal highway building program was launched and the infrastructure was being rebuilt. Capital markets were active with new issues of equity and debt. American industry reached overseas as post-War Europe rebuilt with the help of the Marshall Plan. Legal work and economic activity went hand in hand and the large law firms prospered and steadily grew during the decade of the 1950s. Galanter & Palay refer to "Circa 1960" as "The Golden Age of the Big Law Firm."[157]

---

154. GALANTER & PALAY, *supra* note 50, at 9.

155. W.K. HOBSON *supra* note 152, at 141 et seq, Chapter 5 "Rise of Large Law Firms"; cf. A.H. FREEMAN, THE STYLE OF A LAW FIRM: EIGHT GENTLEMEN FROM VIRGINIA (1989).

156. Cited by Sander & Williams, *supra* note 9, at 436; the Census figures did not distinguish between salaried lawyers and other salaried employees.

157. GALANTER & PALAY, *supra* note 50, at 20-36; See P. HOFFMAN, LIONS IN THE STREET (1973); E. SMIGEL, THE WALL STREET LAWYER: PROFESSIONAL ORGANIZATION MAN? (1969); M. MAYER, THE LAWYERS (1967), at 305-345; B. LEVY, CORPORATION LAWYER: SAINT OR SINNER, Phila. Chilton (1961); A.H. DEAN, WILLIAM NELSON CROMWELL, 1854-1948: AN AMERICAN PIONEER IN CORPORATION, COMPARATIVE AND INTERNATIONAL LAW

A salient feature of law practice—large or small—in this period was the professional sensibility for keeping to one's self not only a client's confidences, but also firm information as to finances, billing, income, relations with clients or firm operations. Discreetness was the rule. Moreover, maintaining a low profile was enjoined by Canon 27 of the 1908 Canons of Professional Ethics[158] which condemned as "unprofessional" various forms of advertising and solicitation and concluded with this admonition:

> Indirect advertisement for business by furnishing or inspiring newspaper comments concerning causes in which the lawyer has been or is engaged, or concerning the manner of their conduct, the magnitude of the interests involved, the importance of the lawyer's positions, and all other like self-laudation, defy the traditions and lower the tone of our high calling and are intolerable.

Thus it was that any attempt in the 1950s (and well into the 1960s) to collect systematically information about law firms met with great resistance. But in the decades that followed, it has been said that the large law firm became "the most conspicuous feature in the American legal landscape."[159]

This "transformation" of large law firms in the 1970s and 1980s has been systematically analyzed, first, by Robert Nelson in his *Partners With Power* and later by Galanter & Palay in their *Tournament of Lawyers* who view the transformation against what they describe as "a dramatic expansion of the scale and scope of the whole world of legal institutions." [160]

The elements of that transformation are the subject of extensive comment.[161] The most obvious feature of the transformation was the

---

(1957); M. MAYER, THE WALL STREET LAWYERS, PART I: THE ELITE CORPS OF AMERICAN BUSINESS AND PART II: KEEPERS OF THE BUSINESS CONSCIENCE, Harper's Magazine (1956); and see L. AUCHINCLOSS, THE GREAT WORLD AND TIMOTHY COLT (1956).

158. The ABA Canons of Professional Ethics were superseded in 1969 by the ABA Code of Professional Responsibility and in 1983 by the ABA Model Rules of Professional Conduct.

159. R.L. ABEL, *supra* note 2, at 182.

160. GALANTER & PALAY, *supra* note 50, at 37.

161. In addition to NELSON and GALANTER & PALAY, *supra* notes 149 and 50, see, for example, S. Brill, *The Law Business in the Year 2000*, American Lawyer (Management Report, June 1989); *Symposium: The Growth of Large Law Firms and Its Effect on the Legal Profession and Legal Education*, 64 IND. L. J. 423 (1989) which includes the following contributions: E. Freidson, "Theory and the Professions," (at 423); B.G. Garth, "Legal Education and Large Law Firms: Delivering Legality or Solving Problems," (at 433); B.C. Danner, "Looking at Large Law Firms - Any Role Left for the Law Schools?," (at 447); J. F. Fitzpatrick, "Legal Future Shock: The Role of Large Law Firms by the End of the Century," (at 461); J.A. Stanley, "Should Lawyers Stick to Their Last?," (at 473); R.E. Rosen, "The Inside Counsel Movement, Professional Judgment and Organizational Representation," (at 479); L. M. Friedman, Robert W. Gordon, Sophie Pirie and Edwin Whatley, "Law, Lawyers and Legal Practice in Silicon

exponential growth in the size of firms, to which the structure and mode of operation of the larger firms was highly conducive. The rate of growth in the very largest firms was truly phenomenal. The average size of the 20 largest firms grew more than fourfold from 1968 (128 lawyers) to 1987 (527 lawyers). While the median number of lawyers in the 200 largest firms between 1975 and 1987 grew from 68 lawyers to 205, the number of firms with more than 100 lawyers grew from 45 in 1975 to 247 in 1987.[162]

Galanter & Palay present a compelling demonstration of the inevitability of such exponential growth when law firms are structured around a system that maintains a leveraged ratio of associates-to-partners combined with a fixed policy of "up-or-out/ promotion-to-partner."[163] Strict adherence to such a system compels an increasing number of associates to be made partners and hiring still more associates to replace the new partners.[164] This in turn compels a continuing search for more legal business to utilize fully the firm's legal resources.

It was in such circumstances that many large firms during the 1970s, in their efforts to retain old clients and to acquire new, began to scatter branch offices and to open foreign offices sometimes in multiple jurisdictions. Specialization became more intense and additional specialties were added so as to offer a "full product line" of services.[165]

At the same time, the firms found their relations with their business clients less enduring.[166] Corporate clients had substantially increased the size of their law departments during the 1950s and began to draw more and more of their legal work in-house. During the 1970s and 1980s they discontinued comprehensive retainer agreements of a single firm and shifted to having their in-house

---

Valley: A Preliminary Report," (at 555); J. Flood, "Megalaw in the U.K.: Professionalism or Corporatism? A Preliminary Report," (at 569); D.A. MacDonald, "Speculations by a Customer About the Future of Large Law Firms," (at 593). *See also*, M. STEVENS, POWER OF ATTORNEY: THE RISE OF THE GIANT LAW FIRMS (1986).

162. See R.L. ABEL, *supra* note 2, at 182-184.

163. GALANTER & PALAY, *supra* note 50, at 77-110; See A.W. Thorner, *Legal Education in the Recruitment Marketplace: Decades of Change*, 1987 DUKE L. REV. 276, 278.

164. The authors postulate that the progressive growth rate of many law firms reached a point in the early 1970s of "exponential" growth which would continue until operation policies were modified either by choice or the compulsion of circumstance.

165. The National Association for Law Placement's *Directory of Legal Employers* indicates that nearly all firms with more than 100 lawyers list over a half-dozen specialties covering most major areas of corporate law (even though many are best known for a single specialty). Cited in Sander & Williams, *supra* note 150, at 436 fn. 14.

166. It has been suggested that 25% of the corporations going public change law firms in the process. R.L. ABEL, *supra* note 2, at 184.

general counsels, as sophisticated shoppers for legal service, arrange *ad hoc* engagements of outside law firms.[167] For large hotly-contested one-of-a-kind transactions, in-house general counsel shopped for law firms who had assembled specialty groups with a variety of relevant competencies. Outside counsel were also engaged for major litigation which required special staffing, but more routine litigation and support for litigation were frequently kept in-house.

Some changes in relations between law firms and their business clients have been industry-specific, as in the case of insurance defense counsel. Ever since courts accepted the principle of insurance companies retaining defense counsel for their insureds, it has been common for stable relationships to exist between insurance companies and the law firms they retain as defense attorneys. But today with the changing profile of the insurance industry, the traditional relationships are no longer secure as companies draw more work in-house, experiment with cost-cutting devices such as "reverse" contingency agreements, and even the acquisition of entire law firms to handle their defense work.[168]

As a consequence, a new and open competitiveness among large law firms emerged. Operations became more profit-oriented. More and more firms resorted to lateral hiring and many to mergers to broaden their lines of legal expertise or to gain new clients. Some turned even to diversifying outside of the law into what they described as ancillary businesses.[169]

The intense competition by an increased number of large firms for top law school graduates to fill what seemed to be an ever-increasing need for more top-flight associates led not only to dramatic increases in associate compensation, but also to expanded recruiting programs to a broader roster of schools. In addition, there was a significant expansion in the hiring of law students for summer employment and at generous levels of compensation.[170]

For the lawyer recruits, large-scale hiring by individual firms (frequently recruiting 40 to 50 lawyers each year) tended to obscure the differences in their experiences that awaited them in practice. Professor Fischer has written that much of the growth in demand for legal services in the 1980s occurred in sharply expanding fields of practice, such as, "new business formation, mergers and acqui-

---

167. See Chapter 2.D, *infra*, regarding in-house counsel.
168. *See* G. Taylor, *Party's Over in Insurance*, NAT. LAW JOUR. (Sept. 23, 1991), at 1, 26.
169. J.W. Jones, *The Challenge of Change: The Practice of Law in the Year 2000*, 41 VAND. L. REV. 683 (1988).
170. A.W. Thorner, *supra* note 163, at 277, 281.

sitions, international trade and finance, malpractice, consumer protection, environmental concerns, tax reforms and litigation." He went on to identify 35 specialties practiced by law firms in Boston in 1986.[171] The experiences of the new lawyers and the tasks they are called upon to perform will vary as widely as the array of legal work within the firms.

In due course, to help maintain the leveraging ratio of associates to partners, many firms lowered their rate of promotion-to-partner, while others introduced multi-tiered staffs of senior lawyers, specialists, a second tier of associates, as well as an increased number of non-lawyer professionals.[172]

In the newly competitive, profit-oriented environment of large firms, a fresh focus was placed on business-like management. Professional managers to run the business side of law offices became commonplace and the Association of Legal Administrators came to boast more than 5000 members.[173] Some firms hired marketing directors, a position unknown in 1980, but by 1985 a National Association of Law Firm Marketing Administrators had also been established.[174] A whole service industry has now grown up to work with law firms: search firms for associates, partners and law-firm mergers; attorney out-placement consultants; law-firm management consultants; special computer support centers; lawyer-software systems providers; and public relations specialists for law firms.

Fanning the fires of competition and aggressively promoting this new service industry for law firms, has been the new legal press which began publishing in the late 1970s in the wake of the Supreme Court's decision in the *Bates* case[175] striking down the ban on lawyer advertising. The ethical restraints dropped one by one and the once opaque practices and internal affairs of large law firms gradually became public information, helping to complete the change in dominant law firm culture, from that of a restrained professional organization, to that of a competitive entrepreneurial enterprise with a growth strategy.

The *National Law Journal*, soon joined by its publishing competitors, lent media support for the growth strategy by focusing attention upon the comparative size of law firms and annually

---

171. T.C. FISCHER, *supra* note 39, at 77, 80-81.
172. *Id.*, at 283.
173. B. Johnson, *Administration Grows Up*, 8(33) National Law Journal 17 (April 28, 1986).
174. S. Schmidt, *Firm Development Mobilized by a 'New Breed' of Resource*, NAT. L. JOUR. (August 25, 1986), at 15.
175. *Supra* note 45, 433 U.S. 350 (1977).

compiling successively longer lists of the nation's largest law firms with a catalog of their branch offices. When the *American Lawyer* began publication in the late 1970s, it shifted the focus from counting lawyers and offices to the economics of law and the business of lawyering.

The investigative reporting of the *American Lawyer* began to pry out information from the previously private financial records of law firms and by 1985 the publisher was able to initiate an annual report in the style of the Fortune 500, with estimates of the financial results of those law firms believed to have the greatest gross revenues. Meanwhile, Prentice-Hall in 1987 began publishing annually "The Of Counsel 500" report which embraces a substantial part of today's large firm segment of more than 100 lawyers. It is published as a "management report for law firms" and reports on marketing practices, "billing rates of firms nationwide," salary figures for corporate counsel and law firm associates and upon the growth of corporate law departments.

Sander & Williams, by combining Census data with the *American Lawyer* data, confirm that the biggest firms have grown at a remarkable rate: the 20 largest law firms had average receipts of $14.7 million in 1972 and by 1987 $158 million.[176] The authors point out that, even adjusting for inflation, this is a fourfold increase in revenues in 14 years. At the same time, law remained a very decentralized industry, with substantially less concentration than in accounting; in engineering, architecture and surveying; in advertising; or in management consulting and public relations; although one of great inequality in the economic rewards.[177]

For at least 50 years, the law has been viewed as the most unequal of all the professions in the incomes of its members.[178] For a period during three decades, 1941 to 1969, incomes within the lawyer population gradually became more equal, but in the 1970s that trend reversed and the inequality of income became increasingly severe.[179] The rapid increase in partner and associate income in the largest firms was not shared in by many firms of lesser size and it appears that after 1972 there was in fact a decline in real income among medium-sized and small firms.[180] Moreover, in the

---

176. Sander & Williams, *supra* note 9, at 437, 438 (Table 4).

177. GALANTER & PALAY, *supra* note 50, at 123 (Table 7).

178. A government study of eight major professions in the 1940s found that lawyers had the most unequal distribution of income. U.S. Dept. of Commerce, *Survey of Current Business* (May 1944): in 1941, the most affluent 5% of lawyers accounted for 28% of all lawyer income.

179. Sander & Williams, *supra* note 9, at 446-51 (Table 10).

180. *Id.*, at 466-67 (Table 14).

economic downturn in the early 1980s the income of sole practitioners fell a stunning 46%.[181]

The continuing lawyer boom during the 1970s and 1980s was
not, however, confined to the very large firms. There was substantial and prosperous growth in the amount of legal work done generally for corporate clients. The relative size of the "corporate
customer" base grew at a steady rate and around 1980 for the first
time it passed the "individual consumer" sector as the dominant
purchaser of lawyers' services.[182] From 1967 to 1982 "personal" legal
services rendered by lawyers grew at only a 4.7% rate (after adjusting for inflation) while "business" legal services grew at a real rate
of 8%.[183] Overall demand for legal services grew more rapidly in the
business sector than in the consumer sector, and most rapidly with
respect to large corporations.[184]

For law firms with receipts of $1,000,000 or more (which would
include a substantial majority of the 5,000 odd firms we have identified as medium or large firms), over 70% of firm receipts have come
from business and less than 25% from individuals, (which propor-
tions appear to have remained quite stable over time).[185]

Ripple Effects of Large Firms

The extent to which law firms of lesser size, who were engaged
primarily in a "corporate" practice, have shared in the phenomenal
success of the largest firms, may well have turned on how the firms
perceived of themselves and how closely they held to the elitist model
of the traditional "Wall Street" firm, to which the business community has customarily turned for help with complex and difficult
problems. Sander & Williams suggest:

> The elite firms *are* elite because, in their view, they provide a special
> type of legal service . . . . [T]he common specialty shared by all elite
> firms is complex law . . . the most difficult and esoteric legal issues.[186]

They go on to contrast this practice of "complex law" concerned
with determining the relevant issues and engaging in exhaustive

---

181. *Id.*, at 450-51. It is appropriate to note that the less systematic and more
limited surveys done by independent consulting firms and published in the legal press
failed to report the general decline in the pattern of income, but focused instead only
on the general prosperity of "the most elite end of the lawyer spectrum."

182. *Id.*, at 441 (Table 5).

183. *Id.*, at 440-41.

184. *Id.*, at 475.

185. *Id.*, at 441. Included in receipts from individual clients are the contingent
fees paid plaintiffs' lawyers in personal injury and product liability cases. There are
firms of every size, including many medium-sized firms, who specialize in handling
these cases on a contingent fee basis.

186. *Id.*, at 475.

research to advance their business clients' interests, with what they perceive as the non-elitist practice which for the most part involves the application of standard legal doctrine to common problems of individual clients.[187]

Such a dichotomy of law practice into two spheres undoubtedly obscures many of the nuances in practice settings and differentiation among law firms, which are important to lawyers in practice or those planning to enter, but as a generalization, it accords with the earlier findings of Heinz & Laumann[188] and with the more recent analysis by Galanter & Palay.[189]

Dean Robert McKay in 1990 wrote of the "sharply increased need for law-trained people in the major law firms." He referred to "the triggering influence of the major firms" which had "defined the task, fixed the rules, and determined the conditions of labor, including compensation and billable hours." Perhaps speaking prophetically, Dean McKay went on to observe that it might be "too much to say that the whole apparatus, from legal education through every form of practice, depends on the large firm's somewhat uneasy structure," but that "at least we can say that collapse or serious damage to that imposing structure would have serious implications for every element of the legal profession," and that the "ripple effect on the way down would be no less dramatic than the impact occasioned by the abrupt rise of great aggregations of lawyers within the new megafirms."[190]

For law firms of all sizes which have a predominately business practice, the 1990-92 downturn in the economy has made apparent how closely linked corporate law practice has become to the general level of economic activity. The new ad hoc relationships between corporations with their own in-house law departments and outside law firms, as well as the special staffing by law firms to serve particular corporate legal needs, made business law firms particularly vulnerable not only to general corporate cost-cutting programs, but also to the loss of the kinds of law business during the 1980s, such as mergers and acquisitions, for which the special staffs had been assembled.[191]

With the demand for complex corporate legal work falling for

---

187. *Id.*, at 475-76.

188. *Supra* note 7.

189. *Supra* note 50.

190. R.B. McKay, *The Rise of the Justice Industry and the Decline of Legal Ethics*, 68 WASH. UNIV. L. QUARTERLY 829 (1990), at 846.

191. E.J. Pollock, *Big Firms Learn That They, Too, Are A Cyclical Business*, WALL ST. JOUR. (August 15, 1991), at 1.

the first time since the lawyer boom began in the 1970s, many firms have had to face the reality that in their entrepreneurial ardor they may have over-expanded. As a result, many law firms have followed the lead of their corporate clients and adopted a strategy of "down-sizing." This has been accomplished not only by reducing and deferring the hiring of new associates, but also by the forced separation of associates and even partners.

The recent down-sizing of law firms has special implications for law students. Since 1970 law graduates entering private practice have displayed an increasing preference to begin their careers in large law firms. This trend was identified by Zemans & Rosenblum (1981)[192] and Heinz and Laumann (1982).[193] The trend continued up through 1989 when it appears to have peaked, as the following NALP survey data reflects:[194]

**Percent of graduates entering private practice
in firms of more than 100 lawyers**

1984	1985	1986	1987	1988	1989	1990
16.6%	20.0%	22.4%	23.2%	27.7%	29.4%	28.4%

The recent slowing in what had been the exponential growth of large firms had an immediately depressing effect on this segment of the lawyer job market. In May 1991, *Of Counsel* reported a drop of at least 5% in associate-hiring of law graduates by large firms and that lateral hiring dropped by an even larger 10%.[195] While the large firm segment continued to grow, the overall growth rate of large firms for three years showed a progressive decline from 9-10% (1985-88) to 7.7% (1989) to 4.6% (1990).[196]

One result of the widespread down-sizing among large firms has been to create an unusually large pool of experienced lawyers looking for jobs. In the past, when lawyers left large firms they invariably had already found other employment, frequently with a smaller firm or corporate law department. However, the forced separations during the 1990-92 downturn were not ordinary turnovers and resulted, at least temporarily, in a market glut.

---

192. ZEMANS & ROSENBLUM, *supra* note 3, at 70.

193. HEINZ & LAUMANN, *supra* note 7, at 18.

194. NALP National Summary Reports for 1984 (at 83), 1985 (at 108), 1986 (at 166), 1987 (at 161), 1988 (at 112), 1989 (at 14) and 1990 (at 15).

195. *The Of Counsel 500* (May 6, 1991). The report indicates that one out of every three new-hires by large firms is a lateral recruit or by merger.

196. *Id.* In the 1991 "NLJ 250," 44% of the firms had shrunk from the preceding year (as compared with 17% a year earlier and 12% the year before that). For the first time, the number of lawyers needed for a firm to be included among the 250 largest dropped: from 131 to 129.

What sustained the modest overall growth rate among the large firms during 1990-91 was a continuing increase in the number of branch offices of the firms. By branching into new locations, large law firms enlarged their markets, as well as the number of firms with whom they competed. The list of the 250 largest firms shows offices of these firms in 44 states in over 120 cities (some of which might more appropriately be referred to as "edge cities" in the terminology of Joel Garreau, describing the new collections of commercial towers removed from central city).[197]

The most pronounced growth during 1990-91, but by a relatively small number of firms, was expansion outside the United States. Foreign offices of these firms are now located in 48 cities in 33 foreign countries and are reported to employ 2152 U.S. and foreign lawyers.[198] Multinational law practice seems to be the latest avenue of expansion for the large corporate law firms. While a few American law firms since the 1930s have had offices in Europe, South and Central America and East Asia, political events of the last several years have had profound repercussions in international commerce and finance, creating new capital markets, channels of trade and wholesale privatizations, all of which portend new law and regulation and the need for expert legal counsel equipped to advise both government and private enterprise regarding an emerging new international legal regime.

The European Common Market has brought European lawyers into a new legal arena along with American law firms. Eastern Europe's turn toward market economies, organization of stock markets and broad scale privatization of national enterprises have created a demand for multinational legal assistance from experienced U.S. lawyers. Meanwhile, Japan has slowly accepted the presence of American law firms, and now from Hong Kong southward and westward: Malaysia, Australia, through a changing India and even into Africa, economic and financial linkages are being forged in which American corporate lawyers are beginning to find public and private clients eager for their knowledgeable services. (It should be noted that in this latter region, with its long history of English law covering its commerce and banking, British solicitors are still the dominate providers of multinational legal services.)

---

197. J. GARREAU, EDGE CITY, LIFE ON THE NEW FRONTIER, (1991). The percent of lawyers in the Nation's 250 largest law firms who work in branch offices rose from 26.2% in 1986 to 33.9% in 1991. NAT. L. JOUR. (October 21, 1991), at 34.

198. NAT. L. JOUR. (October 21, 1991), at S3.

The Future of the Large Firm

In the present environment there appears to be a growing body of opinion that the outer limits of law-firm size may have been reached and that the law will not follow the accounting profession into the formation of a few giant firms that dominate the profession. Rather, it is thought to be more likely in the highly differentiated legal profession, that large business-law practice will increasingly diversify and experiment in firm organization and that lack of concentration will continue to be a principal feature of the profession.[199]

The professional ideal of a unitary profession with its core body of knowledge, skills and values, common educational requirements and shared professional standards has, to a significant degree, survived the profession's profound transformation in the 1970s and 1980s.[200] It has survived despite the enormous pressures within and without the profession to capitulate completely to commercialization and to divide into a series of economic sub-markets in which separate groups of lawyers sell highly specialized legal services to different consumer groups with little or no interaction among the various lawyer groups.[201]

It now appears that the continuous-growth strategy of the large firms with their "up-or-out/promotion-to-partner" system will continue to give way to more bureaucratized, closely-controlled forms of law firm management which conform growth to actual increases in demand, but which recognize the effective limits of rationalization and standardization in the conduct of a corporate law practice with its inherent complexity and the inevitably personalized nature of the professional services involved.[202]

With growth rates falling, large firms are designing diverse firm-missions aimed at different clienteles, focusing on new specialties and coming to look less and less alike, and beginning to display the same range of diversity in their practice as has been common for firms of lesser size all along.

---

199. See GALANTER & PALAY, *supra* note 50, at 121, Table 7, at 123; see also S. Brill, *supra* note 161; D. Bradlow, *The Changing Legal Environment, The 1980s and Beyond*, ABA JOURNAL (December 1988), at 72.

200. See infra Chapter 3.

201. Cf. R.L. ABEL, *supra* note 2, at 179 ("The Eclipse of the Paradigm of the Independent Professional"); at 182 ("The Rise of the Large Law Firm - Numbers"); at 184 ("Success and Failure in the New Marketplace"); at 188 ("Regionalizing, Nationalizing and Internationalizing Law Practice"); at 190 ("Extending and Intensifying Capitalist Relations of Production"); at 199 ("Bureaucratizing Management"); at 200 ("Assimilating the Professional Firm to the Corporate Client"); at 202 ("Professional Stratification"); at 208 ("One Profession or Many?").

202. See GALANTER & PALAY, *supra* note 50, at 138; S. Brill, *supra* note 161.

Galanter & Palay conclude their *Tournament of Lawyers* with these observations:

> The big-firm form carried an inadvertent commitment to exponential growth, but that growth was sufficiently slow to be compatible for a long period with "professional" forms of governance. So law practice never suffered the separation of ownership from control; control of work by others was, in aspiration at least, only temporary. Compared to other business services, law remained relatively unconcentrated, decentralized, unbureaucratic, and worker-managed. As the big firm becomes a less congenial vehicle, lawyers enjoy new opportunities to use their institution-shaping skills to reorganize the formats of professional work to make it produce the services and protections desired by society while making it fulfilling for those who do the work.[203]

In recent years, jobs in law firms with substantial business clienteles have been the positions of choice for large numbers of law students. Many law schools, "enlarged in numbers and expanded in student body, depend to a considerable degree on the apparently insatiable demands of the major firms for the annual crop of warm bodies."[204] Until the last year or two, the corporate law firms were steadily expanding and recruiting an ever larger segment of law school graduating classes. However, legal services for the business community are closely linked to economic activity. They are largely discretionary services for which demand rises in times of business prosperity and quickly falls when businesses contract or postpone to the future transactions calling for specialized legal services. The result has been a sudden contraction in the number of positions available in many law firms serving principally business clients. At the same time, record numbers are seeking admission to law school and enrolling in J.D. programs.

What do these circumstances portend? The rise, growth and prominence of the large law firm has had a profound effect not only upon the legal profession but also upon legal education.[205] Law schools shaped their curricula to respond to the needs of the corporate practice of large law firms,[206] while law students viewed the large law firm as the pathway to success in the profession and shaped their career plans toward what they perceived to be the challenge and the special rewards of such practice. Nowhere in the law is the

---

203. *Id.*, at 138.
204. R.B. McKay, *supra* note 190, at 853.
205. See *Symposium: The Growth of Large Law Firms and Its Effect on the Legal Profession and Legal Education, supra* note 53 and 161.
206. Cf. Descriptive material on George Mason University School of Law in The Official Guide to U.S. Law Schools 1991-92 at 159.

interdependence of law school with the practice of law more starkly apparent.

D. In-House Counsel

Private corporations today generate more than half the legal business of American lawyers. It was lawyers who created the corporation: an artificial person under the law, capable of continuous existence independent of the existence of its owners and having powers and liabilities distinct from those of any natural person. When the corporation became the dominate way of doing business, lawyers became indispensable to the organization, the financing and the operation of business in accordance with corporate law.

To respond to the legal needs of corporate business, the corporate law firm was developed, reshaping an entire segment of private law practice which grew and prospered performing corporate legal services.

However, from the late 19th century a few large corporations found law so pervasive to their operations that they hired lawyers to work full time in the management of the business and called them "general counsel." As demands grew, additional lawyers were added to corporate payrolls and corporate law departments gradually grew in size and number. In addition, in larger corporations, matters of corporate governance in the course of time came to be centered in the office of the corporate secretary and it became common to have lawyers serve in that position and on the secretary's staff when the function was not a part of the law department's responsibilities.

Some general counsel have remained partners in law firms while serving in that position, but substantially all in-house lawyers are now salaried employees of the corporation for which they work.

Today, approximately 10% of the legal profession is employed in legal work on a salaried basis by for-profit and not-for-profit corporations.[207] In addition, as law school training and legal experience came to be viewed as useful preparation for careers in business, the number of law-trained persons employed by corporations in non-legal work has also grown.

The hiring of lawyers by corporations began at a time when the bar, dominated by lawyers in private practice, was strengthening its professional organizations, unifying training and locating it in

---

207. AMERICAN BAR FOUNDATION, 1988 SUPPLEMENT TO THE LAWYER STATISTICAL REPORT (1991), at 4.

universities, raising and enforcing entry rules and instituting codes of ethics which included rules against lawyers using the corporate form for their practice because of the corporation's independent existence and limited liability against suit. Moreover, the number of salaried associates at the time was negligible in the few law firms which had them. In such circumstances, a lawyer going to work for a corporation as a salaried employee was in a sense defying the dominate culture of the profession and was seen, by some, as "leaving" the practice of law whatever might be the individual's role in the corporation.[208] However, as the large law firms themselves grew more institutional and employed increasing numbers of salaried associates and the differentiation in practice settings multiplied, the place of corporate counsel in the profession was gradually accepted together with the right of corporations to have "self service" for their legal work by staff attorneys.

In the early years of the century, lawyers were brought into corporations primarily as a response to the increasing pervasiveness of governmental regulations, which required frequent consultation with lawyers by corporate management, who sought legal advice from someone knowledgeable about the company's business and more aware than an outsider of the objectives of the enterprise. The in-house lawyer's role came to be seen in many companies as keeping the corporation free of legal trouble (some would call this "preventive law")[209] rather than the more traditional lawyer's role of getting the client out of trouble.[210]

On the other hand, among the first corporations to establish law departments were the railroads and the insurance companies who assembled in-house staffs to handle their large volume of more or less routine legal work involving leases and damage claims for the railroads and policy claims for the insurance companies. Although a few large companies in other fields created law departments early, it was not until the New Deal legislation of the 1930s and World War II regulations that the need for legal advice in virtually every area of business became pervasive.[211]

By 1948, the number of lawyers in private employment reached something over 3% of the lawyers accounted for by Martindale-

---

208. See W.K. Hobson, *supra* note 152, at 141.

209. See L. Brown & E. Dauer, *A Synopsis of the Theory and Practice of Preventive Law*, in THE LAWYER'S HANDBOOK (A.B.A. rev.ed. 1982); L. Brown, *Corporate Counsel at the Forefront of Preventive Law*, CAL. ST. B. JOUR. Vol. 42 (March-April, 1967).

210. *See* J.D. DONNELL, THE CORPORATE COUNSEL—A ROLE STUDY (1970), at 27-28.

211. *Id.* See also Q. JOHNSTONE & D. HOPSON, LAWYERS AND THEIR WORK Chapter 6: Corporate Law Departments (1967).

Hubbell,[212] but the following decade was the period in which there was the greatest increase in the percentage of lawyers finding corporate employment, as the following figures reflect:

Year	Percent of total lawyers	
1951:	5.7%	(Total lawyers: 221,605)
1954:	6.9%	
1957:	8.3%	
1960:	10.0%	(Total lawyers: 285,933)[213]

During the 1960s, the percentage of lawyers in private employment rose by another 1% (of a rapidly growing profession) and in 1970 reached its high point of around 11% of all lawyers.[214]

As corporate law departments began their period of growth in the early 1950s, a few corporate counsel directed their attention to raising what they perceived to be the low professional status of in-house counsel and how they were perceived by the members of the bar who were in private practice. One of the first such efforts was taken at the Association of the Bar of the City of New York. While the Association first resisted creating a committee on corporate law departments, the Association did sponsor continuing legal education programs specifically directed to in-house lawyers and the participation of house counsel in bar activities thereafter grew in New York and in other cities where law department staffs were concentrated.[215]

Corporate counsel were successful in the early 1960s in getting the attention of the leadership of the American Bar Association for some of the special problems confronting lawyers employed in the corporate sector, but their efforts to have the ABA create a separate section for corporate counsel were unsuccessful. Their principal section affiliation and activity has remained with the Business Law Section (formerly the Corporation, Banking and Business Law

---

212. R.L. ABEL, *supra* note 2, at 300 (Table 37c).

213. *Id.* 1960 figures from B.A. Curran, *American Lawyers in the 1980s: A Profession in Transition* (1986), at 27 (Table 3). This reflects growth for in-house lawyers of more than 126% compared with 29% for the profession as a whole.

214. *Id.*

215. E. Nobles Lowe, Esq., one of the leaders of this movement, has provided an account of this initiative among corporate counsel as well as of the creation in the same year of the American Society of Corporate Secretaries. "Corporate secretary" at the time was an umbrella title frequently combined with corporate "treasurer" and assigned a variety of miscellaneous duties. A majority were lawyers, but their linkage to the organized bar and their professional status were tenuous at best and dependent on an individual lawyer's voluntarily participating in general bar activities.

Section).[216] However, in 1962-63 and again in 1968-69, general counsel of major corporations served as presidents of the ABA.[217]

While the profession as a whole during the 1970s and 1980s grew from some 355,000 lawyers to over 720,000, the percentage of lawyers in private employment hovered close to 10% as appears in the following table:[218]

Lawyers in Private Employment (Percent of Total Lawyers)			
1970	1980	1985	1988
39,100 (11%)	54,200 (10%)	68,800 (10.5%)	70,700 (9.8%)

Prior to the 1970s, corporate law departments had generally drawn their staffs by hiring experienced lawyers laterally from law firms;[219] however, during the 1970s their direct recruiting of law school graduates increased significantly and the NALP annual reports reflected a surge between 1979 and 1985 in the direct recruiting of law graduates to a high of around 11% (although it should be noted that as many as 45% of the respondents were hired for what was reported as non-legal employment in the business concerns).[220] After 1985 there appears to have been some decline in the corporate hiring of law graduates and in the latest year for which figures are available on law graduates (1990), the percent of graduates going directly into positions in commerce and industry was 6.9% of the graduates.[221] While the total number of lawyers employed by corporations continued to grow into the 1980s, the annual rate

---

216. In 1972-73 the Westchester-Fairfield Corporate Counsel Association was formed as a specialty bar association to serve lawyers whose primary interest is in practicing in business corporations in the greater New York area. It is reported to have 1,000 members from more than 200 companies. The American Corporate Counsel Association was established in the early 1980s with headquarters in Washington, D.C. It is reported to have 35 local, state and regional chapters and has sought to promote bar admissions rules which facilitate multistate practice.

217. ABA Redbook 1991-92, at 408.

218. See Chapter 1 *supra*; AMERICAN BAR FOUNDATION 1985 SUPPLEMENT TO THE LAWYER STATISTICAL REPORT at 3 (Private Industry and Private Association total); 1988 SUPPLEMENT TO THE LAWYER STATISTICAL REPORT at 4 (Private Industry and Private Association total).

219. R.L. ABEL, *supra* note 2, at 176.

220. National Association of Law Placement, *Employment in Business Concerns— Ten Year Comparison*" (1990), at 119; see also R.L. ABEL, *supra* note 10, at 176; the American experience is in marked contrast with the northern European countries where as many as one out of every three law graduates is immediately employed in commerce and industry.

221. NALP, CLASS OF 1990, EMPLOYMENT REPORT AND SALARY SURVEY (1991), at 8-10.

of growth, as measured by one analyst, was substantially slower (3%) than that of the large law firms (13%).[222]

Employment in corporate legal departments has attracted many lawyers as being less hierarchical than the large law firm. At times corporations have seemed to be more receptive to the increasing supply of minority and female law school graduates under the effects of corporate personnel policies. Corporate legal positions may also be perceived as less competitive, stressing contribution to the corporation rather than individual advancement. Many corporate legal departments have been more advanced than law firms in addressing personnel needs, more flexible with regard to part-time work, maternity leave and similar matters.[223]

Studies suggest that there are between five and seven thousand for-profit corporations nationwide that employ in-house lawyers. This leaves some 120,000 businesses with 100 or more employees with no inside counsel at all, presumably still sending substantially all of their legal business to lawyers in private practice.[224]

Nonetheless, a substantial quantity of corporate legal work has been moved in-house ever since the 1950s and there has been in the past 20 years a significant change in the relationships between law firms and their business clients who have large law departments.[225] For the past twelve years, Prentice-Hall has published an annual *Law & Business Directory of Corporate Counsel*. The 1991-92 edition lists approximately 26,000 in-house counsel in some 5,100 for-profit companies and an additional 2,200 lawyers employed by 1700 not-for-profit organizations.[226] The Directory lists 17 primary areas of practice by in-house counsel and, indicative of the extent of specialization in the law today, lists an additional 139 "other areas of practice" together with a further list for non-profit organizations of 10 "other areas of practice."

Almost half of all the lawyers employed in business in 1980 were

---

222. T.C. Fischer, *supra* note 39, at 84-85, citing Csaplar & Bok study for the years 1979-1983.

223. T.C. Fischer, *supra* note 39, at 88. See also E. Spangler, *supra* note 15, at 70-106 ("Company Men Through and Through - Corporate Staff Counsel").

224. Id., at 87. See Glaser & Glaser, *Law and Business Directory of Corporate Counsel, 1991-92* (1991). The *1991 National Directory of Non-Profit Organizations* lists more than 167,000 non-profit organizations with reported annual income in excess of $100,000. The publisher states that they constitute a $350 billion market.

225. See *supra* discussion of the effect of these developments on large law firms.

226. The non-profit organizations are listed under the following ten categories: Colleges/Universities, Credit Unions, Foundations/Charitable, Health Care/Hospitals, Labor Unions, Miscellaneous (including various public interest organizations), Museums, Professional Societies, Religious Organizations and Trade Associations. See C. MacLachlan, *Washington, D.C.'s Hidden Bar*, Nat. Law Jour. (Apr. 22, 1991), at 1.

employed by Fortune 500 industrial companies or by one of the Fortune 50 largest companies in selected industries, as reflected in the following table:[227]

1980

Industry Classification	% of Industry Lawyers N = 54,626
Fortune 500 Industrials	29.2
Fortune 50 Retail	2.0
Fortune 50 Transportation	1.9
Fortune 50 Utilities	4.1
Fortune 50 Life Insurance	3.6
Fortune 50 Diversified Financial	4.3
Fortune 50 Banks	4.0
Other Insurance	6.3
Other banks	8.9
All Others	35.5
Total	99.8

A further analysis of the employment of in-house lawyers in 1980 indicated that a little less than a third (30.5%) of the lawyers worked for companies with one to three lawyers, while something more than a third (37.1%) worked for companies with four to 50 lawyers and another third (32.4%) for companies with over 50 lawyers.

Today, the 250 largest industrial companies identified by the *National Law Journal* have law departments that range in size from no in-house lawyers to 446 lawyers.[228]

The movement to bring more corporate legal work in-house which developed during the 1950s was concentrated in the large corporations with substantial law departments. As these corporate law departments developed, their paramount concern became the cost-effective use of legal services. This is a multifaceted problem. Internal corporate organization seeks to assure that functional areas generating legal work reflect the costs of that work in pricing and in management reporting. Corporate law departments therefore try to help their internal clients make cost-effective decisions about the level of legal services they need. Increasingly, senior management has demanded that internal lawyers account for their time by charging it to internal clients.

---

227. B.A. Curran, *supra* note 152, at 36.
228. National Law Journal, *The NLJ Client List* (July 8, 1991 supplement).

Improving economic efficiency by allocating appropriate tasks internally to in-house counsel also requires an analysis of the cost-effectiveness of the alternatives. This in turn became a major function of in-house counsel. It is maintained by some corporate law departments that the cost per hour for in-house counsel is half that for outside counsel, making the further point that in-house counsel are familiar with the corporate culture and with personnel. Thus, it is argued that the cost of communicating to a lawyer a problem that requires a lawyer's review, is lower when a corporation employs in-house counsel. The issue then becomes deciding whether or not the in-house counsel already has, or can cost-effectively acquire, the legal expertise the problem demands.

On the other hand, developing long-term relationships with particular firms and with particular lawyers within those firms can achieve many of the cost advantages that bringing work inside the corporation can achieve and many long-term relationships with outside counsel continue. The role of corporate law departments in managing the costs of outside counsel has gained increased prominence in recent years. Internal lawyers must decide prospectively what work they should send outside, whom they should select to do it, how much they are willing to pay, and retrospectively judge the quality of the work they have received. A 1991 survey of the general counsels of 350 major companies reported "intense pressure from management to reduce [legal] costs" and more than a quarter of the general counsels said that their own compensation was linked to controlling legal costs.[229]

Two-thirds of the responding general counsels in the 1991 survey said that they planned during the next year to use outside firms for an international legal matter, most often for European Community work,[230] and many expressed the intention to retain outside counsel for patent and trademark and for environmental work, in which fields they have great difficulty in finding qualified lawyers to bring in-house.[231] Other areas for which general counsels expected to retain outside lawyers were labor, mergers and acquisitions, real estate, bankruptcy and antitrust.[232]

Writing in 1967, Johnstone and Hopson found that "[o]ne of the

---

229. B. Lyne, *The Pressure Is On*, Nat. Law Jour. (Corporate Counsel supplement, Sept. 9, 1991), at 51.

230. See W.S. Lipsman, *American Corporate Counsel As In-House Advisers Overseas*, ACCA Docket (Spring 1991), at 18.

231. *Id.*, at 52.

232. *Id.*; 49 percent said their companies had underwent a merger or acquisition in the past five years, but nearly half of those law departments remained stable in size.

most significant developments by the American legal profession is the growth of corporate law departments."[233] It continues to be true. Professor Fischer concluded in his New England study that "the growth of corporate law departments had not seriously reduced corporate demand for outside legal counsel," but that the change in the nature of the relationship between large corporations and the corporate law firms had had "a considerable impact on the structure of legal work and employment" given the high volume of legal services.[234]

With a general stabilization in the size of corporate law departments and the recent recessionary pressures, the role of general counsel has increasingly become one of "managing the legal function of a business enterprise." It remains a stressful position at the center of the tension between company culture and professional ideals. The sometimes competing interests of officers, directors, employers and stockholders lead to recurring questions for in-house counsel as to the client to be served. However, many appear to have made a successful accommodation between the dual roles of loyal corporate officer and responsible professional.[235]

Serving as inside or staff counsel to a business or eleemosynary institution is today an established practice-setting for as many as 10 percent of the legal profession. Such employment places the individual lawyer in the dual position of being responsible to and sharing the culture both of the profession of which he or she is a member and of the institution by which he or she is employed. It is important that new lawyers entering this organizational setting of dual cultures be acquainted with how in-house counsel can properly accommodate in a principled manner to the two cultures and conduct themselves faithfully to the profession's ethical rules. It suggests the desirability that instruction in professional ethics address issues commonly faced by in-house counsel and their appropriate resolution.

E. Lawyers for Government

According to the 1987 Census of Governments, there were 83,237 governments in the United States. In addition to the national and 50 State governments, the Census enumerated the following units of local government:

---

233. JOHNSTONE & HOPSON, *supra* note 211, at 199.
234. T.C. FISCHER, *supra* note 39, at 88-89.
235. J.D. DONNELL, *supra* note 210, at 163-67.

3,141   county governments (county, boroughs and parishes);

19,289   municipalities—providing general local government through municipal corporations (cities, villages and towns);

16,691   town governments (governmental divisions of States and counties);

14,721   school districts;

29,532   special taxing districts.

Virtually every governmental unit requires some legal services. Historically, most such services were provided by private attorneys. Today the legal work of the larger governmental units has been brought "in-house" to be performed by full-time salaried employees, but there remains a substantial amount of the public's legal work done by part-time and fee-charging private attorneys, serving municipalities, school districts and special taxing districts.

Having set apart for separate consideration the judicial branch and the lawyers serving in that distinct function,[236] we may properly view the public sector of the profession at the three levels of government: local, state and federal.

Lawyers for Local Governments

There are approximately 39,000 local government units with police powers in the United States. Of these about 33,000 have populations of less than 10,000.[237] In these smaller units of government, it is customary to hire private attorneys on a part-time or a fee-work basis and there is no composite record of such retainers. Similarly, special taxing districts for schools, fire protection, water, libraries, sewers, waste disposal and other public services generally look to the private bar to serve their legal needs. While there is no count of the number of lawyers serving local governmental units in this manner, it is fair to conclude, based on the number of local governmental units to be served, that as many as 40,000 private attorneys may be retained to provide legal services to local governmental units.

As for the salaried lawyers employed by local governments (both elected and appointed to office), they have a variety of legal roles to fill and a broad range of legal problems to handle. Law enforcement and criminal justice are the quintessential functions of local government, generally led by a district attorney principally responsible for criminal prosecutions. The National District Attorneys Association reported in 1991 that there were 2,800 elected or appointed district attorneys and estimated that there was a total of

---

236. See *infra* Chapter 3.C.

237. The information on local governments and their employment of attorneys was provided by the National Institute of Municipal Law Offices, October 1991.

between 20,000 and 22,000 district attorneys and assistant district attorneys in the United States today. Also part of the local criminal justice system are salaried government lawyers serving as defense counsel in public defenders' offices, as well as in probation, parole and corrections.

On the civil side, there are salaried lawyers variously employed in offices of county and city attorneys (the latter frequently identified as "corporation counsels"); municipal departments of education, city universities, or city school boards; welfare, health and hospital and other agencies of local governments; rail, air and water transportation authorities and public utilities.

The legal work on the civil side of local government is richly varied. It commonly involves land use regulation and real property issues such as cable television rights of way, easements for compatible uses, multiple permits, temporary takings, environmental regulation and questions of just compensation. Municipal tort liability and contractual disputes of public agencies are the core work of many local government lawyers, while others focus on public highways and construction projects. Still others are involved in the legal issues relating to welfare services, as well as health and hospital issues. Discrimination and civil rights are local government concerns, as well as at the state and federal level; as are revenue measures, bond financing and user fees in lieu of taxes.

The lawyers employed to handle this array of civil legal work by more than 5000 governmental units are scattered over the 50 states and no composite record measures their actual number. However, from a canvas of the national organizations of Municipal Law Offices and County Governments it has been possible to arrive at a reasonable approximation of the minimum number of 50,000 lawyers so employed in local governments.[238]

Lawyers for State Governments

The focus of legal activity at the state level is in the offices of the State Attorneys General. According to a recent survey by the National Association of Attorneys General, the chief legal officers

---

238. This minimum estimate is based on information provided by the National Institute of Municipal Law Offices (NIMLO), the *Municipal Yearbook* published by the International City and County Management Association, and the National Association of Counties (NACO). This minimum estimate of 50,000 is substantially larger than the number counted in the Lawyer Statistical Reports prepared by the American Bar Foundation. The ABF Lawyer Statistical Reports are based on data gathered by Martindale-Hubbell for its directory, but the failure of many lawyers in public employment to provide listing information to the publisher apparently results in a substantial undercount of lawyers in government.

of the 50 states and of six other jurisdictions[239] employed in their offices 8,278 full-time and 236 part-time attorneys as of January 1, 1991, supported by staffs of 14,996 non-attorney clerical workers, paralegals, investigators and technical assistants.[240]

Ordinarily separate from the Attorney General's department are the lawyers working for the state regulatory departments of banking, insurance, securities and public utilities, each of which employs staff attorneys.[241] Consumer affairs offices are now operated by most states, sometimes within the Attorney General's department while in other states as a separate department. Wherever the function is located, staff attorneys play a key role in consumer protection.

Varying from State to State is the role of the Attorney General in the legal work for other state agencies including those with responsibility for child welfare, civil rights, corrections, drug abuse, ethics, fair employment, housing codes, juvenile delinquency, labor, law enforcement, occupational licensing, liquor control, health and mental health, highway and occupational safety, parole, taxation and workers compensation.

The legislative branch of state governments also is a substantial employer of lawyers on both a part-time and a full-time basis. Legislative staff attorneys work on bill drafting, law revision, legislative review of administrative regulations, general support for committees and in their conduct of hearings, and counseling and assistance for constituents.[242] (Large numbers of lawyers also work for the judicial branch of government in state and local courts and are discussed in Chapter 3.D, *infra*.)

Similar to lawyers employed by local government units, many employed by state departments and agencies also seem to find no purpose in providing listing information to the *Martindale-Hubbell Directory* with the result that the count of lawyers in state government contained in the Lawyer Statistical Report is substantially less than the number indicated by the organizations of state officials.[243]

---

239. The six jurisdictions are District of Columbia, Northern Mariana Islands, Puerto Rico, American Samoa, Guam and the Virgin Islands.

240. NAAG, *Statistics on the Office of Attorney General* (1991).

241. See the enumeration of state regulatory departments in the *Lawyer's Almanac 1992*, at 1111-15, 1117-21, 1130-1141.

242. See EHRLICH & HAZARD, *supra* note 16 and 19, at 76 ("The Legislative Assistant").

243. The American Bar Foundation in its 1980 and 1988 Lawyer Statistical Reports counted only 30,358 lawyers in 1980 in local and state government combined and that this figure increased only to 34,700 in 1988. The 1980 total was broken down as

Studies currently in process seek a more reliable measure of lawyers employed in the public sector. A more accurate appraisal of the size of this segment of the lawyer population awaits the completion of those studies.[244]

Lawyers for the Federal Government

Since the creation of the Republic, lawyers have played a central role in designing and in administering the federal government. At the Constitutional Convention those trained in the law were in the majority. For the next 200 years at all times lawyers were prominent in the executive branch of government.

As the role of the federal government grew so did the number of lawyers employed by the federal government departments and agencies.[245] The progressive era and the New Deal brought many additional lawyers into government as administrative law developed and flourished.[246] As agencies took on quasi-judicial functions, hearing officers multiplied and eventually came to be acknowledged as administrative law judges. Dean Griswold has pointed out that the *Federal Register* in 1937, the first full year of its publication, filled 3,450 pages. In 1990 (even after several years of "deregulation") the total was 53,618 pages.[247]

When the ABF sought in 1980 to enumerate the lawyers in the federal government it found 20,132 lawyers scattered in a host of departments and agencies, reflecting the rich diversity in subject matter in which lawyers in federal service are engaged. The distribution of lawyers among the departments and agencies in 1980 was reported as follows:[248]

---

follows:

State Attorney General's offices	5,130
Prosecutor's offices (state and local)	11,415
Other state departments or agencies	7,286
Other local departments or agencies	1,670
Unidentified state or local departments or agencies	4,857
Total lawyers in local and state government	30,358

B.A. Curran, *American Lawyers in the 1980s: A Profession in Transition*, 20 LAW & SOC'Y REV., at 36 (Table 14) (1986).

244. In 1991 the ABA created a new Division for Government and Public Sector Lawyers. The first task of the new division is to gather more complete information on lawyers in government than has been available heretofore.

245. See Lawyer's Almanac 1992, *supra*, at 965-80 and 981-88.

246. As to the work of lawyers employed by federal agencies, see E.L. BROWN, LAWYERS, LAW SCHOOLS AND THE PUBLIC SERVICE (1948).

247. E.N. GRISWOLD, OLD FIELDS, NEW CORNE, at 119 (1991).

248. B.A. Curran, *supra* note 243, at 35 (Table 13) and 1988 SUPPLEMENT TO THE LAWYER STATISTICAL REPORT, at 20.

Department or Agency	Percent of 20,132 Federal Lawyers
Department of Justice	17.9%
Internal Revenue Service	9.4%
Department of Defense and Armed Services	8.4%
Department of Health and Human Services	6.5%
National Labor Relations Board	4.8%
Congress	4.5%
Veterans Administration	3.5%
Department of Energy	3.1%
Securities and Exchange Commission	3.0%
Federal Trade Commission	3.0%
Department of Labor	2.9%
Department of Commerce	2.7%
Department of Housing and Urban Development	2.3%
Department of the Treasury	2.2%
Department of the Interior	2.0%
Department of State	2.0%
Environmental Protection Agency	1.8%
Department of Transportation	1.7%
Interstate Commerce Commission	1.6%
Federal Communications Commission	1.5%
Department of Agriculture	1.2%
Equal Employment Opportunity Commission	1.1%
Small Business Administration	1.1%
All other departments and agencies	11.9%

In 1989 the Federal Office of Personnel Management reported that there were 20,000 "general attorneys" according to their count in the employ of the federal government. If this were intended to be an inclusive number, it appears to have been a significant understatement of the actual number of lawyers in federal service. The ABF's 1988 Lawyer Statistical Report, subject to its inherent limitation in the counting of government lawyers, accounted for 23,042 lawyers in federal service (an increase of 2900 over the 1980 count). But in 1991 the Department of Justice alone reported that it had 7,280 attorneys in the units of that one department. There were 93 United States attorneys and approximately 4,000 assistant United States attorneys in 1991,[249] with the remainder scattered among the various units of the Department, including the Immigration and Naturalization Service, Bureau of Prisons, Drug Enforcement

---

249. The work, role and functioning of United States Attorneys is described in J. EISENSTEIN, COUNSEL FOR THE UNITED STATES (1978).

Administration, Federal Bureau of Investigation and the United States Marshals Service.[250]

If the Justice Department continues to account for about the same 18% of the lawyers in federal service that it did in 1980, the Justice Department figures would suggest that the total number of lawyers in federal service today exceeds 40,000.[251] This would seem reasonable when one considers the overall growth in the profession during the 1980s, which increased by 40%, and particularly when one takes into account the extent of the increased legal work performed by private lawyers in so many subject areas of federal law and regulation.[252]

The Needs of Public Sector Lawyers

The responsibilities of government lawyers under various legal provisions may include authority concerning legal matters that ordinarily reposes in the client in private client-lawyer relationships. For example, lawyers for government agencies may have authority on behalf of the government to decide upon settlement or whether to appeal from an adverse judgment. They may also have authority to represent the "public interest" in circumstances where a private lawyer would not be authorized to do so. The ABA Rules of Professional Conduct expressly state that the Rules do not abrogate any such authority given to government lawyers by law. (*See* the Scope of the Model Rules.)

However, in the absence of such special provisions, the government lawyer is no less subject than any other lawyer to the rules regulating professional conduct. Moreover, the special public responsibilities placed upon government counsel carry with them special duties of public trust, as when the prosecutor exercises prosecutorial discretion.[253]

Lawyers entering the public sector have need of special instruction to prepare them for their governmental responsibilities. Law

---

250. These figures are taken from the National Association of Attorneys General's *Statistics on the Office of Attorney General* (1991), at 29-20.

251. A significant addition to the number of lawyers in federal service was the expanded committee and subcommittee staffs of the 22 standing committees of the House of Representatives and the 16 standing committees of the Senate, as the number of subcommittees multiplied, many with staffs largely made up of lawyers. See the *Lawyer's Almanac 1992, supra,* at 1084-1100.

252. See *supra* Chapter 2.C.

253. For a discussion of the work life of lawyers in various civil service positions, see E. SPANGLER, *supra* note 15, at 107-143 ("Good Soldiers—Civil Service Attorneys").

schools and the organized bar should take this need into account in planning programs of instruction and offering support for lawyers entering public service to assist them in their professional development.

Chapter Three
The Organization and Regulation of the Profession

A. The Beginnings of the Profession
B. The Bar's Identity in Learning, Skills and Professional Values
C. Law School: The Unifying Experience
D. The Judiciary: The Profession's Gatekeeper
E. The Survival of a Single Public Profession

A. The Beginnings of the Profession

In colonial and post-Revolutionary War America, there was little beyond one's local community to link one lawyer to another and the idea of a legal profession to which all lawyers belonged was virtually inchoate. The most common method of preparation for a legal career was through apprenticeships in offices of members of the bar.[1] The aspiring attorney paid an established lawyer a fee to study under his tutelage.[2] Many distinguished attorneys served as apprentices, including Thomas Jefferson, Joseph Story, Daniel Webster, James Kent, John Adams, John Marshall, and John Quincy Adams. By late colonial times, apprenticeships were considered mandatory in urban areas; very few attorneys began their practice without one.[3]

Although many considered apprenticeships crucial to a legal

---

1. McManis, *A History of First Century American Legal Education: A Revisionist Perspective* 59 WASH. U.L.R. 597, 601-606 (1981). Two other methods available included studying in England at the Inns of Court and studying independently. Before the Revolution, many young men studied at the Inns of the Court, which was perceived as socially desirable. *Id.* However, during the period when most Americans were admitted, the Inns had deteriorated educationally, and many used study at the Inns as a way to frequent London society, not as a method to study law. *Id.* Independent study was not a popular method because of difficulties, including the severe shortage of books in existence and in print. *Id.*; *see also* Bard & Bamford, *The Bar: Professional Association or Medieval Guild?* 19 CATH. U.L.R. 393, 395. The "universal text for reading at law" was *Coke on Littleton*—at least until Blackstone published his *Commentaries*. E. Coke, INSTITUTES OF THE LAW OF ENGLAND (1628); W. BLACKSTONE, COMMENTARIES ON THE LAWS OF ENGLAND (1765); *see* McManis at 605, n.52, 53.
2. HARNO, LEGAL EDUCATION IN THE UNITED STATES 19 (1953). This fee could add up to an impressive amount for an attorney with several apprentices at the same time. In 1780, the price ranged from $100-200, but could go up as high as $500 for a prestigious attorney. McManis, *supra* note 1, at 605 (*citing* Gewalt, *Massachusetts Legal Education in Transition*, 17 AM. J. LEGAL HIST. 27, 34 1973)).
3. R.B. STEVENS, LAW SCHOOL: LEGAL EDUCATION IN AMERICA FROM THE 1850'S TO THE 1980'S 3 (1983); White, *Legal Education in the Era of Change: Law School Autonomy*, 1987 DUKE L.J. 292, 292- 93.

education, they were not universally admired. Such prominent American lawyers as Thomas Jefferson criticized the apprenticeship as an inadequate method of professional training. The experienced attorney received cheap labor in exchange for the use of his library, but provided the apprentice with very little in the way of actual legal training.[4] Often, experienced attorneys were too busy practicing law to spend time with their apprentices.[5] There was no guarantee that a skilled practitioner was an adequate teacher.[6] Many apprentices spent their time tediously copying documents for their masters, not studying legal tenets.[7] The emphasis was practical, not theoretical.[8]

In the period leading up to the Civil War, the place of lawyers generally in American society had greatly diminished from that which the relatively small number of lawyers had occupied in the early years of the Republic. As Professor Friedman has written:

> The country was flooded with lawyers who were mediocre or worse. Few states controlled admission to the bar through a single agency or court . . . . Where local courts each passed on admission to their bar, the exams were usually oral, and so cursory as to be almost a joke.[9]

Moreover, in the populist era of Andrew Jackson, disdain for lawyers as a self-created, professional elite reached full flower and some legislatures abolished all educational or training requirements,[10] allowing any adult citizen to be a member of the bar, no matter how lacking in training competence or legal skill, (although some courts, in defiance of their legislatures, continued to screen those whom the courts would admit to practice before them).[11]

---

4. McManis (1981), *supra* note 1, at 604 (citing 1 *The Papers of Thomas Jefferson* 23-24 [J. Boyd ed. 1974]).

5. WARREN, A HISTORY OF THE AMERICAN BAR 83 (1911).

6. McManis, *supra* note 1, at 604 (citing Warren (1911), id. at 167.

7. *Id.* at 605.

8. HARNO, *supra* note 2, at 39. This division was enhanced by those who had studied at the Inns of the Court, which supported the idea that a legal education should be separate from a university education. *Id.*

9. L.M. FRIEDMAN, A HISTORY OF AMERICAN LAW, 2nd Ed. (1985) at 652.

10. For example, Maine (1843-59), New Hampshire (1842-72), Wisconsin (1849-59) and Indiana (from 1851 on); id. at 653- 54.

11. Robert Stevens provides the following summation:

> Professional standards in 1860 had been largely nonexistent. In that year, a specific period of law study, as a necessary qualification for admission to the bar, was required in only nine out of thirty-nine jurisdictions, and even law study had come to be thought of as less an apprenticeship and more a clerkship. The bar examination, although required in all states but Indiana and New Hampshire, was everywhere oral and normally casual. In only nine states was there anything approaching a bar examining committee. The leaders of the legal profession, surveying the situation, came to the conclusion that the status quo could not and

Moreover, there continued to be little present to bond lawyers together or to promote any sense of profession across the increasingly diverse and expanding country. There was no consensus as to

- what a lawyer's education and training should be,
- how one became a lawyer,
- what regulation there should be of lawyers, or
- for what functions a lawyer's services should be employed.

Following the Civil War, groups of lawyers—many of whom had elite practices serving the new economic interests and were distressed by the lack of standards and the low estate to which the bar had fallen in their local communities, launched a movement to raise standards and to promote a sense of profession. During the 1870s the seeds of professional organization and regulation were planted by such leaders of the bar which grew to provide an identity for the profession of which a stressful interdependence between the profession and the law schools became a part; a unique relationship of the bar to the judicial branch of government became a second part; and all came to be part of a system of professional self-regulation under the authority of the judiciary.

B. The Bar's Identity in Learning, Skills and Professional Values

In the 1870s an identity for the American legal profession began to be framed in the organization of bar associations, first in a few major cities,[12] then in a few states,[13] and in 1878 nationally with the

---

should not be maintained.
R.B. STEVENS, *supra* note 3, at 25.

12. New York in 1870, Cincinnati in 1872, Cleveland in 1873, St. Louis and Chicago in 1874, Memphis and Nashville in 1875, and Boston in 1876.

13. Dates of the initial organization of state bars:

1873	New Hampshire
1874	Iowa
	District of Columbia
1875	Connecticut
1876	New York
1877	Illinois
1878	Alabama
	Nebraska
	New Jersey
	Vermont
	Wisconsin
1880	Missouri
	Ohio

establishment of the American Bar Association.[14] At its organizational meeting, the ABA established a Standing Committee on Legal Education and charged it with developing a program which visualized a unitary legal profession with common admissions and educational requirements for the entire country.

Meanwhile, Christopher Columbus Langdell had left the practice of law in New York City and had become dean of the Harvard Law School, which at the time, along with a few other law schools, was striving to move into the mainstream of American university education and out of what had been their subordinate educational role. The 1870s was the time that the university in America was beginning to flourish, the intellectual community was infatuated with the "new sciences" which were driving industrial development, and technical training became the badge of contemporary achievement. It was in such circumstances that Dean Langdell introduced the "case method" and began the promotion of legal education as the study of a "science," with the "case method" providing the laboratory in which legal doctrines and principles could be explored and developed out of the opinions of appellate courts.[15]

While these were schools that continued the earlier methods of instruction, the Langdellian reorganization of legal education into an academic discipline acceptable to the university community assured law schools of a place in the modern university at the same time as it presented the profession with an educational program for lawyers that could raise both the standing and the standards of the bar.

The ABA upon its founding became a strong ally of the law schools in their efforts to establish their niche in American university education. In 1881 the ABA initiated what became a century-long campaign, passing a resolution recommending attendance at law school for three years and that all states give credit toward required-apprenticeship, for time spent in law school. With bar leaders advocating the notion that a uniform type of academic law school was needed to control entry into the bar, a national alliance developed between the newly organized bar and the burgeoning law schools.[16]

At the ABA Annual Meeting in 1893, steps were taken to organ-

---

14. Some 75 lawyers from 21 states and the District of Columbia came together for the organizational meeting of the ABA in the upstate New York resort of Saratoga, in response to a call of the Connecticut Bar Association based on a resolution adopted a year earlier by the American Social Science Association which had commended the future of the legal profession to the emerging law schools of the country. See GOETSCH, ESSAYS ON SIMEON E. BALDWIN, 24-30, cited by R.B. STEVENS, *supra* note 3, at 34; G. CARSON, A GOOD DAY AT SARATOGA, (1978).

15. *See* R.B. STEVENS, *supra* note 3, Chapter 4, at 51 to 72.

16. Id. at 92-93.

ize a separate section of the Association for legal education, it being thought that the general ABA meetings were inadequate to discuss issues of legal education and bar admissions and to act on recommendations of the Standing Committee. The Section was to complement the standing committee and be a forum with a considerable measure of autonomy. It would have the power to elect its own officers, schedule programs, debate and pass motions, although its recommendations would still go to the Committee for approval before Association action.

Judge Simeon E. Baldwin of the Yale Law School Faculty and later Chief Justice and Governor of Connecticut was appointed Temporary Chairman. (In 1878 he had been the principal convener of the meeting in Saratoga at which the ABA was organized.) As Chairman, he stated the Section's purposes to be to "serve as an important feeder to the Association" and second, to provide an opportunity for discussion of legal education "with more fullness [sic] than might always be agreeable for the Association to entertain at its open meetings."

Toward the end of the century, the ABA called for the establishment of an organization of "reputable" law schools and in 1900 the Association of American Law Schools was founded with thirty-two charter-member schools. Membership was open to schools rather than individuals, and schools were required to meet certain minimum standards.[17] For the next fourteen years, AALS met regularly with the ABA until World War I, when the ABA heedlessly scheduled its annual meeting to conflict with the academic term.[18]

However, the separation of AALS meetings from those of the ABA beginning in 1915 breathed new vigor into the AALS. By 1920, its leadership, convinced that the schools could do little by themselves to raise requirements for admission to the bar, urged law faculties of the member-schools to work actively with the ABA in a standards-raising effort. With the active participation of a large body of law professors at the 1920 meeting of the ABA Section of Legal Education and Admissions to the Bar, a special committee on legal education was established chaired by the lawyer-statesman Elihu Root. The Root Committee reported in 1921 that "only in law school

---

17. W.A. Seavey, *The Association of American Law Schools in Retrospect.* 3 JOURNAL OF LEGAL EDUCATION 153 (1950) at 157-58: the requirements for Association membership: (1) accept students for admission only who had a high school or equivalent education; (2) require 10 hours-a-week of instruction for at least two years; (3) only graduate students after an examination; and (4) provide students with access to a law library having reports of the state in which located and of the U.S. Supreme Court.

18. Id. at 160.

could an adequate legal education be obtained"; that two years of college should be required before admission to law school; and that the ABA should invest a council on legal education with power to accredit law schools. The report was accepted by the Section, and Root and Chief Justice Taft piloted it to approval by the 1921 ABA convention.[19]

A major accomplishment of the ABA, born of its relationship with the law schools, was to wrest legal education from the local control of the practicing profession during the early years of the 20th century and to place it increasingly in the law schools. When state-wide admissions standards were first prescribed by newly-established boards of law examiners in the late 19th century, it was common to require at least one year of law school preceded by two years in either a law office or a law school,[20] but the growing sentiment among legal educators, supported by the organized bar, led to the call for requiring that the entire three years be spent in law school, which ultimately became the rule.

Today, all but seven states require all applicants for admission to have graduated from a three-year law school program (or its part-time equivalent). California, Vermont, Virginia and Washington do permit law office study (for the few who wish it) to be a substitute for law school graduation, and Maine, New York, and Wyoming permit a combination of law school and law office study as a substitute for law school graduation.[21]

For a profession to create for itself an identity, it must not only claim as its own a special body of learning and skills—for which the legal profession looked increasingly to the law schools—but it must also embrace a core body of values which sets members of the profession apart and justifies their claim to an exclusive right to engage in the profession's activities. "Professionalism" lies in adherence to such values.

In response to the Jacksonian attempt to democratize the bar and to strip it of any special standing, individual lawyers sought to articulate standards for the profession. A central value of the stan-

---

19. *See* R.B. STEVENS, *supra* note 3, at 115 and Seavey, *supra* note 17, at 161-62; cf. A.Z. REED, TRAINING FOR THE PUBLIC PROFESSION OF LAW (1921).

20. If the applicant for admission were a college graduate, it was common to require a year less of "law" training. See, for example, the first New York State Admissions Standards prescribed in 1895. J. Newton Fiero, *Albany Law School Semi-Centennial Remarks* (1901).

21. See "Minimum Requirements for Admission to Legal Practice in the United States," at 75-82 of the ABA REVIEW OF LEGAL EDUCATION, Fall, 1990 and Chart III: Legal Education, at 10-11 of the ABA COMPREHENSIVE GUIDE TO BAR ADMISSIONS REQUIREMENTS, 1991- 92.

dards which they articulated was "objectivity," based upon the lawyer's personal detachment from the client and the client's problems. The "independence" of lawyers was to be furthered by their avoiding conflicting public and private obligations and personal self-interest that might detract from the objectivity of counsel. The various ethical standards articulated in these early models were to be voluntarily assumed by lawyers and were recognized as going beyond those required by law of the ordinary citizen. In addition, they visualized that the lawyer as an individual professional would assume a responsibility for all others in the profession upon whom the standards were equally binding.

Such a model was set out by David Hoffman of the Baltimore bar in 1836 in his "Fifty Resolutions in Regard to Professional Deportment." Later such standards were more elegantly expressed by Judge George Sharswood from his chair of law at the University of Pennsylvania in his seminal lectures for young lawyers in the 1850s on "The Aims and Duties of the Profession of the Law." It was from Judge Sharswood's lectures that Thomas Goode Jones later drew the pioneering Alabama Code of Ethics of 1887.

Reflective of the attention the profession was devoting in the 1880s to its continuing act of self-creation, by articulating its values, was the work done by Thomas Goode Jones in writing a Code of Ethics for the bar of Alabama. Here was a lawyer, who served as Speaker of the House and as Governor of Alabama—and later as a United States District Judge—drawing upon the lectures of Judge Sharswood thirty years before, to set forth a Code of Duties for Attorneys: duties to courts and judicial officers, to each other, to clients and to the public, concluding with the duty to be a friend to the defenseless and the oppressed.

It took another 20 years for the ABA to develop the first national code of conduct for lawyers. This code was set forth in thirty-two *Canons of Professional Ethics* and promulgated in 1908. The Preamble included this general admonition:

> No code or set of rules can be framed, which will particularize all the duties of the lawyer in the varying phases of litigation or in all the relations of professional life. The following canons of ethics are adopted by the American Bar Association as a general guide, yet the enumeration of particular duties should not be construed as a denial of the existence of others equally imperative, though not specifically mentioned.

The 1908 Canons began with "1. The Duty of the Lawyer to the Courts" and what followed were essentially a series of rules for the advocate with little guidance for the lawyer providing other legal services.

In 1928 thirteen additional Canons were added by the ABA which addressed some matters of more general concern to the profession, such as "Partnership—Names" and "Approved Law Lists," but the focus remained on the lawyer as advocate. Canon 45 relating to "Specialists" simply stated:

> The canons of the American Bar Association apply to all branches of the legal profession; specialists in particular branches are not to be considered as exempt from the application of these principles.

In 1933 various Canons were further amended by the ABA but again without changing their focus on the advocate. One new Canon added in 1933 pertained to the permissible manner of giving "Notice of Specialized Legal Service." Additional amendments were made to the Canons in 1937 and the final Canon 47 was added, relating to "Aiding the Unauthorized Practice of Law." It provided:

> No lawyer shall permit his professional services, or his name, to be used in aid of, or to make possible, the unauthorized practice of law by any lay agency, person or corporate.

In the successive writings of Hoffman, Sharswood and Jones, and finally in the ABA *Canons*, there gradually evolved a concept of professionalism for the American lawyer, based upon obligations and responsibilities both voluntarily assumed and required by society. They sought to capture and distill the diverse traditions of the law in America not only for the guidance of practitioners, but so they might be passed along to new lawyers entering the profession. By the mid-1960s the need for updating the 1908 Canons was apparent and the ABA undertook the preparation of a new Code of Professional Responsibility to replace the Canons. With changes in the law and society accelerating, the ABA in the 1980s sought in the Model Rules of Professional Conduct to articulate the responsibilities of the lawyer today as he or she fulfills a variety of roles and is confronted by vastly changed circumstances, socially, economically and politically.

The American legal profession to this time has succeeded in maintaining its overall identity and seems in some respects to have come together as possibly a more unified profession than in the past. In 1880 only 552 of the more than 64,000 lawyers in America were members of the ABA. In 1929 only 18% of the lawyers were ABA members. Today the ABA has approximately 375,000 members, which represents about half the lawyers in the country. In addition, the vast majority of non-ABA members belong to State and local bar associations (with lawyers in at least 35 states required to belong in order to practice. See *infra*, Chapter 3.D).

The bar of America is today a more organized and unified profession than at any time in its history, despite its great size and diverse fragmentation. Its aspired-for identity is now declared in the opening sentence of the Preamble to the Model Rules of Professional Conduct:

> A lawyer is a representative of clients, an officer of the legal system and a public citizen having special responsibility for the quality of justice.

The profession has successfully created for itself a loosely defined but distinct identity in learning, skills and values with which most lawyers can identify. Indispensable to the creation have been the development of formal legal education as the common gateway to the profession and the universal control by the judiciary over entry providing a strongly unifying effect despite the ever-increasing diversity and extraordinary growth of the profession.

C. Law School: The Unifying Experience

At the time in the early 1920s that the Council of the ABA Section of Legal Education and Admissions to the Bar became an accrediting body for law schools, AALS had as members less than half the nation's 143 law schools, and its member-schools enrolled only a minority of the approximately 27,000 law students.[22] However, its select membership had succeeded in raising standards among its own, had successfully established law teaching by full-time scholar-teachers in university-related schools as a new profession and made the law school, rather than the law office, the principal place for training new lawyers. Nonetheless, the AALS member law schools were losing the competition for students to the proprietary, more practical and less academically-inclined schools.[23]

In 1923 in the initial implementation of the Root Report the ABA issued its first list of approved law schools, and in 1927 appointed the secretary of AALS as its first full-time adviser on legal education. Thereafter, the two associations continued their coordinated efforts to raise the standards of law schools and of bar admissions,

---

22. W.K. Hobson, *The American Legal Profession and the Organization Society 1890-1930* (1986), at 108.

23. See Seavey, *supra* note 17, at 159-161: from 1901 to 1919 attendance at AALS schools increased 25 percent, but in non-Association schools it increased over 100 percent.

and of placing the control of the principal gateway to the profession in duly approved law schools.

However, by the late 1920s only about half the country's law schools were ABA-approved (65 schools in 1927) and only about one-third of the law students were in these approved schools. Moreover, 32 states still had no formal requirement for pre-law studies and 11 others required merely high school graduation or its equivalent. In 1927, *no* states as yet required attendance at law school in order to be admitted to the bar.

On the other hand, by 1928 every jurisdiction, except Indiana, had a compulsory bar examination and the tide was clearly beginning to turn. By 1938, there were 101 ABA-approved law schools with about two-thirds of the nation's law-students. As the country entered World War II, with its attendant debilitation of both the law schools and the entire profession, the approved law schools were fast becoming the principal gateway for entry into the profession.

The immediate post-war years witnessed a significant nation-wide consolidation of ABA-approved law schools in their position at the profession's gateway. With the financial aid of the GI Bill, veterans opted for the accredited law schools and the percentage of law students attending ABA-approved schools shot up in 1947 and 1948 to more than 85 percent of all law students. There were at the time approximately 40,000 students enrolled in J.D. programs at the ABA-approved law schools. The combination of wartime attrition and the GI Bill for returning veterans proved fatal to a significant part of the unapproved, marginal law schools (with the salient exceptions of schools in California and Georgia where admission to the bar nominally disregarded the legal education of applicants).[24]

In 1965 there were 136 ABA-approved law schools with 56,510 students enrolled in J.D. programs. Over the next 15 years, 35 law schools were added to the list of accredited schools. In 1980, the then 171 approved schools had 119,501 students enrolled in their J.D. programs. Since that time the number of approved law schools has risen to as high as 176 with a record J.D. enrollment in 1991-92 of 129,580.

The magnitude of the present law school enterprise and of the

---

24. *See* R.B. STEVENS, *supra* note 3, at 207-09, 220-21 (fn. 32, 33), 244-45. California has continued up to today generally to use the bar examination as the exclusive control on admissions to the bar, but recently it has flirted with taking a quite contrary approach under which law schools would be required to offer certain courses of study and applicants for admission to the bar would be required to show that they had completed specifically approved courses. *See infra* Chapter 3.C.

role it plays today in preparing lawyers for practice is highlighted by a contrasting glimpse at the past. From 1829 to 1845 Joseph Story constituted half the entire faculty of Harvard Law School at the same time as he served as a justice of the U.S. Supreme Court.[25] During the 25 years, toward the end of the century, when Langdell served as dean there was only one full-time instructor for every 50 students (8 for 400 students at the end of his term), yet under his successor, Dean James Barr Ames, Harvard's full-time faculty-to-student ratio fell even lower to 1 to 78 and persisted at that level into the 1920s.[26] Meager faculties were the rule at law schools around the country as their enrollments generally grew.

Not until 1915 did AALS find it feasible to fix the modest requirement that its member schools have at least three full-time instructors. At that time, only 35 of the AALS members had as many as three full-time faculty.[27] Not until after the ABA accreditation program was established did the faculty-to-student ratio begin to rise. Since 1950 law school faculties have grown substantially to the point that they are now treated as a distinct segment of the total lawyer population.

In the 1980 Lawyer Statistical Report, 6,606 lawyers were counted in educational institutions, and the 1988 Supplement to the Lawyer Statistical Report found that the ranks of lawyers in academia had swollen to 7,575, approximately one percent of the lawyers in the United States.[28] In 1991 the ABA-approved law schools reported the following total faculties:

5,585	full-time teachers (1,455 women, 586 minorities);
3,718	part-time teachers (902 women, 308 minorities);
1,365	deans and administrators (722 women, 187 minorities); and
1,182	librarians (792 women, 134 minorities)

Today, the educational continuum for virtually all lawyers commences in the accredited law school. There the professional development for each individual lawyer begins. For the vast majority, admission to law school followed by the successful completion of the law school's program are requisite for admission to the bar. What law schools require of their students in educational performance can significantly affect the stage of professional development reached by graduates when they seek admission to the bar. In recent

---

25. Seavey, *supra* note 17, at 153.
26. *See* A.E. SUTHERLAND, THE LAW AT HARVARD (1967) at 277.
27. Seavey, *supra* note 17, at 160- 61.
28. AMERICAN BAR FOUNDATION 1988 SUPPLEMENT TO THE LAWYER STATISTICAL REPORT, at 20.

years, law schools have given increasing attention to their role at the entry point to the profession and as the initiators for each student's professional development.

D. The Judiciary: The Profession's Gatekeeper

The federal Constitution in Article III, Section 1, created the third branch of government by vesting all "judicial Power" in the Supreme Court and such other courts as the Congress might establish. While assuring tenure to federal judges, no eligibility for judicial office was prescribed in the Constitution and none has been prescribed by Congress. Alexander Hamilton in his Federalist No. 78, item 25, argued that there were "two necessary requirements for proper judges, namely, "skill in the laws" and "integrity," but he stopped well short of suggesting that judges must be members of the bar or have any particular legal experience.

It is clear that the Revolutionary generation of lawyers had no special relationship to the judicial branch of government at the time. Nine states had established distinct branches of judicial power (Delaware, Georgia, Maryland, Massachusetts, New Hampshire, North Carolina, Pennsylvania, South Carolina and Virginia),[29] but lay judges were commonplace in all. Of the eleven men who served on the Superior Court of Massachusetts between 1760 and 1774, nine had never practiced law and six had never even studied law.[30] Both England and the colonial tradition contemplated lay judges as well as judges learned in the law, and New Jersey and New York in their state constitutions, continued well into the 19th century, courts of last resort in which laypersons could play key roles.[31]

How judges were chosen and how they were to act were lively political issues in the early years of the Republic,[32] and, they remained major issues into the middle of the 19th century. By 1850, the popular election of judges had become more and more accepted as normal.[33] Professor Friedman notes that

[t]he elective principle undermined the idea that no one but lawyers

---

29. See Federalist No. 81, item 7. See M. L. CHADWICK ed., THE FEDERALIST (1987) at 439.

30. L.M. FRIEDMAN, *supra* note 9 at 125, citing W.E. NELSON, AMERICANIZATION OF THE COMMON LAW: THE IMPACT OF LEGAL CHANGE ON MASSACHUSETTS SOCIETY 1760-1830 (1975) at 32- 33.

31. Id.

32. See Friedman, *supra* note 9, at 124- 138.

33. Id. at 371.

had the right to determine the proper outcome of cases, and that strict legal principles were the only tools that belonged in the toolshed of judges.[34]

However, the politicalization of the judicial process gave rise to calls for reform and lent impetus and mission to the newly organized bar associations in the 1870s.[35] Full professional status for judges and heightened status and standards for the legal profession went hand and hand, and as they progressed over the next 50 years the relationship between bench and bar became indissoluble. The lay judge virtually disappeared from the judicial branch, except at the very bottom of the judicial pyramid, and the organized bar came to view the judiciary as an off-shoot of the bar, for which and to which, in theory, all lawyers had a special public responsibility. Lawyers came increasingly to be described as "officers of the court."

The 1988 Lawyer Statistical Report (published in 1991) counted 2,551 lawyers in the federal judiciary and 16,520 lawyers in state and local courts.[36] Not all lawyers who work in the judicial branch are judges. Up to twice as many lawyers are court officials (such as clerks of court and staff attorneys), law clerks to judicial officers and other support personnel, as are judges.[37]

Today, the entire Federal Judiciary are lawyers: Justices; Circuit Judges; District Judges; Judges of the Tax Court and Court of International Trade; Bankruptcy Judges; U.S. Magistrates; and of the Court of Military Appeals. In 1990, 2,143 judicial officers were accounted for by the Administrative Office. In addition, substantially all of the federal administrative law judges, functioning outside the judicial branch, are also lawyers.[38] Moreover, there are now over

---

34. Id. at 372.

35. Id. at 648-49.

36. THE 1988 SUPPLEMENT TO THE LAWYER STATISTICAL REPORT, at 4: "National Lawyer Population."

37. B.A. Curran, *American Lawyers in the 1980s: A Profession in Transition*, 20 LAW & SOC'Y REV. 19 (1986) at 31, 33 (Table 11). According to the surveys of the American Bar Foundation the number of lawyers in the judicial branch more than doubled between 1960 and 1980 (from 9,000 to 19,160). From 1980 to 1988, ABF reports no growth, but rather a small decline, to 19,071 lawyers in the judicial branch. However, both the number of lawyers counted in the federal judiciary and in state and local judiciary appear to be substantially understated when compared with those statistics that are available from the Administrative Office of the Federal Courts and the National Center for State Courts. (The ABF figures for lawyers in the judiciary are based solely on Martindale-Hubbell's listings of lawyers.)

38. There are more than 1,500 administrative law judges at the federal level (ALJs and AJs) and possibly as many as three times that number in the States. More and more they are dealing with benefit and enforcement cases involving trial-type resolution of disputes in which government is a contending party. See D.L. Skoler, *The Administrative Law Judiciary: Change, Challenge and Choices*, ANNALS AM. ACAD. POL. SC. (July 1982).

2,600 law clerks to federal judges and magistrates (for many of them, their first position after graduating from law school).[39]

The National Center for State Courts reports that in the 50 States, Puerto Rico and the District of Columbia there were in 1989 the following judges and justices:

Courts of Last Resort	356
Intermediate Appellate Courts	827
Courts of General Jurisdiction	9,250
Courts of Limited Jurisdiction	18,738
Total number of judges/justices	29,171[40]

Today the Judiciary, both State and Federal, is unmistakably a "lawyers branch" of government and the relationship of bar to bench is central to the core values of the legal profession. On the other hand, while litigation remains the forte of a large segment of the legal profession, the practice of law for a majority of lawyers (in private practice, in-house and in government) has moved from the courtroom to the lawyer's office. For the majority, after they are inducted by the court into the bar, it is unlikely that they will ever return to a courtroom in a lawyer's capacity.

Nonetheless, for a variety of reasons, both historical and relating to the role the profession has assumed in the legal system, judicial regulation of *all* lawyers is a principle firmly established today in every state. Today the highest courts of the several states are the gatekeepers of the profession both as to competency and as to character and fitness. As to competency, most state courts rely on graduation from an ABA-accredited law school and on a written bar examination which includes the Multistate Bar Exam. As to character and fitness, the state courts provide for their own investigations under guidelines generally adapted from the ABA guidelines pertaining to character and fitness.[41]

With the authority of the courts standing behind them, the legal profession is able to be largely self-governing under court delegation and supervision. Establishing requirements for admission to the bar, administration of bar examinations and the admissions process, promulgation of ethical rules, and lawyer discipline and disbarment, all are matters in conjunction with the courts in which the organized bar plays a central role. The courts' assumption of control over the

---

39. *See* 1990 ANNUAL REPORT OF THE DIRECTORS OF THE ADMINISTRATIVE OFFICE OF THE UNITED STATES COURTS, at 41 (Table 28).

40. Data gathered from the 1989 State Trial and Appellate Court statistical profiles.

41. See Code of Recommended Standards for Bar Examiners, III. Moral Character and Fitness, published in the ABA's ANNUAL REVIEW OF LEGAL EDUCATION IN THE UNITED STATES; see also Chapter 8, *infra*.

bar as a whole was an essential part of the legal reform movement of the late 19th and early 20th centuries, together with the organization of bar associations and the reshaping of legal education into a respected academic discipline.

It was the courts' exercise of authority over admissions to the bar and over lawyer discipline that enabled the profession to make graduation from an approved law school a virtually universal requirement for bar admissions, as well as to give force and effect to the rules of professional conduct developed by the bar. However, the courts' exercise of control over the bar has neither been exclusive nor unchallenged.

The courts have claimed an inherent power over lawyers as "officers of the court" for more than a century. The Supreme Court in 1856 declared:

> It has been well settled, by the rules and practice of common-law courts, that it rests exclusively with the court to determine who is qualified to become one of its officers, as an attorney and counsellor, and for what cause he ought to be removed.[42]

On the other hand, legislatures exercising their general police powers have frequently asserted control over the profession and put themselves into potential conflict with the judiciary by legislating with respect to the bar. Such legislation has included eliminating virtually all qualifications for admission;[43] granting to graduates of particular law schools the "diploma privilege," providing admission without bar examination;[44] exempting certain law students from a general educational requirement;[45] or countermanding the disbarment of a lawyer.[46]

Some commentators have argued that with a majority of the bar now "office lawyers" rather than "courtroom lawyers," the legislatures rather than the courts should regulate members of the bar "to promote the interests of the consumers of legal services" and that lawyers should not be exempt from ultimate legislative control.[47] Such arguments ignore the accommodations that have been reached between legislatures and the courts and the pattern of delegation

---

42. *Ex parte Secombe*, 19 How. 9, 60 U.S. 9, 15 L.Ed. 565, (U.S. Minn., Dec Term 1856).

43. *Supra* note 10.

44. *In re Cooper*, 22 N.Y.67 (1960).

45. *In re Day*, 181 Ill. 73, 54 N.E. 646 (1899).

46. *Ex rel. Thacher*, 22 Ohio Dec 116 (1912); cf. *In re Saddler*, 55 Okla. 510, 130 P. 906 (1913).

47. See T.M. Alpert, *The Inherent Power of the Courts to Regulate the Practice of the Law: An Historical Analysis*, 32 Buff. L. Rev. 525-26, 556 (1983).

under which the courts and the bar function today: Eight states by constitutional provision have expressly granted to their courts power over the practice of law.[48] Thirty-five states, territories and the District of Columbia have a unified or integrated bar, created either by statute or by court rule, to which all lawyers must belong and for which ultimate control is expressly placed in the jurisdiction's highest court.[49] Over the years the ABA and state bars successfully lobbied legislatures to require bar examinations for admission to the bar and in many states there are specific delegations to the judiciary of power to establish a board of bar examiners or to provide for lawyer discipline.[50]

The ABA Commission on Evaluation of Disciplinary Enforcement in its May 1991 report made the following comment regarding legislative regulation of the bar:

> The Commission believes that legislative regulation will impair the independence of lawyers. While historically legislative regulation was benign, it was also laissez faire, so much so that courts assumed regulatory control to stop ethical abuses. See e.g., *People ex rel. Karlin v. Culkin*, 248 N.Y. 465, 162 N.E. 487, 60 A.L.R. 851 (N.Y., 1928).[51] Legislative regulation that did exist mostly concerned admissions requirements. Modern proponents of legislative regulation would have legislatures regulate aspects of the lawyer-client relationship to protect "consumer" interests. It is precisely in this area that the protection of the client must be delicately balanced with the independence of the lawyer from political pressure. History offers no basis for comparison.

---

48. Arkansas, Florida, Kentucky, New Jersey, Indiana, Louisiana, Ohio and South Carolina.

49. See 1991 DIRECTORY OF BAR ASSOCIATIONS published by the ABA Division for Bar Services.

50. *See* R.B. STEVENS, *supra* note 3, at 99; see ABA/NCBE COMPREHENSIVE GUIDE TO BAR ADMISSION REQUIREMENTS 1991-92.

51. In the *Karlin* case, Chief Judge Cardozo of the New York Court of Appeals, sustaining the power of the judiciary to conduct an investigation of "ambulance chasing," wrote:

> A petition by three leading bar associations . . . gave notice to the court that evil practices were rife among members of he bar. "Ambulance chasing" was spreading to a demoralizing extent. As a consequence, the poor were oppressed and the ignorant overreached. . . . Wrongdoing by lawyers for claimants was accompanied by other wrongdoing, almost as pernicious, by lawyers for defendants. . . . The bar as a whole felt the sting of the discredit thus put upon its membership by an unscrupulous minority.
>
> The appellant was received into that ancient fellowship [of lawyers] for something more than private gain. He became an officer of the court itself, an instrument or agency to advance the ends of justice. His cooperation with the court was due, whenever justice would be imperiled if cooperation was withheld.
>
> If the house is to be cleaned, it is for those who occupy and govern it, rather than for strangers, to do the noisome work.

As for the protection of the consumers of legal services, the Supreme Court in recent years, invoking the First Amendment and the antitrust laws, struck down bar-promoted prohibitions on group legal services;[52] prohibitions on advertising;[53] and the promulgation of minimum fee schedules.[54] At the same time, state courts have largely withdrawn from their once aggressive role of protecting the profession from any and all competitive pressures.[55] The ABA's Commission on Professionalism summed up the case law of the 1970s and 1980s in this way:

> What these cases and more recent decisions involving attempted state regulation of lawyer practices suggest is a consistent prohibition of rules which operate to limit the extent to which members of the Bar must compete both in the acquisition of business and the charging of fees. Rhetoric about the "Special" character of the profession remains, but the reality is that, as a matter of law, lawyers must now face tough economic competition with respect to almost everything they do.

E. The Survival of a Single Public Profession

The Preamble to the ABA Model Rules expressly affirms the lawyer's several responsibilities as a representative of clients, an officer of the legal system and a public citizen having special responsibility for the quality of justice. To the extent lawyers have met these responsibilities of their professional calling, government regulation has been obviated and the profession has been permitted to remain largely self-governing under the ultimate authority of the courts.

The Preamble further notes that self-regulation helps maintain the legal profession's independence from government domination, permitting the profession to be an important force in preserving government under law, standing ready to challenge the abuse of authority. However, as the Preamble concludes, the legal profession's relative autonomy carries with it special responsibilities of

---

52. *NAACP* v. *Button*, 371 U.S. 415 (1963); *Brotherhood of R.R. Trainmen* v. *Virginia ex rel. Va. State Bar*, 377 U.S. 1 (1964); *United Mine Workers* v. *Illinois State Bar Association*, 389 U.S. 217 (1967); *United Transport Union* v. *State Bar*, 401 U.S. 576 (1971).

53. *Bates* v. *State Bar of Arizona*, 433 U.S. 350 (1977); *In re RMJ*, 455 U.S. 191 (1982).

54. *Goldfarb* v. *Virginia State Bar Assn.*, 421 U.S. 773 (1975).

55. Cf. *Illinois State Bar Association* v. *People's Stock Yards State Bank*, 344 Ill. 462, 176 N.E. 901 (1931).

self-government. Thus every lawyer is responsible for observance of the rules of professional conduct. Neglect of professional responsibilities compromises the independence of the profession and the public interest which it is to serve.

Together, the law schools and the organized bar can have no more important function than to pass to each succeeding generation of lawyers an understanding of the profession's relationship to the American legal system. If a single public profession of shared learning, skills and professional values is to survive into the 21st century, the law schools together with the bar and the judiciary must all work for the perpetuation of core legal knowledge together with the fundamental lawyering skills and professional values that identify a distinct profession of law throughout the United States.

Part II.
A Vision of the Skills and Values Which New Lawyers Should Seek to Acquire

Chapter Four
Formulating a Statement of Skills and Values

A. Reasons for a Statement

When the Task Force began to consider how the preparation of lawyers for practice could be improved, it felt the need to develop a conception of the object of this preparation, in the form of a compendium of the skills and values that are desirable for practitioners to have. Such an inventory was useful to provide a focus for the thinking of the Task Force itself, but the Task Force believed that it might be even more useful as a jump-off point and stimulus for thinking within the profession as a whole. After the Task Force had reviewed prior writings on the subject and examined the range and complexity of lawyers' work (described in Part I of this Report), two points became quite apparent:

First, the Task Force itself could not hope to write a comprehensive statement of skills and values that all members of the profession would—or could reasonably be expected to—accept as definitive. Whether or not such a project would ever be feasible, it

123

was certainly not feasible in the current state of the art or for any single group of individuals.

Second, for precisely this reason, there was considerable value in putting together the best comprehensive statement which the Task Force itself could develop, so as to begin a process through which, in the years ahead, discussion in all sectors of the profession could be focused on questions about the nature of the skills and values that are central to the role and functioning of lawyers in practice. By hammering out this kind of a statement, the Task Force would refine and guide its own analysis of immediate steps that might be taken to enhance the quality of lawyers' preparation for practice; by disseminating the statement, the Task Force would encourage the profession to examine it critically and to improve upon the thinking that went into it.

B. Focus of the Statement

An analysis of skills and values necessarily must take account of the phenomena of specialization and of division of labor within law firms, described in Part I. These developments are not inconsistent, however, with the traditional vision of law as a unitary profession whose members share a common calling. Regardless of their particular fields of practice or specialties, lawyers are united by their pursuit of certain values, which this Statement terms the "fundamental values of the profession." These values inform and shape the lawyer's use of professional skills. *See, e.g.*, McKay, *What Law Schools Can and Should Do (and Sometimes Do)*, 30 N.Y.L. SCH. REV. 491, 509-10 (1985).

Moreover, notwithstanding the increasing demand for specialized knowledge and skills, competent representation of a client still requires a well-trained generalist—one who has a broad range of knowledge of legal institutions and who is proficient at a number of diverse tasks. This is so because any problem presented by a client (or other entity employing a lawyer's services) may be amenable to a variety of types of solutions of differing degrees of efficacy; a lawyer cannot competently represent or advise the client or other entity unless he or she has the breadth of knowledge and skill necessary to perceive, evaluate, and begin to pursue each of the options. Indeed, the lawyer is not even in a position to diagnose the client's problem adequately unless the lawyer has the range of knowledge and skill necessary to look beyond the client's definition of the problem and identify aspects of the problem and related problems which the client has not perceived.

The focus of this Statement is on the skills and values with which a well-trained generalist should be familiar before assuming ultimate responsibility for a client. Different lawyers will emphasize different skills, and practitioners will often be concerned with matters outside the scope of the Statement, such as attracting and retaining clients. The Statement is concerned with what it takes to practice law competently and professionally.

The Statement recognizes that a lawyer functioning as a member of a team need not be familiar with all of the skills and values analyzed in the Statement, so long as the team as a whole can mobilize and effectively apply the full range of skills and values in representing a client and making professional judgments. For similar reasons, the Statement recognizes that new members of the profession need not become acquainted with the full roster of skills and values while they are in law school or even before they are admitted to the bar. If, as frequently happens, an entry-level lawyer practices under the supervision of a more experienced attorney—and if the attorney who bears the ultimate responsibility for representing and advising the client is truly in a position to protect the client's interests and to ensure that the client receives competent representation—the entry-level attorney may appropriately work on the matter without possessing all of the qualifications envisioned by this Statement.

Whether a lawyer is working alone or as a member of a team, substantive knowledge—and often highly specialized substantive knowledge—is necessary to complement the skills and values that are the subject of this Statement. In choosing to focus on skills and values, the Task Force did not ignore or underestimate the important role that substantive knowledge plays in the provision of competent representation and in the process of preparing for competent practice. The Task Force fully appreciated that attention has been, and surely will continue to be, given to the question of what aspects of substantive law should be included in a course of preparation for all new members of the profession. But, the Task Force concluded, this issue is sufficiently distinct from an analysis of skills and values that the Statement should not attempt to address both.

C. Formulation of the Statement

The Task Force began its classification of lawyers' skills and values by reviewing an extensive bibliography on the subject compiled by its Reporter. The Task Force then formed a subcommittee to consider the utility and feasibility of preparing a systematic statement of skills and values and to explore the possible focus and content of such a statement. The subcommittee examined additional literature and proposed the format and a rough inventory of the topics to be covered in a Statement of Skills and Values. These were reviewed and approved by the Task Force, which also approved the subcommittee's recommendation that a special consultant be engaged to work with the subcommittee in preparing a first draft of the Statement.

Considerable information and a wide range of views pertinent to the subject of the Statement of Skills and Values were generated at a series of hearings conducted by the Task Force. (*See* Appendix C.) Observations and ideas were received from practicing lawyers, judges, law teachers, bar examiners, and representatives of bar associations about the demands of legal practice, the capabilities that it requires, and the extent and nature of the deficiencies that entry-level practitioners experience or exhibit.

Drawing on the prior literature as well as the information gathered at the hearings, the subcommittee prepared a first draft of the Statement. This draft and successive drafts reworked by the subcommittee were reviewed and progressively refined by the Task Force.

A Tentative Draft produced by this process was circulated nationally to members of the Bar and law school faculties in June 1991, with a request for comments on the substance of the draft, its form and content, and the uses to which a statement of skills and values might be put. This produced a considerable number of responses, including comments by representatives of American Bar Association sections and committees, the Association of American Law Schools, the Appellate Judges Conference, the Conference of Chief Justices, and state and local bar associations, as well as judges, law school deans and faculty members, practitioners, and professionals in other fields who regularly work with lawyers. The Task Force gave careful consideration to each of these comments and made numerous changes in the document as a result. These included the addition of sections dealing with skills and values omitted in the Tentative Draft, the reformulation of some skills and values discussed in the Tentative Draft, and the expansion or compression, particularization or generalization of others.

D. Uses of the Statement

Range of Possible Uses

Uses by Law Students. The Statement of Skills and Values can serve as an aid to law students in preparing for practice. As noted on page 228 of this Report, many law students are passive consumers of legal education: They lack an adequate understanding of the requirements for competent practice, the process by which a new member of the profession prepares for practice and attains competence, and the role that law schools play in that process. If the Statement of Skills and Values is distributed to all law students at the time they enter law school, students will begin their legal education with a clearer sense of the importance of acquiring skills and values in the course of professional development. Students will be encouraged to seek out opportunities to develop these skills and values while they are in law school (in law school courses, extra-curricular activities, and part-time and summertime employment) and after law school (in postgraduate education, continuing legal education, judicial clerkships, and legal practice). Moreover, students will be assisted to reflect upon and learn from these experiences and to develop for themselves a considered long-range educational agenda aimed at attaining professional competence and eventually excellence.

Familiarity with the Statement of Skills and Values will also enable law students to play a more active role in shaping the educational opportunities available to them while in law school and afterward. Thus, for example, law students will be able to participate more thoughtfully in their law schools' curricular planning and to offer suggestions to part-time and summertime employers about what types of experiences would complement the learning that takes place in law school. In this manner, law schools, employers, and other providers of legal education and training can benefit from a better informed consumer's perspective.

Finally, providing the Statement of Skills and Values to entering law students will allow them to take part in the process of refining the Statement and the profession's understanding of skills and values. As Chapter 4.A explains, the Task Force sees the Statement as the starting point for an ongoing exchange within the profession about the skills and values needed for competent practice and the best means to teach and learn these skills and values. By contributing their perspective, law students can substantially enrich this exchange.

Uses by Law Schools. The Statement of Skills and Values can serve as an aid to law schools in curricular development. The empirical data collected by the Task Force suggest that many schools are experimenting with a variety of curricular changes intended, *inter alia*, to enhance the quality of preparation for legal practice. *See* Chapter 7.B *infra*. This is as it should be. By providing the beginnings of a shared vocabulary in which local innovations as well as traditional law school courses designed to teach skills and values can be discussed, compared and debated, the Statement should facilitate the trade and refinement of ideas about curricular needs and directions.

Law schools can use the Statement as a focus for examining proposals to modify their curricula to teach skills and values more extensively or differently than they now do. Such modifications might include, for example:

- revisions of conventional courses and teaching methods to more systematically integrate the study of skills and values with the study of substantive law and theory;
- revisions of existing skills courses or programs, or the creation of new ones, to better achieve pedagogical goals;
- development of courses or programs concerned with professional values.

The Statement of Skills and Values can also be of use to law schools when conducting the Self-Study required by Standard 201(a) of the American Bar Association Accreditation Standards. As the most complete (and, as of the date of this report, the most current) analysis of the skills and values needed for practice, the Statement can serve as a useful tool when a law school assesses the extent to which its curriculum "provide[s] a sound legal education and accomplish[es] the objectives of [the school's] . . . educational program" (Standard 201(b)), "offer[s] instruction in professional skills . . . [and] the duties and responsibilities of the legal profession" (Standard 302(a)(iii)-(iv)), and provides "an educational program that is designed to qualify its graduates for admission to the bar" (Standard 301(a)). Although the Statement is not meant to serve as a blueprint or a measure of performance in the accrediting process (*see* Chapter 7.C *infra*), it is an instrument that faculties may wish to consider when developing and evaluating their educational programs.

Uses by Developers of Programs for Continuing Legal Education. In addition to informing the design and content of postgraduate courses in law schools, the Statement of Skills and Values can serve as an aid to the development and enrichment of programs for postgraduate education outside law school (including, for example,

Continuing Legal Education (CLE) and bridge-the-gap programs). To assist new lawyers to acquire necessary skills and values, it is particularly important that providers of postgraduate legal education be encouraged to develop programs in which:

- Instruction includes exercises that require students to participate actively in role.
- Those teaching in the program have special expertise and training as teachers of skills and values.
- Teaching occurs in a context that allows students to receive immediate feedback on their applications of lawyering skills and values.

The Statement of Skills and Values can serve as a guide to commercial and non-profit organizations for continuing legal education—as well as to local, state, and national bar associations—in developing appropriate programs. It also can serve as a reference source for state bars, state supreme courts, and other entities responsible for overseeing the bar, in assessing the need for mandatory continuing legal education and evaluating the adequacy of existing programs of continuing legal education.

Uses by Law Offices in Designing In-House Training for New Lawyers. Many law firms, government agencies, corporate counsel, and other types of law offices have training programs for newly hired attorneys. These programs often provide training in lawyering skills and values in addition to teaching specialized substantive knowledge relevant to a particular field of practice.

The Statement can serve as a guide to the designers of law office programs in evaluating the adequacy of existing programs and, where appropriate, revising and expanding such programs. In particular, the Statement can inform judgments about the nature and amount of training that all lawyers should receive before beginning to represent clients and before assuming ultimate responsibility for a client.

Uses by Practicing Lawyers in Self-Evaluation and Self-Development. Although the Statement of Skills and Values is primarily directed at new lawyers and the means by which they prepare for practice, the Statement recognizes that the process of learning and refining professional skills continues long after a lawyer has commenced practice. Indeed, the Statement explicitly states that lawyers should be committed to the value of seeking out and taking advantage of opportunities to increase their knowledge and improve their skills in order to remain competent within their chosen field and in order to attain excellence. *See* Value § 4 & Commentary; *see also* Value § 1.2 & Commentary to Value § 1.

The Statement's analysis of skills and values can be useful to practicing lawyers in evaluating their capabilities for the purpose of identifying areas in which further study would be beneficial. *See also, e.g.,* AMERICAN LAW INSTITUTE-AMERICAN BAR ASSOCIATION COMMITTEE ON CONTINUING PROFESSIONAL EDUCATION, A PRACTICAL GUIDE TO ACHIEVING EXCELLENCE IN THE PRACTICE OF LAW: STANDARDS, METHODS, AND SELF-EVALUATION (1992) ("offer[ing] . . . a method by which all lawyers can assess their own skills, knowledge, ethical standards, and overall competence," *id.* at xiii). In addition, practicing lawyers can use the Statement's analysis of skills and values as a reference when selecting courses of study and as a framework when reflecting upon and learning from lawyering experiences. *See* Value § 4.1.

Facilitating the Proposed Uses of the Statement

The Creation of a National Institute. In later sections of this Report, the Task Force sets forth a proposal for a national institute for the practice of law. *See* Chapter 10 *infra.* Such a national institute could play a central role in furthering the various uses of the Statement proposed above. It could stimulate and facilitate discussion and critical analysis of the Statement and a progressive refinement of thinking about the subjects of the Statement within the profession. It could develop modes of instruction, course materials, problems, and methods of assessment to assist law schools to teach skills and values more effectively. And it could create and serve as a clearinghouse for model curricula, instructional materials, and teacher training for providers of continuing legal education and law office programs.

The Use of the Statement as a Vehicle for Organizing Resources. Several of the proposals set forth above will require the creation of new modes of instruction and the development of new instructional materials. Later sections of this Report will suggest various ways in which the proposed national institute, bar associations, and other organizations can assist law schools and providers of continuing legal education in these endeavors. *See* Chapters 7-10 *infra.* It appears likely, however, that law schools and providers of continuing legal education will need increased funding to implement the reforms suggested in this Report. The Statement of Skills and Values can serve as a vehicle for organizing the resources of providers and securing the requisite funding.

Refinement of the Statement of Skills and Values Through

Discussion Within the Profession. As Chapter 4.A explains, the Task Force views the Statement of Skills and Values as a work in progress. The document is intended to serve as a stimulus and starting point for an ongoing exchange within the profession about the skills and values that a legal practitioner should have and about the types of education and training that lawyers should receive at various stages of their careers.

Dissemination of the Statement throughout the profession would allow the Statement to perform these functions. As suggested above, the Statement should be distributed not only to current members of the profession but also to law students, so that the exchange of views can include those of consumers of legal education. The profession's thinking about skills and values also should take into account the perspective of another population of consumers—the consumers of legal services. *Cf.* Garth, *Rethinking the Legal Profession's Approach to Collective Self-Improvement: Competence and the Consumer Perspective*, 1983 Wis. L. Rev. 639.

The profession's views on the teaching and attainment of skills and values will inevitably change over time, not only as a result of further discussions of the Statement but also as a result of experience in using the Statement (and courses and materials that grow out of it) and changes in the nature and demands of practice. It is the hope of the Task Force that the Statement will be periodically revised to reflect these changes, so that it can continue to fulfill its intended purpose of sparking and informing discussion of the means by which new lawyers prepare for practice.

E. Abuses of the Statement to Be Avoided

The Statement would disserve its aims and the profession if it were used in ways not contemplated in its drafting. Specifically:

> *The Statement is not, and should not be taken to be, a standard for a law school curriculum.*

As later sections of this Report explain, the Task Force concluded after extensive study that the law schools and the practicing bar must share responsibility for giving new members of the profession the training needed to practice competently. This training is best provided through a combination of law school education and opportunities for learning outside the law school environment. Such a division of responsibility has the additional benefit of leaving both the schools and the Bar free to pursue a broader mission.

The Statement of Skills and Values is concerned with the limited goal of ensuring practice at a minimum level of competency. All law schools and the legal profession rightly aspire to assist lawyers to practice not merely capably but excellently. Excellence cannot be promoted by the kind of standardization involved in formulating any particular list of prescriptions and prerequisites. It is best supported by encouraging pluralism and innovativeness in legal education and practice. This Statement should therefore not be viewed as denigrating the development of skills and values not included in it. Such skills and values will frequently mark the difference between an able lawyer and an outstanding one.

The Statement is not designed to be used as a measure of performance in the accrediting process.

The Statement should not be used by site inspection teams, by the Accreditation Committee and Council of the Section of Legal Education and Admissions to the Bar, or even by law schools themselves, as a standard for judging a law school's program. To the extent that the Statement plays any role in the accrediting process, it should be the limited one suggested in Chapter 4.D—as a resource for law schools when they conduct self-studies pursuant to Standard 201(a).

The Statement is not an enumeration of ingredients that are either necessary or sufficient to avoid malpractice.

The Statement has nothing to do with the standards governing malpractice liability, disciplinary infractions, or ineffective assistance of counsel. It is concerned with the elements which equip a lawyer for capable practice, not with the lawyer's actual performance. Just as an adequately equipped lawyer may sometimes perform below the level of his or her abilities, so may an inadequately equipped lawyer sometimes manage to take appropriate actions in a particular situation. Preparation to handle situations necessarily involves an ability to deal with more contingencies than turn out to occur. That kind of preparation is the hallmark of professionalism; its contents are the subject of this Statement.

The Statement should not be used as a source for bar examinations.

The Statement employs analytic models to describe the skills and values with which practicing lawyers should be familiar. While bar examinations may, and generally do, attempt to evaluate whether applicants have acquired certain of these skills and values, it would be neither possible nor desirable to test students' familiarity with the models themselves. Moreover, any attempt to test on particular portions of the Statement—or to reduce it to a set of general principles for testing purposes—would be at odds with the Statement's central approach of analyzing skills and values in a holistic way. In any event, the Statement was never intended to serve as a list of the skills and values in which every lawyer must be versed before he or she is admitted to the bar. Rather, as explained in Chapter 4.B, the Statement is concerned with the skills and values with which a lawyer should be familiar at the point at which he or she first accepts ultimate responsibility for clients.

Chapter Five
The Statement of Fundamental Lawyering Skills and Professional Values

A. Organization of the Statement
B. Overview of the Skills and Values Analyzed
   Fundamental Lawyering Skills
   Fundamental Values of the Profession
C. The Analysis of Skills and Values

A. Organization of the Statement

The Statement first analyzes the fundamental lawyering skills essential for competent representation. It begins with two analytical skills that are conceptual foundations for virtually all aspects of legal practice: problem solving (Skill § 1) and legal analysis (Skill § 2). It then examines five skills that are essential throughout a wide range of kinds of legal practice: legal research (Skill § 3), factual investigation (Skill § 4), communication (Skill § 5), counseling (Skill § 6), and negotiation (Skill § 7). The Statement next focuses upon the skills required to employ, or to advise a client about, the options of litigation and alternative dispute resolution (Skill § 8). Although there are many lawyers who do not engage in litigation or make use of alternative dispute resolution mechanisms, even these lawyers are frequently in a position of having to consider litigation or alternative dispute resolution as possible solutions to a client's problem, or to counsel a client about these options, or to factor the options into planning for negotiation. To accomplish these tasks, a lawyer needs to have at least a basic familiarity with the aspects of litigation and alternative dispute resolution described in Skill § 8. Skill § 9 identifies the administrative skills necessary to organize and manage legal work effectively. This section reflects the perception that adequate practice management skills are an essential precondition for competent representation of clients. Finally, Skill § 10 analyzes the skills involved in recognizing and resolving ethical dilemmas.

The analysis of professional values recognizes that "training in professional responsibility" should involve more than "just the specifics of the Code of Professional Responsibility and the Model Rules of Professional Conduct"; it should encompass "the values of the profession," including "the obligations and accountability of a professional dealing with the lives and affairs of clients." McKay,

135

supra, at 509-10. Value § 1 examines the value of competent representation, analyzing the ideals to which a lawyer should be committed as a member of a profession dedicated to the service of clients. Value § 2 considers the value of striving to promote justice, fairness, and morality; it examines the ideals to which a lawyer should be committed as a member of a profession that bears "special responsibilit[ies] for the quality of justice" (Model Rules, Preamble). Value § 3 addresses the value of striving to improve the profession; it explores the ideals to which a lawyer should be committed as a member of a "self-governing" profession (*ibid.*). Finally, Value § 4 examines the value of professional self-development, analyzing the ideals to which a lawyer should be committed as a member of a "learned profession" (*ibid.*).

Each section is divided into a *statement* of the respective skill or value and a *commentary*. In the skills sections, the statements contain the bulk of the analysis, with the commentaries providing background on the particular skill and the manner in which it is analyzed. In the values sections, the statements tend to be briefer; the commentaries contain more analysis. These differences in style reflect a basic difference in the kinds of discourse best suited to express skills on the one hand and values on the other, particularly in a prescriptive format. Legal skills are illuminated by dissection and precise elaboration; values are better explicated in broad formulations nuanced by discussion.

The skills and values in this Statement are analyzed separately in order to promote clarity in examining the components of each one. However, the vision of legal practice underlying the Statement recognizes that individual skills and values cannot be neatly compartmentalized. There are numerous relationships between individual skills. Thus, for example, the formulations of the skills of counseling (Skill § 6), negotiation (Skill § 7), and litigation (Skill § 8) explain that these skills may require the application of the skills of legal analysis, legal research, and factual investigation (*see, e.g.*, Skill §§ 6.2(a)-(b), 7.1(b), 8.1(c), 8.3(d)); the analysis of the skill of negotiation explains that counseling skills are ordinarily employed to help a client decide whether to accept or reject the best terms obtained from the other side in a negotiation session (Skill § 7.3(a)); and the skill of problem solving typically requires that a lawyer employ interviewing skills to gather the facts needed to identify and diagnose the client's problem (*see* Skill § 1.1). Similarly, there are relationships between individual values. For example, both the value of competent representation (Value § 1) and the value of professional self-development (Value § 4) call for a commitment to continuing study, although the former section conceives of such study as a means of maintaining competence while the latter treats it as a means of attaining excellence.

Moreover, there is a relationship between the skills and the values. As Value § 1 explains, the specific skills examined in Skill §§ 1-10, together with the more general skill of self-appraisal (which is discussed in the text and Commentary of Skill § 1) are essential means by which a lawyer fulfills his or her responsibilities to a client and simultaneously realizes the ideal of competent representation. The process of preparing to represent clients competently is a matter both of accepting certain professional values and of acquiring the skills necessary to promote these values.

These relationships between skills and values were taken into account in deciding the order in which to present the various skills and values. Thus, for example, the Statement analyzes skills before values because familiarity with Skill §§ 1-10 is essential for understanding the ideal of competent representation which is discussed in Value § 1. General foundational skills such as problem solving (Skill § 1) and legal analysis (Skill § 2) are addressed before other skills that build upon them, just as the value of continuing study for the purpose of maintaining competence (Value § 1) is addressed before the value of continuing study for the purpose of attaining excellence (Value § 4). Otherwise, the order in which skills or values are presented does not reflect any views about their relative importance in the practice of law or in the process of preparing for practice.

The arrangement of skills is also not descriptive of the sequence in which they may be used in handling a client's legal problem. Effective lawyering is rarely, if ever, a linear, step-by-step process. Although skills such as problem solving and legal analysis are ordinarily applied at an early stage of the process, they are also relevant throughout a lawyer's representation of a client. As the analyses of these skills explain, a lawyer must constantly reassess a plan for solving a client's problem or a legal theory when new information becomes available (*see* Skill §§ 1.4(d), 1.5, 2.1(c)(iii)). In much the same manner, other sections recognize that the acquisition of new information may require that a lawyer reassess the validity of a plan for legal research (Skill § 3.3(d)(ii)) or an investigative strategy (Skill § 4.2(b)(i)(B)), that he or she counsel a client about the advisability of reconsidering a decision or adopting a new course of action (Skill § 6.5(c)), and that the lawyer re-evaluate the goals for a negotiation or the negotiating strategies or tactics which he or she previously selected to achieve those goals (Skill § 7.2(c)).

B. Overview of the Skills and Values Analyzed

Fundamental Lawyering Skills

Skill § 1: *Problem Solving*

In order to develop and evaluate strategies for solving a problem or accomplishing an objective, a lawyer should be familiar with the skills and concepts involved in:

1.1 Identifying and Diagnosing the Problem;
1.2 Generating Alternative Solutions and Strategies;
1.3 Developing a Plan of Action;
1.4 Implementing the Plan;
1.5 Keeping the Planning Process Open to New Information and New Ideas.

Skill § 2: *Legal Analysis and Reasoning*

In order to analyze and apply legal rules and principles, a lawyer should be familiar with the skills and concepts involved in:

2.1 Identifying and Formulating Legal Issues;
2.2 Formulating Relevant Legal Theories;
2.3 Elaborating Legal Theory;
2.4 Evaluating Legal Theory;
2.5 Criticizing and Synthesizing Legal Argumentation.

Skill § 3: *Legal Research*

In order to identify legal issues and to research them thoroughly and efficiently, a lawyer should have:

3.1 Knowledge of the Nature of Legal Rules and Institutions;
3.2 Knowledge of and Ability to Use the Most Fundamental Tools of Legal Research;
3.3 Understanding of the Process of Devising and Implementing a Coherent and Effective Research Design.

Skill § 4: *Factual Investigation*

In order to plan, direct, and (where applicable) participate in factual investigation, a lawyer should be familiar with the skills and concepts involved in:

4.1 Determining the Need for Factual Investigation;
4.2 Planning a Factual Investigation;
4.3 Implementing the Investigative Strategy;
4.4 Memorializing and Organizing Information in an Accessible Form;

4.5 Deciding Whether to Conclude the Process of Fact-Gathering;

4.6 Evaluating the Information That Has Been Gathered.

Skill § 5: *Communication*

In order to communicate effectively, whether orally or in writing, a lawyer should be familiar with the skills and concepts involved in:

5.1 Assessing the Perspective of the Recipient of the Communication;

5.2 Using Effective Methods of Communication.

Skill § 6: *Counseling*

In order to counsel clients about decisions or courses of action, a lawyer should be familiar with the skills and concepts involved in:

6.1 Establishing a Counseling Relationship That Respects the Nature and Bounds of a Lawyer's Role;

6.2 Gathering Information Relevant to the Decision to Be Made;

6.3 Analyzing the Decision to Be Made;

6.4 Counseling the Client About the Decision to Be Made;

6.5 Ascertaining and Implementing the Client's Decision.

Skill § 7: *Negotiation*

In order to negotiate in either a dispute-resolution or transactional context, a lawyer should be familiar with the skills and concepts involved in:

7.1 Preparing for Negotiation;

7.2 Conducting a Negotiation Session;

7.3 Counseling the Client About the Terms Obtained From the Other Side in the Negotiation and Implementing the Client's Decision.

Skill § 8: *Litigation and Alternative Dispute-Resolution Procedures*

In order to employ—or to advise a client about—the options of litigation and alternative dispute resolution, a lawyer should understand the potential functions and consequences of these processes and should have a working knowledge of the fundamentals of:

8.1 Litigation at the Trial-Court Level;

8.2 Litigation at the Appellate Level;

8.3 Advocacy in Administrative and Executive Forums;

8.4 Proceedings in Other Dispute-Resolution Forums.

Skill § 9: *Organization and Management of Legal Work*

In order to practice effectively, a lawyer should be familiar with the skills and concepts required for efficient management, including:

9.1 Formulating Goals and Principles for Effective Practice Management;

9.2 Developing Systems and Procedures to Ensure that Time, Effort, and Resources Are Allocated Efficiently;

9.3 Developing Systems and Procedures to Ensure that Work is Performed and Completed at the Appropriate Time;

9.4 Developing Systems and Procedures for Effectively Working with Other People;

9.5 Developing Systems and Procedures for Efficiently Administering a Law Office.

Skill § 10: *Recognizing and Resolving Ethical Dilemmas*

In order to represent a client consistently with applicable ethical standards, a lawyer should be familiar with:

10.1 The Nature and Sources of Ethical Standards;

10.2 The Means by Which Ethical Standards are Enforced;

10.3 The Processes for Recognizing and Resolving Ethical Dilemmas.

Fundamental Values of the Profession

Value § 1: *Provision of Competent Representation*

As a member of a profession dedicated to the service of clients, a lawyer should be committed to the values of:

1.1 Attaining a Level of Competence in One's Own Field of Practice;

1.2 Maintaining a Level of Competence in One's Own Field of Practice;

1.3 Representing Clients in a Competent Manner.

Value § 2: *Striving to Promote Justice, Fairness, and Morality*

As a member of a profession that bears special responsibilities for the quality of justice, a lawyer should be committed to the values of:

2.1 Promoting Justice, Fairness, and Morality in One's Own Daily Practice;

2.2 Contributing to the Profession's Fulfillment of its Responsibility to Ensure that Adequate Legal Services Are Provided to Those Who Cannot Afford to Pay for Them;

2.3 Contributing to the Profession's Fulfillment of its Responsibility to Enhance the Capacity of Law and Legal Institutions to Do Justice.

Value § 3: *Striving to Improve the Profession*

As a member of a self-governing profession, a lawyer should be committed to the values of:

3.1 Participating in Activities Designed to Improve the Profession;

3.2 Assisting in the Training and Preparation of New Lawyers;

3.3 Striving to Rid the Profession of Bias Based on Race, Religion, Ethnic Origin, Gender, Sexual Orientation, or Disability, and to Rectify the Effects of These Biases.

Value § 4: *Professional Self-Development*

As a member of a learned profession, a lawyer should be committed to the values of:

4.1 Seeking Out and Taking Advantage of Opportunities to Increase His or Her Knowledge and Improve His or Her Skills;

4.2 Selecting and Maintaining Employment That Will Allow the Lawyer to Develop As a Professional and to Pursue His or Her Professional and Personal Goals.

C. Analysis of Skills and Values

1. Problem Solving

In order to effectively develop and evaluate strategies for solving a problem or accomplishing an objective[1] presented by a client

---

1. The text of this section will hereafter refer simply to "problem solving." The term "problem" is conceived as including the entire range of situations in which a lawyer's assistance is sought in avoiding or resolving difficulties, realizing opportunities, or accomplishing objectives—situations as diverse as those in which a dispute has arisen between the client and another individual or entity; those in which a client may need to define legal rights or relationships in a contract, lease, will or other instrument; and those in which a government agency may wish to promulgate or amend a rule.

As the text of § 1.1 indicates, a "problem" cannot be defined solely in terms of legal constructs: It must take into account a wide range of fact-specific variables as well as the client's goals, attitudes, and feelings. Section 1.1 describes the process by which a lawyer and client can work together to identify the precise circumstances and needs that make a situation a "problem" for the client.

or other entity that has employed the lawyer's services,[2] a lawyer should be familiar with the skills and concepts involved in problem solving: identifying and diagnosing a problem, generating alternative solutions and strategies, developing a plan of action, implementing the plan, and keeping the planning process open to new information and ideas:

1.1 *Identifying and Diagnosing the Problem.* A lawyer should be familiar with the skills and concepts involved in obtaining an accurate and complete understanding of the client's situation and objectives, including:

(a)   The precise circumstances and needs that make the situation a problem for the client. This assessment should take into consideration:

(i)   The client's definition of the problem;

(ii)   Aspects of the problem that the client may not have perceived;

(iii)   Additional problems that the client may not have perceived;

(b)   The legal, institutional, and interpersonal frameworks in which the problem is set;

(c)   The information available from the client and others about economic, technological, and other factors relating to the problem (such as the nature of the client's business operations or the lessons of the client's experience in similar situations in the past) which create or constrain possible solutions or are relevant to the prediction of the consequences of actions or inaction;

(d)   The client's "goals"—the resolution of the problem that the client would consider optimal and the range of alternative possible outcomes ranked in accordance with the client's preferences, needs, and interests;

(e)   The courses of action that the client considers possible as means for achieving his or her goals, ranked in accordance with the client's preferences, needs, and interests;

(f)   The limits of what is presently known, including:

---

2. The text of this section will hereafter refer simply to "the client." It should be understood, however, that the principles set forth apply equally in situations in which a lawyer acts without a client (such as, for example, when counsel for a governmental agency is asked to act on behalf of the agency).

(i) The extent to which factual or legal information needed to analyze or refine the problem is as yet unknown;

(ii) The likelihood that this information will become known at some point in the future;

(iii) The time frame in which additional information will become known;

(iv) The costs of acquiring additional information; and

(v) The precise impact of informational gaps on the planning process, including the need to keep some courses of action flexible and the possibility that some plans may need to be changed as more information becomes known;

(g) The optimal timetable for resolving the problem, taking into account:

(i) The client's preferences and the factors that influence his or her preferences;

(ii) Any tactical advantages that may accrue if the resolution of the problem is accelerated or postponed;

(iii) The feasibility of advancing or delaying the resolution of the problem and the means for doing so; and

(iv) The ethical limitations upon the use of delay tactics when delay is in the client's interest;

(h) The financial resources which a client is prepared to devote to the solving of the problem and, when economy is required, the courses of action or potential solutions which the client is willing to forgo because of their comparative cost;

1.2 *Generating Alternative Solutions and Strategies.* A lawyer should be familiar with the skills and concepts involved in the process of systematically and creatively generating potential approaches to the problem, drawing upon both the client's insights (*see* § 1.1(c)—(e) *supra*) and the lawyer's independent analysis in considering:

(a) Possible solutions to the problem, including:

      (i)   An inventory of the full range of alternative possible solutions consistent with the practicalities of the client's situation;

      (ii)   An assessment of the extent to which these possible solutions conflict with each other, and any measures that can be taken to reconcile or minimize these conflicts; and

      (iii)   To the extent the conflicts cannot be reconciled, an identification of the choices that must be made and the timetable for making each of these choices;

(b)   Possible means for achieving each of the potential solutions to the problem. This should include the same type of exhaustive generation of alternatives and assessment of conflicts between alternatives described in § 1.2(a)(i)-(iii) *supra;*

(c)   Limitations upon or potential inaccuracies of the solutions or means that have been generated, including:

      (i)   Aspects of the analysis that could not be performed or that may have been overlooked altogether because of current gaps in factual or legal information (along with an analysis of the extent to which it is feasible and desirable to obtain the missing information and thereby complete the analysis, and the optimal timetable for obtaining any such information);

      (ii)   Aspects of the analysis which depend upon questionable assumptions of the client, other providers of information, or the lawyer;

      (iii)   Aspects of the analysis which depend upon assertions of the client or other providers of factual information which the lawyer has a reason to doubt;

1.3   *Developing a Plan of Action.* A lawyer should be familiar with the skills and concepts involved in developing a plan of action with the client, including:

(a)   Identifying the full range of possible plans of action;

(b)   Evaluating the comparative efficacy and desirability of the alternative possible plans of action, comparing and ranking them on the basis of:

(i)   The extent to which each plan of action is likely to achieve the client's objectives and satisfy his or her priorities and preferences;

(ii)   The benefits and costs of each plan of action;

(iii)   The probabilities of successful implementation of each plan of action;

(iv)   The likely consequences of unsuccessful implementation of each plan of action (including those of both total and partial failure);

(v)   The extent to which each plan of action is consistent with the financial resources which the client is able and willing to devote;

(vi)   The extent to which each plan of action is consistent with a timetable which is strategically desirable and which satisfies the client's wishes and needs;

(c)   Tentatively settling upon a plan of action, which should take into account:

(i)   All of the contingencies that may require revision of the plan or recourse to an alternative plan of action;

(ii)   All of the factual or legal information that is as yet unknown, and the portions of the plan that may need to be revised as the missing information is acquired;

1.4 *Implementing the Plan.* A lawyer should be familiar with the skills and concepts involved in implementing a plan of action, including:

(a)   Giving careful consideration to the question of which person (or people) should implement the plan, including:

(i)   Assessing whether the matter should be referred (in whole or in part) to another lawyer because it requires a degree of experience, knowledge, or skill greater than the lawyer personally possesses. This assessment should take into account:

(A)   A realistic appraisal of the degree of experience, knowledge, or skill required for each of the aspects of the plan that should be handled by a lawyer;

(B) A realistic appraisal of one's own ability to competently carry out each of the aspects of the plan that should be handled by a lawyer;

(C) To the extent that one's own degree of experience, knowledge, or skill is insufficient, realistically assessing:

(I)   Whether it is feasible and appropriate to compensate for any such limitations by seeking advice or assistance from more experienced lawyers; or

(II) Whether the professional obligation to provide competent representation requires that the matter be referred in whole or in part to another lawyer;

(ii) Assessing whether some aspects of the plan require expertise in fields other than law and, if so:

(A) Making a judgment about whether it is desirable to retain or consult with experts in the pertinent fields, taking into account the potential value of expert assistance, the cost of retaining or consulting an expert, and the extent of the client's financial resources;

(B) Counseling the client about the lawyer's judgment, including the reasons why the lawyer believes that the potential advantages of retaining or consulting with an expert either do or do not justify the expense;

(iii) Assessing whether some aspects of the plan may appropriately be delegated to law clerks, paralegals, investigators, or support staff in order to maximize the efficient use of the lawyer's time and in order to limit the client's expenses;

(iv) Assessing whether it is appropriate to enlist the aid of the client or the client's associates, relatives, or friends, either because this will facilitate the implementation of some aspect of the plan or because it will make it possible to limit the client's expenses;

(b) Determining the optimal timetable for the completion of each of the tasks that should be performed (either by the lawyer or by any other individual) in the course of implementing the plan;

(c) Monitoring the timely implementation of the plan, including:

(i) Monitoring the performance of any tasks which have been delegated to others;

(ii) Critically evaluating one's own performance and considering whether it is appropriate to seek advice or assistance from more experienced lawyers or to refer the matter to a more experienced lawyer because the implementation of the plan— or some particular issue or problem that has arisen in the course of its implementation—requires a degree of experience, knowledge, or skill greater than one's own;

(d) As tasks are completed, new information is learned, or unanticipated events take place, reviewing the need to revise:

(i) The plan of action;

(ii) The allocation of responsibilities for its implementation; or

(iii) The timetable for its implementation;

1.5 *Keeping the Planning Process Open to New Information and Ideas.* A lawyer should be familiar with the skills and concepts involved in assuring that appropriate account is taken of the ebb and flow of events, information, thoughts, and feelings throughout the process of analyzing a client's problem and working it through to resolution, including:

(a) Monitoring aspects of the client's situation that may change and arranging to be kept constantly informed of new factual developments;

(b) Keeping in touch with the evolution of the client's thinking and attitudes regarding the problem;

(c) Maintaining sufficient flexibility in planning to permit consideration of the latest available information before significant action is taken at each stage, and systematically reviewing new information at appropriate points in the process;

(d)   Adjusting the pace of decisionmaking to the availability of evolving information, to the extent practicable, so as to base decisions on the firmest accessible information base;

(e)   Assuring that the client has had adequate opportunity to reflect on his or her preferences, judgments, and decisions before those are acted upon, so that their stability over time can be appraised consistently with the importance of the interests affected by the action, without the loss of opportunities through indecision.

Commentary

Several of the models that have been developed for teaching or evaluating lawyers' competency recognize the importance of the conceptual skills involved in problem solving. *See, e.g.*, AMERICAN LAW INSTITUTE–AMERCIAN BAR ASSOCIATION COMMITTEE ON CONTINUING PROFESSIONAL EDUCATION, A MODEL CURRICULUM FOR BRIDGE-THE-GAP PROGRAMS (Discussion Draft 1988) (setting forth a model curriculum to teach "'essential components of law practice'" to "'recent graduates [of law school] and new members of the bar'" (*id.* at 7), which lists the skills of "Analyzing and Selecting Appropriate Options" and "Designing and Implementing a Plan of Action" among the "sub-skills to be acquired by the neophyte lawyers" (*id.* at 13)); Cort & Sammons, *The Search for "Good Lawyering": A Concept and Model of Lawyering Competencies*, 29 CLEVE. ST. L. REV. 397, 406, 441-43 (1980) (describing the "Model of Lawyering Competency" developed by the Competency-Based Task Force of Antioch School of Law, which includes "Problem-Solving Competency" as one of the six categories of major "lawyering functions" required for competent lawyering); STATE BAR OF CALIFORNIA COMMITTEE OF BAR EXAMINERS, INFORMATION REGARDING PERFORMANCE TESTS 14-16 (1988) (setting forth standards for testing "problem solving," one of four "broad categories of lawyering competency" assessed in the performance test of the California Bar Examination (*id.* at 5)). *See also, e.g.*, AMERICAN LAW INSTITUTE–AMERICAN BAR ASSOCIATION COMMITTEE ON CONTINUING PROFESSIONAL EDUCATION, A PRACTICAL GUIDE TO ACHIEVING EXCELLENCE IN THE PRACTICE OF LAW: STANDARDS, METHODS, AND SELF-EVALUATION § 2.1(c) & Comment (1992) (describing the process by which lawyers "develop an initial strategy of legal problem solving . . . in collaboration with the client'"); Barnhizer, *The Clinical Method of Legal Instruction: Its Theory and Implementa-*

tion, 30 J. LEGAL EDUC. 67, 77 (1979) (listing the teaching of "strategy, tactics, and decision-making" among the goals of legal education and explaining that "a lawyer must . . . be able to choose between the issues and alternatives and select those most appropriate for obtaining the most beneficial consequences for the client"); Rosenthal, *Evaluating the Competence of Lawyers*, 11 LAW & SOCIETY 256, 270-71 (1976) (stating that "[l]awyers essentially perform a problem solving service," and proposing a model for evaluating lawyer competency by focusing on "five sequential sets of activities" involved in "systematic problem solving"); Strong, *The Pedagogic Training of a Law Faculty*, 25 J. LEGAL EDUC. 226, 230 (1973) (presenting a "Catalogue of Components of Legal Education" based upon the work of Karl Llewellyn, and listing "[p]roblem formulation" and "[p]roblem resolution" among the "[p]erceptional (essentially cognitive)" components).

One of the most extensive explorations of the conceptual skills involved in the problem-solving aspects of legal practice can be found in Amsterdam, *Clinical Legal Education—A 21st-Century Perspective*, 34 J. LEGAL EDUC. 612 (1984). This article describes a conceptual process it terms "ends-means thinking," "a process by which one starts with a factual situation presenting a problem or an opportunity and figures out the way in which the problem might be solved or the opportunity might be realized." *Id.* at 614. The process begins with a systematic identification of all the possible goals ("the 'end points' to which movement from the present state of affairs might be made"), and then reasons "backward from [these] goals, . . . mapping the various roads that might be taken to each goal, . . . proceeding backward step by step along each road and asking what steps have to be taken before each following step can be taken." *Ibid.* Each of the possible means to achieve the respective goals is inventoried, and then the various ends and means are examined for potential conflicts. Conflicts are reconciled to the extent possible, and those which prove truly incompatible are prioritized.

The analysis of the skill of problem solving in this Statement incorporates several of the elements common to the formulations in the above-described literature. An emphasis was placed on the aspects of problem solving essential to minimal competency, and therefore some of the more sophisticated aspects described in the literature were excluded. For example, Amsterdam describes the use of "best-case/worst-case" scenarios for relating ends and means in the light of risks. *See* Amsterdam, *supra*, at 614. Other forms of analysis, such as cost/benefit analyses and minimax analyses, can be used for similar purposes. While such refined analytical techniques are certainly useful and do enhance the quality of problem solving, it was concluded that these are refinements which can be learned at a later stage of a lawyer's career.

This formulation of the skill of problem solving also includes some elements and emphases not found in the literature. This Statement explicitly calls for a holistic approach to the assessment of a client's situation, considering the "legal, institutional, and interpersonal frameworks in which the problem is set." § 1.1(b) *supra*. The importance of these non-legal factors is readily apparent: A lawyer would ill-serve a client if, for example, the lawyer settled upon a possible solution to the client's legal problems without considering the devastating effect the selected alternative could have on the client's family, current employment, future career opportunities, relationships to others in the workplace or the community, and the like. This Statement also includes, and indeed emphasizes, practical constraints on the problem solving process. Factors such as the financial resources that a client is able and willing to devote and the effects upon the client of accelerating or delaying the resolution of the problem are quintessential aspects of any analysis of the best way to solve a client's legal problems.

This Statement's formulation of the skill of problem solving includes certain other conceptual skills that are crucial for the effective application of virtually all of the skills analyzed in the Statement:

The first of these is the skill of creativity. Whether the task at hand is the generation of possible solutions and strategies for solving a client's problem (§ 1.2 *supra*), the formulation of legal or factual theories (Skill §§ 2.2, 4.2 *infra*), or the conceptualization of the subject of a negotiation (Skill § 7.1(e) *infra*), competent lawyering requires a person with a creative mind—a person who is willing to look at situations, ideas, and issues in an openminded way; to explore novel and imaginative approaches; and to look for potentially useful connections and associations between apparently unrelated principles (Skill § 2.5(b)(i)(A)), facts (Skill § 4.6(b)), negotiating points (Skill § 7.1(d)(i)), or other factors.

Second, effective problem solving (like the effective use of other skills in the Statement) requires sound judgment. In identifying the range of possible solutions, a problem solver must exercise judgment in determining which options deserve serious consideration. Similarly, judgment must be exercised in comparing viable options. *See, e.g.*, Amsterdam, *supra*, at 614-15 (discussing the analytical skills which lawyers use when engaging in "[d]ecisionmaking in situations where options involve differing and often uncertain degrees of risks and promises of different sorts," *id.* at 614).

Yet, it is not enough for a problem solver merely to have the capacity for sound judgment: He or she also must be capable and willing to exercise judgment in an independent manner. Effective problem solving requires a person who is not content to follow customary practices blindly or to accept the advice of a more experienced attorney uncritically. It requires a person who is willing to engage in independent thinking to determine what approach is best suited to the particular situation and who is willing to search for his or her own insights and ideas.

Finally, effective use of the skill of problem solving (as well as other lawyering skills) requires a realistic view of one's own abilities and limitations. Previous studies of lawyer competence have stressed the importance of a lawyer's appreciating the limits of his or her own competence. *See, e.g.,* AMERICAN BAR ASSOCIATION, FINAL REPORT AND RECOMMENDATIONS OF THE TASK FORCE ON PROFESSIONAL COMPETENCE 4, 18, 32 (1983); AMERICAN BAR ASSOCIATION SECTION OF LEGAL EDUCATION AND ADMISSIONS TO THE BAR, REPORT AND RECOMMENDATIONS OF THE TASK FORCE ON LAWYER COMPETENCY: THE ROLE OF THE LAW SCHOOLS 10 (1979). As explained in §§ 1.4(a)(i), 1.4(c)(ii) *supra*, this Statement's formulation of problem solving (and other skills) assumes that a lawyer will refer a matter to a more experienced attorney when this is necessary to ensure that a client receives competent representation.

2. Legal Analysis and Reasoning

In order to effectively analyze the application of legal rules and principles to a client's problem, a lawyer should be familiar with the skills and concepts involved in identifying legal issues, formulating legal theories, elaborating and enhancing the theories, and evaluating and criticizing the theories:

2.1 *Identifying and Formulating Legal Issues.* In order to analyze a factual situation so as to identify each of the distinct legal issues presented by the facts, a lawyer should be familiar with the skills and concepts involved in:

(a) Analyzing the facts so as to:

(i) Identify all potentially relevant facts known at the present time (*see* Skill § 1.1 *supra*), breaking down complex factual situations into parts susceptible to systematic analysis;

(ii) Examine each fact critically, distinguishing between levels of "fact" (such as observational data, inferences, characterizations, conclusions, and so forth);

(iii) Tentatively evaluate the reliability of each fact, developing standards and processes for continuing re-evaluation of the reliability of these facts as more factual information is gathered;

(iv) Identify inconsistencies between facts and evaluate the possible significance of each inconsistency;

(b) Identifying and accurately formulating any pertinent rules or principles of law bearing on the factual situation. This will typically require legal research (*see* Skill § 3 *infra*)—with its specialized techniques for reading and analyzing court decisions, statutes, and other primary texts (*see* Skill § 3.2(b) *infra*)—to supplement or refine the lawyer's pre-existing knowledge of rules or principles;

(c) Using the legal rules and principles to:

(i) Identify the specific facts that frame each legal issue and its possible resolutions;

(ii) Group, categorize, and characterize facts in terms of the concepts or language of legal rules and principles (while ensuring that the facts are described objectively and accurately, and that all pertinent facts are accounted for);

(iii) Identify the additional factual information that is needed. Methods and processes should be developed for gathering the requisite factual information and integrating it into the legal analysis;

2.2 *Formulating Relevant Legal Theories.* In order to formulate relevant legal theories, a lawyer should be familiar with the skills and concepts involved in analyzing and synthesizing the pertinent legal rules and principles in the light of the facts, including:

(a) Breaking legal rules down into their component parts (elements, "factors," "considerations," competing interests, and so forth), and relating the facts at hand to each of these components;

(b) Articulating the reasoning by which a particular legal rule or principle applies to the facts at hand and calls for a specified result;

2.3 *Elaborating Legal Theory.* A lawyer should be familiar with the skills and concepts involved in elaborating and enhancing legal theories, including:

(a) Combining legal theories by shifting the level of theoretical discourse and reconceptualizing the theories in terms of "overarching concepts," "common themes," and the like;

(b) Formulating legal theories in the alternative and either cumulating them or sequencing them in terms of "fallback" positions;

(c) Identifying arguments in different dimensions (such as, for example, doctrine, history, practicality, justice and equity), that can be brought to bear to support (or oppose) the legal theories that have been formulated, and:

   (i) Analyzing the extent to which each of these possible arguments can be used to enhance the effectiveness of each of the theories that has been formulated;

   (ii) Analyzing whether the arguments will be more persuasive if presented cumulatively, individually, or in various combinations;

2.4 *Evaluating Legal Theory.* In order to evaluate the likely efficacy of a legal theory or theories in persuading a decisionmaker (or class of decisionmakers) to make a particular decision or to reach a particular result, a lawyer should be familiar with the skills and concepts involved in identifying and assessing:

(a) Considerations that are likely to bear on the decisionmaker's (or decisionmakers') reactions to a legal theory, including:

   (i) Whether a theory requires an extension of a legal rule or principle beyond its previously recognized applications, and, if so: (A) the potential implications of the extension; (B) the likely reactions of the decisionmaker(s) to the extension and its potential implications; and (C) the feasibility of avoiding a negative reaction on the part of the decisionmaker(s) by articulating a basis for limiting the extension so as to avoid untoward results;

(ii)   Whether a theory requires that a competing rule or concept be rejected or limited, and, if so: (A) the potential implications of any such rejection or limitation of the competing rule or concept; (B) the likely reaction(s) of the decisionmaker(s) to the rejection or limitation of the competing rule or concept or any of the possible implications of these results; and (C) the feasibility of persuading the decisionmaker(s) that it is appropriate to reject or limit the competing rule or concept;

(iii)   Whether a theory is consistent or inconsistent with current trends in the evolution and application of legal rules and principles, and, if so: (A) the extent to which its compatibility with current trends can be used to persuade the decisionmaker to accept the theory; (B) the extent to which its incompatibility with current trends can be minimized or overcome by limiting or reframing the theory;

(b)   The likely predispositions of the decisionmaker (or class of decisionmakers), as evidenced by:

(i)   Patterns of previous decisionmaking;

(ii)   The reasons articulated for previous decisions;

(iii)   Institutional considerations that tend to produce a particular mind set or perspective;

(iv)   Personal biases as revealed in prior decisions or statements;

(c)   Factors present in the particular factual situation that are likely to engage the sympathetic or antipathetic reaction of the decisionmaker(s) (such as, for example, the "equities" inherent in the situation);

2.5   *Criticizing and Synthesizing Legal Argumentation.* In order to objectively evaluate the validity and limitations of theories and arguments (including, in a litigative or other adversarial context, the theories and arguments likely to be put forward by the opposing side), a lawyer should be familiar with the skills and concepts involved in:

(a)   Critically examining the legal "rules" on which the theories and arguments are based, putting these rules into perspective in the light of their purposes, derivations, the circumstances under which they were announced, and so forth;

(b)   Critically examining any reasoning upon which legal argumentation is based, making:

  (i)   An evaluation of the validity of, and limitations upon, various forms of argument, including:

    (A)   The validity of reasoning by analogy, and the extent to which analogies are or are not appropriate to particular aspects of the theory or theories;

    (B)   The inevitable extensions of chosen lines of logic and the points at which such extensions can be plausibly resisted;

  (ii)   An evaluation of potential flaws in reasoning, including:

    (A)   Underlying premises or assumptions which are questionable;

    (B)   Questionable applications of inductive or deductive logic;

    (C)   Failures to take into account factors or conditions that may call for a different analysis or conclusion;

(c)   Identifying and evaluating other possible legal theories by:

  (i)   Identifying and isolating the component parts of facts, doctrines, theories, concepts, and the like;

  (ii)   Recombining these component parts in new patterns; and

  (iii)   Examining the extent to which the new patterns suggest new legal theories (and, if so, repeating each of the above steps to formulate, elaborate, evaluate, criticize, and synthesize the new theories).

Commentary

The importance of the skill of legal analysis is universally acknowledged. *See, e.g.*, AMERICAN BAR ASSOCIATION SECTION OF LEGAL EDUCATION AND ADMISSIONS TO THE BAR, REPORT AND RECOMMENDATIONS OF THE TASK FORCE ON LAWYER COMPETENCY: THE ROLE OF THE LAW SCHOOLS 11 (1979) (the "foundation for competent practice" that law schools attempt to provide to law students "includes solidly developed skills of legal analysis"); Cort & Sammons, *The Search for "Good Lawyering": A Concept and Model of Lawyering Competencies*, 29 CLEVE. ST. L. REV. 397, 415 (1980) ("[i]f legal educators agree on anything, it is that legal analysis is taught in law schools").

This section attempts to break down the process of legal analysis into its component parts. These may or may not take the form of a series of discrete steps, although their description necessarily does. To many experienced lawyers, the process has become second nature and they can perform it in much less time than is required to detail what they are doing. Less experienced laywers have to go through it more methodically and articulately until they habituate the knack.

This Statement's formulation of the skill of legal analysis reflects the prevailing conception of legal analysis as a means of reasoning from existing law and applying rules and principles established in prior judicial decisions (as well as other sources of law) to a new factual situation. *See, e.g.*, Amsterdam, *Clinical Legal Education - A 21st-Century Perspective*, 34 J. LEGAL EDUC. 612, 613 (1984). However, the Statement diverges from the traditional case-method approach to teaching legal analysis in that it takes into account two critical aspects of the ways in which legal analysis is conducted in actual practice. First of all, in practice, it is frequently necessary to develop legal theories at a stage of the case at which the facts are only partly known; in classroom applications of the case method, although hypotheticals do provide factual diversity, each hypothetical asks the students to accept a given set of facts as a closed universe of facts. The above formulation takes into account the possibility of additional facts becoming known at a later time and requiring a re-evaluation of the legal analysis, of the assessment of facts underlying the legal analysis, or of both. *See* §§ 2.1(a)(iii), 2.1(c)(iii) *supra*. Second, in the case method, students develop legal analyses in situations in which they are familiar with the law to be applied—namely, the legal rules and principles emerging from the judicial decision(s) under discussion. In contrast, in practice, lawyers are often called upon to develop legal analyses in situations in which the lawyer is not familiar with the applicable law. The above formulation takes into account the possible need for legal research to supplement or refine a lawyer's knowledge of the applicable law. *See* § 2.1(b) *supra.*

In explaining the process of evaluating legal theory, § 2.4 uses the terms "decisionmaker" and "class of decisionmakers." It should be emphasized that these terms are not intended to refer solely to decisionmakers in the traditional litigative sense of a judge, jury, or other neutral arbiter. In a wide variety of other contexts, an individual or an organization is in a position to make decisions affecting the client, and a lawyer may need to use legal reasoning to gauge the best possible approach for dealing with that individual or organization. This is true, for example, in the negotiation of a commercial transaction, where legal reasoning may inform a lawyer's approach to the party with whom he or she is negotiating.

3. Legal Research

In order to conduct legal research effectively, a lawyer should have a working knowledge of the nature of legal rules and legal institutions, the fundamental tools of legal research, and the process of devising and implementing a coherent and effective research design:

3.1 *Knowledge of the Nature of Legal Rules and Institutions.* The identification of the issues and sources to be researched in any particular situation requires an understanding of:

   (a) The various sources of legal rules and the processes by which these rules are made, including:

      (i) Caselaw. Every lawyer should have a basic familiarity with: (A) The organization and structure of the federal and state courts of general jurisdiction; general concepts of jurisdiction and venue; the rudiments of civil and criminal procedure; the historical separation between courts of law and equity and the modern vestiges of this dual court system; (B) The nature of common law decisionmaking by courts and the doctrine of *stare decisis*; (C) The degree of "authoritativeness" of constitutional and common law decisions made by courts at the various levels of the federal and state judicial systems;

      (ii) Statutes. Every lawyer should have a basic familiarity with: (A) The legislative processes at the federal, state, and local levels, including the procedures for preparing, introducing, amending, and enacting legislation; (B) The relationship between the legislative and judicial branches, including the power of the courts to construe ambiguous statutory language and the power of the courts to strike down unconstitutional statutory provisions;

(iii)   Administrative regulations and decisions of administrative agencies. Every lawyer should have a basic familiarity with the rudiments of administrative law, including: (A) The procedures for administrative and executive rulemaking and adjudication; (B) The relationship between the executive and judicial branches, including the power of the courts to construe and pass on the validity and constitutionality of administrative regulations and the actions of administrative agencies;

(iv)   Rules of court;

(v)   Restatements and similar codifications (covering non-official expositions of legal rules that courts tend to view as authoritative);

(b)   Which of the sources of legal rules identified in § 3.1(a) *supra* tend to provide the controlling principles for resolution of various kinds of issues in various substantive fields;

(c)   The variety of legal remedies available in any given situation, including: litigation; legislative remedies (such as drafting and/or lobbying for new legislation; lobbying to defeat pending legislative bills; and lobbying for the repeal or amendment of existing legislation); administrative remedies (such as presenting testimony in support of, or lobbying for, the adoption, repeal, or amendment of administrative regulations; and lobbying of an administrator to resolve an individual case in a particular way); and alternative dispute-resolution mechanisms (formal mechanisms such as arbitration, mediation, and conciliation; and informal mechanisms such as self-help);

3.2 *Knowledge of and Ability to Use the Most Fundamental Tools of Legal Research*:

(a) With respect to each of the following fundamental tools of legal research, a lawyer should be generally familiar with the nature of the tool, its likely location in a law library, and the ways in which the tool is used:

   (i)   Primary legal texts (the written or recorded texts of legal rules), including: caselaw reporters, loose-leaf services, and other collections of court decisions; codifications of federal, state, and local legislation; collections of administrative regulations and decisions of administrative agencies;

   (ii) Secondary legal materials (the variety of aids to researching the primary legal texts), including treatises, digests, annotated versions of statutory compilations, commentaries in loose-leaf services, law reviews, and Shepard's Compilations of citations to cases and statutes;

   (iii) Sources of ethical obligations of lawyers, including the standards of professional conduct (the Code of Professional Responsibility and the Model Rules of Professional Conduct), and collections of ethical opinions of the American Bar Association and of state and local bar associations;

(b) With respect to the primary legal texts described in § 3.2(a)(i) *supra*, a lawyer should be familiar with:

   (i)   Specialized techniques for reading or using the text, including:

      (A) Techniques of reading and analyzing court decisions, such as: the analysis of which portions of the decision are holdings and which are *dicta*; the identification of narrower and broader possible formulations of the holdings of the case; the evaluation of a case's relative precedential value; and the reconciliation of doctrinal inconsistencies between cases;

(B) Techniques of construing statutes by employing well-accepted rules of statutory construction or by referring to secondary sources (such as legislative history);

(ii) Specialized rules and customs permitting or prohibiting reliance on alternative versions of the primary legal texts (such as unofficial case reporters or unofficial statutory codes);

(c) With respect to the secondary legal materials described in § 3.2(a)(ii) *supra*, a lawyer should have a general familiarity with the breadth, depth, detail and currency of coverage, the particular perspectives, and the relative strengths and weaknesses that tend to be found in the various kinds of secondary sources so that he or she can make an informed judgment about which source is most suitable for a particular research purpose;

(d) With respect to both the primary legal materials described in § 3.2(a)(i) *supra*, and the secondary legal materials described in § 3.2(a)(ii) *supra*, a lawyer should be familiar with alternative forms of accessing the materials, including hard copy, microfiche and other miniaturization services, and computerized services (such as LEXIS and WESTLAW);

3.3 *Understanding of the Process of Devising and Implementing a Coherent and Effective Research Design.* A lawyer should be familiar with the skills and concepts involved in:

(a) Formulating the issues for research:

(i) Determining the full range of legal issues to be researched (*see* Skill § 2.1 *supra*);

(ii) Determining the kinds of answers to the legal issues that are needed for various purposes;

(iii) Determining the degree of confidence in the answers that is needed for various purposes;

(iv) Determining the extent of documentation of the answers that is needed for various purposes;

(v) Conceptualizing the issues to be researched in terms that are conducive to effective legal research (including a consideration of which conceptualizations or verbalizations of issues or rules will make them most accessible to various types of search strategies);

(b)   Identifying the full range of search strategies that could be used to research the issues, as well as alternatives to research, such as, in appropriate cases, seeking the information from other people who have expertise regarding the issues to be researched (for example, other attorneys or, in the case of procedural issues, clerks of court);

(c)   Evaluating the various search strategies and settling upon a research design, which should take into account:

(i)   The degree of thoroughness of research that would be necessary in order to adequately resolve the legal issues (*i.e.*, in order to find an answer if there is one to be found, or, in cases where the issue is still open, to determine to a reasonable degree of certainty that it is still unresolved and gather analogous authorities);

(ii)   The degree of thoroughness that is necessary in the light of the uses to which the research will be put (*e.g.*, the greater degree of thoroughness necessary if the information to be researched will be used at trial or at a legislative hearing; the lesser degree of thoroughness necessary if the information will be used in an informal negotiation with opposing counsel or lobbying of an administrator);

(iii)   An estimation of the amount of time that will be necessary to conduct research of the desired degree of thoroughness;

(iv)   An assessment of the feasibility of conducting research of the desired degree of thoroughness, taking into account:

(A)   The amount of time available for research in the light of the other tasks to be performed, their relative importance, and their relative urgency;

(B)   The extent of the client's resources that can be allocated to the process of legal research; and

(C)   The availability of techniques for reducing the cost of research (such as, for example, using manual research methods to gain basic familiarity with the relevant area before using the more expensive resource of computerized services);

(v)   If there is insufficient time for, or the client lacks adequate resources for, research that is thorough enough to adequately resolve the legal issues, a further assessment of the ways in which the scope of the research can be curtailed with the minimum degree of risk of undermining the accuracy of the research or otherwise impairing the client's interests;

(vi)   Strategies for double-checking the accuracy of the research, such as using different secondary sources to research the same issue; or, when possible, conferring with practitioners or academics with expertise in the area;

(d)   Implementing the research design, including:

(i)   Informing the client of the precise extent to which the scope of the research has been curtailed for the sake of time or conservation of the client's resources (*see* § 3.3(c)(v) *supra*); the reasons for these curtailments; and the possible consequences of deciding not to pursue additional research;

(ii)   Monitoring the results of the research and periodically considering:

(A)   Whether the research design should be modified;

(B)   Whether it is appropriate to end the research, because it has fully answered the questions posed; or, even though it has not fully answered the questions posed, further research will not produce additional information; or the information that is likely to be produced is not worth the time and resources that would be expended;

(iii) Ensuring that any cases that will be relied upon or cited have not been overruled, limited, or called into question; and that any statutes or administrative regulations that will be relied upon or cited have not been repealed or amended and have not been struck down by the courts.

Commentary

It can hardly be doubted that the ability to do legal research is one of the skills that any competent legal practitioner must possess. *See, e.g.*, AMERICAN BAR ASSOCIATION SECTION OF LEGAL EDUCATION AND ADMISSIONS TO THE BAR, REPORT AND RECOMMENDATIONS OF THE TASK FORCE ON LAWYER COMPETENCY: THE ROLE OF THE LAW SCHOOLS 9 (1979); Baird, *A Survey of the Relevance of Legal Training to Law School Graduates*, 29 J. LEGAL EDUC. 264, 273-74 (1978); Barnhizer, *The Clinical Method of Legal Instruction: Its Theory and Implementation*, 30 J. LEGAL EDUC. 67, 78 (1979); Mudd & LaTrielle, *Professional Competence: A Study of New Lawyers*, 49 MONT. L. REV. 11, 17 (1988); Schwartz, *The Relative Importance of Skills Used by Attorneys*, 3 GOLDEN GATE L. REV. 321, 324-33 (1973).

This Statement employs a broad definition of the range of knowledge and skills required for legal research. It recognizes that a prerequisite for effective research is an understanding of the nature of legal remedies and the processes for seeking these remedies. It treats legal research as far more than a mechanical examination of texts; the formulation and implementation of a research design are analyzed as processes which require a number of complex conceptual skills.

The description of the process of researching legal issues parallels the treatment of problem solving in Skill § 1 as a process consisting of: diagnosis of the problem; identification of the range of possible solutions; development of a plan of action; and implementation of the plan. This parallelism is appropriate because legal research is in essence a process of problem solving.

4. Factual Investigation

To effectively plan, direct, and (where applicable) participate in the process of factual investigation, a lawyer should be familiar with the skills, concepts, and processes involved in determining whether factual investigation is needed, planning an investigation, implementing an investigative strategy, organizing information in an accessible form, deciding whether to conclude the investigation, and evaluating the information that has been gathered:

4.1 *Determining the Need for Factual Investigation.* To resolve the threshold question of whether any factual investigation is necessary (or, if not actually necessary, worthwhile), a lawyer should be able to:

(a)   Organize and critically evaluate the factual information already in hand (such as, for example, factual information acquired from the client or documents which he or she furnished);

(b)   Integrate the foregoing analysis of the factual information in hand with an analysis of the law, to assess what, if any, factual information is still needed in the light of the applicable legal rules and principles (*see* Skill § 2.1(c)(iii) *supra*);

(c)   If additional factual information is needed, then:

(i)   Make a determination of whether the information is worth seeking by assessing the likely accessibility of the information, the amounts of time and resources that are likely to be required to obtain the information, the extent of the client's resources, and other pertinent considerations; and

(ii)   If the lawyer concludes that the information is not worth seeking, counsel the client about the decision and advise him or her of the possible consequences of failing to investigate;

4.2 *Planning a Factual Investigation.* In order to acquire relevant facts efficiently, a lawyer must be familiar with the following skills, concepts, and processes:

(a)   Formulating a "working hypothesis" of the legal and factual theories upon which the lawyer will rely to achieve his or her objectives (which the lawyer treats as merely a tentative and flexible plan and which he or she modifies whenever revisions are warranted by the acquisition of new information or other factors). The formulation of a working hypothesis requires:

(i)   An analysis of the pertinent legal rules and principles to formulate the range of relevant legal theories (*see* Skill §§ 2.2, 2.3 *supra*);

(ii)   Use of the legal theories (and the underlying legal rules and principles) as an analytical framework to identify the range of factual theories that will make it possible to prove each of the factual propositions necessary to prevail. The process of identifying factual theories requires:

(A) An understanding of basic forms of logical connection in reasoning about facts, as guides to the identification of information necessary to construct lines of proof;

(B) An understanding of the standards and processes by which any pertinent decision-maker assesses the reliability of information, as guides to the identification of information necessary to accredit or discredit lines of proof;

(b) Devising a coherent and effective investigative strategy by:

(i) Using the working hypothesis to determine the initial directions of investigation (including the facts to be gathered and the order in which to gather them), while keeping in mind:

(A) The need to guard against overly restricting the investigation to the current working hypothesis and thereby excluding information that is potentially germane;

(B) The need to constantly be alert to the possible advisability of revising the current working hypothesis as new facts are learned;

(ii) Analyzing whether the legal issues that have been formulated (*see* Skill § 2.1 *supra*) suggest factual questions that are susceptible to investigation and that warrant investigative directions or priorities other than those indicated by the working hypothesis;

(iii) Evaluating the most efficient way of using investigative tools to address the factual questions that have been identified, which requires:

(A) An understanding of the basic methods of factual investigation, their relative strengths and weaknesses, benefits and costs;

(B) Systematic analysis of the possible sources of factual information and the relationships among them so as to generate and follow up on leads efficiently;

(c)   Determining the degree of thoroughness that is required of the investigation in light of the purposes of the investigation, the time available, the client's resources, and other pertinent variables. If the lawyer concludes that some potentially fruitful sources of information should be excluded, then he or she should be able to:

  (i)   Re-evaluate previously made decisions (and, if necessary, reconceptualize issues) in the light of the information or assurance lost by limiting the depth or breadth of the investigation;

  (ii)   Consult with the client about:

    (A) The process of analysis and decisionmaking through which the client's lack of resources, the need for a quick response, and similar constraints are taken into consideration in determining the depth and breadth of the investigation;

    (B) The lawyer's judgment that the depth or breadth of the investigation should be limited, and the potential consequences of such limitations;

4.3 *Implementing the Investigative Strategy.* In order to implement an investigative strategy effectively, a lawyer should be able to follow the strategy systematically, monitoring results as they are obtained and modifying the strategy whenever appropriate. Depending upon the nature of a client's legal problem, the implementation of an investigative strategy may include:

(a)   Interviewing fact witnesses. To interview a fact witness effectively, a lawyer should be familiar with the following skills, concepts and processes:

  (i)   Planning an interview effectively, which requires:

    (A) An understanding of the basic communications processes and interpersonal dynamics involved in interviewing (*see* Skill § 5 *infra*);

    (B) Viewing a situation from the perspective of the witness and anticipating his or her concerns, expectations, assumptions, and attitudes (*see* Skill § 5.1 *infra*);

(C) Identifying the subject-matter focus of the interview on the basis of the presently available information;

(D) Engaging in contingency planning to prepare for:

   (I) The possibility that the lawyer has misjudged the witness's concerns, expectations, etc.;

   (II) The possibility that the lawyer has failed to accurately identify the subject-matter focus;

   (III) Other contingencies that may be anticipated in the light of the facts presently known about the client's legal problem and the individual to be interviewed;

(ii) Conducting an interview effectively, which requires:

(A) An understanding of the basic communication processes and interpersonal dynamics involved in interviewing (*see* Skill § 5 *infra*), and an application of that understanding in:

   (I) Ascertaining the witness's motivations, reinforcing positive motivations and abating negative motivations (and, where necessary, overcoming hostility or an unwillingness to cooperate);

   (II) Paying attention to, and correctly interpreting, verbal and nonverbal communications;

(B) Effective application of question-asking techniques and other devices for conducting an investigative interview, which include:

   (I) Techniques of question-formulation, such as the uses of open and closed questions, consecutive and non-consecutive questions, and so forth;

(II)   Specialized questioning techniques, such as the "walk-through" technique of story-telling, experiential recall, demonstrations, and so forth;

(III) Alternatives to direct questioning, such as inviting narration, encouraging association, repeating, and restating;

(IV)   Probing beneath abstractions and conclusions;

(C) Employment of the process of formulating and revising hypotheses (*see* § 4.2(a) *supra*) in the course of the interview to consider whether the information supplied by the witness militates for revising the original plan for the interview by adding previously unforeseen topics or by avoiding topics about which the lawyer had planned to ask;

(b) Document analysis. In order to work with documents effectively, a lawyer should be familiar with the skills and processes required for:

(i)   Identifying the types of documents that are pertinent to a client's legal problem or its possible resolution(s);

(ii) Acquiring the pertinent documents, which requires:

(A) An identification of the likely sources of the various documents;

(B) An identification of the most effective means of acquiring the documents from these sources in an expeditious manner;

(C) A systematic inventory and review of the documents that have been acquired to ascertain any documents that were not obtained (for example, documents that were not produced in response to the lawyer's request or subpoena; or documents that the lawyer failed to request or subpoena because he or she did not previously know of their existence);

(iii)   Analyzing the documents, including:

(A)   Identifying significant passages or portions of the documents and assessing the implications of the facts contained in these passages or portions for the present factual and legal theories;

(B)   Identifying significant omissions (by, for example, analyzing what information logically should be recorded but is not), and assessing the implications of these omissions for the present factual and legal theories;

(C)   Developing a system or process for reviewing the documents at later points in time to identify:

(I)   Information which does not presently appear significant but whose significance may become apparent in light of subsequently learned information;

(II)   Information which is not presently significant because of the current legal or factual theories but which may turn out to be significant in light of later revisions of legal or factual theories;

4.4   *Memorializing and Organizing Information in an Accessible Form.* In order to effectively memorialize and organize factual information as it is gathered (and/or at the conclusion of the fact-gathering process), a lawyer should be familiar with the skills and processes for memorializing and organizing factual data in a form that:

(a)   Maximizes efficiency in retrieving and using the data throughout the period of time in which the information may need to be used; and

(b)   Is appropriately responsive to:

(i)   Legal requirements for recording and preserving factual information;

(ii)   Legal requirements for disclosure or discovery of factual information which may make it strategically undesirable to memorialize information (other than that which must be memorialized as a matter of law);

4.5   *Deciding Whether to Conclude the Process of Fact-Gathering.* In order to determine whether it is appropriate to conclude an investigation, a lawyer should be familiar with the skills and processes involved in:

   (a)   Assessing whether:

      (i)   The investigation has yielded as much of the desired information as it is practicably likely to yield; or that

      (ii)   Further investigation is not worthwhile, in the light of the information it is likely to produce, the amount of time and resources it is likely to consume, and other pertinent variables;

   (b)   Consulting with the client about the lawyer's judgment that the investigation should be concluded, including advising the client of:

      (i)   The process by which the lawyer reached this decision;

      (ii)   The factors he or she considered, including the extent to which he or she factored in the extent of the client's resources;

      (iii)   The possible consequences of deciding not to pursue additional investigation;

4.6   *Evaluating the Information That Has Been Gathered.* In order to effectively evaluate factual information that has been gathered (a process which ordinarily takes place as each new fact is gathered and again at the conclusion of the investigation), a lawyer should be familiar with the skills and processes involved in:

   (a)   Scrutinizing facts critically to assess their accuracy and reliability;

   (b)   Analyzing facts in order to:

      (i)   Identify patterns of information (how the facts that have been gathered fit together) and thereby acquire a better understanding of the facts;

      (ii)   Identify facts that are inconsistent with other facts that have been gathered and evaluate the possible reasons for the inconsistencies;

(c) Reasoning from the facts that have been gathered in order to:

    (i) Determine the conclusions that they support, and the courses of action that are appropriate in light of these conclusions;

    (ii) Examine whether there are alternative ways of analyzing the facts that would lead to conclusions other than those which the lawyer has drawn, and, if so:

        (A) Assessing the relative validity of the various possible conclusions; and

        (B) Determining the courses of action that may be warranted in light of the range of alternative possible conclusions that may be drawn from the facts (including, where appropriate, deciding to investigate further to resolve ambiguities or inconsistencies in the facts that have been gathered thus far).

Commentary

The skill of factual investigation plays a central role in the lawyering process and in the professional life of the legal practitioner. *See, e.g.*, D. BINDER & P. BERGMAN, FACT INVESTIGATION: FROM HYPOTHESIS TO PROOF 2-4 (1984); G. BELLOW & B. MOULTON, THE LAWYERING PROCESS: MATERIALS FOR CLINICAL INSTRUCTION IN ADVOCACY 290-92 (1978). Surveys of practitioners attest to the practicing bar's recognition of the importance of factual investigation. *See, e.g.*, F. ZEMANS & V. ROSENBLUM, THE MAKING OF A PUBLIC PROFESSION 125-26 (1981); Baird, *A Survey of the Relevance of Legal Training to Law School Graduates*, 29 J. LEGAL EDUC. 264, 273, 281 (1978); Schwartz, *The Relative Importance of Skills Used by Attorneys*, 3 GOLDEN GATE L. REV. 321, 324-25 (1973).

This Statement's formulation of the skill of fact investigation attempts to strike a balance between the conceptual and practical aspects of the skill consistent with the needs of lawyers in all spheres of practice. Thus, the formulation sets out the fundamental conceptual skills that are critical for planning and directing fact investigation, such as the skill of "[h]ypothesis formulation and testing in information acquisition." *See* Amsterdam, *Clinical Legal Education—A 21st-Century Perspective*, 34 J. LEGAL EDUC. 612, 614 (1984). *See also* AMERICAN LAW INSTITUTE–AMERICAN BAR ASSOCIATION

COMMITTEE ON CONTINUING PROFESSIONAL EDUCATION, A PRACTICAL GUIDE TO ACHIEVING EXCELLENCE IN THE PRACTICE OF LAW: STANDARDS, METHODS, AND SELF-EVALUATION, Comment to § 6.2, at 327-28 (1992) ("Fact investigation strategy"). The Statement further recognizes that a general "understanding of the basic methods of factual investigation" is necessary to "us[e] . . . investigative tools efficiently" (*see* § 4.2(b)(iii) *supra*). But the Statement consciously refrains from a more detailed analysis of the practical techniques that may be used in conducting an investigation (such as, for example, the process by which a lawyer or investigator takes a written statement from an adverse witness).

Its formulation recognizes that factual investigation may take very different forms—and may require very different skills—depending upon the nature of a client's legal problem. Section 4.3 illustrates this point by using two common forms of factual investigation: interviewing of fact witnesses and analysis of documents. Other forms of investigation may call upon the lawyer to employ other skills and perhaps also other substantive knowledge. For example, lawyers often have to gather facts about technological or scientific matters, a process that may require specialized interviewing skills (to interview experts in the relevant fields) and that also may require (or that would be facilitated by) some knowledge of the relevant fields or disciplines (*see also* Value §§ 1.1(b), 1.2(b), 1.3(b), 4.1(b), 4.1(c) *infra*).

As in previous sections, references to a "decisionmaker" (*see* § 4.2(a)(ii)(B) *supra*) are not intended to refer narrowly to a decisionmaker in an adversarial litigative context. Rather, the term is meant to refer to a wide range of contexts and types of decisionmakers. *See* Commentary to Skill § 2 *supra*.

5. Communication

Lawyers employ communicative skills—including both written and oral forms of communication—in a wide variety of ways and in a wide range of contexts. These include: communications designed to advocate or persuade (such as, for example, written briefs; oral arguments on motions; bargaining with an adversary); to advise or inform (for example, opinion letters to a client; orally counseling or giving legal advice to a client; briefing a senior partner); to elicit information (for example, interviews of clients or witnesses; discovery letters, interrogatories, and other informal or formal requests for discovery); and to establish legal obligations or effectuate legal transactions (for example, drafting of contracts, wills, trust instruments, corporate charters, separation agreements, leases, documents transferring interests in real property, consent decrees, statutes, and administrative regulations).

While these various types of communication differ substantially in substance and form, certain fundamental skills are essential to effective communication in each of these contexts. These skills include the following:

5.1 *Effectively Assessing the Perspective of the Recipient of the Communication* (the client, decisionmaker(s), opposing counsel, witnesses, and so forth), and using this assessment to:

(a) View situations, problems, and issues from the perspective of the recipient of the communication, while taking into account the possibility that one's ability to adopt the perspective of another person may be impeded by, *inter alia*:

(i) One's own partisan role and perspective;

(ii) An insufficient understanding of the other person's culture, personal values, or attitudes;

(b) Anticipate the concerns, assumptions, expectations, and objectives of particular individuals in a given situation, while taking into account:

(i) The limitations of such predictions about other individuals; and

(ii) The need for planning techniques, such as contingency planning, to guard against becoming a prisoner of one's own preconceptions;

5.2 *Using Effective Methods of Communication*: To communicate effectively, a lawyer should be familiar with:

(a) The general prerequisites for effective written or oral communication, including:

(i) Presenting one's ideas or views in an effective way, which includes:

(A) Organizing the presentation effectively;

(B) Expressing ideas or views with precision, clarity, logic, and economy;

(C) Choosing appropriate terms, phrases, and images;

(D)   Applying the mechanics of language (grammar, syntax, punctuation) in an effective manner;

(E)   Attending to detail (for example, using defined terms consistently; proofreading written communications);

(ii)   Accurately perceiving and interpreting the communications of others (whether these be written, oral, or nonverbal communications); reading, listening and observing receptively; and responding appropriately;

(iii)   Attending to emotional or interpersonal factors that may be affecting the communications;

(b)   Specialized requirements for effective communications in the legal context, such as:

(i)   Requirements for effective use of factual material, including:

(A)   Selecting the proper facts to include and the proper facts to emphasize;

(B)   Developing facts at an appropriate level of detail;

(C)   Determining whether facts should be presented in an abstract or concrete fashion;

(ii)   Requirements for effective elaboration of legal reasoning, including:

(A)   Articulating relevant legal theories coherently (*see* Skill §§ 2.2–2.3 *supra*);

(B)   Providing appropriate documentation for legal theories (*see* Skill §§ 2.2–2.5 *supra*);

(C)   Selecting the most powerful arguments in the particular setting (*see* Skill §§ 2.3–2.4 *supra*);

(D)   Making appropriate determinations of whether to anticipate and answer objections, to dismiss them summarily, or not to address them at all;

(iii)   Substantive and technical requirements for specialized kinds of legal writing, including those applying to:

(A)   Drafting of executory documents (for example, contracts, wills, trust instruments, covenants, consent decrees, separation agreements, and corporate charters);

(B)   Drafting of litigation documents (for example, pleadings, motions, affidavits, briefs, and memoranda of law);

(C)   Legislative drafting (for example, drafting of statutes, administrative regulations, and ordinances);

(iv)   Requirements for legal citation form;

(c)   Methods of effectively tailoring the nature, form, or content of the written or oral communication to suit:

(i)   The particular purpose of the communication (whether that purpose is, for example, to advise a client or to present an argument to a court);

(ii)   The audience to which the communication is directed (for example, using a style that conforms to the reader's or auditor's expectations for the particular kind of communication; predicting the reader's or auditor's substantive predilections and adapting the communication appropriately);

(d)   The strategic considerations involved in deciding what material should be included and what material should *not* be included in a given communication (for example, the tactical advantages of withholding certain information from opposing counsel until a later stage in the process; giving consideration to the risk that raising a subject which may not otherwise arise may produce unnecessary controversy);

(e)   Methods for effectively recording or memorializing oral communications.

Commentary

There is a general recognition among legal educators and the practicing bar that effective communication skills are essential to competent legal practice. *See, e.g.*, AMERICAN BAR ASSOCIATION SECTION OF LEGAL EDUCATION AND ADMISSIONS TO THE BAR, REPORT AND RECOMMENDATIONS OF THE TASK FORCE ON LAWYER COMPETENCY: THE ROLE OF THE LAW SCHOOLS 9 (1979) (listing the skills of "writ[ing] effectively" and "communicat[ing] orally with effectiveness" among seven "fundamental skills" required for "[l]awyer competence"); B. G. GARTH, D. D. LANDON & J. MARTIN, American Bar Foundation Study "Learning Lawyering: Where Do Lawyers Acquire Practice Skills?" (Appendix B to this Report); F. ZEMANS & V. ROSENBLUM, THE MAKING OF A PUBLIC PROFESSION 125-26 (1981); Baird, *A Survey of the Relevance of Legal Training to Law School Graduates*, 29 J. LEGAL EDUC. 264, 273-74 (1978); Mudd & LaTrielle, *Professional Competence: A Study of New Lawyers*, 49 MONT. L. REV. 11, 18-19 (1988).

This Statement's formulation of the skill of communication diverges from previous analyses in that, for the most part, it does not differentiate between written and oral forms of communication. This approach was deemed appropriate because, at the conceptual level at which the skill of communication has been analyzed, the abilities, concepts, and processes required for effective communication are essentially the same, regardless of whether a communication is in oral or written form.

There is, however, one central respect in which legal writing differs from oral communication. As this formulation recognizes, there are a number of substantive, technical, and strategic considerations that must be taken into account when drafting executory instruments, litigation pleadings, and certain other forms of legal writing. *See* Skill § 5.2(b)(iii) *supra*.

6. Counseling

In a wide variety of contexts, lawyers counsel clients about decisions the clients have to make or courses of action they are considering. In a litigative context, this may take the form of, for example, counseling a client about a settlement offer in a civil case or a plea offer in a criminal case. In a non-litigative context, it may take the form of, for example, counseling a client about estate planning or whether to file a bankruptcy petition. In order to counsel a client effectively, a lawyer should be familiar with at least the skills, concepts, and processes involved in establishing a proper counseling relationship with a client, gathering information relevant to the decision to be made by the client, analyzing the decision to be made by the client, counseling the client about the decision, and implementing the client's decision:

> 6.1 *Understanding the Proper Nature and Bounds of the Law-yer's Role in a Counseling Relationship.* Effective counseling requires:

(a) An understanding of the various ethical rules and professional values that shape the nature and bounds of a counseling relationship between lawyer and client, including those applying to:

    (i) The division of authority between lawyer and client in making decisions that affect the resolution of a client's legal problem (*see* Skill § 10.1(c)(i) *infra*);

    (ii) The extent to which it is proper for a lawyer, in counseling a client, to attempt to persuade the client to take certain courses of action that the client is not inclined to take (or to dissuade the client from taking courses of action that he or she is inclined to take), because the lawyer believes these measures are necessary to safeguard the client's welfare or best interests;

    (iii) The extent to which it is proper for a lawyer, in counseling a client, to take account of considerations of justice, fairness, or morality, by:

        (A) Attempting to persuade the client to modify his or her decisions or actions to accommodate the interests of justice, fairness, or morality (*see* Value § 2.1(b) *infra*); and

        (B) In the event that the client is not willing to modify his or her decisions or actions to accommodate the interests of justice, fairness, or morality:

            (I) Taking action to safeguard the interests of third parties or the general public (*see* Value § 2.1(a) *infra*); or

            (II) Withdrawing from representation of the client (*see ibid.*);

(b) Sensitivity to the lawyer's need to strike a proper balance between two conflicting considerations when counseling clients:

    (i) The lawyer's need to maintain dispassion and objectivity—despite the role of partisan advocate for the client—in order to:

        (A) Perceive issues or options which the client has failed to perceive or appreciate because of self-interest, emotional involvement, or other factors;

(B) Determine whether it is appropriate (within the bounds of ethical rules, professional values, and the nature of the relationship with the particular client) to counsel the client about any such issues or options which he or she has failed to perceive or appreciate, and if so, the proper means of any such counseling;

(ii) The lawyer's need to guard against being so dispassionate and objective as to be unable to:

(A) View issues and options from the client's perspective;

(B) Counsel the client in a manner that communicates to him or her that the lawyer is committed to furthering the client's objectives and interests;

6.2 *Gathering Information Relevant to the Decision to Be Made.* An essential prerequisite for effective counseling is that the lawyer be able to acquire information pertaining to the decision to be made, including:

(a) Relevant factual information (using factual investigation to the extent necessary (*see* Skill § 4 *supra*));

(b) Relevant legal information (using legal analysis (*see* Skill § 2 *supra*) and, to the extent necessary, legal research (*see* Skill § 3 *supra*));

(c) Information about the client's perspective on the decision to be made (*see* Skill § 1.1(c) - (e) *supra*), including:

(i) The client's objectives regarding the decision to be made:

(A) The outcomes which the client would view as desirable;

(B) The outcomes which the client would view as undesirable;

(C) The precise factors or considerations which cause the client to view certain outcomes as preferable to others;

(ii) The client's concerns about the decision to be made, including concerns about:

    (A) The possible costs or consequences of certain options;

    (B) The potential risks which some options entail;

(iii) The extent to which (and the ways in which) the client's perspective, perceptions, or judgment may differ from those of the lawyer because of:

    (A) Differences in personal values or attitudes;

    (B) Cultural differences;

    (C) Differences in emotional reactions to the situation;

    (D) Interpersonal factors in the relationship between attorney and client;

6.3 *Analyzing the Decision to Be Made.* In order to adequately analyze a decision to be made by a client so as to effectively counsel the client about it, a lawyer should be familiar with the following skills, concepts, and processes:

(a) Analyzing a decision in the light of the client's conceptualization of the relevant issues, objectives, and concerns:

    (i) Systematically identifying each of the options that enable the client to achieve his or her objectives fully or partially;

    (ii) Systematically evaluating the extent to which each of these options:

        (A) Achieves outcomes the client regards as desirable or avoids outcomes the client regards as undesirable;

        (B) Avoids costs or risks the client regards as unacceptable and minimizes costs or risks the client regards as undesirable;

    (iii) Comparing the various options and ranking them in terms of their relative capacity to achieve the client's objectives and satisfy his or her priorities or preferences while avoiding or minimizing costs or risks;

(b)   Examining whether alternative conceptualizations (of the issues, objectives, concerns, and so forth) produce other options which should be presented to the client, and, if so, analyzing these additional options with the same processes described in § 6.3(a)(ii)-(iii) *supra*;

6.4   *Counseling the Client About the Decision to Be Made.* In order to counsel a client effectively, a lawyer should be familiar with the following skills, concepts, and processes:

(a)   Presenting issues, concepts, and options in terms and vocabulary suitable for the particular client's comprehension level and frame of reference;

(b)   Assuring that the client understands his or her legal rights and responsibilities with regard to the processes of making and implementing the decision, including the relative roles of the attorney and client in these processes (*see* § 6.1(a) *supra*);

(c)   Explaining to the client all of the options available to him or her with regard to the decision to be made, including:

(i)   The potential benefits of each option, including any potential positive effects on the client's legal rights or responsibilities;

(ii)   The potential costs or risks which each option entails, including any potential adverse effects on the client's legal rights or responsibilities;

(d)   Assisting the client in evaluating the various options available to him or her by:

(i)   Providing the client with the benefit of the lawyer's legal expertise (as it bears upon the decision to be made), including:

(A)   Informing the client of any legal rules, principles, procedures, or other aspects of the law or legal processes that may bear upon the decision or the desirability of any of the options;

(B)   Assisting the client in assessing the proper weight to be accorded any of the legal consequences that may attach to the decision to be made (*see* § 6.4(b)–(c) *supra*);

(C) To the extent that the lawyer's experience in the present case or in prior cases provides him or her with a basis for assessing the likelihood of particular legal or factual contingencies, advising the client of the lawyer's predictions and the precise bases for the predictions (consistent with maintaining the confidentiality of other clients);

(ii) Working with the client to identify and evaluate the various options, their potential benefits, and their potential costs, in a manner that is:

(A) Methodical and systematic;

(B) Realistic about the likelihood of consequences, the need to make choices, and so forth;

(C) Conscious of inhibitions or distortions produced by emotional or interpersonal factors;

(iii) If the client wishes the lawyer's advice about the relative desirability of the various options, advising the client of:

(A) The extent to which the various options satisfy the objectives, concerns, values, and priorities which the client has expressed (explaining to the client the precise nature and bases of the lawyer's reasoning);

(B) The extent to which the various options satisfy other objectives, concerns, values, or priorities, which the client has not expressed but which the lawyer believes to be consistent with the client's own welfare (explaining precisely the factors the lawyer is considering, the reasons why he or she believes these factors to be appropriate, and the client's absolute prerogative to reject these factors and/or the lawyer's reasoning (*see* § 6.1(a)(ii) *supra*));

(iv) If considerations of justice, fairness, or morality are relevant to the client's decision or to the selection of particular options, counseling the client about these considerations to the extent required or permitted by ethical standards (*see* § 6.1(a)(iii) *supra*; Value § 2.1(b) *infra*);

(v)   To the extent that effective counseling of the client may call for giving advice other than legal advice (such as, for example, business advice or personal advice):

(A)   Determining the propriety of exceeding the traditional bounds of the lawyer's role, by considering, *inter alia*:

(I)   The extent to which the lawyer is competent at, and feels comfortable with, giving advice of this sort;

(II)   The extent to which the client seeks advice of this sort;

(III) The extent to which the client's resolution of the legal issue or problem will benefit from advice of this sort;

(B)   Advising the client of the fact that advice of this sort exceeds the traditional bounds of the lawyer's role, and informing the client of the extent of (and limitations of) the lawyer's expertise in giving advice of this sort;

(e)   If the client concludes that none of the available options adequately fulfills his or her objectives or concludes that each of these options entails unacceptable costs or risks:

(i)   Examining whether a reconceptualization of the problem or issues results in the identification of any new options;

(ii)   To the extent that reconceptualization does produce new options, counseling the client about these options by employing the processes set forth in § 6.4(c)-(d) *supra*;

6.5   *Ascertaining and Implementing the Client's Decision.* In order to effectively ascertain and implement a client's decision, a lawyer should be familiar with the following skills, concepts, and processes:

(a)   Assuring that the client fully understands the decision to be made;

(b)   Ascertaining the client's decision, including:

   (i)   If the lawyer must take certain actions to implement the client's decision, advising the client of the various actions that must be taken and obtaining the client's informed consent to each of the various actions;

   (ii)   If it may prove impossible to implement the client's decision and if it is strategically desirable to develop alternative or "fallback" positions or plans, collaborating with the client in developing these alternatives by going through each of the steps set forth in § 6.3 *supra*;

(c)   Implementing the client's decision. If, in the course of implementing the decision, the lawyer discovers any changes of circumstances that relate to the decision itself or to the anticipated benefits, costs, or risks of the decision, the lawyer should be able to:

   (i)   Advise the client of the change of circumstances and its possible implications;

   (ii)   If the change of circumstances militates for reconsidering the decision, and if it is still practicable to reconsider the decision (because the decision has not yet been implemented or because the decision is revocable without undue cost or prejudice to the client):

      (A)   Identify and analyze the full range of options available to the client in the light of the change of circumstances (including examining whether reconceptualization of the problem, issues, or the original decision results in any new options becoming apparent);

      (B)   Counsel the client about the various options available if he or she does and if he or she does not reconsider the decision;

   (iii)   If the change of circumstances militates for reconsidering the decision but the decision is no longer open to reconsideration (because it has been fully implemented and either is irrevocable or is revocable only at undue cost or prejudice to the client):

(A) Identify and analyze the full range of options available to the client in the light of the change of circumstances (including examining whether reconceptualization of the problem, issues, or the original decision results in any new options becoming apparent);

(B) Counsel the client about the various options available to him or her;

(d) When the client's decision has been fully implemented, advise the client of that fact, and ensure that the client understands and accepts any effects that the implementation of the decision has had (or is likely to have) on his or her posture with regard to the underlying legal problem and/or on his or her legal rights or responsibilities.

Commentary

The skill of counseling is generally perceived to be one of the fundamental skills required for competent legal practice. *See, e.g.*, AMERICAN BAR ASSOCIATION SECTION OF LEGAL EDUCATION AND ADMISSIONS TO THE BAR, REPORT AND RECOMMENDATIONS OF THE TASK FORCE ON LAWYER COMPETENCY: THE ROLE OF THE LAW SCHOOLS 10 (1979); Baird, *A Survey of the Relevance of Legal Training to Law School Graduates*, 29 J. LEGAL EDUC. 264, 273-74 (1978); Schwartz, *The Relative Importance of Skills Used by Attorneys*, 3 GOLDEN GATE L. REV. 321, 324-25 (1973). In recent years, counseling has been the subject of intensified study by legal educators and scholars. *See, e.g.*, D. BINDER, P. BERGMAN & S. PRICE, LAWYERS AS COUNSELORS: A CLIENT-CENTERED APPROACH (1991); R. BASTRESS & J. HARBAUGH, INTERVIEWING, COUNSELING, AND NEGOTIATING: SKILLS FOR EFFECTIVE REPRESENTATION (1990).

As explained in § 6.1(a) *supra*, effective counseling requires an understanding of the ethical rules and professional values that define the relationship between attorney and client. The subject of ethical concerns is discussed further in Skill § 10 *infra*. The professional value of promoting justice, fairness, and morality, which is discussed in §§ 6.1(a)(iii) and 6.4(d)(iv) *supra*, is discussed further in Value § 2.1 *infra*.

7. Negotiation

In order to negotiate effectively, a lawyer should be familiar with the skills, concepts, and processes involved in preparing for a negotiation, conducting a negotiation, counseling a client about the terms obtained from the other side in a negotiation, and implementing the client's decision:

7.1 *Preparing for Negotiation Effectively*, which requires that a lawyer be able to:

    (a)   Ascertain whether the purpose of the negotiation is to resolve a controversy about a past event ("dispute-resolution negotiation") or to establish terms for a future interchange or for a continuing relationship between the parties ("transactional negotiation"), or some combination thereof, and:

        (i)   Identify any strategic implications of the classification of the negotiation as a "dispute-resolution" or "transactional" negotiation (such as, for example, the importance of avoiding an unfavorable termination of the negotiation in situations in which the parties will have an ongoing relationship);

        (ii)   Consult with the client about the implications of the classification for negotiation strategies;

    (b)   Evaluate whether the client's legal problem can be solved by means other than negotiation and, if so, evaluate the likely efficacy of any such alternatives to negotiation by:

        (i)   Acquiring the pertinent factual and legal information (using, to the extent necessary, fact investigation (Skill § 4 *supra*), legal analysis (Skill § 2 *supra*), and legal research (Skill § 3 *supra*));

        (ii)   Assessing the factual and legal information objectively and interpreting it accurately;

    (c)   Determine the "settling point" (or "bottom line") that is appropriate in negotiating on behalf of the client: the point on the continuum of possible settlements that represents the least favorable terms that the client can appropriately accept to resolve the problem through negotiation (and the point below which it is in the client's interest to terminate the negotiation without agreement).[3] The determination of an appropriate settling point requires that a lawyer:

(i)   Evaluate the various alternatives to negotiation, by considering:

(A)   The range of possible consequences of each alternative, and the probable impact of each alternative on the client's situation and objectives;

(B)   The range of possible costs of each alternative, and the probability that such costs would be borne;

(C)   The range of risks that each alternative entails;

(ii)   Fully and adequately advise the client of each of the options, and their comparative benefits, risks, and costs;

(iii)   Work with the client to select and refine the appropriate settling point in the light of the best information bearing on it that the lawyer and the client can develop;

(d)   Identify and rank a roster of outcomes of the negotiation that are preferable to the "settling point" and that should be obtained if possible. This requires working with the client (and, where appropriate, experts in the pertinent field) to:

(i)   Identify the range of plausible combinations or "packages" of possible benefits and concessions;

(ii)   With regard to each of the packages, ascertain its comparative advantages and disadvantages, and assess the likelihood of obtaining the package;

(iii)   Identify the optimal package, and rank the remaining packages in order of their desirability;

(e)   Effectively conceptualize the subject of the negotiation, including:

---

3. The text of this section will hereafter refer simply to the "settling point." The principles set forth apply *mutatis mutandi* to situations such as transactional negotiations in which the client's "bottom line" is determined by considerations different from those that would be taken into account in calculating a client's "settling point" in a typical dispute-resolution negotiation.

(i)   Evaluating whether the situation is necessarily viewed (or, from the client's perspective, best viewed) in:

    (A)   "Zero-sum" terms, as a controversy in which each party's satisfaction necessarily comes at the expense of the other party; or

    (B)   "Non-zero-sum" terms, as a situation in which gains to one party do not necessarily equal losses to the other party; or

    (C)   Both kinds of terms, as a situation which combines zero-sum and non-zero-sum elements;

(ii)   Evaluating whether the client's objectives are best achieved by analyzing the situation from a:

    (A)   "Competitive" (or "adversarial") perspective, in which the lawyer analyzes the situation exclusively in terms of maximizing the client's interests;

    (B)   "Cooperative" (or "problem-solving") perspective, in which the lawyer analyzes the situation in terms of maximizing the interests of both parties;

(iii)   Identifying the best ways of framing or articulating the issues, including:

    (A)   Articulating issues in either a concrete or abstract manner (for example, articulating the issues at a level of abstractness at which the parties can more easily cooperate);

    (B)   Combining or connecting some or all of the issues in controversy;

(f)   Devise an appropriate negotiating plan, which requires the ability to:

(i)   Anticipate the other party's likely "settling point" (*see* § 7.1(c) *supra*) by:

    (A)   Taking the perspective of the other party (*see* Skill § 5.1 *supra*) and assessing his or her likely objectives, concerns, values, and attitudes;

(B)   Taking the perspective of counsel for the other party and assessing that attorney's likely analysis of the appropriate settling point for his or her client and the attorney's likely choice of strategies, by:

(I)   Identifying the factual and legal information probably known to the other side; and

(II)   Assessing this information with the analytic processes set forth in §§ 7.1(a)–(e) *supra*, while factoring in the other attorney's thinking patterns, values, attitudes, personality, and usual negotiating tactics (as revealed in prior negotiations or communications);

(ii)   Consider alternative possible means of moving towards an agreement favorable to the client (such as, for example, a series of reciprocal concessions);

(iii)   Identify and plan for all realistic contingencies, including:

(A)   The possibility that factual or legal information unknown to the lawyer may emerge during negotiation;

(B)   The possibility that the lawyer has misjudged the goals, settling point, or negotiating strategies of the other side;

7.2   *Conducting a Negotiation Session Effectively.* In order to negotiate effectively, a lawyer should be able to:

(a)   Communicate effectively with the opposing side and evaluate the other side's positions, demands, and offers objectively and accurately (*see* Skill § 5.2 *supra*);

(b)   Analyze the statements and negotiating behavior of the opposing side to ascertain:

(i)   Relevant information that he or she is not revealing;

(ii)   The nature of the other side's analysis of the situation (including the other side's settling point);

      (iii)   Other information about the other side's thought processes, assumptions, values, or attitudes that may be useful in understanding his or her objectives and resolving the negotiation in a manner favorable to one's own client;

   (c)   Re-evaluate and, if necessary, modify one's own goals, strategies, and tactics in the light of the other side's negotiating behavior;

7.3 *Counseling the Client About the Terms Obtained From the Other Side in the Negotiation and Implementing the Client's Decision.* A lawyer should be familiar with the skills required for:

   (a)   Counseling a client about whether to accept or reject the best terms obtained from the other side (*see* Skill § 6 *supra*);

   (b)   If the client wishes to accept these terms, implementing the client's decision by:

      (i)   Giving consideration to, and counseling the client about, the question of whether it is in the client's interest to raise with the other side and attempt to resolve:

         (A) Issues relating to the implementation or enforcement of the agreement;

         (B) Contingencies affecting the rights or responsibilities of the parties under the agreement;

      (ii)   Giving consideration to possible alternative forms for embodying the agreement and choosing an appropriate form;

   (c)   If the client does not wish to accept the terms, counseling the client about alternative options (*see* Skill § 6 *supra*), including the option of further negotiation to seek terms the client would find satisfactory.

Commentary

Like the skill of counseling analyzed in the preceding section, the skill of negotiation is a fundamental part of legal practice (*see, e.g.*, AMERICAN BAR ASSOCIATION SECTION OF LEGAL EDUCATION AND ADMISSIONS TO THE BAR, REPORT AND RECOMMENDATIONS OF THE TASK FORCE ON LAWYER COMPETENCY: THE ROLE OF THE LAW SCHOOLS 10

(1979); F. ZEMANS & V. ROSENBLUM, THE MAKING OF A PUBLIC PROFES-
SION 125 (1981); Baird, *A Survey of the Relevance of Legal Training
to Law School Graduates*, 29 J. LEGAL EDUC. 264, 273-74 (1978)),
which has increasingly become a subject of study for legal educators
and scholars (*see, e.g.*, R. BASTRESS & J. HARBAUGH, INTERVIEWING,
COUNSELING, AND NEGOTIATING: SKILLS FOR EFFECTIVE REPRESENTATION
(1990); R. FISHER & W. URY, GETTING TO YES (1981); R. FISHER & S.
BROWN, GETTING TOGETHER (1988); D. GIFFORD, LEGAL NEGOTIATION:
THEORY AND APPLICATIONS (1989); Menkel-Meadow, *Toward Another
View of Legal Negotiation: The Structure of Problem Solving*, 31
U.C.L.A. L. REV. 754 (1984); *see also, e.g.*, AMERICAN LAW INSTITUTE–
AMERICAN BAR ASSOCIATION COMMITTEE ON CONTINUING PROFESSIONAL
EDUCATION, A PRACTICAL GUIDE TO ACHIEVING EXCELLENCE IN THE
PRACTICE OF LAW: STANDARDS, METHODS, AND SELF-EVALUATION § 6.6
(1992)). There is also an extensive social scientific literature on the
subject of negotiation. *See, e.g.*, H. RAIFFA, THE ART AND SCIENCE OF
NEGOTIATION (1982); J. RUBIN & B. BROWN, THE SOCIAL PSYCHOLOGY
OF BARGAINING AND NEGOTIATION (1975).

As in prior sections, this Statement's formulation of the skill of
negotiation attempts to strike a balance between conceptual and
practical aspects of the skill that is consistent with the needs of
lawyers in all spheres of practice. It recognizes that certain aspects
of negotiation theory—such as the dichotomy between "cooperative" and "competitive" negotiation, and the concepts of "zero-sum"
and "non-zero-sum"—are essential for planning and conducting a
negotiation effectively. (For further discussion of these concepts,
see, e.g., Menkel-Meadow, *supra*.) But the Statement consciously
excludes a more extensive development of theoretical aspects of the
negotiation process, such as game theory models, economic models,
and social-psychological bargaining theories. (For an overview of
these aspects of negotiation theory, *see, e.g.*, R. BASTRESS & J.
HARBAUGH, *supra*, at 349-404.) While an understanding of these
theoretical aspects of negotiation is certainly conducive to effective
negotiation, it was felt that such an understanding is not critical for
minimum competency in using the skill of legal negotiation. Similarly, while some practical aspects of negotiation are essential for
effective use of the skill and therefore are included in this formulation, it was felt that an extensive knowledge of the various techniques that have been developed for effective negotiation is not
essential for mimimum competency. (For an overview of these techniques, *see, e.g.*, R. BASTRESS & J. HARBAUGH, *supra*, at 429-522.)

8. Litigation and Alternative Dispute-Resolution Procedures

In order to effectively employ, or to advise a client about, the options of litigation or alternative dispute resolution, a lawyer should have an understanding of the potential functions and consequences of these courses of action in relation to the client's situation and objectives (*see* Skill § 1 *supra*) and should have a working knowledge of the fundamentals of trial-court litigation, appellate litigation, advocacy in administrative and executive forums, and alternative dispute resolution:

8.1 *Knowledge of the Fundamentals of Litigation at the Trial-Court Level*, which should include:

   (a) An understanding of the litigative process, including:

   (i) The functions and general organization of the trial courts;

   (ii) Basic concepts of jurisdiction;

   (iii) The availability of alternative forums and the importance of the choice of forum;

   (iv) The basic procedural rules and principles governing litigation in a trial court of general jurisdiction;

   (v) The basic rules and principles of evidence;

   (vi) Knowledge of the means by which additional pertinent rules of procedure and evidence may be efficiently ascertained (including legal research (*see* Skill § 3 *supra*));

   (b) An understanding of the processes for initiating litigation, including:

   (i) The lawyer's ethical obligation to screen the merits of a case before instituting litigation;

   (ii) The types of factors that should be considered in deciding whether to institute litigation (including the likely length and cost of trial-court litigation and any appeals that might ensue, and the comparative utility of alternative dispute-resolution mechanisms (*see* Skill § 8.4 *infra*)), as well as the analytical processes for evaluating and weighing these factors;

(iii) The types of factors that should be considered in determining what relief to seek (or to oppose) in litigation, and the analytical processes for evaluating and weighing these factors;

(iv) The types of factors that should be considered in selecting the forum in which to initiate litigation, and the analytical processes for evaluating and weighing these factors;

(c) An understanding of the skills and processes required for preparing a case for trial, including:

(i) Effective acquisition of relevant factual and legal information, which requires:

(A) Developing an effective plan for information acquisition, by:

(I) Formulating legal theories (*see* Skill § 2 *supra*) and working hypotheses to guide fact investigation (*see* Skill § 4.2 *supra*);

(II) Analyzing the appropriate degree of thoroughness of factual investigation and legal research by considering the relative need for the information and the extent of the client's resources, and by consulting the client about any decisions to curtail information acquisition (*see* Skill §§ 1.1(h), 3.3(c), 4.1 *supra*);

(III) Determining the appropriate timing of factual investigation and legal research by considering the degree of exhaustiveness of information needed at each stage of the case (*see* Skill § 3.3(c)(ii) *supra*) and the possibility that delaying acquisition of information may result in a saving of the client's resources in the event of a resolution of the case short of trial (for example, in a situation where the applicable rules require more thorough information acquisition for particular stages of litigation than counsel considers necessary to effect a satisfactory settlement on the basis of the information already acquired);

(B) Using legal research to acquire the necessary legal information (*see* Skill § 3 *supra*);

(C) Using fact investigation to gather the necessary factual information (*see* Skill § 4 *supra*);

(ii) Effective drafting of pleadings, which requires:

(A) An understanding of the various skills, concepts, and processes involved in effective written communication (*see* Skill § 5 *supra*);

(B) The ability to engage in legal analysis (including formulating, evaluating, and criticizing possible legal theories (*see* Skill § 2 *supra*));

(C) An appreciation of the impact of the choice of legal theories on:

(I) The issues to be litigated at trial;

(II) The admissibility and evaluation of evidence at trial;

(iii) Effective use of processes for informal and formal discovery, which requires the development of a discovery plan, and which may require a variety of skills (such as the use of communication skills (*see* Skill § 5 *supra*) in drafting discovery documents); and the use of problem-solving skills (*see* Skill § 1 *supra*) and witness examination skills in conducting depositions);

(iv) Effective use of procedures for filing and litigating pretrial motions, which requires:

(A) Strategic assessment of what motions to file;

(B) Strategic drafting of motions;

(C) Strategic use of evidentiary hearings on pretrial motions;

(D) Effective argument of motions (*see* Skill §§ 2.3–2.5 and 5 *supra*);

(v)   Effective evaluation of the choice between a bench trial and a jury trial, considering, *inter alia*:

(A)   The extent to which a jury may be swayed by emotional factors prejudicial to the client;

(B)   The existence of evidence favorable to the client which is more likely to be credited by a jury than a judge, or *vice versa*;

(C)   The existence of evidence (either favorable or unfavorable to the client) which is likely to be excluded from a jury trial but which may be heard by a judge in a bench trial (for example, in the course of ruling on an evidentiary objection);

(D)   Ancillary benefits or consequences of choosing a bench or jury trial (such as, for example, in civil cases, expediting the trial by opting for a bench trial; or in criminal cases, receiving consideration from the judge at sentencing (in the event of conviction) for choosing a bench trial);

(d)   An understanding of the skills and processes required for effectively conducting a trial, including:

(i)   The process of developing a theory of the case and a trial strategy;

(ii)   The skills of preparing and conducting witness examinations;

(iii)   The skills of anticipating and making strategic use of evidentiary objections;

(iv)   The procedures for handling documentary and real evidence;

(v)   The skills of organizing, formulating, and presenting opening statements and closing arguments;

(e)   An understanding of the processes available for securing post-trial relief at the trial court level;

8.2   *Knowledge of the Fundamentals of Litigation at the Appellate Level*, which should include:

(a)   An understanding of the appellate process, including:

       (i)   An understanding of the functions and general organization of the appellate courts;

      (ii)   General familiarity with the procedural rules and principles governing the appellate process;

    (iii)   Knowledge of the means of efficiently researching procedural rules and principles governing the appellate process;

(b)   An understanding of the processes for taking an appeal, including:

       (i)   The types of factors that should be considered in deciding whether to take an appeal, and the analytical processes for evaluating and weighing these factors;

      (ii)   Once the decision to appeal has been made, the analytical processes for identifying the range of potentially appealable issues and selecting the particular issues to raise in the appeal;

(c)   Familiarity with the skills and techniques required for effective brief writing, including:

       (i)   The various skills, concepts, and processes required for effective written communication (*see* Skill § 5 *supra*);

      (ii)   The types of factors to consider, and the analytical processes for considering, which arguments to make and whether it is effective to make alternative arguments;

    (iii)   Organizing argumentation;

(d)   Familiarity with the skills and techniques required for effective oral argument, including, *inter alia*, the skills required for effective oral communication (*see* Skill § 5 *supra*);

8.3   *Knowledge of the Fundamentals of Advocacy in Administrative and Executive Forums*, which should include:

(a)   An understanding of the functions and structure of administrative agencies and executive departments;

(b)   Knowledge of the processes for ascertaining the substantive and procedural rules and principles governing administrative and executive proceedings;

(c)   An understanding of the factors to consider in deciding whether to seek relief in administrative or executive forums and in selecting the particular forum or avenue for relief;

(d)   Familiarity with the skills required for effective advocacy in formal adjudicative or rulemaking proceedings, including:

    (i)   Formulation of a working hypothesis (*see* Skill § 4.2 *supra*);

    (ii)   Integration of legal research (*see* Skill § 3 *supra*) and factual investigation (*see* Skill § 4 *supra*);

    (iii) Drafting pleadings, applications, and requests;

    (iv)   Participation in administrative investigative proceedings;

    (v)   Preparing and presenting documentary evidence;

    (vi)   Preparing and presenting witness examinations;

    (vii) Organizing argumentation, drafting written argument, and formulating and presenting oral argument;

(e)   Familiarity with the skills and processes required for effective advocacy in informal administrative or executive proceedings, including:

    (i)   Efficient acquisition of information about the processes of decisionmaking involved in, and the factors that bear upon the outcome of, administrative and executive proceedings;

    (ii)   Designing a theory of persuasion;

    (iii) Preparing and presenting written submissions;

    (iv)   Oral communications with administrative or executive staffpersons;

8.4   *Knowledge of the Fundamentals of Proceedings in Other Dispute-Resolution Forums*, which should include:

(a)   An awareness of the range of non-litigative mechanisms for resolving disputes, including arbitration, mediation, and conciliation;

(b)   Familiarity with the basic concepts and dynamics of these alternative mechanisms, including:

(i)   The types of outcomes that may be achieved through the various mechanisms;

(ii)   The relative degree of procedural formality surrounding the use of the various mechanisms;

(iii)   The extent to which the various mechanisms depend upon the use of a third-party decision-maker or facilitator and the processes by which such decisionmakers or facilitators are selected;

(iv)   The sources of norms that govern or guide decisionmaking in the various mechanisms (for example, substantive legal doctrines, industry conventions, equitable considerations);

(v)   The opportunities which the various mechanisms afford for the presentation of proofs and arguments;

(c)   An understanding of the factors that should be considered in determining whether to pursue one or another alternative dispute-resolution mechanism, including:

(i)   The types of situations in which one or another mechanism is likely to prove particularly effective or ineffective;

(ii)   The extent to which a party may benefit by having a third-party decisionmaker or facilitator with specialized expertise in the subject matter of the dispute;

(iii)   The comparative expense of the various mechanisms;

(iv)   The amount of time which is likely to be expended in arranging for and employing particular mechanisms;

(v)   The comparative efficacy of the mechanisms in producing a resolution that is:

(A)   Binding upon the parties;

(B)   Final (in that it is not subject to review and modification or is subject to review and modification only under very limited circumstances);

(C)   Enforceable through procedures or mechanisms that are likely to be readily available,
effective, and not unduly costly or time-
consuming;

(d)   Familiarity with the means for acquiring additional
knowledge about the availability, relative merits, processes, and procedures of the various alternative dispute-resolution mechanisms, including:

(i)   National, state, or local agencies or organizations
that may offer assistance in learning about or
making use of alternative dispute-resolution
mechanisms;

(ii)   Libraries, directories, or other resources that contain lists of, or other forms of information about,
alternative dispute-resolution mechanisms.

Commentary

This section sets forth the fundamentals of litigation and alternative dispute resolution that should be known by any lawyer whose
practice calls for the use of either or both of these courses of action,
or who advises a client about either or both of these options, or who
engages in any type of problem solving or planning in a situation in
which these options are available. While it is certainly true that there
are many lawyers who do not engage in litigation or employ alternative dispute-resolution mechanisms, even these lawyers must have
a basic familiarity with the fundamentals of litigation and alternative dispute resolution in order to competently represent their clients
or make professional judgments in the latter situations.

The analysis of litigation here considers the range of skills
involved in pretrial, trial and post-trial litigation. It identifies the
principal conceptual and practical skills involved in deciding whether
litigation should be pursued, in defining the goals and structuring
the general outlines of a lawsuit, in designing a litigation strategy
and developing a theory of the case, in conducting investigation and
discovery and preparing the case for trial, and in handling pretrial
motions and the trial itself. It also recognizes that effective litigation
(or effective consideration of the option of litigation) requires an
understanding of appellate remedies, administrative remedies, and
forms of alternative dispute resolution. A lawyer cannot effectively
assess the advisability of initiating or maintaining litigation unless
he or she has a general familiarity with alternatives to litigation and

with the scope and limitations of appellate remedies for errors committed at the trial-court level.

However, the section does not undertake to catalogue all of the specialized skills required to handle particular kinds of litigation. It contemplates that a lawyer who lacks the skills necessary for effective litigation of a given case will take appropriate steps to associate with or substitute another lawyer having those skills. *See* Skill §§ 1.4(a)(i), 1.4(c)(ii), and the last paragraph of the Commentary to Skill § 1 *supra*. On this assumption, and in keeping with the Statement's focus upon skills needed by lawyers in a wide variety of kinds of practice, the section avoids particularizing such skills as "preparing and conducting witness examinations" and does not, for example, detail specific techniques of cross-examination or impeachment or for questioning expert witnesses.

In addition to analyzing the skill of litigation, the section identifies basic skills and concepts involved in alternative forms of dispute resolution. As in other sections of the Statement, this analysis proceeds at a level of generality that is appropriate to the needs of practitioners in all spheres of practice. The section is premised on the view that a well-trained generalist need not be familiar with the intricacies of the various forms of "primary" and "hybrid" alternative dispute-resolution mechanisms but should know enough to recognize when the use of alternative dispute resolution may be indicated, to evaluate the potentialities of its various forms, and to effectively gather whatever additional information may be needed to select and use the most suitable mechanism.

9. Organization and Management of Legal Work

In order to organize and manage legal work effectively, a lawyer should be familiar with the skills, concepts, and processes required for efficient management, including appropriate allocation of time, effort and resources; timely performance and completion of work; cooperation among co-workers; and orderly administration of the office:

9.1 *Formulating Goals and Principles for Effective Practice Management.* In order to develop effective systems and procedures of practice management, a lawyer should first formulate the goals to be achieved by the systems and procedures. These should include:

(a)   Efficient allocation of time, effort and resources (*see* § 9.2 *infra*);

(b)   Ensuring that work is performed and completed at the appropriate time (*see* § 9.3 *infra*);

(c)   Effectively working with other people (*see* § 9.4 *infra*);

(d)   Efficient office administration (*see* § 9.5 *infra*);

9.2   *Developing Systems and Procedures to Ensure that Time, Effort, and Resources Are Allocated Efficiently,* including systems and procedures for ensuring that time, efforts, and resources are properly allocated to the various tasks required for:

(a)   Daily practice;

(b)   Any long-term objectives of expanding or modifying the practice;

(c)   Other aspects of the lawyer's professional life (such as *pro bono* service (*see* Value § 2.2 *infra*); membership in professional organizations (*see* Value § 3 *infra*); and assisting in the training and preparation of new lawyers (*see ibid.*));

(d)   Continuing professional education and development of professional skills (*see* Value §§ 1.2(a)–(b), 4 *infra*);

9.3   *Developing Systems and Procedures to Ensure that Work is Performed and Completed at the Appropriate Time,* including systems and procedures for:

(a)   Setting and meeting deadlines, including procedures for:

(i)   Calendaring and docket control; and

(ii)   Seeking an extension in a timely fashion when it becomes apparent that a deadline cannot be met;

(b)   Regularly communicating with clients, so as to inform the client of:

(i)   New developments or the acquisition of new information;

(ii)   Extensions of deadlines, changes of dates, and factors that may affect the timing of events;

(c)   Attending to, and completing, all work as promptly as possible;

(d)   Monitoring the status of all ongoing work and doing appropriate follow-up where necessary;

(e)   Monitoring the status of present commitments, and avoiding the undertaking of additional commitments when this is improvident;

9.4   *Developing Systems and Procedures for Effectively Working with Other People,* including systems and procedures for:

(a)   Collaborating with other attorneys in the same office or other offices;

(b)   Training, organizing, directing, supervising, and working with paralegals, investigators, law librarians, law clerks, secretaries, and other support personnel;

(c)   Delegating work to others when appropriate, including:

     (i)   Providing the other person with enough information at the outset to enable him or her to handle the assignment, such as:

         (A)   The precise task(s) to be performed;

         (B)   The time that may be spent on the assignment and any specific deadlines that must be met;

         (C)   To the extent it may prove helpful in performing the task, background information about the reasons why the task needs to be performed;

     (ii)   Establishing procedures for the other person to obtain additional guidance or answers to questions that arise in the course of handling the assignment;

     (iii)   Monitoring the other person's work to ensure that the work is being performed properly and at an appropriate pace;

     (iv)   At the conclusion of the assignment, providing the other person with an evaluation of his or her work and constructive suggestions for performing future assignments;

9.5   *Developing Systems and Procedures for Efficiently Administering a Law Office,* including systems and procedures for:

(a)   Handling cases;

(b) Maintaining files (including client files, billing files, and subject matter files);

(c) Identifying conflicts of interest between current clients or between a current client and a previously represented client;

(d) Monitoring office operations, including the work of paralegals, secretaries, and other support personnel;

(e) Attending to the financial aspects of maintaining a law office, including:

   (i)   Setting fees and obtaining retainers from clients;

   (ii) Billing and collection of payments from clients;

   (iii) Paying office bills;

   (iv) Managing cash flow;

   (v)   Maintaining appropriate trust accounts and guarding against commingling of funds;

(f) Maintaining and upgrading equipment;

(g) Regularly reviewing and evaluating the efficacy of the systems and procedures that have been developed for administering the office, so as to identify problems, correct deficiencies, and continually improve procedures and routines.

Commentary

As studies have recognized, efficient organization and management of legal work is an essential precondition for competent practice. *See, e.g.*, AMERICAN BAR ASSOCIATION, FINAL REPORT AND RECOMMENDATIONS OF THE TASK FORCE ON PROFESSIONAL COMPETENCE 17-18, 22, 31 (1983); AMERICAN LAW INSTITUTE–AMERICAN BAR ASSOCIATION COMMITTEE ON CONTINUING PROFESSIONAL EDUCATION, A PRACTICAL GUIDE TO ACHIEVING EXCELLENCE IN THE PRACTICE OF LAW: STANDARDS, METHODS, AND SELF-EVALUATION 241 (1992) ("[a]ll too often, a lawyer's incompetence can be traced to poor management skills and practices"). Lawyering ability and experience are of little avail if a lawyer misses a deadline or fails to detect a conflict of interest as a result of inadequate office procedures.

This Statement's formulation of the skill focuses on central aspects of practice management—efficient allocation of time, compliance with deadlines, and effective collaboration with others—

which are applicable regardless of whether a lawyer is a solo practitioner, a partner or associate in a firm, or a lawyer in public service practice. The Statement also calls for some understanding of systems for administering a law office because even though new lawyers will rarely serve in the role of administrator, a certain degree of familiarity with such procedures is useful for effective functioning within a law office.

As with other skills analyzed in this Statement, this section's analysis of practice management rests upon a certain vision of professional values. It assumes a lawyer who is committed not only to competent representation (*see* Value § 1 *infra*) but also to *pro bono* work (§ 9.2(c) *supra*; *see* Value § 2.2 *infra*); improving the profession (§ 9.2(c) *supra*; *see* Value § 3 *infra*); and professional self-development (§ 9.2(d) *supra*; *see* Value §§ 1.2(a)-(b), 4 *infra*).

10. Recognizing and Resolving Ethical Dilemmas

In order to represent a client consistently with applicable ethical standards, a lawyer should be familiar with the skills, concepts, and processes necessary to recognize and resolve ethical dilemmas:

10.1 *Familiarity with the Nature and Sources of Ethical Standards*, including:

(a) The basic concept of law as an ethical profession, which:

(i) Imposes upon each member of the profession certain ethical obligations to clients, the legal system, the profession, and the general public; and

(ii) Defines those obligations in terms which involve their interpretation both by individual attorneys at the level of conscience and by authorized organs of the profession;

(b) Primary sources of ethical rules, which include:

(i) Constitutional, statutory, or common-law rules or principles bearing upon the ethical obligations of a lawyer (such as, for example, caselaw construing the Sixth Amendment standard for effectiveness of counsel in criminal cases; federal or state statutes, rules, or caselaw defining the scope of the attorney-client privilege; federal or state statutes or rules establishing sanctions for certain types of misconduct by lawyers);

(ii) The rules of professional conduct which have been formally adopted by the jurisdiction in which the lawyer is practicing (which may include some or all of the provisions of the American Bar Association's Model Rules of Professional Conduct or Code of Professional Responsibility);

(iii) Interpretations of the applicable rules of professional conduct by:

  (A) The courts of the jurisdiction in which the lawyer is practicing;

  (B) State or local bar associations;

  (C) Other entities that are authorized to issue binding or persuasive interpretations of ethical rules;

(iv) Model rules of ethics which have not been adopted by the jurisdiction in which the lawyer practices, but which shed light on the ethical obligations of lawyers generally or of practitioners in a particular field of practice. These may include:

  (A) The American Bar Association's Model Rules of Professional Conduct;

  (B) The American Bar Association's Code of Professional Responsibility;

  (C) The American Bar Association's Standards for Criminal Justice;

  (D) The American Bar Association's Standards of Practice for Lawyer Mediators in Family Disputes;

(v) Aspects of ethical philosophy bearing upon the propriety of particular practices or conduct (such as, for example, general ethical precepts calling for honesty, integrity, courtesy and respect for others; general ethical prohibitions against lying and misrepresentation);

(vi) A lawyer's personal sense of morality, particularly to the extent that it causes the lawyer to:

  (A) Question and research the ethical propriety of practices before employing them (including practices urged upon the lawyer by a supervisor or practices long accepted by lawyers within the particular field of practice);

(B) Question and seek guidance with regard to practices that are not addressed by existing rules or the opinions interpreting them;

(c) The fundamental ethical rules that shape the profession and define what it means to be a legal professional, including:

(i) The rules and principles defining the respective roles of attorney and client in setting the objectives of representation and making decisions in the course of the representation;

(ii) The duties which a lawyer owes to a client, including:

(A) The duty to provide competent representation;

(B) The duty to work zealously and diligently on the client's behalf;

(C) The duty to avoid conflicts of interest that undermine or appear to undermine the lawyer's loyalty to the client;

(D) The duty to preserve the client's confidences and secrets;

10.2 *Familiarity with the Means by Which Ethical Standards are Enforced*, including:

(a) The lawyer's duty to engage in self-scrutiny and to guard against unethical conduct by:

(i) Critically evaluating the ethical propriety of practices which the lawyer himself or herself is contemplating or which are being urged upon the lawyer by a supervisor, colleague, advisor, client, or other person or entity;

(ii) When appropriate, consulting other lawyers in the process of critical evaluation described by § 10.2(a)(i) *supra*, through procedures that respect applicable concerns of confidentiality;

>> (iii)   When appropriate, seeking guidance from advisory organs (such as state or local bar associations or offices of bar counsel), through procedures that respect applicable concerns of confidentiality;

> (b)   The lawyer's duty to report unethical conduct by other lawyers in certain circumstances. A lawyer should be familiar with:

>> (i)   The rules establishing the circumstances under which it is necessary or appropriate for a lawyer to report unethical conduct by other lawyers; and

>> (ii)   The procedures by which misconduct of this sort is reported to the relevant authorities;

> (c)   The procedures by which questions of unethical conduct are authoritatively considered and resolved in the jurisdiction in which the lawyer is practicing;

10.3   *Familiarity with the Processes for Recognizing and Resolving Ethical Dilemmas*, including:

> (a)   Constantly being alert to the possible existence of ethical dilemmas;

> (b)   Being familiar with the warning signs of ethical problems and paying adequate attention to such warning signs when they appear;

> (c)   Responding to ethical problems by:

>> (i)   Diagnosing the precise nature of the problem;

>> (ii)   Researching the applicable ethical rules and principles;

>> (iii)   Identifying a solution that satisfies the applicable ethical rules and principles while at the same time accommodating any competing interests of a client;

> (d)   When appropriate, enlisting the aid of other lawyers or of advisory organs to identify, diagnose, research, or resolve ethical problems, through procedures that respect applicable concerns of confidentiality.

Commentary

This section analyzes the body of knowledge and skills with which a practitioner must be familiar in order to assure that he or she will consistently conform to ethical conduct. Unlike the Code of

Professional Responsibility and the Model Rules of Professional Conduct, the section does not analyze the lawyer's ethical obligations in detail. Rather, it calls upon a practitioner to be familiar with these obligations and with the relevant sources of ethical standards.

This section recognizes that competent, ethical practice requires more than just knowledge of the applicable rules and principles of professional responsibility. It also requires that a lawyer faithfully apply these rules and principles to his or her daily practice by scrutinizing the ethical propriety of practices which he or she is contemplating or which are urged upon him or her by others (§§ 10.1(b)(vi)(A), 10.2(a) *supra*), and, in appropriate circumstances, by reporting unethical conduct of other lawyers (§ 10.2(b) *supra*). As the Model Rules of Professional Conduct explain, the legal profession's "unique" "powers of self-government" require that every member of the profession scrupulously observe ethical rules in his or her own practice and "also aid in securing their observance by other lawyers." Model Rules, Preamble.

Finally, this section takes into account the practical consideration that even lawyers who are aware of their ethical obligations may not adequately perceive the existence of an ethical problem in a particular situation or may not know how to respond to a problem they have perceived. The analysis calls for an understanding of the means of identifying and solving ethical problems in one's own practice (§ 10.3 *supra*) as well as the procedures for reporting unethical conduct by others (§ 10.2(b)(ii) *supra*).

Fundamental Values of the Profession

1. Provision of Competent Representation

As a member of a profession dedicated to the service of clients, a lawyer should be committed to the values of:

1.1 *Attaining a Level of Competence in One's Own Field of Practice*, including:

(a) With regard to lawyering skills, developing a degree of proficiency that is sufficient to enable the lawyer to represent the client competently or to acquire whatever additional degree of proficiency is needed within the time available for doing so and without inappropriately burdening the client's resources;

(b)   With regard to substantive knowledge (including both knowledge of the law and familiarity with fields and disciplines other than law), acquiring sufficient knowledge to enable the lawyer to represent the client competently or to acquire whatever additional knowledge is needed within the time available for doing so and without inappropriately burdening the client's resources;

(c)   Developing a realistic sense of the limits of the lawyer's own skills and knowledge;

(d)   Developing practices that will enable the lawyer to represent clients consistently with the ethical rules of the profession, including the rules that require that a lawyer:

  (i)   Work diligently and zealously on a client's behalf;

  (ii)   Avoid conflicts of interest that undermine or appear to undermine the lawyer's loyalty to a client;

  (iii)   Preserve a client's confidences and secrets;

  (iv)   Refrain from handling matters that are beyond the lawyer's range of competence (*see* Value §§ 1.3(a)(ii), 1.3(b)(ii) *infra*);

1.2   *Maintaining a Level of Competence in One's Own Field of Practice*, including:

(a)   With regard to lawyering skills, engaging in whatever forms of study and learning are necessary to attain the degree of expertise that may be expected of any competent practitioner at the lawyer's level of experience;

(b)   With regard to substantive knowledge, attending to new developments in the law and other relevant fields or disciplines, and engaging in whatever forms of study and learning are necessary to attain the degree of expertise that may be expected of any competent practitioner at the lawyer's level of experience;

(c)   As the lawyer improves his or her skills and expands his or her knowledge of the field, maintaining a realistic sense of the new limits of his or her skills and knowledge;

(d)   Maintaining the conditions of physical and mental alertness necessary for competence, including:

  (i) Remaining constantly alert to the existence of problems that may impede or impair the lawyer's ability to provide competent representation (such as alcohol abuse, drug abuse, psychological or emotional problems, senility, or other types of health problems);

  (ii) To the extent that the lawyer's ability to provide competent representation is impeded or impaired, taking whatever steps are necessary to ensure competent representation of his or her clients, including, when appropriate:

    (A) Seeking treatment to remedy the problems that have resulted in the impairment of the lawyer's abilities;

    (B) Until the lawyer has regained competence, enlisting whatever aid is necessary (including aid from other lawyers) to allow the lawyer to competently represent his or her clients;

    (C) If the lawyer is unable to competently represent a client even with assistance, withdrawing from the representation and referring the client to another lawyer;

1.3 *Representing Clients in a Competent Manner*, including:

 (a) With regard to lawyering skills:

  (i) Applying his or her skills in a competent manner;

  (ii) If the representation of a particular client requires types of skills or a degree of proficiency that the lawyer does not presently possess:

    (A) Assessing whether the client would best be served by the lawyer's acquisition of the requisite skills (assuming it is possible to do so within the time available and without inappropriately burdening the client's resources), or by the lawyer's enlisting the aid of other lawyers or other individuals, or by referring the client to another lawyer;

    (B) Advising the client of the limits of the lawyer's skills and the steps the lawyer intends to take to overcome or compensate for his or her limitations;

(b) With regard to substantive knowledge of the law or of other fields or disciplines:

   (i) Applying his or her knowledge in a competent manner;

   (ii) If the representation of a particular client requires knowledge that the lawyer does not presently possess:

      (A) Assessing whether the client would best be served by the lawyer's acquisition of the requisite knowledge (assuming it is possible to do so within the time available and without inappropriately burdening the client's resources), or by the lawyer's enlisting the aid of other lawyers or experts from other fields, or by referring the client to another lawyer;

      (B) Advising the client of the limits of the lawyer's knowledge and the steps the lawyer intends to take to overcome or compensate for his or her limitations;

(c) Devoting the time, effort, and resources necessary to competently represent the client;

(d) Representing the client in a manner that is consistent with the ethical rules of the profession.

Commentary

As the ABA Task Force on Professional Competence observed, the "goal of serving the public in a competent manner" must be a primary objective of every member of the profession, just as the goal of ensuring competent representation must be a driving concern of the organized bar. AMERICAN BAR ASSOCIATION, FINAL REPORT AND RECOMMENDATIONS OF THE TASK FORCE ON PROFESSIONAL COMPETENCE 2 (1983). This fundamental professional value of competent representation is recognized in the American Bar Association's Model Rules of Professional Conduct as well as its Code of Professional Responsibility. *See* AMERICAN BAR ASSOCIATION, MODEL RULES OF PROFESSIONAL CONDUCT 1.1 (1983) ("[a] lawyer shall provide competent representation to a client"); AMERICAN BAR ASSOCIATION, CODE OF

PROFESSIONAL RESPONSIBILITY, Canon 6 (1969) ("[a] lawyer should represent a client competently").

As this section recognizes, the ideal of competent representation requires first of all that a lawyer strive to attain a certain level of proficiency in lawyering skills and a certain body of substantive knowledge. *See* Model Rules, *supra*, Rule 1.1 ("[c]ompetent representation requires the legal knowledge . . . [and] skill . . . reasonably necessary for the representation"). This would include the relevant aspects of Skill §§ 1–10 *supra* and any additional skills or knowledge required by the particular matter in which the lawyer is acting. Depending upon the type of practice, proficiency may require knowledge not only of the law but also of fields and disciplines other than law. In addition to skills and knowledge, it requires that a lawyer be committed to the values embodied in the ethical rules of the profession, particularly those rules that are designed to promote competent representation. *See also* Skill § 10 *supra*. Finally, as explained in this section and previous sections of the Statement, it requires that a lawyer engage in self-appraisal and acquire a realistic sense of his or her own abilities and limitations. *See, e.g.*, Code of Professional Responsibility, *supra*, DR 6-101(A)(1). *See also* Skill § 1.4 and Commentary.

Yet, as the Model Rules and Code also recognize, it is not enough for a lawyer simply to attain a level of competence. In order to adequately represent clients, a lawyer also must "engage in continuing study and education" in order "[t]o maintain the requisite knowledge and skill." Model Rules, Commentary to Rule 1.1. *See* Code, *supra*, EC 6-1 (a lawyer "should strive to become and remain proficient in his [or her] practice"). As Judge Judith S. Kaye of the New York Court of Appeals has observed, "[t]he increasing codification and complexity of the law, the expansion of the law into wholly new societal areas, the heightened expectation of clients that their lawyers will know even arcane points of law of other jurisdictions in specialized areas, the new technology—all these serve to dramatize the eternal truth that ours is a profession that by its nature demands constant study in order to maintain even the barest level of competence." Kaye, *The Lawyer's Responsibility to Enhance Competence and Ethics*, in AMERICAN LAW INSTITUTE–AMERICAN BAR ASSOCIATION COMMITTEE ON CONTINUING PROFESSIONAL EDUCATION, CLE AND THE LAWYER'S RESPONSIBILITIES IN AN EVOLVING PROFESSION: THE REPORT ON THE ARDEN HOUSE III CONFERENCE 55, 56 (1988).

In analyzing the concept of maintaining a level of competence, this section calls upon lawyers to strive to attain the degree of expertise that may be expected of any competent practitioner at their level of experience. This formulation is designed to protect the rightful expectations of clients. Just as a client who retains a newly admitted lawyer is entitled to expect a certain minimum level of competence, so too a client who retains a lawyer with ten years of experience is entitled to expect a level of knowledge and skill that is considerably more advanced than that of a newly admitted lawyer.

This section's analysis of the concept of maintaining competence also takes into account the physical and mental problems that can prevent a lawyer from functioning competently. As the ABA Task Force on Professional Competence recognized, "[t]he abuse of alcohol or other drugs, emotional problems and more severe psychological disorders, and physical or mental disability may contribute to incompetent legal representation." FINAL REPORT AND RECOMMENDATIONS OF THE TASK FORCE ON PROFESSIONAL COMPETENCE, *supra*, at 20. This section attempts to further the profession's legitimate interest in protecting clients from inadequate representation without unduly intruding into or overly regulating the private lives of lawyers.

Finally, this section's analysis of the concept of competence recognizes that it is often possible and appropriate for a lawyer to acquire (or to refine) particular skills or knowledge in the course of representing a client. As the Model Rules observe, "[a] lawyer can provide adequate representation in a wholly novel field through necessary study"; for this reason, "[a] lawyer may accept representation where the requisite level of competence can be achieved by reasonable preparation." Model Rules, Comment to Rule 1.1. As this section recognizes, there are certain essential preconditions to accepting representation with the expectation of acquiring necessary skills or knowledge in the course of the representation. First, a lawyer must engage in a realistic appraisal of his or her abilities, the skills or knowledge he or she currently lacks, and the degree of study necessary to acquire the requisite skills or knowledge. Second, the lawyer must determine whether the necessary learning can be accomplished within the time available and without inappropriately burdening the client's resources. And finally, the lawyer must advise the client of the lawyer's own limitations and the remedial steps he or she intends to take, so that the client can make an informed decision about whether to seek the services of a lawyer who already possesses the requisite expertise.

2. Striving to Promote Justice, Fairness, and Morality

As a member of a profession that bears "special responsibilit[ies] for the quality of justice" (AMERICAN BAR ASSOCIATION, MODEL RULES OF PROFESSIONAL CONDUCT, Preamble (1983)), a lawyer should be committed to the values of:

2.1 *Promoting Justice, Fairness, and Morality in One's Own Daily Practice*, including:

(a) To the extent required or permitted by the ethical rules of the profession, acting in conformance with considerations of justice, fairness, and morality when making decisions or acting on behalf of a client (*see* Skill § 6.1(a)(iii)(B) *supra*);

(b) To the extent required or permitted by the ethical rules of the profession, counseling clients to take considerations of justice, fairness, and morality into account when the client makes decisions or engages in conduct that may have an adverse effect on other individuals or on society (*see* Skill § 6.1(a)(iii)(A) *supra*);

(c) Treating other people (including clients, other attorneys, and support personnel) with dignity and respect;

2.2 *Contributing to the Profession's Fulfillment of its Responsibility to Ensure that Adequate Legal Services Are Provided to Those Who Cannot Afford to Pay for Them*;

2.3 *Contributing to the Profession's Fulfillment of its Responsibility to Enhance the Capacity of Law and Legal Institutions to Do Justice.*

Commentary

Dean Roscoe Pound observed that the "primary purpose" of a profession is the "[p]ursuit of the learned art in the spirit of a public service." R. POUND, THE LAWYER FROM ANTIQUITY TO MODERN TIMES 5 (1953). This section recognizes that there are three central respects in which a lawyer can and should strive to serve the public and to further the interests of justice, fairness, and morality.

The first of these is the manner in which the lawyer conducts his or her daily practice. In his or her actions on behalf of a client, a lawyer should embrace "those qualities of truth-speaking, of a high sense of honor, of granite discretion, of the strictest observance of fiduciary responsibility that have, throughout the centuries, been compendiously described as 'moral character.' " *Schware v. Board of Bar Examiners*, 353 U.S. 232, 247 (1957) (concurring opinion of Justice Frankfurter). The lawyer should scrupulously refrain from any conduct "that is prejudicial to the administration of justice." AMERICAN BAR ASSOCIATION, CODE OF PROFESSIONAL RESPONSIBILITY, DR 1-102(A)(5) (1969). When, as often happens, a lawyer encounters a situation in which some of the options available for solving a client's problem would result in unfairness or injustice to others, the lawyer should counsel the client to act in a manner "that is morally just." *Id.*, EC 7-8; *accord*, Model Rules, *supra*, Rule 1.2. *See also* Rubin, *A Causerie on Lawyers' Ethics in Negotiation*, 35 LA. L. REV. 577, 591-92 (1975). As § 2.1(c) of this section recognizes, the professional value of promoting justice, fairness, and morality in one's daily practice also calls for according appropriate dignity and respect to all people with whom one interacts in a professional capacity. *See, e.g.*, Model Rules, *supra*, Preamble ("[a] lawyer should demonstrate respect for the legal system and for those who serve it, including judges, other lawyers and public officials"). This necessarily includes refraining from sexual harassment and from any form of discrimination on the basis of gender, race, religion, ethnic origin, sexual orientation, age, or disability, in one's professional interactions with clients, witnesses, support staff, and other individuals. *See, e.g.*, N.Y. LAWYER'S CODE OF PROFESSIONAL RESPONSIBILITY, EC 1-7 (as amended Sept. 1, 1990) ("[a] lawyer should avoid bias and condescension toward, and treat with dignity and respect, all parties, witnesses, lawyers, court employees and other persons involved in the legal process"); MINNESOTA STATE BAR ASSOCIATION, MINNESOTA RULES OF PROFESSIONAL CONDUCT, Rule 8.4 (as amended Dec. 27, 1989) ("[i]t is professional misconduct for a lawyer to . . . harass a person on the basis of sex, race, age, creed, religion, color, national origin, disability, sexual preference or marital status in connection with a lawyer's professional activities").

A second general area of concern has to do with the lawyer's fulfillment of his or her professional responsibility to provide *pro bono* service. It is by now well-accepted that that all lawyers bear a *pro bono* obligation. *See, e.g.*, Model Rules, *supra*, Rule 6.1 ("[a] lawyer should render public interest legal service"); Code of Professional Responsibility, *supra*, EC 2-25 ("[e]very lawyer, regardless of professional prominence or professional workload, should find time to participate in serving the disadvantaged"; "[t]he rendition of free legal services to those unable to pay reasonable fees continues to be the obligation of each lawyer"); AMERICAN BAR ASSOCIATION SPECIAL

COMMITTEE ON PUBLIC INTEREST PRACTICE, RECOMMENDATION AND REPORT (Approved by ABA House of Delegates, August, 1975) ("Montreal Resolution") ("it is the basic professional responsibility of each lawyer engaged in the practice of law to provide public interest legal services"); AMERICAN BAR ASSOCIATION YOUNG LAWYERS DIVISION, RECOMMENDATION AND REPORT (Approved by ABA House of Delegates, August, 1988) ("Toronto Resolution") ("the American Bar Association . . . [u]rges all attorneys to devote a reasonable amount of time, but in no event less than 50 hours per year, to *pro bono* and other public service activities that serve those in need or improve the law, the legal system, or the legal profession"). Yet, it appears that many lawyers fail to honor this obligation. *See, e.g.*, AMERICAN BAR ASSOCIATION COMMISSION ON PROFESSIONALISM, ". . . IN THE SPIRIT OF PUBLIC SERVICE": A BLUEPRINT FOR THE REKINDLING OF LAWYER PROFESSIONALISM 84 (1986). As Chief Justice Rehnquist has observed, the drive for "profit-maximization" has caused modern lawyers to ignore the "public aspect" of the profession, including the obligation to serve the community by doing " 'pro bono' work." Rehnquist, *The State of the Legal Profession*, 59 N.Y. ST. BAR J., Oct. 1987, at 18, 20. This section reaffirms that it is the responsibility of every lawyer to provide *pro bono* service. While the service may take any one of a number of different forms (*see, e.g.*, Model Rules, *supra*, Rule 6.1), a lawyer has the obligation to provide service of some sort and to organize his or her practice in a manner that makes this possible (*see* Skill § 9.2(c) *supra*).

Finally, "a lawyer should assist in improving the legal system." Code of Professional Responsibility, *supra*, Canon 8. *Accord*, Model Rules, *supra*, Preamble ("a lawyer should cultivate knowledge of the law beyond its use for clients . . . [and] employ that knowledge in reform of the law"); *id.*, Rule 6.1. Lawyers play a critical role in the ongoing process of rationalizing and civilizing the law and legal institutions. As the Code of Professional Responsibility states, "lawyers are especially qualified ["[b]y reason of education and experience"] to recognize deficiencies in the legal system and to initiate corrective measures therein." EC 8-1. *See also* A. Z. REED, TRAINING FOR THE PUBLIC PROFESSION OF THE LAW 3 (1921). These "corrective measures" include "proposing and supporting legislation and programs to improve the system" (EC 8-1); endeavoring to change "[r]ules of law . . . [that] are not just, understandable, and responsive to the needs of society" (EC 8-2); and seeking other changes in rules of law, legal procedures or the legal system that are "in the public interest" (EC 8-4) or necessary in order to "advance[] . . . our legal system" (EC 8-9).

3. Striving to Improve the Profession

As a member of a "self-governing" profession (AMERICAN BAR ASSOCIATION, MODEL RULES OF PROFESSIONAL CONDUCT, Preamble (1983)), a lawyer should be committed to the values of:

3.1 *Participating in Activities Designed to Improve the Profession*;

3.2 *Assisting in the Training and Preparation of New Lawyers and the Continuing Education of the Bar*;

3.3 *Striving to Rid the Profession of Bias Based on Race, Religion, Ethnic Origin, Gender, Sexual Orientation, Age, or Disability, and to Rectify the Effects of These Biases.*

Commentary

As this section recognizes, membership in a self-governing profession such as the legal profession imposes upon lawyers an affirmative responsibility to participate in efforts to "assure that . . . [the profession's] regulations are conceived in the public interest and not in furtherance of parochial or self-interested concerns of the bar." Model Rules, *supra*, Preamble; *see also id.*, Rule 6.1; AMERICAN BAR ASSOCIATION, CODE OF PROFESSIONAL RESPONSIBILITY, EC 6-2 (1969). There are numerous ways in which lawyers may contribute to the improvement of the profession. These include participation in national, state, or local bar associations or in organizations that represent alternatives to traditional bar associations; participation in processes for regulating the practice of law, such as the processes for admitting new lawyers to the bar or for disciplining lawyers who have committed ethical infractions; service on commissions and similar bodies concerned with aspects of the administration of justice; and giving speeches or writing articles that criticize the profession and propose reforms.

In addition to expecting contributions that improve the work, regulations and mechanisms of the bar, the profession depends upon its members to assist in the enterprise of educating new lawyers and preparing them for practice. *See* Model Rules, *supra*, Preamble ("[a]s a member of a learned profession, a lawyer . . . [should] work to strengthen legal education"); Code of Professional Responsibility, EC 1-2 ("the bar has a positive obligation to aid in the continued improvement of all phases of pre-admission and post-admission legal education"). These efforts are demanded of lawyers as a means of "maintaining the integrity and competence of the legal profession" (*id.*, EC 1-1) and protecting consumers of legal services from incompetent or unethical representation (*id.*, EC 1-2). Practicing lawyers can productively assist in the training or preparation of new lawyers in a number of ways, including participation in "mentor and buddy systems"—programs administered by state and local bar associations to enable "inexperienced lawyers . . . [to] seek help and guidance from experienced lawyers" (AMERICAN BAR ASSOCIATION, FINAL REPORT AND RECOMMENDATIONS OF THE TASK FORCE ON PROFESSIONAL COMPETENCE 15 (1983)); participation in training programs or support services for new lawyers in one's own office (AMERICAN BAR ASSOCIATION COMMISSION ON PROFESSIONALISM, ". . . IN THE SPIRIT OF PUBLIC SERVICE": A BLUEPRINT FOR THE REKINDLING OF LAWYER PROFESSIONALISM 38 (1986)); and lecturing at or preparing materials for workshops or conferences devoted to the training of new lawyers. In addition to teaching law, strategy, skills, and ethics to new lawyers, experienced practitioners can serve an important function in helping new lawyers make the transition from law school to practice. This includes aiding new lawyers to "understand what they do *not* know, to grasp the limited nature of their education and background in the law" (AMERICAN LAW INSTITUTE–AMERICAN BAR ASSOCIATION COMMITTEE ON CONTINUING PROFESSIONAL EDUCATION, ENHANCING THE COMPETENCE OF LAWYERS: REPORT OF THE HOUSTON CONFERENCE 75 (1981)), as well as assisting them to cope with the paralyzing feelings of incompetence that some new lawyers experience.

Finally, it is incumbent upon all members of the bar to strive to rid the profession of the existence and effects of bias based on race, religion, ethnic origin, gender, sexual orientation, age, or disability. Despite the substantial efforts of the organized bar to eliminate bias within the profession, its effects continue to be felt in numerous ways. *See, e.g.*, AMERICAN BAR ASSOCIATION COMMISSION ON WOMEN IN THE PROFESSION, REPORT TO THE HOUSE OF DELEGATES (Approved by ABA House of Delegates, Aug. 10, 1988) (concluding that "a variety of discriminatory barriers remain a part of the professional culture" and "make it difficult for women to participate fully in the work, responsibilities and rewards of the profession," *id.* at 17); AMERICAN BAR ASSOCIATION TASK FORCE ON MINORITIES IN THE LEGAL PROFESSION, REPORT WITH RECOMMENDATIONS (1986) (finding that "lack of equal opportunity for the minorities in the legal profession persists" (*id.* at 7)). Elimination of bias within the profession is essential in order to preserve "public . . . confidence in the integrity and impartiality" of the profession and "the system for establishing and dispensing [j]ustice" which it administers. AMERICAN BAR ASSOCIATION, CANONS OF PROFESSIONAL ETHICS, Preamble (1908).

4. Professional Self-Development

As a member of a "learned profession" (AMERICAN BAR ASSOCIATION, MODEL RULES OF PROFESSIONAL CONDUCT, Preamble (1983)), a lawyer should be committed to the values of:

4.1 *Seeking Out and Taking Advantage of Opportunities to Increase One's Own Knowledge and Improve One's Own Skills*, including:

(a) Making use of the process of reflecting upon and learning from experience, which entails:

(i) Critically assessing one's own performance so as to evaluate:

(A) The quality of the preparation for the performance, including:

(I) An assessment of the appropriateness of the goals set for the performance and an analysis of whether it would have been possible and desirable to define the goals differently;

(II) An assessment of the appropriateness of the means chosen to pursue the goals and an analysis of whether it would have been possible and desirable to employ different means;

(III) The extent to which the planning process correctly anticipated the contingencies that arose and effectively prepared for these contingencies;

(IV) The accuracy of one's assessments of the likely perspectives, concerns, and reactions of any individuals with whom one interacted (such as, for example, clients, other lawyers, judges, mediators, legislators, and government officials);

(B) The quality of the performance itself, including:

(I) The effectiveness of any applications of lawyering skills;

(II)   The quality of the execution of the plans for the performance;

(III)   The appropriateness and effectiveness of one's reactions to any unexpected events;

(C)   The extent to which ethical issues were properly identified and resolved;

(ii)   Identifying practices that will make it possible to replicate effective aspects of the performance in the future and/or guard against repetition of ineffective ones, including:

(A)   Methods of thinking or analysis that will make it possible to plan more effectively for performances;

(B)   Methods of improving future performances, including one's applications of lawyering skills;

(C)   Methods of improving one's own abilities to perceive or resolve ethical issues;

(b)   Taking advantage of courses of study for increasing one's knowledge of one's own field of practice, other fields of legal practice, and other relevant disciplines;

(c)   Employing a consistent practice of reading about new developments in the law and other relevant fields or disciplines;

(d)   Periodically meeting with other lawyers in one's own field of practice or other fields for the purpose of discussing substantive law, techniques, or topical issues;

4.2   *Selecting and Maintaining Employment That Will Allow the Lawyer to Develop As A Professional and To Pursue His or Her Professional and Personal Goals.*

Commentary

Although the Statement of Skills and Values focuses on competent practice, this section recognizes that a lawyer should not be content with simply attaining the level of competence. The mark of a dedicated professional is that he or she seeks to achieve excellence in his or her chosen field. *See, e.g.,* Model Rules, *supra*, Preamble ("[a] lawyer should strive to attain the highest level of skill");

AMERICAN LAW INSTITUTE–AMERICAN BAR ASSOCIATION COMMITTEE ON CONTINUING PROFESSIONAL EDUCATION, A PRACTICAL GUIDE TO ACHIEVING EXCELLENCE IN THE PRACTICE OF LAW: STANDARDS, METHODS, AND SELF-EVALUATION (1992).

Value § 1 explained that continuing study is an indispensable part of the process of maintaining a level of competence in one's field of practice. This section recognizes that continuing study also is an essential part of the process of attaining excellence. It calls upon lawyers to take advantage of opportunities for continuing learning and improvement, including the use of the process of self-reflection to learn from experience in a "reflective, organized, [and] systematic" manner (Amsterdam, *Clinical Legal Education—A 21st-Century Perspective*, 34 J. LEGAL EDUC. 612, 616 (1984)), and participation in continuing legal education programs and other programs of this sort (*see, e.g.,* AMERICAN BAR ASSOCIATION, FINAL REPORT AND RECOMMENDATIONS OF THE TASK FORCE ON PROFESSIONAL COMPETENCE 7-8, 15 (1983)). The section takes the view that continuing education can improve a lawyer's understanding not only of substantive law and lawyering skills but also of professional responsibility. *See, e.g.,* Kaye, *The Lawyer's Responsibility to Enhance Competence and Ethics*, in AMERICAN LAW INSTITUTE–AMERICAN BAR ASSOCIATION COMMITTEE ON CONTINUING PROFESSIONAL EDUCATION, CLE AND THE LAWYER'S RESPONSIBILITIES IN AN EVOLVING PROFESSION: THE REPORT ON THE ARDEN HOUSE III CONFERENCE 55, 57-62 (1988).

Section 4.2 reflects the practical consideration that a lawyer will not develop as a professional unless the lawyer is in an employment setting where he or she can effectively pursue his or her professional and personal goals. Studies and anecdotal accounts suggest that significant numbers of lawyers experience dissatisfaction in their jobs. *See, e.g.,* AMERICAN BAR ASSOCIATION YOUNG LAWYERS DIVISION, THE STATE OF THE LEGAL PROFESSION, Report # 2 (1991); AMERICAN BAR ASSOCIATION TASK FORCE ON THE GENERAL PRACTITIONER AND THE ORGANIZED BAR, REPORT OF THE TASK FORCE ON THE GENERAL PRACTITIONER AND THE ORGANIZED BAR 38-39 (1984); Dart, *The First Five Years of Practice*, 21 CONN. L. REV. 81, 83-86 (1988); Hirsch, *Are You on Target?*, 12 BARRISTER, Winter, 1985, at 17. A national survey conducted by the ABA Young Lawyers Division in 1984 found that 25 % of the associates and staff attorneys in the sample were dissatisfied with their jobs and intended to change jobs within two years. Hirsch, *supra*, at 18. A follow-up study by the Young Lawyers Division in 1990 found that "[a]cross the board, regardless of job setting, there has been a dramatic 20 % reduction in the number of lawyers indicating that they are very satisfied, accompanied by an increase in dissatisfaction." ABA YOUNG LAWYERS DIVISION, *supra*, at 2. Moreover, this follow-up study found a sharp increase in the number of partners, senior associates, and solo practitioners expressing dissatisfaction: 22% of male partners and 42% of female partners in the sample reported that they are dissatisfied. *Id.*

In order to find employment that is consistent with his or her professional goals and personal values, a lawyer must be familiar with the range of traditional and non-traditional employment opportunities for lawyers. In the past two decades, there have been significant changes in the nature of legal practice, including "[c]hanges in the type of legal services a client requires, [the development of] increased competition among lawyers (and between lawyers and others offering legal services), [and the emergence of] more knowledgeable clients, and a host of new tools available to lawyers." AMERICAN BAR ASSOCIATION TASK FORCE ON THE ROLE OF THE LAWYER IN THE 1980'S, REPORT OF THE TASK FORCE ON THE ROLE OF THE LAWYER IN THE 1980'S, at 2 (1981). A lawyer should have a general familiarity with the effects of these developments on the nature of legal practice as well as an understanding of the processes by which he or she can acquire additional information about fields of legal practice, the nature of practice within these fields, and the types of positions available within the fields.

Part III.
The Educational Continuum Through Which Lawyers Acquire Their Skills and Values

Chapter Six
The Process Prior to Law School

A. Self-Assessment and Commitment to Self-Development
B. The Need for Informed Choice

A. Self-Assessment and Commitment to Self-Development

The responsibility for assessing one's fitness for any career must ultimately rest with the individual, who through careful introspection can make judgments regarding personal strengths, priorities, and other aptitudes and thereby maximize the likelihood of experiencing a satisfying and rewarding professional life. This personal responsibility for self-assessment in beginning one's self-development should continue through professional school and throughout one's professional life.

In commencing the process of self-development, one must learn to ask questions, seek information, continually set standards for one's self and goals to achieve.[1] There ensues the need continually to evaluate one's own performance in the light of the standards and goals one has fixed.

The decision to pursue a career in the law should be a considered choice reached with a full awareness of its implications. Approximately 99,300 people applied for admission to law school in 1991; 53,800 were admitted; and 44,050 matriculated choosing to invest in a legal education at 176 ABA approved law schools. The cost of legal education varies widely from school to school. Three years of tuition alone, and there can be considerable additional expense, ranges from a high of about $50,000 to a low of approximately $5,000. Regardless of the financial cost, the stake of law students in three years of law school is substantial. Law school is more than an economic venture. The experience frequently challenges and permanently alters law students' fundamental values and convictions. For most, law school results in a lifetime commitment to the legal profession. At least three quarters of those who finish law school become career practitioners.

As we have noted, the legal profession is extremely diverse and highly differentiated in practice settings, in areas of specialization,

---

1. See Preface (at 2) of A PRACTICAL GUIDE TO ACHIEVING EXCELLENCE IN THE PRACTICE OF LAW, ALI-ABA (1992).

in clients served, in work experience and in its economic and psychic rewards.[2] Because the profession is diverse, a law degree is frequently depicted as providing its holders with a high degree of professional mobility and flexibility. Yet, over the years, placement statistics from any given law school disclose that the percentages of their graduates who enter specific professional niches are fairly predictable. Graduates of "national" law schools tend to enter practice with large firms; graduates of many state and region-oriented schools are apt to enter practice in small or medium size firms, or even in solo practice.[3] The choice of law school attended correlates strongly with the range of professional career options exercised by students at graduation and may circumscribe or expand the variety of career options available.[4]

Although the decision to become a lawyer means a quest to acquire a common body of learning, particular skills and professional values, the ways in which those qualities will be used and to what ends they will be used are matters that each prospective lawyer must individually weigh. Many profess to select a legal career because of important moral, political, and social values, and view a legal career as an opportunity to contribute to society. It is also likely that some today are motivated by the glamorous life styles and careers depicted on television, and the allure of what are seen as prestigious positions with handsome financial rewards. Some simply select by default after having decided against fields such as science, engineering, business, or medicine, while still others turn to law after having had successful first careers.

But at the threshold of a career in the law, the prospective law student should contemplate the challenges that lie ahead of intellectual discipline, required learning, society's demands and the profession's expectations for its members. Given the aptitude and a commitment to one's self-development, one who is aware of the challenges can enter the educational continuum of professional devel-

---

2. See supra Part I.

3. LEONA M. VOGT, FROM LAW SCHOOL TO CAREER: WHERE DO GRADUATES GO AND WHAT DO THEY DO? A CAREER PATHS STUDY OF SEVEN NORTHEASTERN AREA LAW SCHOOLS (1986). At page 13, it is stated that "the law school attended appears to have the most influence over whether the graduates work in large firms, very small firms or solo practice, i.e, the probability of ending up in these three practice situations seems to be related to the school one attends."

4. The National Association for Law Placement (NALP) annually collects detailed placement information from law schools and, after computer analysis, returns a variety of reports to them. Unfortunately, because these data are considered highly sensitive, no central data bank is maintained. Law school placement professionals generally believe, however, that graduates' ultimate employment is affected (but not necessarily determined) by the law school attended. This belief is shared by Lujuanna Treadwell, NALP executive director.

opment with a reasonable expectation of finding a satisfying life in the law.[5]

B. The Need for Informed Choice

There are three critical stages of decision-making en route to becoming a lawyer: 1) Perhaps the most significant, whether to enter the legal profession at all; 2) which law school to choose; and 3) what career path to enter after law school. Each occasion should be a time for careful reflection and self-assessment based upon sufficient information to make an informed choice. Far too often these decisions are made without sufficient information or thought. Many common factors affect each of these decisions. The three stages of decision-making are parts of an ongoing process of self-development.

Many factors influence each individual's decision. When exploring the possibility of becoming a lawyer, choosing a law school, and finding a practice niche, individuals pursue and rely on a variety of information. They may seek advice from friends, relatives, guidance counselors, professors, lawyers, the popular press, career guidebooks, magazine articles, law school bulletins, and other sources. The consequences flowing from their decisions are important to their career satisfaction, to the legal profession, and to society. Timely and accurate information about the legal profession and the function of law schools as the gateway to the profession helps prepare prospective applicants for a future in law and may help prevent some from becoming locked into a career from which they draw no real satisfaction, for which they are poorly suited, and in which they perform marginally. Such individuals need access to comprehensive and objective information.

The 1990 Report on the State of the Legal Profession, issued by the ABA Young Lawyers Division, presents evidence suggesting that many may have entered the profession with inadequate information regarding a life in the law. While interest in law is at a peak, the survey found that lawyer dissatisfaction had risen.[6] It was noted that, since 1984, "across the board, regardless of job setting, there has been a dramatic 20% reduction in the number of lawyers indi-

---

5. *See* BYERS, SAMUELSON & WILLIAMSON, LAWYERS IN TRANSITION—PLANNING A LIFE IN THE LAW (1988).

6. Career dissatisfaction may not be a new phenomenon. The 1986 Vogt study, *supra* note 3, at 10, found that many lawyers who had received their degrees several years prior to the study were no longer practicing law. It may be inferred that career dissatisfaction was a factor in some cases. See also, Kaye, *Free of the Law*, HARVARD MAGAZINE (Jan. - Feb. 1992), at 60.

cating that they are very satisfied, accompanied by an increase in dissatisfaction." The report also shed light on how expectations had changed between entering law school and graduation.

Career dissatisfaction is not exclusive to law; much is heard about unhappiness in medicine, accounting, teaching, and other professions. Many law school applicants are seeking career changes from other professions because their initial professional pursuits have not met their expectations. It seems clear that better information about career characteristics is needed at the beginning.

Prospective law students generally are not knowledgeable about the profession: what certain jobs entail; what different paths for entry into the profession may be; how students should prepare for their careers; and how law schools may differ in the preparation they offer. Law students tend to be passive consumers of legal education; they simply assume that the law school experience adequately prepares them for practice. To the extent that this is not accurate, efforts should be made to inform students how to identify the skills they will need to be competent attorneys, and how to enable themselves to take an active role in their education by seeking appropriate training for those skills.

Law school administrators know the strengths and weaknesses of their own institutions and should be candid in discussing them with applicants. Catalogs and application materials should provide the kinds of information that will enable candidates to make informed decisions. Unfortunately, this is not always the case. It has become routine, for example, to talk about skills training and clinical opportunities, but there may be no mention of enrollment restrictions nor of the chances of being accepted into these courses. Information may also be incomplete with regard to writing opportunities, seminars, and courses that are likely to be of particular interest to certain groups of students. Schools could be the source of considerable information about such concerns, about the pressures of law school and practice, about the kinds of work their graduates do, and about the financial and personal implications of different legal careers.

A review of catalogs and entries in the *Official Guide to U.S. Law Schools*, published by the Law School Admission Council in cooperation with the American Bar Association and the Association of American Law Schools, provides evidence that schools are not doing a good job distinguishing themselves from one another. Many appear to be all things to all people. This is unfortunate, because it prevents law school applicants from making intelligent and informed choices as to which law schools would be good matches for them.

The provision of high-quality information at an early stage would be a significant step in this direction.

The perceived lack of adequate information coming from law schools themselves has resulted in a plethora of materials purporting to fill the vacuum. These include articles, books, and a variety of law school ratings which have attracted considerable attention. Many legal educators have commented on the defects in these materials, especially the ratings, but little has been done to address the underlying problem. It is now time to do so.

With regard to the selection of a law school, the following kinds of information would be helpful to a prospective student:

a   Admissions data
b.   Tuition, costs, and financial aid data
c.   Enrollment and graduation data
d.   Composition of faculty and administration
e.   Curricular offerings and class sizes
f.   Library resources
g.   Physical plant
h.   Housing availability
i.   Financial resources available to support educational program
j.   Placement and bar passage data[7]

This list is not exhaustive; there is much more information that one could seek in selecting a law school. A good deal of that data is submitted annually to the ABA Consultant on Legal Education's office by every law school approved by the American Bar Association. It is considered confidential and is not released. The Task Force recommends that, to the extent that such information is relevant, accurate, and useful in decision-making, the current policy of absolute confidentiality should be reconsidered.

Other steps could include:

• Distributing to all LSAT registrants a statement indicating that there are differences between law schools, describing broadly what those differences are, explaining that schools' reputations do differ, and providing relevant information from the front of the *Official Guide to U.S. Law Schools.*
• Sending to each LSAT registrant a letter from the ABA and/or AALS and/or LSAC outlining the kinds of ques-

---

7. This list is taken from a February 1992 draft interpretation of a proposed ABA Standard for Approval of Law Schools, which would require the release by a law school of "basic consumer information."

tions an applicant should ask admissions personnel in order to obtain the kinds of information upon which to base a decision.

• Expanding the ABA's *Annual Review of Legal Education* and the *Official Guide's* key facts, providing some of the information listed above. These materials might be mailed to LSAT registrants.

With regard to career path information, there are various helpful sources of information on the legal profession which identify key factors that should be considered by prospective law students when making the decision to become a lawyer.[8] Such books profile attorney lifestyles in different practice settings and generally describe law school and the nature of legal education, but the subject matter today is so immense that any one of these books can serve only as a starting point in one's exploration of law as a career. There is clear need for a more comprehensive way in which to address today's diverse and changing legal profession and the practice of law in its myriad settings. This suggests that the ABA give consideration to producing a regularly updated volume of materials on careers in the law. Such information, augmented by current data available from law school placement professionals, could be extremely helpful to those considering law as a career.

Most prelaw counseling takes place only after individuals have already decided to become lawyers and are seeking information to assist them in selecting the law schools to which to apply. The need for advice at an earlier time in the decision-making process is apparent.

The organized bar's programs in primary and secondary school of law-related education provide useful instruction at an early stage of choosing one's career direction; but greater attention should be given by the bar to providing guidance during the undergraduate years on the factors to be considered in selecting law as a career.

We suggest that during undergraduate years the following considerations should be brought to the attention of prospective law students:

• prelegal education is crucial to the development of future

---

8. See, for example, *Susan J. Bell, Full Disclosure: Do You Really Want to Be A Lawyer?*, ABA Young Lawyers Division (1989); *V. Countryman, T. Finman, & T.J. Schneyer, The Lawyer in Modern Society*, 2nd Ed. (1976); *T. Ehrlich & G. Hazard, Going to Law School? Readings on a Legal Career* (1975); *Eve Spangler, Lawyers for Hire, Salaried Professionals at Work* (1986). *Cf.* F. UTLEY & G.A. MUNNEKE, FROM LAW STUDENT TO LAWYER (1984), from the ABA Career Series, which is published as "A Career Planning Manual" for students while in law school.

lawyers. As early as 1953, the AALS issued a Statement on Prelegal Education, calling attention to the quality of undergraduate instruction that AALS believed fundamental to the later attainment of legal competence, and to the fact that quality of prelaw education was important to the development of basic skills and insights needed in the study and practice of law. The Statement pointed to the importance of:

- comprehension;
- oral and written expression;
- critical understanding of the human institutions and values with which the law deals;
- creative power in thinking.

The AALS Statement's emphasis on communication, oral and written, is underlined by the recent ABF survey on legal education and the profession, "Assessing the New Generation of Lawyers," Appendix B. The two most important skills as defined by beginning practitioners are oral and written communication, but most of these practitioners do not believe that they learned these skills primarily in law school. It is important for them to come to law school as prepared as possible in these skills. Prospective law students should be encouraged to review the AALS Statement when planning their undergraduate studies.

In addition, we point out that the ABA Special Committee for a Study of Legal Education identified in 1980 some specific areas of the undergraduate curriculum which can be helpful to would-be lawyers. It is also important that undergraduates know that selection of a law school can significantly impact one's career options. For example, attendance at a "national" school may enhance one's chances of entering large firm practice, but may discourage entering practice in other settings.

Course selection in law school may be important to certain law firm interviewers, but generally does not open or foreclose later opportunities. Students may make curriculum choices with an eye toward honing particular skills, producing the best possible grade-point average, passing a bar examination, coming into contact with the best teachers, or pleasing potential future employers. These different goals are likely to require somewhat different approaches to curriculum planning.

Finally, the Task Force recommends that its Statement of Fundamental Lawyering Skills and Professional Values be made available to prospective and entering law students to inform them about the skills and values they will be expected to possess as lawyers. This will help them to seek appropriate educational opportunities both in law school and beyond to develop these skills and values.

Chapter Seven
Professional Development During
Law School

A. The Law Schools' Role in Professional Development

Prior to the advent of the clinical legal education movement in the 1960s, the role of law schools in the professional development of lawyers was confined, with few exceptions, to the teaching of analytical skills, substantive law, and the techniques of legal research. In 1973, the American Bar Association adopted its Standards for approval of law schools incorporating, in Standard 302, requirements for the teaching of the "core" curriculum, "the duties and responsibilities of the legal profession," and training in a limited number of "professional skills." The Standards were subsequently amended by adding a requirement for "at least one rigorous writing experience," and by an amendment of the "professional skills" Standard to reflect a more expansive view of skills instruction.

233

Standard 302, however, which defines curriculum requirements in terms of categories of courses ("core" curriculum) or categories of instruction ("skills," "writing experience," and "duties and responsibilities of the legal profession") bears little relationship to the detailed set of skills and values described in this Task Force's Statement of Skills and Values. Moreover, the Standards, which apply only to law schools, cannot reflect the powerful message that emerges from the Statement—that the teaching of these skills and values is the joint responsibility of law schools and the practicing bar.

While these observations suggest a continuum in which law schools and the practicing bar should participate jointly in the professional development of lawyers, it is important for legal educators and practicing lawyers to recognize that they have different capacities and opportunities to impart these skills and values to future lawyers.

Specifically, law schools should continue to emphasize the teaching of "legal analysis and reasoning," and "legal research," as described in the Statement. Indeed, the unfortunate tendency to define "skills instruction" as dealing with skills other than legal analysis and research has obscured the obvious fact that appellate-case analysis—the technique for teaching traditional courses—involves the teaching of important professional skills. Moreover, it is now apparent that a well-structured clinical program also provides an important vehicle for the development of the skills of legal analysis and research. These skills can no longer be viewed as teachable only in the traditional classroom setting.

As the next section of this Report demonstrates, law schools, through their clinical programs, have developed the capacity to teach other lawyering skills—those associated with practice—that had previously been considered as incapable of being taught other than through direct practice experience. The skills of "problem solving," "factual investigation," "communication," "counseling," "negotiation," and "litigation" are being taught in many, perhaps most, law schools in ways that emphasize the conceptual underpinnings of these skills.

While even well-structured law school clinical programs would rarely be able to duplicate the pressures and intensity of a practice setting, law schools provide a unique opportunity for exposing students to the full range of these practice skills, an opportunity that might not be readily available in actual practice. Moreover, the organized instruction in these skills, in a simulated or live-client context in law schools, enables students to relate their later practice experience to concepts that they have learned in law school, just as students are able to place the substantive knowledge that they acquire after law school in the framework of the concepts they have learned in their substantive courses.

Law schools also have an important, and varied, role to play in developing the skill of "recognizing and resolving ethical dilemmas." Although the teaching of professional responsibility in law schools has been criticized for being too rule-oriented, this criticism ignores the opportunity that clinical programs provide for sensitizing students to ethical issues. Moreover, a rich body of teaching materials has emerged during the past fifteen years that has enriched both professional responsibility and clinical courses.

Thus, law schools can help students to recognize ethical dilemmas and can provide the rudiments of training for resolving them. It must be emphasized, however, that the exposure of students to these issues in law school clinical programs, or in the classroom, is very limited compared to the variety and complexity of the ethical dilemmas that students confront in practice. Although law schools have taken seriously their responsibilities with regard to the teaching of ethical standards and professional values, a young lawyer's ethical standards are likely to be shaped far more by his or her mentors in the early years of practice than by the experiences one acquires in the limited practice setting available in law school. Too often, practicing lawyers fail to appreciate their own responsibilities in this area.

In a similar vein, a well-structured clinical program, particularly in the live-client context, can help students understand the importance of the skill of "organization and management of legal work," but it remains for the first employer, or mentor, to translate this awareness into a functioning reality. Even the strongest proponents of courses in "law office management" would probably concede the importance of the early years of practice in developing this skill.

Turning to the "fundamental values of the profession," as set forth in the Statement of Skills and Values, law schools, from which the vast majority of lawyers enter the profession, have a responsibility to stress that these values are at least as important as the substance of courses or the skills of practice. Students must be made aware of the fundamental professional values of "competent representation," of "striving to improve the profession," and of "professional self-development." Law schools can, and should, teach these values in clinical and traditional courses and should instill in students the desire to achieve them in the course of their professional careers. The efforts of law schools, however, will mean little if the practicing bar shuns its own responsibilities for inculcating professional values.

Practicing lawyers can teach by the power of example. Practicing lawyers influence students during their law school years, through contact in part-time work or through summer jobs. Later, in a young lawyer's early years of practice, partners, associates, other mentors, and adversaries may be more significant than law teachers in teaching these professional values.

Finally, the Statement of Skills and Values identifies, as a fundamental professional value, the need to "promote justice, fairness, and morality." Law school deans, professors, administrators and staff must not only promote these values by words, but must so conduct themselves as to convey to students that these values are essential ingredients of our profession. Too often, the Socratic method of teaching emphasizes qualities that have little to do with justice, fairness, and morality in daily practice. Students too easily gain the impression that wit, sharp responses, and dazzling performance are more important than the personal moral values that lawyers must possess and that the profession must espouse. The promotion of these values requires no resources and no institutional changes. It does require commitment.

And it is the clear responsibility of the practicing bar to impress on students that success in the practice of law is not measured by financial rewards alone, but also by a lawyer's commitment, in practice and in the lawyer's other activities, to a just, fair, and moral society.

B. Assessing Current Instruction in Skills and Values

In 1983, the Final Report of the Task Force on Professional Competence stated,

> Recent research on American legal education concludes that the strength of legal education is teaching substantive law and developing analytical skills—often described as "teaching students to think like lawyers." There appear to be no problems in law school curricula or pedagogy as they relate to the competence goal of making lawyers knowledgeable about the fields of law in which they practice. Law schools do well in teaching substantive law and developing analytic skills. The problems and issues in American legal education involve chiefly the teaching of other lawyering skills.

The courses then described as "teaching substantive law and developing analytical skills" comprise the core of contemporary law school curricula. They constitute the bulk of law school offerings and students are both required and encouraged to take them. In addition, traditional bar examinations mandate a basic knowledge of many of these subjects.

For the decade before 1983 and in the decade since then, however, law schools have steadily added, expanded or enhanced courses encompassing a broad range of other professional skills.[1] The great majority of law schools now offer a variety of skills courses spread over the entire three year curriculum. Many of these schools have advanced beyond simply offering a broad blend of skills courses and have begun implementing sequences of courses.[2] In either case, there is an increased probability that skills instruction is available in the full spectrum of professional skills outlined in the Statement of Skills and Values. The variety of single unsequenced offerings and the existence of sequences enhance students' opportunities to acquire skills at the time and in the manner most suited to their learning styles, and provides for advanced learning through repetition and a "building block" approach to skills education. The law school community deserves credit for its accomplishments to this time in developing the components of a robust skills curriculum.

Data on skills courses are available for three distinct modes of instruction—clinics, externships, and simulations—plus a catch-all

---

1. For the National Conference on Professional Skills and Legal Education in Albuquerque, New Mexico, (October 15-19, 1987), 24 law schools submitted materials describing professional skills courses and programs at the schools. These materials were compiled by the Consultant on Legal Education to the American Bar Association and published in September 1988.

At the conference of the ABA Standing Committee on Lawyer Competence in St. Louis, Missouri, November 1-3, 1990, papers were presented on the conference theme: "Making the Competent Lawyer: Models for Law School Action." A compilation of the papers is available from the Standing Committee.

A description of the Competency-Based Curriculum of the University of Montana School of Law was provided to the Task Force in 1992 and will be lodged in the Office of the Consultant on Legal Education. This curriculum seeks to ensure that each graduate has the knowledge, skills, perspective and personal qualities essential for entry-level competence in the general practice of law.

The Task Force was also provided in 1992 with a description of the University of Maryland School of Law's "Legal Theory and Practice" program which will be lodged in the Office of the Consultant on Legal Education. This program links together legal theory, doctrine and the provision of legal assistance to poor and marginalized people as part of a systematic public service curriculum and includes live-client clinical experience for all students.

2. Much of the data in this section are premised on a survey done by the Task Force. In response to a Task Force survey question, almost half of the responding law schools identified skills course sequences in their curricular. Sequences included writing, litigation practice, and other skills courses as prerequisites to live client clinic courses. Some schools sequence basic and advanced substantive law courses and include a skills dimension in them, e.g., tax or business practice. In most reported course sequences, students are given the option of taking the full sequence or only part. This gives them the opportunity to explore areas of possible interest and to "specialize" in those most appropriate for them.

"other" category.[3] One can trace the growth in simulation and "other" skills course offerings by comparing data gathered for 1974-75 with data for 1984-86 and with data for 1990.[4] Such a comparison shows that in 1974-75,[5] 109 schools reported 834 courses. A decade later, in 1984–86, a survey of 164 schools[6] showed 1576 courses, an increase of 25.7% per school. A survey of 119 schools in 1990[7] found 1763 courses, a further increase of 54.1% per school over the 1984–86 figures.

Clinics have made, and continue to make, an invaluable contribution to the entire legal education enterprise. They are a key component in the development and advancement of skills and values throughout the profession. Their role in the curricular mix of courses is vital. Much of the research leading to the advancement of knowledge about lawyering, the legal profession and its institutions is found in the work of clinicians, and many are recognized to be among the most dedicated and talented teachers in law schools. Clinics provide students with the opportunity to integrate, in an actual practice setting, all of the fundamental lawyering skills. In clinic courses, students sharpen their understanding of professional responsibility and deepen their appreciation for their own values as well as those of the profession as a whole.

Historical data comparable to those on simulation and other courses are not as readily available for in-house clinics and extern-

---

3. Throughout this section reference will be made to four forms of professional skills education. The American Bar Association, in its instructions to law schools which accompany its annual questionnaire, defines these teaching methods as follows:

Client Contact   "Client contact" programs are those which involve students in representing actual clients. (Throughout this section courses using this method and in which law teachers teach through working with the students on client cases are called "clinics" to distinguish them from placements.)

Simulation   "Simulation" programs include programs which use simulation exercises to teach interviewing, counseling, negotiation, trial practice, etc.

Placement   "Placement/Externship" refers to courses or programs in which students are placed with non-law school agencies or offices.

Other   The "other" category includes any program conducted by the school deemed to be skills instruction which does not fall within the other categories.

4. Unfortunately available data do not distinguish between courses using simulation and "other" skills courses as defined above. Therefore, all such courses are grouped together in this analysis.

5. Data from a study by the Council on Legal Education for Professional Responsibility (CLEPR), reported by E. Gordon Gee and Donald W. Jackson. See discussion, *infra*.

6. These data come from a study by the American Bar Association's Office of the Consultant on Legal Education and reported by William Powers. See discussion, *infra*.

7. These data come from a study by this Task Force. See discussion, *infra*, this chapter.

ship programs. The Council on Legal Education for Professional Responsibility (CLEPR) annual reports[8] show in-house clinics funded by that organization in 94 to 104 schools during the period from 1975 to 1979. The American Bar Association annual questionnaire data from 1985 to 1991 show that between 129 and 138 schools reported in-house clinics. Thus, if the CLEPR reports included most clinics, there has been growth from the late seventies to the late eighties on the order of 25% in the number of schools offering in-house clinics. At a minimum it is clear that from among schools on which there is data, the proportion of those schools offering in-house clinics has fluctuated between 75 to 82 percent for more than one decade.

The number of clinics offered by this group of schools has not been annually reported, but in 1987 147 in-house clinics were reported by 70 schools for an average of 2.1 clinics per school.[9] The Task Force found 314 clinics from 119 schools in 1990 for an average of 2.64 clinics per school.

Comparing the American Bar Association Curriculum study data to those of the Task Force survey, it would seem that the number of externship programs is holding steady at approximately an average of 3 per school.

Maturing professional skills programs have become increasingly sophisticated in content, in articulating the theoretical underpinnings of lawyering skills and in teaching methodologies.[10] For example, courses in pre-trial practice, trial practice, appellate advocacy, interviewing and counseling, negotiation and alternative dispute resolution, and legal writing and research are common, and many courses set in a substantive law context, such as business planning

---

8. These reports, unlike the American Bar Association questionnaires, do not come from all accredited law schools. In the period in question between 127 and 139 schools reported. Given that CLEPR was the primary source of external funding for clinics during this period, it is likely that most schools with clinics, whether in-house or extern, submitted reports to CLEPR.

9. *See* data from the Association of American Law Schools Clinical Legal Education Section study reported by McDiarmid and discussed *infra* this chapter. Because the CLEPR studies by Gee and Jackson, *supra* note 6, reported externs and in-house clinics as one category, that information is of little help in determining the correct number.

The ABA Curriculum study, *supra* note 7 (at 12) reports in excess of 600 clinics (as distinguished from externships) from 164 schools reporting in 1984-86 for an average of 3.75 clinics per school. When compared to other data gathered by CLEPR, McDiarmid and the Task Force, this figure seems high. Part of the difference may lie in the definition of clinic, stricter in the McDiarmid data than in either the ABA Curriculum or the Task Force report. However, it is unlikely that this is the entire explanation.

10. See section on "methodologies," *infra*.

and family law, now include skills components. At many schools, imaginative introductory courses in legal writing, research and other professional skills have been added to the mandatory first year curriculum as well.

Offsetting this clear pattern of growth in the numbers and sophistication of skills offerings are data generated by the Task Force study and from other sources which demonstrate that relatively few law students have exposure to the full range of professional skills offerings. The Task Force found that the majority of graduating law students had four or fewer skills "experiences" (simulated skills, clinics, externships or others)[11] while in law school. When classes of first year 'Introduction to Lawyering' (29% of students enroll), first year and advanced legal writing and research (85% of students enroll), trial advocacy (58% of students enroll) and moot court (41% of students enroll) were removed from the list, the majority of graduating students had only one (32%) or no (28%) additional exposures to professional skills instruction.

The following graph shows the number of skills courses taken by graduates (other than courses of Introduction to Lawyering, Introduction and Advanced Legal Writing and Research, Trial Advocacy and Moot Court.).

Graduates' Skills Exposure
Number of skills courses taken

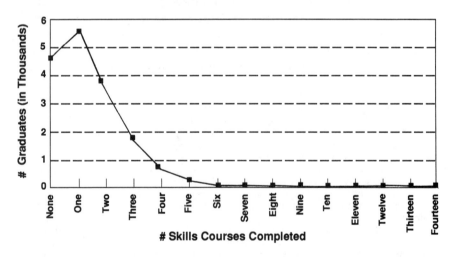

11. Not all courses which fall in these categories effectively teach professional skills. Those which lack sufficient organization, faculty involvement and supervision will not provide the requisites for effective instruction as discussed in the section on "methodologies," *infra*.

These data are consistent with findings that clinical programs are generally available to only 30 percent of law students at schools where live client clinics are offered.[12] Using data from the American Bar Association questionnaire for 1990-91,[13] it appears that professional skills training occupies only nine (9%) percent of the total instructional time available to law schools.

The growth in the professional skills curriculum may be attributable to a number of factors including a heightened awareness of the importance of the law schools' role in preparing graduates for practice, the hiring of faculty with intellectual interests in the nature of lawyering and legal institutions, the development of new teaching methodologies suited for professional skills instruction, student demand, and pressure from the profession. Students' lack of exposure to a full range of skills instruction may be attributable to a number of factors. The first is that the labor intensive nature of such instruction with its resultant cost may limit offerings. There may also be a lack of interest on the part of some faculty in either learning new teaching methods or in the nature of the skills material itself. Finally, the fact that sophistication in the handling of this material has developed relatively recently may account for the dearth of opportunities.

The Task Force's Survey and Other Studies

In April 1990, the Task Force initiated a survey of ABA approved law schools in an effort to gain a concrete, detailed sense of the nature and extent of professional skills instruction currently being offered. The survey was designed to obtain a better understanding of the contribution law schools are making, and are capable of making, in providing students with the opportunity to acquire the skills and values required for competent representation of clients.

The survey instrument was mailed to all ABA approved law schools with a request that the schools provide narrative descriptions of all professional skills instruction offered during the 1989-90 academic year, together with descriptions of the specific competencies sought to be developed and methodologies used in each course. For all reported courses, law schools were asked to supply information about the course type and title, number of sections offered, total enrollment, course credits, instructor type and student/faculty ratio. For students graduating in the class of 1990, schools were to

---

12. Marjorie Anne McDiarmid, *What's Going on Down There in the Basement: In-House Clinics Expand their Beachhead*, 35 N.Y.L. SCH. L. REV. 239, 280-81 (1990) [hereafter *'Basement'*]. For a discussion of this study see section on "methodologies," *infra*.

13. See tables C9-8990 and G2-9091 from the ABA Office of the Consultant on Legal Education.

list all of the professional skills training acquired and pertinent employment data. (The complete Task Force questionnaire is Appendix C to the Report.)

The conclusions reached in this chapter are premised not only on the Task Force survey, but also on reports of previous investigations. The first of these are the annual reports of the Council on Legal Education for Professional Responsibility (CLEPR), the arm of the Ford Foundation largely responsible for the funding growth in clinical programs during the 1970's. CLEPR also conducted an important study in 1974-75 of the make up of law school curricula. The results of that study were published in 1975 by E. Gordon Gee and Donald W. Jackson in *Following the Leader? The Unexamined Consensus in Law School Curricula and Bread and Butter? Electives in American Legal Education.*

In 1986 the American Bar Association's Office of the Consultant on Legal Education conducted a significant study which paralleled the CLEPR curricula project. Results of that study, organized by William Powers, were published in *A Study of Contemporary Law School Curricula* in 1986 and *A Study of Contemporary Law School Curricula II: Professional Skills Courses* in 1987. These studies provide bench marks against which current data were measured.

A more narrowly focused, but more detailed study of live client, in-house clinics was undertaken by a sub-committee of the Clinical Legal Education section of the Association of American Law Schools[14] in 1987. The study was conducted by Marjorie Anne McDiarmid and her personal views as to its findings are set forth in *What's Going On Down There in the Basement: In-House Clinics Expand Their Beachhead.*[15] Raw data from that study were also made available to the Task Force.

In addition to these previous studies and reports aimed at analyzing professional skills education, data from the American Bar Association annual law school questionnaires was also used.

The Methodologies Employed for Teaching Skills and Values

As noted in Part II of this report, the Task Force's Statement of Fundamental Lawyering Skills and Professional Values (Statement) seeks to provide an inventory of the skills and values new members of the profession should seek to acquire. The concepts articulated

---

14. The AALS has not been asked to and has not adopted the findings of this report.
15. '*Basement*', *supra* note 12.

there are keyed to lawyers' work and professional activities. Focusing on those skills in an educational setting involves: 1) developing students' understanding of lawyering tasks, 2) providing opportunities to them to engage in actual skills performance in role, and 3) developing their capacity to reflect upon professional conduct through the use of critique.

Many aspects of the skill of legal analysis and reasoning, an important element of professional training, have long been effectively taught through appellate case analysis. Other skills and values described in the Statement require more versatile and extensive instruction than can be accomplished solely through the analysis of appellate cases. The data from the law school studies tell us that techniques are available for teaching most of these skills and exposing students to an examination of the relevant values, beginning as early as the first year in law school. The techniques are various: live-client clinics, simulations, externships and "other." Effective teaching of skills and values analyzed in the Statement ordinarily involves these components:

1) Development of concepts and theories underlying the skills and values being taught;
2) Opportunity for students to perform lawyering tasks with appropriate feedback;
3) Reflective evaluation of the students' performance by a qualified assessor.

A simple illustration: the ability to organize and develop a thesis is an important step in the development of an effective writer. A legal writing instructor may teach students to "discuss general assertions before qualifications, important subjects before less significant ones, more widely held theories before idiosyncratic ones, and more conventional views before radical ones."[16] Giving the students an opportunity to translate these "skills concepts" into practice by repeatedly engaging in the act of writing adds a necessary developmental step; finally, critical analysis of the written product and the writer's approach to the task serves to deepen and improve the performance of the skill. Performance of skills followed by critical analysis reinforces concept development, and learning concepts improves performance and provides a principled basis for critical analysis.

Because skills education is three dimensional, having reference

---

16. This example, from GERTRUDE BLOCK, EFFECTIVE LEGAL WRITING, 218 (1992), is of a particular technical skill that may be taught in a legal writing class or included in other courses.

points in concept development, performance and critical analysis of performance, a great variety of teaching methods are employed, including lecture, assigned reading, discussion and Socratic dialogue, demonstration, simulation and role-playing, computer-assisted learning, planning exercises, problems, writing and research exercises, supervised clinical experience, peer review and other evaluative techniques.

The diverse methodologies described in the reports of 2425 professional skills offerings detailed in the Task Force survey can be grouped according to the characteristic of skills education which they chiefly promote. Some methodologies are principally employed to develop student thinking about concepts and legal principles, others promote student performance of lawyering tasks and the remainder primarily support the critique of student work. Because the processes of concept development, performance and critique are interrelated and all instructional methodologies have at least some capacity to promote all three processes, the groupings are somewhat artificial.

Methods principally used to develop concepts
1. Lecture
2. Assigned reading
3. Discussion and Socratic dialogue
4. Demonstration and modeling
5. Computer assisted learning
6. Alternative presentations[17]

Methods supporting student performance of lawyering tasks
1. Writing exercises
2. Research problems
3. Simulation and role-play
4. Oral presentations
5. Instructor posed problems
6. Clinical practice
7. Computer simulation
8. Performance examinations

Methods used in critique of student performance
1. Professor critique and evaluation
2. Critique and evaluation by third party experts
3. Peer review
4. Self evaluation
5. Computer feedback

---

17. These include observation of court house activity, guest speakers and interviews with litigators.

Although effective skills instruction using these methods has been elaborated with increasing sophistication in contemporary legal education,[18] only a minority of students is receiving this kind of instruction outside of courses in trial advocacy. The challenge is to make such instruction broadly available to students and attorneys during and after law school.

The Faculty Employed in Teaching Skills and Values

In order to meet the challenge of making skills instruction broadly available, law schools should assign primary responsibility for instruction in professional skills and values to permanent full-time faculty who can devote the time and expertise to teaching, and developing new methods of teaching skills to law students. In addition, law schools should continue to make appropriate use of skilled and experienced practicing lawyers and judges in professional skills and values instruction with guidance, structure, supervision and evaluation of these adjunct faculty by full-time teachers.

Commitment to teaching skills, experience, training, knowledge of the growing literature of clinical scholarship, an ability to contribute to that scholarship, and reflection and attention to educational theory are all required of an effective professional skills teacher. In addition, a willingness to be highly accessible to students, patience and sensitivity are required. As with any faculty, skills faculty benefit from experience and study. Law schools should identify, retain and reward faculty who possess the requisite attributes to teach skills and values and who are able to contribute to the advancement of knowledge about them.

The survey data collected by the Task Force does not distinguish between full-time skills faculty and traditional faculty who incorporate skills components into their teaching. One phenomenon has been the development of courses by traditional faculty which have substantial skills components, including, in a number of schools, small limited purpose clinics as well as simulated and other skills instruction. Some faculty teach both traditional and skills courses. The picture of two distinct faculty groups, skills teaching and traditional, is not as clear as is suggested by the data. For many who consider themselves traditional, rather than skills faculty, skills education has acquired increased significance despite their lack of training as or close cooperation with full-time skills faculty.

Part-time and non-permanent faculty add another important

---

18. In addition to the findings of the Task force survey, see '*Basement*', *supra* note 12, at 247-250.

ingredient to skills education. The presence of judges, practitioners and others willing to contribute to skills instruction on a part-time basis adds to law faculties' knowledge of practice and to the practitioner's understanding of legal education. The full-time skills instructor, however, is more likely to have time to devote to the design, organization and management of skills courses, to be available to students outside of class, and to have access to the resources of the law school, including other skills instructors. Supervision of part-time and non-permanent faculty can therefore be more effectively accomplished by someone in this position.

The following table details the distribution, by course subject matter, of faculty assigned to professional skills education as reported in the Task Force survey.

Types of Faculty Assigned to Professional Skills Education in 1989-90

NOTE: FTP (Full-Time Permanent), PT/PTNP (Part-Time/Part-Time Not Permanent), FTNP (Full-Time Not Permanent)

COURSE A: (First Year "Introduction to Lawyering")

FTP(56%)	PT/PTNP(28%)	FTNP(16%)	TOTAL
159	81	46	286

COURSE B: (First Year Research, Writing, or Drafting)

FTP(36%)	PT/PTNP(36%)	FTNP(28%)	TOTAL
638	642	485	1765

COURSE C: (Advanced Research, Writing or Drafting, e.g., business planning. Does not include supervised independent research, traditional seminars, or law review work)

FTP(52%)	PT/PTNP(26%)	FTNP(22%)	TOTAL
261	129	111	501

COURSE D: (Interviewing and/or Counseling)

FTP(74%)	PT/PTNP(11%)	FTNP(15%)	TOTAL
62	9	13	84

COURSE E: (Negotiation and/or Alternative Dispute Resolution)

FTP(67%)	PT/PTNP(20%)	FTNP(13%)	TOTAL
166	48	32	246

COURSE F: (Trial Practice/Trial Advocacy)

FTP(25%)	PT/PTNP(40%)	FTNP(35%)	TOTAL
372	603	528	1503

COURSE G: (Pretrial Litigation Practice)

FTP(36%)	PT/PTNP(24%)	FTNP(40%)	TOTAL
86	56	95	237

COURSE H: (Appellate Advocacy, Including Moot Court)

FTP(33%)	PT/PTNP(56%)	FTNP(11%)	TOTAL
342	575	119	1036

COURSE I: (Lawyering Courses Set in Specific Substantive Contexts With Non-Litigation Focus, e.g., Business Planning)

FTP(55%)	PT/PTNP(31%)	FTNP(14%)	TOTAL
224	128	55	407

COURSE J: (Combination of Two or More Topics Listed in D, E, F, G, H, or I, e.g., "Interviewing, Counseling and Negotiation" or "Trial and Appellate Practice" or "General Lawyering Skills")

FTP(47%)	PT/PTNP(41%)	FTNP(12%)	TOTAL
201	176	51	428

COURSE K: (Externships/Internships)

FTP(32%)	PT/PTNP(52%)	FTNP(16%)	TOTAL
509	843	261	1613

COURSE L: (Clinics)

FTP(65%)	PT/PTNP(13%)	FTNP(21%)	TOTAL
609	124	200	933

COURSE M: (Other)

FTP(65%)	PT/PTNP(22%)	FTNP(13%)	TOTAL
124	42	25	191

TOTALS:

FTP(3753)	PT/PTNP(3456)	FTNP(2021)	TOTAL
41%	37%	22%	100%

Our data show an uneven pattern in the use of full-time faculty (permanent and non-permanent) for professional skills instruction. Overall, 63 percent of the 9230 skills courses shown in our survey are taught by full-time faculty, 37 percent by part-time faculty. In three areas, however, trial practice, appellate advocacy, and externships, part-time faculty play on average a more significant instructional role. If we were to remove these three offerings from our sample, the percentage of skills courses taught by full-time faculty rises to nearly 72.

We can draw several inferences from these data. The use of full-time faculty, not only in the areas where traditionally law schools have taught skills, such as first year writing and research, but also in areas more sounding of practice, like negotiation, interviewing, counseling, and "introduction to lawyering," suggests a growing recognition that law schools should offer a broad range of skills instruction, under the direction of faculty with the time, the teaching experience, and the incentive to contribute to their students' intellectual and professional growth.

At the same time, the survey shows that in these latter practice areas, although full-time faculty now play the dominant teaching role, the absolute number of offerings remains quite small;[19] also, in some instances, other data suggest that student to faculty ratios may be higher than desirable.[20] In an effort to expand the availability of skills instruction without weakening student to faculty ratios, some schools have used approaches such as hiring more full-time faculty; encouraging faculty to integrate skills components into their traditional courses; using judges and practitioners in the classroom, closely monitored by full-time faculty; and creating externships supervised by faculty and accompanied by a classroom component.

The Allocation of Law School Resources for the Professional Development of Students

Over the course of the past 15 years, with even greater acceleration during the last four years from 1987-88 to 1991-92, law schools have expanded their investment in clinical legal education at a rate considerably in excess of inflation. In addition, the schools have significantly increased the number of faculty teaching professional skills courses as well as the number of students enrolled in skills instruction, including not only live client clinics, but also skills simulation courses and external placements or internships.[21]

Budget expansion. The Task Force compared the clinical (live

---

19. For example, our survey shows only 84 interviewing and/or counseling, 286 introduction to lawyering, and 246 negotiation and/or ADR offerings.

20. For example, interviewing and counseling classes average 18 students to one full-time faculty member; see text at page 251, note 29, *infra.*

21. No data of this type are available on students enrolled in other skills courses as defined in note 3, *supra.*

client only) budgets of law schools in academic years 1977-78 with those in 1987-88 and 1991-92 on the basis of the questionnaires submitted by schools to the American Bar Association each Fall. While the 1977 and 1987 data encompassed 156 law schools (only 164 law schools were accredited as of 1977 and eight submitted data that could not be utilized for either 1977 or 1987) and the 1991 data covered only 136 of 177 law schools,[22] the adjusted growth is nonetheless noteworthy:

Clinical Expenditures in Millions of Dollars

Source	1977-78	1987-88	1991-92	1977-78 in 1991-92 Dollars	Real Increase
From School's Own Resources	8.819	27.172	39.831	15.001	165.5%
From Overall Resources	16.472	31.716	58.228	28.019	107.8%

Unfortunately no similar data are available for other forms of skills education. However, given the increase in both faculty numbers and salaries reflected in the ABA questionnaire data,[23] there is every reason to believe that the costs of those programs have risen as well.

In reviewing these figures it is important to keep in mind that the increase in the costs of legal education in general has consistently outstripped the rise in clinical costs. Data on total law school costs are not available for 1991-92, but in the period from 1977-78 to 1987-88 the overall costs of legal education rose 173.9% while the rise in clinical education expenditures for that period was 92.5%.[24] Clinical costs in fact rose more slowly during that period than did any other segment of the law school budget.[25] As a result, clinical

---

22. Seventeen schools had not submitted clinical budget data as of April, 1992, including some schools with substantial live client programs, and 24 had no live client programs and, thus, no budget to report.

23. See discussion of "faculty expansion," *infra*.

24. John R. Kramer, *Who Will Pay the Piper or Leave the Check on the Table for the Other Guy*, 39 J. OF LEGAL ED 655, 661 (1989) [hereafter *Kramer*]. These numbers are calculated from the figures set forth in Table D in that article.

25. *Kramer, supra* note 24, at 661, Table D.

Law School Overall Budget

	1977-78	1987-88	Change
Instruction	$152,652,000	$ 389,379,000	155.08%
Library	$ 56,205,000	$ 150,471,000	167.72%
Supporting Personnel	$ 49,018,000	$ 167,186,000	241.07%
Research	$ 14,070,000	$ 27,616,000	96.28%
Financial Aid	$ 29,326,000	$ 86,956,000	196.52%
Potpourri	$ 39,082,000	$ 124,134,000	217.62%
Other	$ 11,254,000	$ 30,516,000	171.16%
Clinical Education	$ 16,472,000	$ 31,716,000	92.54%
TOTAL	$368,079,000	$1,007,974,000	173.85%

education actually dropped as a percentage of the law school budget from 4.5% to 3.1% during this period.[26]

The increased investment derives primarily from direct law school revenues (tuition and state subvention), but also from a variety of sources, whose underwriting of clinics is relatively recent. This encompasses such Federal sources as Title IX of the Higher Education Act (slightly over $5 million in 1991-92, expected to grow to $8 million in 1992-93) and the Legal Services Corporation Act (almost $2 million), private funding from the bar through IOLTA grants ($1.3 million), the award of attorneys' fees in fee-shifting cases ($1.6 million), and foundation and other grants ($6.8 million in all).

The following is an approximate breakdown of the sources of clinical funding (the individual categories do not add up to the total expenditures because of irregularities in the underlying data):

	Millions of dollars	Percent
All expenditures	58.228	
Law School/University budget	39.831	68.4
Title IX	5.011	8.6
Legal services corporation	1.981	3.4
IOLTA	1.336	2.3
Other grants	4.657	8.0
Attorneys' fees	1.586	2.7
Alumni donations	.486	.8
Other non-law school agencies	2.189	3.8

Sixty-five of the schools reported receiving Title IX funding in 1991-92; 28, Legal Services grants; 35, IOLTA funds; and 34, attorneys' fees. The average school clinical budget was $428,000; the median, $280,000.

Again, no data are available as to the source of expenditures in other forms of skills education.

Faculty expansion. The determinative factor in the cost of effectively taught (as described *infra*) live client clinics, externships and simulation courses is the size of the faculty because of the low student-faculty ratios required to provide meaningful skills education. The Task Force data reveal that live client clinics have an average ratio of eight students to one full time faculty member (8:1),[27] externships

---

26. *Kramer, supra* note 24, at 661, Table D.
27. The ratios discussed here, unlike those set forth above relating to full-time faculty, include part-time faculty and faculty who are full time but not permanent.

have a mean ratio of four students to one full time teacher (4:1),[28] interviewing and counseling classes average eighteen to one (18:1),[29] trial practice courses have a mean of sixteen to one (16:1),[30] the appellate advocacy mean is fourteen to one (14:1),[31] and combined skills offerings average eighteen to one (18:1).[32] In response to the annual questionnaire from the American Bar Association, 155 schools reported that the number of full-time professional skills faculty[33] increased dramatically in 1991-92 over 1990-91, with traditional tenure track teachers expanding from 233 to 255 or 9% (at an average salary of $69,342), special separate tenure track faculty climbing from 137 to 186 or 36% (with an average salary in 1991-92 of $62,331), and those on short-term contracts growing from 119 to 156 or 31% (at an average salary of $48,592). It is not clear how much of this increase reflects an expansion in the number of full-time faculty as opposed to a change in the classification of existing faculty as a result of ABA Standard 405(e).

In any event, the gross salary costs of these 597 skills teachers in 1991-92 (as opposed to 489 in 1990-91 or a reported increase of 22 percent over the course of one year) amounted to $37.3 million. These 597 skills instructors represent nearly 11 percent of the 5,555 full-time faculty in all law schools and, therefore, may be as much as 15 percent of those teaching in the 155 schools which supplied data.

Student enrollment expansion. In 1991-92, 155 law schools reported the number of their students enrolled in skills instruction courses including live client clinics, externships and simulated skills classes. Seventy-two thousand and eighty-three (72,083) students in these 155 schools (nearly all of them presumably enrolled as J.D.

---

28. It is not known what proportion of faculty workload goes into this externship supervision. If little teaching credit is given for faculty involvement in externship programs, then the ratio revealed by these data imply an intensity of supervision which does not exist.

29. It is not clear whether all courses listed in this category meet the profile of theory, performance and critique espoused here. To the extent that some element of this process is omitted, it is likely that the course will be less faculty intensive. Therefore, it is likely that this mean ratio of students to teacher is higher than would occur if all aspects to the instruction model set forth here were implemented.

30. See note 29, *supra.*

31. See note 29, *supra.*

32. See note 29, *supra.*

33. The questionnaire instructions provide:

A professional skills program is that portion of a law school's curriculum in which student performance in lawyering roles is paramount. Teaching 'professional skills' involves teaching and evaluating law student performance on live cases or problems, or in simulation of the lawyer's role, for mastering of basic lawyering skills, and the better understanding of professional responsibility, substantive and procedural law and the theory of legal practice.

students in their second and third year full-time or second through fourth year part-time) were enrolled in:

Course Type	Number	Percentage
School-operated live client clinics	9,343	13.0
Skills simulation courses	52,045	72.2
Placements/externships	10,695	14.8

These numbers understate the total number of students in such courses because many of the non-reporting schools are known to have skills programs of a substantial size, even if accurate student body counts are not available.

The total number of student course enrollments in skills training in these 155 reporting schools constitute approximately 10 percent of all such enrollments involving second and third year full-time and second through fourth year part-time students in those same schools (60,351 and 13,503 students, respectively), assuming that full-time students take ten courses a year and part-timers take seven. There appears to be nearly one skills training course available per student (72,083 for 73,854 students), although that overlooks the fact that students frequently take more than one offering in the three categories. Indeed, excluding legal research and moot court, the majority of students enrolled in one to two skills training courses according to the Task Force's survey.

Live client clinics are usually restricted to full-time third year students, of whom there were a total of 29,428 in those same 155 schools in 1990-91. Accordingly, 31.7 percent of all graduating students in 1992 could well have participated in one live client clinic prior to graduation, assuming that multiple enrollment by any student in such scarce and costly courses is universally disallowed.[34]

On the basis of the Task Force survey, which placed mean live client clinical credits at 4.1, mean externship credits at 3.5, and mean simulation course credits at 2.5, the slightly over 200,000 credit hours earned in skills training courses constituted nearly 11 percent of the total credit hours earned by those students this year, assuming that full-time students average 27 credit hours in their second and third years, while part-time students take an average of 20 credit hours.

---

34. The Task Force data show enrollment of 20% of students in live client clinics; the AALS Clinical section study, *Basement, supra* note 12, at 280-81, shows that live client, in-house clinics in 1987 had the ability to accommodate on average 30 percent of their student bodies.

These data indicate that skills training constitutes at least 10 percent of all upper-class legal education.

Eighty percent of the surveyed 155 law schools had live client clinics (124), which correlates with both the Task Force survey (75 percent) and the data published by Marjorie McDiarmid[35] (80 percent as well), while 96.1 percent offered simulated skills training (149), and 83.9 percent conducted externships (130). The median number of live client clinic slots among the 124 schools was 60; of places in simulated skills training classes offered by 149 law schools, 286; and of externship placements in the 130 law schools which undertook them, 57.

The increase in student participation in skills training in recent years appears to have been significant. However, there has been a perceptible shift in the distribution of student enrollments among school-operated live-client clinics, skills simulation and externships. The following table shows the actual increases over a four year period in the number of students enrolled in each type of course (the data from 35 schools for which there was no comparable data for 1986-87 has been excluded):

Type of Course	1986-87	1990-91	% Increase
School-operated live-client clinics	7,547	8,701	15.3
Skills Simulation	36,919	47,870	29.7
Placements/externships	7,754	10,261	32.3
All Skills	52,220	66,833	28.0

The greatest percentage increase occurred in externships, despite accreditation standards which some thought would limit their growth. But 74.9 percent of the entire increase from 52,220 to 66,833 student slots was focussed on simulated skills training, with only 7.9 percent on live client clinics and 17.1 percent on externships.

Of the 143 schools surveyed in both 1986-87 and 1990-91, the change in numbers of students enrolled in these various courses over this period are reflected in the following table of increases and decreases:

---

35. *Basement, supra* note 12, at 241-42.

1986-87 to 1990-91

Type of Course	# Up	% Up	# Down	% Down	# No Change	% No Change
All Skills	109	76.2	34	23.8	--	--
Live Client Clinic	92	64.3	30	21.0	21	14.7
Simulated Skills	100	69.9	42	29.4	1	.7
Placements Externships	81	56.6	49	34.3	13	9.1

The data collected for 1977-78 and especially 1987-88 (1986-87 for enrollments), when compared with the data available for 1991-92 (1990-91 for enrollments), suggest that skills training is alive and well and in an expansionary mode in most law schools, with more faculty and students involved and more budget dollars invested, and the rate of growth even more pronounced in the most recent years.

Whether these increases will continue in the face of likely budgetary stringency is uncertain. Despite its small percentage of law school budgets (3.1% in 1987-88) live client clinics are seen as expensive. Costs of other forms of skills instruction are less well documented, but it is clear that the method advocated here of theory instruction, performance and critique is more costly than placing large numbers of students in a large class with a single instructor. There will likely be some pressure within law schools to diminish the rate of growth of these forms of education.[36] It would be a mistake to do so. It is clear that skills can be taught and that the profession increasingly expects them to be taught in law schools. The gains of recent years must be maintained and continued.

The Skills and Values Content of Law School Courses

Grouped according to the specific skills and values noted in Part II of this report are samples, taken from their narrative submissions,

---

36. A goal of offering enrollment in a live client in-house clinic to every student before he or she graduates may not be feasible from a budgetary perspective for some time. If there are 38,000 graduates a year, fewer then 9,500 of whom now are enrolled in live client clinics and 28,500 are not, the cost of expanding live client clinics to cover the additional 28,500 could well exceed $170.4 million (2591 faculty needed at a ratio of 11 to 1 at an average salary of $65,800 or midway between the average of a traditional tenure track clinician and a separate tenure track clinician). This would represent somewhere between 15-20% of the 1987-88 law school budget. While we can expect that overall budget increases would reduce this share to something approaching 10-15%, it is unlikely that law schools are going to be able to quickly increase their commitment (3.1% in 1987-88) to this form of skills teaching. Nevertheless, the Task Force encourages schools to recognize the value of live-client clinical experiences and to explore ways to expand the availability of courses that offer such experiences.

of how teachers describe their goals with respect to their skills instruction. The parenthetical number included in each topic heading indicates the number of courses in which teaching the competence was specifically identified as a goal of the course as reported in the Task Force's law school study.

1. Problem solving or decision making (88 courses)
   - case analysis and planning
   - identifying client objectives
   - strategic planning: students focus on strategic choices made for practical, ethical and purely legal reasons in representation of clients
   - students hopefully develop an appreciation for the existing and potential choices that exist in terms of approaching the resolution of a dispute
   - developing a sense of the likely future consequences of present actions
   - viewing problems and transactions from multiple angles and learning to integrate all relevant legal and related principles-evaluating alternatives and trade-offs
   - study the theories and various approaches to conflict resolution including comparisons among and between adjudication, arbitration, mediation, med-arb, mini-trials, and community dispute centers
2. Legal analysis and reasoning (291 courses)
   - introduce students to the nature of legal doctrine and its operation in our legal culture
   - legal reasoning skills, including problem identification, analysis and synthesis
   - analyzing statutory and case law and applying that law to a given fact pattern to determine the legal issues raised and to perform a complete written legal analysis.
   - an understanding of the sources of law
   - statutory interpretation
3. Legal research (397 courses)
   - students learn to analyze real life fact patterns and select the most successful research tools available to answer the problem in the shortest amount of time. Tools would include advance computer research techniques, use of sophisticated administrative law materials, including Federal Register and the Code of Federal Regulations and the Commercial Index to those sets; for one example, students learn the best and most effective tools to research other subject areas

including research tools in environmental law, international law, labor law, criminal law and procedures, etc.

- students learn the legal research process; that is, they learn how to analyze legal problems so as to identify legal issues, design research strategies necessary to explore those issues and find the authority needed to develop well-documented analyses of the issues and to formulate well documented positions on how the issues can be resolved.
- specifically, the students learn how to identify and find the primary and secondary authority applicable to a variety of particular research problems. They learn the methods for finding the most pertinent and up-to-date case law, constitutional and statutory law and administrative law as well as law review articles, encyclopedia entries, restatements, looseleafs and treatises. The students also learn correct citation form.

4. Factual investigation (63 courses)
   - the investigation of facts related to a client's case.
   - the course attempts to teach the students how to plan factual investigations. Specifically, the course attempts to teach students to develop factual theories and to identify systematically the potential witnesses, exhibits and other sources of information which would be likely to support or undermine those factual theories. It also attempts to teach the students to set priorities in obtaining factual information.
   - students develop proficiency in interviewing witnesses, drafting interrogatories and other discovery requests, and taking depositions

5. Communication (1938 courses)
   - this course focuses on developing a method, or way, of drafting that is transferrable from topic to topic. Students are exposed to a variety of drafting problems such as tone/voice and audience, ambiguity and vagueness, structure and layout, plain language drafting. The need to begin drafting by thinking before even touching a paper is emphasized. Some attention is also paid to problems of fact gathering as a source of information for drafting and to negotiations.
   - improvement in oral advocacy skills
   - listening and observing, creating conditions for effective communication, responding and reacting skillfully to others, using acceptable language and

grammar, organizing information, speaking effectively, identifying and evaluating relevant facts, identifying and evaluating legal issues, analyzing and selecting appropriate options, designing and implementing a plan of action, responding to constructive criticism, reviewing and editing a draft work product, identifying and responding to audience, identifying appropriate focus and tone of legal writing.
- write clearly reasoned arguments with clear indicators of logical connection.

6. Counseling (280 courses)
- questioning techniques for fact-gathering and rapport— development at the initial interview; counseling techniques to assist the client in decisions concerning the legal matter
- students learn the importance of a proper greeting, of allowing the clients freedom to explain the problem as seen by the client, assuring the client of attention and concern with open-ended questions. Students likewise learn the importance of involving the client in problem solving with a counseling technique which utilizes the skills and information base of the client for those things in which the client excels.

7. Negotiation (400 courses)
- students will develop, it is hoped, competence in lawyering skills, evaluating cases, determining negotiation tactics and strategies, communicating with clients and adversaries, and resolving ethical problems encountered in the negotiation process; expose students to the process of negotiation as a pervasive lawyering activity; to increase the awareness of the technical, interdisciplinary, and ethical dimensions of the process; to introduce the concept of the lawyer's role as problem-solver; to enable students to experiment with and consider thoughtfully the various forms and techniques of negotiation and dispute resolution; and to provide students an opportunity to assess their own capabilities within those contexts.

8. Litigation and ADR procedures (444 courses)
- how to do trial practice, direct examination, cross examination, introducing and handling evidence, voir dire, opening and closing statements, trial strategy. Interview witnesses and prepare witnesses.
- pretrial litigation: Assess and evaluate all aspects of pretrial stages commencing with initial client contact.

Formulate litigation strategy and tactics at pretrial stage. Formulate creative solution to various litigation problems. Draft pleading, discovery requests and responses, motion papers, and other litigation documents. Take and defend depositions.

- Identify, assess and take steps to eliminate evidently problems at pretrial level. Specific skills. organization and management of legal work.
- how to work within the "formal" and "informal" criminal justice system.

9. Organization and management of legal work (48 courses)

- organization/management skills, timekeeping/billing, substantive systems, administrative systems, planning, marketing, applied ethics (e.g.-escrow funds, conflicts, fees), drafting, computers, and personnel administration.
- ability to file documents and instruct others on how to do so; ability to organize, maintain and rearrange an office file system; ability to maintain a tickle calendar system for insurance purposes and malpractice avoidance; enhance skills in obtaining and retaining clients; ability to act "professionally" with lawyers, judges and clients.
- basic components of law firm management are reviewed, including firm organization records handling; financial control; quality control, client relations, and charging strategies. Critical procedural routines such as client screening, document preparation, time keeping and accounting are also examined with special emphasis on enhancement through the use of microcomputer and digital communication technologies.

10. Recognizing and Resolving Ethical Dilemmas (135 courses)[37]

- ethical issues in drafting
- understanding of ethical issues
- ethical considerations in trial work
- an ability to recognize and rehearse the appropriate resolution of multiple ethical issues of law practice.
- an ability to communicate more effectively with a client, recognizing the psychological and economic

---

37. The Survey instrument did not seek information explicitly about values issues. Therefore, this number should be viewed as a gross understatement of the courses in which ethics education figures.

conflicts that lead to ineffective counseling, manipulation, violation of client autonomy, or failure to limit the client to legally permissible goals or means to achieve legitimate goals.

- an ability to recognize how the ethics of advocacy and the rhetoric of zealous representation can bind a lawyer in the gathering of information, in the isolation of alternative courses of behavior, or in recognizing the short term and long term consequences of the lawyer's actions on behalf of a client.

11. Values (57 courses)[38]

- an ability to recognize the economic, psychological and institutional pressures that make professional behavior difficult.
- an ability to recognize the various ways in which the organized bar had made our society dependent on the law and lawyers, and the various institutional and individual ways in which lawyers can make effective and affordable legal services available in our society.
- a recognition that with ineffective bar screening and discipline individual self-regulation is an essential element of professional growth.

Enhancing Skills and Values Instruction

The achievement of the last 25 years in creating new methods to teach lawyering skills and professional values reflect great determination and creativity. The data generated by the Task Force's 1991 survey give many reasons for encouragement, and we should take special care to engender further experimentation.

The Task Force was mindful of the risks inherent in externally imposed requirements that may stifle experimentation. Our recommendations for enhancing skills and values instruction therefore emphasize law school self-study and initiative. The Task Force recommends that each law school undertake a study to determine which of the skills and values identified in the Statement are presently being taught in its curriculum. It further recommends that each faculty develop a coherent agenda of skills instruction, not limited to the development of research, writing and litigation skills. As noted above, the data from the law school study show that a majority of students has completed courses in legal writing, research and trial advocacy, but only a minority has gone beyond these courses and,

---

38. Because the Survey instrument did not seek information on this issue, no data as to the number of courses incorporating values training are available. See note 33 *supra*.

of that minority, only a small number has taken more than one additional skills training offering that employs the methodologies of skills instruction.

After review of the Statement of Fundamental Lawyering Skills and Professional Values and other relevant literature, each faculty should determine how its school can best improve the process of helping students acquire the skills and values that are important in the practice of law, keeping in mind not only the resources presently available at the school, but the characteristics of effective skills instruction described above. After this determination is made, law schools should describe the skills and values content of their courses and make the information available to students as an aid in course selection and so that students will understand which skills and values need further development and mastery before they assume primary responsibility for the representation of clients. In addition, law schools should work with the organized bar to assure that the development of lawyering skills continues beyond law school and that such education also incorporates the characteristics described.

C. The Accreditation Process and Instruction in Skills and Values

The progressive steps by which law schools came to provide the vast majority of those entering the profession with the unifying experience of a common three-year academic program has been previously sketched. We have also traced the role played by the ABA in the creation of the Association of American Law Schools and the early efforts of the two organizations to enhance the quality of legal education.[39] In that progression, the accreditation process, initiated by the ABA during the 1920s, was central to placing the law schools into the position they occupy today in relation to the profession.

The ABA commenced its role as an accrediting body of legal education in 1923 responding largely to the perceptions that the profession was rapidly increasing in size, that the practice of law was growing in complexity, and that many law schools were not preparing their students effectively for the profession. While it has been suggested that social class and ethnic issues were involved, the major purpose underlying the ABA's decision to establish an accreditation process was improvement of the level of education of lawyers.

The early accreditation standards were not particularly

---

39. See Chapter 3, *supra*.

demanding and the review of the law schools was informal. However, they helped assure that the educational program, faculty, facilities and students met certain minimum standards, as well as the school's own specific goals. The process also encouraged the adoption in most states of policies generally requiring those taking the local bar examination to be graduates of an ABA-accredited law school. This not only assured the basic quality of beginning lawyers, but strengthened the ABA-approved schools in relation to their unaccredited colleagues. The latter schools then tended, as the requirements became more universal, to seek accreditation.

The result over the years was that substantial improvements were made in many schools, based upon the accreditation requirements. Based upon four decades of experience, the ABA House of Delegates in 1961 authorized the Council of the Section of Legal Education and Admissions to the Bar to develop new Accreditation Standards. The ensuing process consumed more than a decade of development, drafting, commentary and revision before the new Standards were adopted in February 1973.

The Standards as approved in 1973 (at a time of great ferment in society and change in the legal profession) remain today the foundation of the ABA's accreditation process. In the meantime, various additions and amendments have been made and numerous formal interpretations developed. It is widely acknowledged that a number of the changes in legal education over the past several decades have been in substantial part generated by this development of the Standards, the various additions and amendments, and by their application in the approval of law schools.

Standard 301(a) provides the broad basic Standard for educational programs:

> A law school shall maintain an educational program that is designed to qualify its graduates for admission to the bar.

This focus upon the qualification of graduates to become lawyers is hardly a set requirement, but rather a generalization that lays down the philosophical basis and educational emphasis for the Standards that follow. The standard was adopted shortly after the Council of the ABA Section of Legal Education and Admissions to the Bar and the Board of Managers of the National Conference of Bar Examiners in July 1971 had expressly acknowledged that bar admissions authorities "should determine that the content of the applicant's education is such that, upon admission he [or she] will be able to adequately serve the public," underscoring the need for a suitable level of skills and values education prior to admission. Consistent with the thesis of this report, we would favor a clarifying amendment of Standard 301(a) adding:

> . . . . and to prepare them to participate effectively in the legal profession.

Subsection (b) of Standard 301 recognizes the breadth of the law and the differentiation within the legal profession, declaring:

> A law school may offer an educational program designed to emphasize some aspects of the law or the legal profession and give less attention to others.

Nevertheless, the Standard tacitly assumes the prevalence of broad educational programs and, consonant with principles of full disclosure, adds:

> If a school offers such a program, that program and its objectives shall be clearly stated in its publications, where appropriate.

Subsection (c) of Standard 301 rounds out the general prescription for program design with the admonition that:

> The educational program of the school shall be designed to prepare the students to deal with recognized problems of the present and anticipated problems of the future.

This Standard forms the generalized basis for requiring programs that at least educate law students for the type of practice to which they plan to go. While Standards 302 and 303, which follow, have tended to this time to be the litmus tests of a valid educational program, subsections (a) and (c) of Standard 301 do provide in the changed legal environment of today a useful touchstone for evaluating law school programs.

While the Standards since the 1970s have provided general support for the development in law schools of lawyering skills and professional values, they have laid down a specific requirement only with respect to the teaching of professional values, first, as a general requirement of "instruction in the duties and responsibilities of the legal profession," but in August 1974, in the wake of Watergate, with the following specification in Standard 302(a)(iv):

> Such required instruction need not be limited to any pedagogical method as long as the history, goals, structure and responsibilities of the legal profession and its members, including the ABA Code of Professional Responsibility are all covered. Each law school is encouraged to involve members of the bench and bar in such instruction.

Standard 302(a) sets the major criteria by which law school

programs are judged.[40] As originally adopted in 1973, Standard 302 set three specific programmatic objectives for all students:

(1) instruction in subjects in the core curriculum;

(2) training in professional skills; and

(3) instruction in the legal profession.

In 1981 the Standard was amended, largely as a result of the reports of the Task Force on Lawyer Competency in 1979[41] and the earlier Devitt committee.

The present Standard 302 dating from 1981, now requires instruction for *all* students of three kinds: in subjects in the core curriculum; in the legal profession (including the ABA Model Rules of Professional Conduct); and "at least one rigorous writing experience," but the Standard excludes professional skills instruction as a requirement for *all* students and only prescribes that schools "offer instruction in professional skills" (302(a)(iii)). In addition, the examples of professional skills instruction, formerly enumerated in Standard 302(a), were dropped and placed in an Interpretation of the Standard in a more detailed manner.[42]

---

40. Standard 302:

(a) The law school shall:

   (i)   offer to all students instruction in those subjects generally regarded as the core of the law school curriculum;

   (ii) offer to all students at least one rigorous writing experience;

   (iii) offer instruction in professional skills;

   (iv) require of all candidates for the first professional degree, instruction in the duties and responsibilities of the legal profession. Such required instruction need not be limited to any pedagogical method as long as the history, goals, structure and responsibilities of the legal profession and its members, including the ABA Model Rules of Professional Conduct [MRPC substituted for CPR in earlier Standard] are all covered. Each law school is encouraged to involve members of the bench and bar in such instruction.

41. Commonly referred to as the Cramton Report, the report was entitled "Lawyer Competency: The Role of the Law Schools" (1979).

42. Interpretation 3 of 302(a)(iii) provides: Such instruction need not be limited to any specific skill or list of skills. Each law school is encouraged to be creative in developing programs of instruction in skills related to the various responsibilities which lawyers are called upon to meet, utilizing the strengths and resources available to the law school.

Thoughtful professional studies have urged that trial and appellate advocacy, alternative methods of dispute resolution, counseling, interviewing, negotiating, and drafting be included in such programs. (August, 1981; June, 1988)

There are today the following three further Interpretations of Section 302(a)(iii):

Interpretation 1 of 302(a)(iii): this section requires training in professional skills. To which of the many professional skills the curriculum will give special attention is left to the individual schools. (August, 1975; June, 1990)

Interpretation 2 of 302(a)(iii): A law school's failure to offer adequate training in professional skills, whether through clinics or otherwise, violates Standard 302(a)(iii).

Adding to the difficulties in construing the present Standards and Interpretations is the use in Standard 302(a)(i) of the phrase "subjects generally regarded as the core of the law school curriculum," which seems to suggest something set at a point in time representing some immutable collection of courses and not reflecting changes in legal education. It has been common among law school faculties to believe that there are two essentials: substantive coverage and intellectual problem-solving which are defined, for want of a better word, as "core." Perhaps for this reason, the Standard has not been a major force in developing change in the law schools. Accreditation requirements with respect to both core curriculum and skills instruction have tended to be seen as an endorsement of the status quo and to have had little impact upon curriculum reform.[43]

The requirement of Standard 302(a)(ii), first imposed in 1981, of "at least one rigorous writing experience" for all students, has been frequently an issue in accreditation. Deficiencies have been found and questions have been raised at a number of schools regarding the allocation of resources, student time and faculty effort in this area. The specific requirement and accreditation process have undoubtedly been helpful in bringing greater focus in the law schools on the development of writing skills, but the continuing complaints heard by the Task Force concerning law graduates' writing skills suggest that further concerted effort is required to teach writing at a better level than is now generally done both in the law schools and in bridge-the-gap programs after law school.

The requirement of Standard 302(a)(iv) for a fairly detailed form of instruction in the legal profession and professional ethics, does seem to have played an important part in the development of this educational field in the law schools. The recent study of the American Bar Foundation,[44] following up on the Zemans-Rosenblum study of 1979[45] which was made before the requirement was detailed in

---

(May, 1980)

Interpretation 4 of 302(a)(iii): There is no ABA ruling that a student requesting enrollment in an advocacy course must be admitted to that course. The Standard in question states merely that the law school shall offer training in professional skills. (February, 1990)

43. Changes in the "core curriculum" have occurred, in some cases, substantial, as well as in skills instruction. The internal content of many individual courses and materials reflect changes in emphasis, incorporating social issues such as race and poverty (*see* F.L. Ansley, *Race and the Core Curriculum in Legal Education*, 79 CALIF. L. REV. 1511-1597 (1991)), less common law and more statutory and administrative law and regulations, as well as changes in the methods of teaching first-year and other fundamental courses.

44. "Learning Lawyering: Where Do Lawyers Acquire Practice Skills?", Appendix B.

45. *See* ZEMANS AND ROSENBLUM, THE MAKING OF A PUBLIC PROFESSION (1981).

the Standard, indicates today a much greater sensitivity to these issues and much greater evaluation of their importance on the part of the bar. This subject matter is given to philosophical and scholarly analysis and fits traditional course criteria. New courses and casebooks have been developed and the material to a significant extent has been integrated into the educational program.[46]

The provision of Standard 302(a)(iii) that "The law school shall offer instruction in professional skills" is the one that most directly impacts on the skills portion of the work of this Task Force. The 1981 revision of the Standard substituted the word "instruction" for the rather craft-oriented word "training" in the prior Standard. This change reflected the growing appreciation of the intellectual quality of effective skills education and was in keeping with the more recent scholarly appraisals of professional skills teaching and newly developed methods for its teaching.

In lieu of the listing of some skills as had been done in the original 1973 Standard, the elaboration on skills instruction was placed in the new Interpretation 3 of 302(a)(iii), as we have noted, and adopted at the same time as the new Standard. This Interpretation has two components: the first encourages schools to be creative in developing programs of skills instruction related to the various responsibilities lawyers are called upon to meet, considering the strengths and available resources of the individual law school. The second component makes reference to the professional studies which had preceded the adoption of the new Standard and Interpretation,[47] and urges the inclusion in educational programs of skills instruction in "trial and appellate advocacy," "alternative methods of dispute resolution," "counseling," "interviewing," "negotiating" and "drafting."

It is unclear just what part the existing Standard and Interpretations have played in the development and expansion of programs of skills instruction. Beginning in 1968 funding from CLEPR and from federal and state governments, and more recently from Interest on Lawyers' Trust Accounts ("IOLTA") sources, together with greater student interest in these programs, have contributed to a general recognition by law schools that they do need to introduce their students to some of the fundamental lawyering skills. Amplifying the effect of other factors has been the development of larger numbers of professional skills faculty members, their organization in both the AALS and the ABA, and the closely knit nature of their common commitments, helping to create a growing sense that skills

---

46. See *Teaching Legal Ethics: A Symposium*, 41 JOUR. LEGAL ED. (No. 1 1991).

47. The Task Force's Report, together with the Statement of Skills and Values, now make a substantial new contribution to the professional studies previously existing.

instruction is indeed central to essential legal education.

The status of professional skills faculty has improved under the requirements of Standard 405(e);[48] the number of full-time professional skills faculty has continued to increase; and schools have added to the resources expended upon skills instruction. But progress has not been uniform, and at some institutions, it has come slowly and without the commitment that is necessary to develop and maintain skills instruction of a quality commensurate with the school's overall educational aspirations. In these cases, the lack of a more substantial expansion of lawyering skills education may be due at least in part to the schools' failure to value the importance of these programs to the training of lawyers to become competent professionals.

If professional competence is the goal, the fact is troubling that so many young lawyers are seen as lacking the required skills and values at the time the lawyer assumes full responsibility for handling a client's legal affairs. Much remains to be done to improve the preparation of new lawyers for practice, both in law school and after law school, in bridge-the-gap and other skills-oriented CLE programs.

We believe that the Task Force's Statement of Skills and Values will permit each law school faculty to evaluate its present curriculum and facilitate its review of the actual skills education components and opportunities, as well as the extent of transmission of professional values. In doing this, we suggest that the faculty ask as to each course, what skills and what values are being taught along with the coverage of a substantive field.

While the emphasis in basic first-year courses may be on the skills of "problem solving" and "legal analysis and reasoning," instruction should not be limited to those two skills. In addition, virtually every school offers a first-year course that focuses in differing levels on the skill of "legal research" and the written aspects of "communication." In a similar vein, we suggest that faculty for all advanced courses in a school's program should at least consider the skills content that might be effectively included in such courses and the professional values implicated.

---

48. Standard 405(e) provides:

The law school should afford to full-time faculty members whose primary responsibilities are in its professional skills program a form of security of position reasonably similar to tenure and perquisites reasonably similar to those provided other full-time faculty members by Standards 401, 402(b), 403 and 405. The law school should require these faculty members to meet standards and obligations reasonably similar to those required of full-time faculty members by Standards 401, 402(b), 403 and 405.

We look upon the proposed national institute for the practice of law as a potential major resource for furthering effective skills education in law schools. Model programs, courses and methods of instruction could suggest ideas and lead the way, reducing planning and organizational time for those schools choosing to adopt them.

We emphasize that the Statement of Skills and Values is not a blueprint, but a document which can serve as a basis for discussion and further development. Any direct, compelled use of the Statement in the accreditation process would be antithetical to its purposes and goals.

We do believe the Statement should be an essential reference in the accreditation process. Specifically , we recommend that an Interpretation to Standard 201(a),[49] on the self-study process, require that law schools evaluate their programs in the light of Standard 301(a) and (c). We recommend that the Interpretation for a school's self-study refer to the Statement of Skills and Values and other scholarly evaluations of the roles and qualifications of lawyers as material which should be reviewed and used by the school in evaluating its curriculum.

We also recommend an Interpretation of Standard 302(a)(iii) which would recognize the special needs for students who expect to go into a relatively unsupervised practice to have opportunities for education in the skills needed in such a practice setting. Competence in the use of these skills may not be assured in law school but an introduction to them should be available.

As noted earlier, Standard 302(a) does need to be clarified in the light of the Statement of Skills and Values and developments delineated in this Task Force Report, as well as the other literature that has been authored since the Standards were adopted in 1973 and amended in 1981. The interaction between core subjects, treated in 302(a)(i), and professional skills, treated in 302(a)(iii), should be revisited and clarified.

Teaching certain of the skills enumerated in the Statement of Fundamental Lawyering Skills and Professional Values, such as problem solving, legal analysis and reasoning, legal research, and legal writing, has long been a part of the required education for all law students. Today's law schools tend to offer instruction in most of the other skills elucidated in the Statement, either in clinical programs

---

49. Standard 201(a) provides:

Through development and periodic reevaluation of a written self-study, the law school shall articulate the objectives of the school's educational program consistent with the Standards.

and discrete courses, or integrated into the teaching of traditional subjects. Since law schools have demonstrated their capacity to teach effectively skills and values previously considered learnable only through post-graduation experience in practice, law schools should strive to develop or expand instruction in all components of the Statement of Fundamental Lawyering Skills and Professional Values.

D. Employment Experience as a Complement to Law School

Part-Time Employment

The employment of students on a part-time basis during the academic year has long been a matter of concern for law faculties and national legal education organizations. It is believed that excessive time spent in outside employment detracts from the educational experience, that students often give priority to work obligations, and that employers use students as cheap labor on assignments that usually do not complement or enhance their studies.

All of this may be true in many, perhaps most, situations. But it is also a fact that law schools generally have been unable or unwilling to deal with this problem. Students with bills to pay will seek a source of income; those with placement concerns will view a clerkship as a "foot in the door" and an opportunity to better define career goals; those who are bored with second- and third-year courses will find employment a welcome break from the classroom and a chance to view law practice in the "real" world. So, schools have tended to focus simply on enforcing the ABA's twenty-hour employment limitation on full-time students—an effort which, at many schools, has not been particularly successful.

Zillman and Gregory (*The New Apprentices: An Empirical Study of Student Employment and Legal Education*, 12 J. Contemp. L. 203 (1987)) reported on a survey at the University of Utah College of Law and concluded that

> law schools and law firms are partners in the business of legal education and training for the bar whether they like it or not. Rather than deplore or ignore the partnership, professors and practitioners should assess how it might be used to produce better law students and better lawyers.

The authors then suggest four initial steps toward that goal:

> First, both faculty and practitioners need to address the strengths and weaknesses of law school and clerkships. Both provide instruc-

tion and practice in legal research, writing, and analysis. However, these abilities comprise only a part of the skills needed to practice law. Both training experiences are deficient in important areas, such as drafting documents, gathering facts, counseling, interviewing, and negotiating.

Second, law schools would profit from a review of their curricula and the teaching competencies of members of the faculty. It might prove beneficial to consult with practitioners to encourage them to participate in training experiences. Members of the bar could journey into academia and provide students with real-life drafting problems and feedback about the quality of the student work. Professionals from other areas of expertise could be recruited to teach classes in negotiating, interviewing or counseling within the law school. This would broaden the skills which law students currently must develop on a trial-and-error basis as young attorneys.

Third, faculty members could become more supportive of and involved in clerkships. Most other professions require a practical or internship experience before an individual meets graduation and/or licensure requirements. Clinical programs are initial steps in this direction. However, if law school faculty begin to offer guidelines and structure for clerkships, the clerkships could better advance educational goals. Law students would then be better able to make choices as to what skills they want to develop and what types of law they want to learn. Faculty members may be able to assist the firms in increasing the efficiency of the clerking process. Clerks are more likely to get greater quality control of the clerking experience as a result.

Fourth, practicing lawyers can also improve the quality of clerkships. Self-interest should motivate some efforts since figures show that every other clerk will end up as an associate at the firm. Even without this direct incentive, firms should appreciate that they provide one of the major experiences in acculturation to the bar for all law students. Clerkship experiences play a significant role in shaping law students' attitudes towards the practice of law.

Employment experiences, of course, can only constitute a small part of a student's education in the totality of skills and values necessary to practice law. Some commentators agree with the conclusion of Zillman and Gregory that law school resources should be directed toward enhancing the educational potential of employment experiences. It has been suggested that schools consider scheduling the upperclass curriculum with large blocks of time available for clerking, rather than producing a schedule designed to prevent students from getting away from the law school for long.[50] Although

---

50. Susan D. Kovac, *Part-time Employment of Full-time Law Students: A Problem or an Opportunity?* (unpublished 1990 draft). The article includes references to other useful materials on this topic.

this approach may be commendable, it is unlikely to receive serious consideration by more than a few law schools at the present time. Given the longstanding concern about the distractions caused by term-time employment, there will be considerable reluctance to allocate limited resources and modify class schedules to accommodate the needs of employers.

It has also been suggested that a credit-bearing "supporting seminar" might be closely tied to common clerking duties.[51] Because so many students will spend so much time employed by law firms during each semester of their legal education, any attempt to inject educational value into this experience is likely to prove worthwhile.

The Task Force recommends legal employers and law schools should join together to develop models for strengthening the educational content of term-time employment under the auspices of the proposed national institute for the practice of law.

Summer Employment

The possibility of adding an educational element to the summer clerkship experience should also be explored. Summer positions are enthusiastically encouraged by law schools and, today, are used by many firms as the primary vehicle for hiring students after graduation. It is in the best interest of students, schools, and employers to maximize the educational component of summer experiences.

One step in this direction would be the development by law schools of workshops, offered at the beginning of the summer clerkship season, to support the educational aspects of clerking. Coverage might include instruction in advanced legal writing and research skills, an overview of law office management, suggestions for acclimating to firm "culture," and methods for obtaining appropriate supervision and feedback during the clerkship. Law firms might well be prepared to subsidize the costs incurred for such workshops.

In addition, employers should be advised concerning the importance of having a continuing educational component in student clerkships and be provided with both materials for and guidance in undertaking this responsibility. Finally, if the summer experience becomes truly educational, schools may want to build on this background during the academic year.

Employers have a vested interest in summer programs and should be receptive to structuring them in an educationally sound manner. At present, however, there is no consistent way in which a student can obtain information about various aspects of the summer

---

51. *Id.*

opportunities offered by law firms. This gap could be filled by asking the National Association of Law Placement (NALP) to add to its annual employer questionnaire several questions designed to elicit information pertaining to the educational quality of summer programs. Such inquiries might cover the kinds and breadth of assignments typically made, the level of supervision offered, and methods utilized to provide feedback and to ensure that the feedback meets student needs. Information of this sort, centrally compiled, would not only aid students in assessing the value of particular programs but might also stimulate employers (as they fill out the form) to consider whether the educational aspects of their summer clerkships are as sound as they should be.

Insofar as the legal profession involves a career of learning through and in conjunction with practice, this approach to summer employment experience serves to emphasize that the lifetime learning process extends back to the time spent with a legal employer during law school. Accordingly, the Task Force recommends that NALP add to its employment questionnaire items designed to elicit information pertaining to the educational quality of employers' summer programs.

Credit-Bearing Externships

Some law schools permit students to work in externships for credit. It is likely that this practice will increase over time. A significant problem with credit-bearing externships is that the quality of supervision varies considerably depending on the experience of the field placement supervisor and the amount of time he or she is able to devote to such supervision.

In recognition of this problem, the ABA has sought to require law schools to oversee the nature of the supervision. This, alone, may not be sufficient to solve the problem. Further steps should be taken to require faculty involvement in the design, supervision and evaluation of every program of extern experience, and to emphasize the critical importance of faculty responsibility for overseeing extern programs. The Task Force recommends that these principles be emphasized in ABA accreditation Standards.

Faculty-Practitioners and Practitioner-Teachers

Enhancing the ability of both practitioners and law faculty to be effective teachers can be accomplished by having practitioners teach in law schools and faculty engage in practice. A few schools and employers have experimented with leaves of absence, allowing practitioners to teach or faculty to practice. This can help expose students, in the classroom, to the practical perspective of experienced practitioners and enable faculty to benefit from a period of practice.

After such an experience, it is hoped that a returning faculty member brings to the law school and presents to students an expanded view of practice while the returning practitioner might encourage colleagues to take a broader view of the firm's responsibilities in training student clerks and young lawyers.

Chapter Eight
The Transition from Law Student to Practitioner

A. The Licensing Process

The judiciary of each state traditionally has been responsible for setting standards for admission to the state bar. Admissions standards are intended to ensure that candidates have the minimum level of competence and character to practice law. Although admissions standards vary, in almost every state a law school graduate[1] is required to satisfy at least two requirements in order to receive a license to practice law: first, the candidate must pass a bar examination,[2] and second, the candidate must demonstrate the requisite moral character to practice law.

In recent years, state admitting authorities have given increasing consideration to the manner in which admissions requirements

---

1. In the vast majority of states, a bar applicant must graduate from a law school that was accredited by the American Bar Association. In a few, graduates of particular non-accredited law schools are also eligible for admission to the bar. In addition, in some states, applicants for admission may serve an apprenticeship as an alternative to graduating from law school. *See* Chapter 3.A, *supra*.

2. The State of Wisconsin, the sole exception, provides a "diploma privilege" for graduates of law schools within the state; graduates of University of Wisconsin School of Law and Marquette University School of Law may forgo the bar examination. In addition, many states waive the bar examination for attorneys who have practiced in another jurisdiction for a specified number of years.

may ensure that new lawyers have acquired fundamental lawyering skills and professional values. Two possible approaches have been considered. The first approach, which generally has been disfavored, would be for admitting authorities to require applicants to take particular courses as a condition of admission to the bar. The second approach, which merits continued consideration, would be for admitting authorities to devise methods effectively to measure a broader array of professional skills and values than are traditionally tested on state bar examinations. Both approaches are discussed below.

B. Curricular Requirements for Bar Admission

In the overwhelming majority of jurisdictions, licensing authorities influence law school curricula indirectly, through the selection of particular subjects to be tested on the bar examination and through the method of testing.[3] However, in two states, South Carolina and Indiana, rules of court presently dictate a substantial portion of the curriculum of applicants for admission to the bar. Neither requirement is particularly directed at the acquisition of lawyering skills and professional values, although legal writing and research and professional responsibility are among the required courses in both states, and trial advocacy is an additional requirement in South Carolina. Rather, the rules are primarily designed to ensure that new lawyers are exposed to bodies of substantive and procedural law most likely to be employed by practitioners in those states. Thus, South Carolina requires applicants for admission to the bar to take at least one law school course in the following additional areas: business law, civil procedure, commercial law, constitutional law, contracts, criminal law, domestic relations, equity, evidence, property, taxation, and torts.[4] Similarly, Indiana requires applicants to take a designated number of course credits in the following additional areas: administrative law and procedure; business organizations; civil procedure; commercial law and contracts; constitutional law, criminal law and criminal procedure; property; taxation; and torts.[5]

---

3. See Chapter 8.C, *infra*.
4. SOUTH CAROLINA RULES OF COURT, Rule 5A.
5. INDIANA RULES FOR ADMISSION TO THE BAR AND THE DISCIPLINE OF ATTORNEYS, Rule 13(V).

These requirements have been the subject of spirited debate.[6] Both the American Bar Association and the National Conference of Bar Examiners have long opposed provisions which would dictate curriculum content. A statement adopted in July, 1971 and still adhered to by both the Council of the ABA Section of Legal Education and Admissions to the Bar and the Board of Managers of the National Conference of Bar Examiners provided:

> Not only are law schools quite properly experimenting in teaching techniques but they are experimenting in curriculum content. . . . [P]ublic authority should not dictate curriculum content but by examination should determine that the content of the applicant's education is such that, upon admission he [or she] will be able to adequately serve the public.[7]

Consistent with this position, outside of South Carolina and Indiana there has been little serious support for rules mandating, in comprehensive fashion, the course of law school study of applicants to the bar.

In recent years, proposals have been made for bar admissions requirements directed not at the overall content of bar applicants' course of study but at skills instruction in particular.[8] For example, a proposal considered and rejected by the State Bar of California would have required law students to receive 90 hours of lawyering skills instruction in law school as a condition for admission to the bar.[9] The course work would focus on, among other things, client interaction, preventive law planning and analysis for clients, alternative dispute resolution methods, time and practice management, fact gathering and analysis, drafting, negotiating, and pre-trial and trial practice. At least 30 of the class hours would have to be devoted to course work or legal work which had a component of student performance, including some participation in an adversarial proceeding which gives students the opportunity for argument, witness examination and the use of evidence. Courses taken in

---

6. Compare, e.g., Littlejohn, *South Carolina's Rule 5 Works Well*, 54 THE BAR EXAMINER 19 (Aug. 1985) (defending program), with Blackmar, *South Carolina is Out of Line: A Response to Chief Justice Littlejohn*, 55 THE BAR EXAMINER 4 (Feb. 1986) (criticizing program); Letter of Prof. Charles B. Blackmar, 64 JUDICATURE 253 (1981) (same); Letter of Prof. John Burkoff, 64 JUDICATURE 200 (1980) (same).

7. See White, *Lawyer Competency and the Law School Curriculum: An Opportunity for Cooperation*, 53 THE BAR EXAMINER 4, 7-8 (Feb. 1984).

8. Because law schools are already required to provide instruction in professional responsibility in order to receive ABA accreditation, bar admissions authorities have not had reason to consider mandating course work aimed at the development of professional values.

9. REPORT AND RECOMMENDATIONS OF THE COMMISSION ON LAWYERING SKILLS OF THE STATE BAR OF CALIFORNIA 3-6 (Oct. 11, 1991).

fulfillment of the requirement would have to be approved by the State Bar.[10]

Similarly, the Committee on Legal Education and Admission to the Bar of the Association of the Bar of the City of New York recently proposed the development of what it termed a "practice skills requirement."[11] Under the committee's proposal, applicants would be required to attend courses in at least three of the following seven skills: drafting of legal instruments; interviewing and counseling; law office management; negotiation; oral advocacy (appellate and motion argument); trial advocacy; and written advocacy. Applicants would not necessarily be required to take the requisite courses in law school. The committee contemplated that, if its proposal were adopted, bar associations, private concerns such as the Practising Law Institute, bar review course providers, and employers would also develop programs to satisfy the requirement.

Advocates of skills instruction requirements such as those proposed in California and New York recognize that members of the bar who are responsible for representing clients must possess competency in such lawyering skills as fact-gathering, interviewing, negotiation and oral advocacy in order to provide legal services. These skills are not developed in law school by many, if not most, applicants to the bar, since some law students do not elect to take lawyering skills courses and at many schools the number of slots in skills instruction courses are limited. Those who do enroll do not presently receive skills training of uniform quality. Moreover, after graduation and admission to the bar, many new lawyers, particularly those who immediately enter a solo or small practice, may take responsibility for representing clients before receiving adequate training in these fundamental lawyering skills through programs outside the law school. A required course of skills instruction prior

---

10. In January 1990, a Commission on Lawyering Skills was appointed to make recommendations to the Board of Governors of the State Bar of California with respect to the acquisition of lawyering skills in general, and with respect to the proposed pre-admission skills-training requirement in particular. After receiving testimony and written comments, the Commission issued a report that opposed a requirement that applicants to the bar have received training in lawyering skills other than those, such as legal analysis, legal research, legal writing and oral advocacy, that are traditionally developed in law schools, together with instruction in the duties and responsibilities of the legal profession. The Commission proposed, instead, that, within three years following admission to the bar, lawyers in the state be required to receive at least 34 hours of approved training in professional lawyering skills. The recommendations were accepted by the Board of Governors of the State Bar of California in April 1992, and referred for implementation to a Board committee.

11. COMMITTEE ON LEGAL EDUCATION AND ADMISSION TO THE BAR, ASSOCIATION OF THE BAR OF THE CITY OF NEW YORK, DISCUSSION DRAFT REPORT ON ADMISSION TO THE BAR IN NEW YORK IN THE TWENTY FIRST CENTURY—A BLUEPRINT FOR REFORM 22-26 (Jan. 2, 1992) (hereafter "CITY BAR REPORT").

to admission to the bar is seen as a means of ensuring that all newly admitted lawyers possess fundamental lawyering skills before they begin representing clients without supervision.

In addition to the general opposition to requirements which dictate curriculum content, the primary concern about a pre-admission skills-instruction requirement is that it could impair the ability of law schools to perform their traditional roles adequately, by causing them to give so much emphasis to skills instruction that they would have difficulty meeting their other responsibilities. The Task Force agrees that this is a legitimate concern, and licensing authorities and other regulatory bodies should be sensitive to it. It will not serve the public interest if law schools are obliged to overemphasize any aspect of the legal education which is required for students to begin the process of becoming competent lawyers. However, the Task Force is persuaded that an imbalance in emphasis presently exists in legal education and that most law schools can provide enhanced instruction in skills and values without detriment to their other equally important responsibilities.

C. The Bar Examination

Traditional Examinations

Applicants to the bar who have not previously been admitted to practice elsewhere must receive a passing grade on a written examination as a prerequisite to receiving a license to practice law.[12] The traditional bar examination is an entirely closed-book test combining multiple choice and essay questions. Although the examination is intended to test a variety of skills, including the ability to carry out certain types of legal analysis and to communicate effectively, it puts a premium on the knowledge of legal rules drawn from a broad variety of subjects.

The number of subjects tested on the bar examination varies from state to state.[13] For example, the New York State Bar Exami-

---

12. As noted above, the State of Wisconsin is the sole exception. *See* note 2, *supra*.

13. All but a handful of states include as part of their examination the one-day Multistate Bar Examination (MBE) prepared by the National Conference of Bar Examiners. The MBE is a six-hour multiple-choice examination comprised of 200 questions concerning six subjects: torts, contracts, criminal law, real property, evidence and constitutional law. The questions are intended to test the candidate's knowledge of substantive legal principles, reading comprehension and reasoning skills. Several states also include a standardized essay examination, the Multistate Essay Examination (MEE), also prepared by the National Conference of Bar Examiners, which tests knowledge of the same six subjects and three additional ones: federal civil procedure, corporations, and wills, trusts and estates. Those states making use of the MEE also include additional essay questions tailored to other areas of state law.

nation may cover any of the following subjects: business relationships, civil procedure (state and federal), conflict of laws,
constitutional law (state and federal), corporations, criminal law and
procedure, evidence, family law, federal income and estate taxation,
real property, remedies, torts (including statutory no-fault provisions), wills and estates, and Uniform Commercial Code Articles 2,
3, 6 and 9. Until recently, six other subjects were also included among
those that might be tested in New York: administrative law, bankruptcy, insurance (other than statutory no-fault provisions), labor
law, municipal corporations, and suretyship.[14]

The traditional bar examination does nothing to encourage law
schools to teach and law students to acquire many of the fundamental lawyering skills identified in the Statement of Skills and Values.
If anything, the bar examination discourages the teaching and
acquisition of many of those skills, such as problem solving, factual
investigation, counseling and negotiation, which the traditional
examination questions do not attempt to measure. For example, the
examination influences law schools, in developing their curricula, to
overemphasize courses in the substantive areas covered by the
examination at the expense of courses in the area of lawyering skills.
The examination also influences law students, in electing from among
those courses offered, to choose substantive law courses that are the
subject of bar examination questions instead of courses designed to
develop lawyering skills. Finally, the examination discourages law
professors from integrating skills training into their substantive law
courses.

Over the years, critics of bar examinations have raised just such
concerns about the danger that bar examinations will influence law
schools, law professors and law students to take an unduly narrow
approach to legal education. For example, a 1970 study undertaken
by the A.A.L.S. under the direction of Professor George Neff Stevens
determined that "the selection of bar examination subjects does have
a very definite effect upon law school curricula and on the legal
education received by the applicant."[15] A number of the law school
deans polled in the course of that study indicated that their curricula were affected by bar examinations,[16] and many perceived that
law students themselves were influenced by bar examination cover-

---

14. CITY BAR REPORT, *supra* note 11, at 3.
15. A.A.L.S. BAR EXAMINATION STUDY PROJECT, BAR EXAMINATION COVERAGE, LAW
SCHOOL CURRICULA AND THE APPLICANT 37 (Apr. 10, 1970)
16. A minority of deans indicated that bar subject selection restricted the school's
elective offerings. A minority also reported that, because of their inclusion on the bar
examination, some subjects were required which would otherwise be offered as
electives.

age in their choice of electives. One of the most frequent complaints about the impact of the bar examination was that it created a demand for course offerings on local law, particularly in the area of practice and pleading. Some respondents contended that because of the breadth of their coverage, bar examinations "needlessly inhibited educational experimentation."[17] Some recommended that bar examinations shift their emphasis from comprehensive knowledge of legal rules to skills-testing.

The AALS Bar Examination Study preceded the great growth in law school enrollments, faculties, number of elective courses and graduates' mobility from State to State. How much these developments have altered the impact of bar examinations upon legal education is problematic since enrollments in substantive courses that are generally covered in bar examinations remain very high.

However, in the past five years, others have expressed concerns similar to those expressed in the AALS Study,[18] including, most recently, the Committee on Legal Education and Admission to the Bar of the Association of the Bar of the City of New York.[19] That committee has proposed reducing or eliminating multiple choice questions and reducing the number of doctrinal areas tested on the examination from twenty-two subjects to ten: civil practice and procedure; corporations; constitutional law; contracts; criminal procedure; ethics; evidence; property; torts; and wills. In making this proposal, the committee rejected what it considered to be the two-fold premise underlying the current examination: "that one can and should know 'the law' on each and every one of [the twenty-two] subjects before being permitted to practice law and that one can be tested on each one of these subjects in a way that allows one to conclude that the examinee who passes in fact knows these subjects."[20] The committee's alternative approach was said to promote three objectives: it would permit applicants to prepare more meaningfully for the examination and provide more thoughtful examination answers; it would "decrease the role of detail and the importance of memorization"; and it would "emphasize[] that the bar

---

17. *Id.* at 49.

18. For example, in a discussion of courses on estate planning, Professor Jeffrey N. Pennell noted that "topics with a modern relevance are frequently glossed over (if covered at all) to cover traditional material that is frequently relevant in few, if any, real world situations." Pennell, *Introduction: Whither Estate Planning*, 24 Idaho L. Rev. 339, 342 (1987-88). He attributed this, in part, to the fact that "these traditional topics are still tested on the bar exam in most states." *Id.* Thus, insofar as bar examiners are emphasizing knowledge of legal rules, they are often focusing on the wrong rules, in his view.

19. *See* City Bar Report, *supra* note 11, at 5.

20. *Id.* at 32.

examination would not be an endpoint, but a part of a new lawyer's continuing professional development."[21]

Efforts to Measure Lawyering Skills

Over the past decade, bar admissions authorities and others have given increasing consideration to the possibility of devising examinations to measure lawyering skills in addition to those such as legal reasoning and analysis which are measured by traditional bar examination questions. Three states—Alaska, California and Colorado—currently depart from the traditional model by including "performance tests" as part of their bar examinations. The performance tests share several characteristics: first, they are not designed to test the memorization of legal rules; second, they are intended to measure legal analytical skills in addition to those measured by traditional bar examination questions; and, third, they ask "applicants to demonstrate proficiency somewhat as a lawyer actually is asked to perform in actual practice."[22]

In July, 1982, Alaska became the first state to add a performance test to its examination. The purpose of the test was to measure lawyering skills that are not adequately tested by the other, traditional portions of the examination:

> [T]he process of "lawyering" usually involves the assimilation of facts, research of law, development of legal issues and strategies, segregating relevant from irrelevant, and helpful from unhelpful materials, and the exercise of judgment in drawing a conclusion. Few of these processes were thought to be well-tested by either the MBE, which depends for the most part on recognition of accurate or inaccurate discrete statements of law, or the traditional essay question, which generally requires some analysis, and the recitation in a brief period of time of as much of a particular area of law, designated by the question, as possible.[23]

As originally devised, the test required applicants to write a memorandum answering particular questions arising out of a given set of facts. Applicants were provided a complete set of research materials, consisting primarily of cases and statutes, some relevant and some irrelevant.

California has included a performance test on its bar examina-

---

21. *Id.* at 32-33.

22. See Feldman & MacNeille, *Certifying Professional Competence: The Alaska Experiment*, 52 THE BAR EXAMINER 1, 14 (Feb. 1983) (remarks of Armando M. Menocal, III).

23. *Id.* at 6.

tion since 1983.[24] "The tests are designed to examine four broad categories of lawyering competency: legal analysis, fact analysis, awareness of professional responsibility, and problem solving."[25] The test does so by simulating the types of documents with which lawyers work. Applicants are required to complete a written assignment using facts contained in a file that includes memos, letters, police reports, news articles, and the like, and legal material consisting of statutes, cases and restatement sections. They have three hours in which to answer two questions. Drafting assignments have included outlining a deposition, drafting legislation, critiquing an interview plan, writing briefs, writing a closing argument, drafting memoranda, writing a position paper, and writing investigation plans.[26]

Colorado added a performance test to its examination in 1989 with the goal of "test[ing] skills commonly used by lawyers practicing law competently."[27] It consists of two thirty-minute questions which take the place of three essay questions. When the test was first given in February, 1989, the first question, designed to test reading skills and analysis, asked applicants to point out major differences between two evidentiary rules. The second question, which required evaluative reading and issue formulation, asked applicants to review a two-page client statement and prepare a brief memorandum identifying issues that would have to be researched and documents in the client's possession that might usefully provide additional information.

In the past two years, other states have begun considering whether to follow the lead of Alaska, California and Colorado and to follow the urging of the Conference of Chief Justices in 1986, that serious consideration be given to the inclusion of performance tests as part of the bar examination.[28] The National Council of Bar Examiners is currently undertaking the development of standardized performance tests for use nationwide.

Proponents of adding a performance test to the traditional multiple-choice and essay questions emphasize that the test successfully measures attributes necessary for a candidate to provide

---

24. See Smith, *Performance Testing in California, 1983-1989*, 58 THE BAR EXAMINER 17 (Aug. 1989); Smith, *Preparing and Grading the California Performance Test*, 54 THE BAR EXAMINER 1 (Feb. 1984).

25. Smith, *Performance Testing in California, 1983-1989*, 58 THE BAR EXAMINER 17, 19 (Aug. 1989).

26. *Id.* at 19-21.

27. See Ogden, *Performance Testing in Colorado*, 58 THE BAR EXAMINER 19 (Nov. 1989).

28. Conference of Chief Justices, *Promoting Lawyer Competence*, 10 STATE COURT JOURNAL 15 (Fall 1986).

competent legal assistance, including attributes not measured by the traditional bar examination questions.[29]

> The performance test expands the scope of lawyering skills tested by the bar examination. Instead of limiting the bar examination to measuring the applicant's ability to recall specific doctrinal knowledge, to spot issues and to apply fundamental legal principles, the performance questions test the applicant's ability to evaluate undigested facts and integrate law and facts, and then to develop and employ that information using common lawyering tools such as a deposition, interrogatories or an appellate brief. Proponents believe that the performance test offers an effective method of assessing an applicant's ability to perform competently some of the tasks a newly admitted practicing lawyer would perform.[30]

In addition, performance tests may serve the secondary purpose of encouraging the teaching and acquisition of lawyering skills[31]—indeed, they appear to be having such an influence in California at the present time.

A number of criticisms have been leveled, however, at the performance tests that are currently in use. First, in large measure those performance tests focus on (albeit by a different method and more fully) the same lawyering skills of legal analysis and reasoning and written communication that are measured by the traditional examinations. They do not go nearly as far as they might to test the additional lawyering skills identified in the Task Force's Statement of Skills and Values. Second, the variation between how candidates score on the traditional examination and the performance tests, although measurable, is relatively small. Third, the adoption of performance tests increases the burden on bar applicants unless the number of subjects tested by the traditional bar examination questions is reduced to compensate for the need to prepare for the performance questions. Finally, the performance tests may be more expensive to prepare and to grade than the traditional questions.

---

29. *See, e.g.* Feldman & MacNeille, *supra* note 22; Klein & Bolus, AN ANALYSIS OF THE RELATIONSHIP BETWEEN CLINICAL LEGAL SKILLS AND BAR EXAMINATION RESULTS: A REPORT PREPARED FOR THE COMMITTEE OF BAR EXAMINERS OF THE STATE BAR OF CALIFORNIA AND THE NATIONAL CONFERENCE OF BAR EXAMINERS (1982).

30. CITY BAR REPORT, *supra* note 11, at 28.

31. Although the principal purpose of bar examinations is to assist in separating out those who are qualified from those who are unqualified to practice law in the jurisdiction, bar examinations have a secondary, but equally legitimate, purpose of shaping law school curricula. See, e.g., Smith, *Progress in Education for Admission to the Bar*, 7 AM. L. SCHOOL REV. 267, 271 (1931); *Performance Testing: A Valuable New Dimension or a Waste of Time and Money*, 52 THE BAR EXAMINER 12, 21 (Nov. 1983).

Efforts to Measure Professional Values

The licensing process has not played a significant role in either encouraging or measuring the acquisition of the professional values identified in the Statement of Skills and Values. Although candidates for admission are required, in many states, to pass an examination devoted entirely to the subject of professional responsibility, and candidates in all states are required to have the requisite moral character to practice law, neither the bar examination nor the character review process meaningfully contributes to the development of professional values.

Approximately one-third of the states require applicants to take and pass the Multistate Professional Responsibility Exam (MPRE). The MPRE, which may be taken while still in law school, is a fifty-question, multiple-choice test that measures familiarity with the ABA Code of Judicial Conduct and with two professional codes governing the conduct of attorneys: the ABA Code of Professional Responsibility, which is in effect in approximately one-third of the states, and the Model Rules of Professional Conduct, which have been adopted in approximately two-thirds of the states. The examination does not test on areas in which the Code of Professional Responsibility and the Model Rules diverge, and it does not require applicants to engage in extended analysis of questions that are legally uncertain under the professional codes. Thus, the MPRE is not, and was never intended as, a test of one's commitment to professional values; it is, rather, almost exclusively a test of one's mastery of settled principles of law governing the conduct of attorneys and judges. Indeed, some critics have urged that, far from promoting instruction in professional values, the MPRE discourages such instruction; they contend that, because of its narrow focus, the examination may influence law schools to overemphasize professional regulation, at the expense of professional values. The Task Force agrees with these criticisms.

Similarly, the process by which admitting authorities assess the character of applicants to the bar has no influence on the acquisition of professional values. In most jurisdictions, that process involves a review by a committee of volunteer lawyers of a candidate's response to a questionnaire seeking information about prior arrests, convictions, civil judgments and similar problems. Few candidates are rejected in the absence of a public record of misconduct. Thus, the process is not intended to ensure an applicant's familiarity with or adherence to professional values, but simply to weed out the exceedingly small number of candidates whose past misconduct is viewed as a portent of future wrongdoing.

Accordingly, the development in law schools of programs designed to enhance their students' understanding of, and commitment to, professional values, and the increasing importance given to professional values throughout the profession over the years has largely been a response to various factors independent of the licensing process. Chief among those factors have been the efforts of the ABA throughout this century to encourage law schools to promote professional values—efforts which included in 1974 the adoption of a requirement that accredited law schools instruct all students in the duties and responsibilities of the legal profession.

D. Building the Continuum

In setting standards for applicants to the bar, admitting authorities must inevitably give consideration to the fundamental lawyering skills and values identified in the Task Force's Statement of Skills and Values and other relevant literature. However, the Statement is not intended as a list of the skills and values in which every lawyer must be versed before he or she is admitted to the bar, and the process of acquiring and refining the skills and values is seen as a continuum which will span one's legal career. But since this process begins in law school, it is appropriate for admitting authorities both to encourage and support the initiation of that process of professional development during the law school years and to undertake to measure applicants' familiarity with at least some of the lawyering skills and values to ensure that applicants are at an appropriate place in the continuum.

The Task Force believes it is unwise for licensing authorities to consider setting specific curriculum requirements for law schools. To the extent that it may be appropriate to revisit the treatment of skills and values instruction within the law schools, the ABA Standards for Approval of Law Schools provides a vehicle for doing so on a uniform, national basis. The Task Force in this report is recommending that the Section of Legal Education and Admissions to the Bar should revisit the treatment of skills and values instruction in the accreditation process in recognition of the skills and values identified in the Statement of Fundamental Lawyering Skills and Professional Values as those with which a lawyer should be familiar before assuming ultimate responsibility for a client. (See Chapter 7.C., *supra*.) If licensing authorities share our belief that certain of the existing accreditation standards should be reexamined, the appropriate body with which they should communicate is the Council of the ABA Section of Legal Education and Admissions to the Bar.

More direct and possibly more effective ways for ensuring that new lawyers acquire the skills and values requisite to discharge their professional responsibilities would be for licensing authorities to focus upon modifying the bar examination and upon strengthening transition education for bar applicants and new lawyers. Modifying the bar examination to give appropriate weight to the importance of acquiring lawyering skills and professional values would encourage law students in their efforts to develop their personal skills and values.

The importance to competent and responsible practice of strengthening transition education for bar applicants and new lawyers cannot be questioned. The Task Force has concluded that it is unrealistic to expect even the most committed law schools, without help from the Bar, to produce graduates who are fully prepared to represent clients without supervision. Licensing authorities must be concerned with the problem of how to regulate entry into the profession of those partially-prepared lawyers. The Task Force has concluded that the appropriate way for resolving this problem is for licensing authorities, law schools, and the organized bar, with the support of the proposed national institute, to share information and to coordinate their efforts to improve the transition education for lawyers as they enter the profession. The Task Force urges all interested parties to engage in a continuing dialogue to determine the appropriate content, methods, and mix of instruction in skills and values at each stage of the continuum of professional development: in law school, during the licensing process and after admission to practice.

E. Transition Education for Bar Applicants and New Lawyers

A national conference of bar leaders and legal educators, convened in 1963 by the American Law Institute and the American Bar Association, concluded that certain practical skills were not appropriately taught in law school but should instead be offered to the profession through continuing legal education. The conference thought "the public interest would be served" if such bar applicants were required to complete "a comprehensive course in practical skills" prior to final admission; that requirement, however, would only be justified "when the scope and quality of the course offered are found to be adequate to meet the need."[32]

In response to the 1963 conference recommendation, Professor August Eckhard, then at the University of Wisconsin Law School, was asked to serve as reporter for a project to develop standards and a general curriculum in practical skills and methods for newly-graduated lawyers prior to admission to the bar. The product of the project was a report which encouraged "representative states" to institute programs in the recommended format "on a voluntary, experimental basis," and report their experience in the future. There is, however, no published collection of any reports on such experimentation.[33]

United States jurisdictions have responded to the need for training of bar applicants and new lawyers in a variety of ways. A few states have retained a concept of apprenticeships, training the law graduate in a practice setting. Most jurisdictions have developed a wide variety of programs, usually called "bridge-the-gap" programs, which attempt to introduce the law graduate to a variety of practical information. In some jurisdictions these programs are a prerequisite for bar admission; in many jurisdictions the programs are voluntary, sponsored by an assortment of bar organizations, and aimed at newly-admitted attorneys. A few jurisdictions have mandated bridge-the-gap programs for newly-admitted attorneys, usually as part of a more comprehensive mandatory CLE program. Bridge-the-gap programs vary widely in content and quality, but most provide little or no instruction in the fundamental lawyering skills identified in the Task Force's Statement of Skills and Values and are dramatically different from comparable programs in a number of Commonwealth jurisdictions (see *infra*, footnote 34).

In recent years, a number of employers, private law firms, corporate general counsel offices, and government agencies, have established a variety of formal programs for their own newly-admitted attorneys. These programs are conducted on-the-job or "in-house"

---

32. The Conference report was entitled AMERICAN LAW INSTITUTE-AMERICAN BAR ASSOCIATION COMMITTEE ON CONTINUING PROFESSIONAL EDUCATION, ARDEN HOUSE II: TOWARD EXCELLENCE IN CONTINUING LEGAL EDUCATION, THE REPORT OF THE SECOND NATIONAL CONFERENCE ON THE CONTINUING EDUCATION OF THE BAR (1964) [hereafter "ARDEN HOUSE II REPORT"]. The text of the Final Statement of ARDEN HOUSE II can be found as Appendix B to AMERICAN LAW INSTITUTE-AMERICAN BAR ASSOCIATION COMMITTEE ON CONTINUING PROFESSIONAL EDUCATION, CLE AND THE LAWYER'S RESPONSIBILITIES IN AN EVOLVING PROFESSION, THE REPORT ON THE ARDEN HOUSE III CONFERENCE, NOVEMBER 13TH TO 16TH (1987) [hereafter "ARDEN HOUSE III REPORT"], pp. 583-90.

33. *See* AMERICAN LAW INSTITUTE-AMERICAN BAR ASSOCIATION COMMITTEE ON CONTINUING PROFESSIONAL EDUCATION, MEETING THE EDUCATIONAL NEEDS OF THE NEWLY ADMITTED: A PROPOSAL FOR GENERAL PRACTICE COURSES (1967).

and represent a significant new development in providing training for new lawyers. Each of the different responses to the needs of the bar applicants and new lawyers are addressed in the ensuing sections of this Chapter.

Apprenticeships

The apprenticeship is a program for training new lawyers in a practice setting. Although generally required in Commonwealth jurisdictions,[34] the apprenticeship has fallen into disfavor in the United States. At present, only two states—Delaware and Vermont— continue to require law school graduates to serve an apprenticeship. Both programs last approximately half a year and may be begun during law school.[35] While completion of the Delaware clerkship is a requirement for bar admission,[36] the Vermont internship may be completed within two years of admission.[37]

The Delaware apprenticeship is considerably more structured than the Vermont program. The Delaware clerk must complete 32 tasks which are designed to develop the law clerk's lawyering skills in a "learning by doing" atmosphere. For example, the clerk is

---

34. In most Commonwealth countries, a prospective lawyer (or solicitor, if the solicitor/barrister distinction has been retained) must serve a specified period of time under articles (*i.e.*, a law office clerkship) to an admitted lawyer or to a solicitor with an unrestricted license. Problems with the articling periods have led some to call for their reform and others to call for their abolition. *See, e.g.*, David A. Cruickshank, *The Professional Legal Training Course in British Columbia, Canada*, J. PROF. L. EDUC., Dec. 1985, at 111, 111-112 (discussing criticism of Canadian articling system); Margot Costanzo, *The Practical Training Course: Placing It in the Victorian Profession*, J. PROF. L. EDUC., July 1983, at 33, 34-35 (discussing criticisms of articling in Melbourne and in general); Audrey Blunden & Les Handler, *A New Course at the New South Wales College of Law*, J. PROF. L. EDUC., June 1987, at 42, 43 (noting "widespread dissatis-faction" with articling). Often, the usefulness of the articling experience for the clerk depends on the principal's and/or the firm's attitude towards training. Cruickshank, *supra*, at 112 (*citing* Neil Gold, *Pre-Admission Education and Training in Canada: Some Reflections and a Survey*, paper for the Commonwealth Legal Education Association, May 1983 at 3). Ideally, articling is an experience in which a student can expect "to learn the customs, conventions, mores, attitudes, ethics, and social structure of the subculture which is the legal profession." However, it has been said that such information is now "passed along randomly and without certainty," and a clerk-ship all too often consists of "routine, repetitive and mundane tasks."

35. Del. Sup. Ct. Rules (revised June 30, 1989), R.52(a)(8), 52(c); Vt. Sup. Ct. Rules of Admission, § 6(i)(1). Delaware Rules require completion of a not necessarily consecutive five-month, full-time clerkship. The Vermont internship lasts six months.

36. Del. Sup. Ct. Rules (revised June 30, 1989), R.52(a)(8), 52(c). The Delaware clerkship must be completed in a law office, a judge's chambers, or in an office of the Justice Department, the Public Defender, the U.S. Attorney, Legal Aid, or the like.

37. Vt. Sup. Ct. Rules of Admission, § 6(i)2.

required to attend various courts and observe various proceedings[38] in order to become familiar with the Delaware judicial system and its procedures. The clerk must also complete interactive tasks aimed at fostering lawyering skills. For example, the clerk must help prepare a Superior Court motion, a Delaware Supreme Court appeal, papers in connection with the commencement of a lawsuit (including complaint, praecipe, and instructions to Sheriff), as well as three memoranda of law and a will or trust instrument.[39] Both the law clerk and the preceptor are required to certify that the applicant completed the clerkship.

In contrast, the Vermont Rules do not specify any tasks for the neophyte lawyer, and they do not attempt to ensure that specific skills are developed by outlining exercises to be completed, as does the Delaware checklist. The Vermont intern, a graduate of an approved law school, is simply required to "pursue[] the study of law within this state in the office of a judge or a practicing attorney in this state" for the period of the apprenticeship.[40]

Within the past two decades, several other states, including New Jersey, Pennsylvania, and Rhode Island, have replaced the requirement of an apprenticeship with required attendance at a bridge-the-gap program.[41] By way of example, the New Jersey apprenticeship, discontinued in 1963, required a minimum apprenticeship period of nine months in the office of a counselor-at-law engaged in the general practice of law as a prerequisite to bar admission. The clerk was required to be in the practitioner's office for most of the day during business hours, and could not "be engaged in or pursue any business, occupation, or employment incompatible with the full, fair, and bona

---

38. Del. Law Clerk schedule (revised 1/1/90). The Delaware clerk must attend various courts, including the Justice of the Peace Court, family court, the Court of Common Pleas, Superior Court, Court of Chancery, and the District Court. The proceedings to be observed include a complete civil trial, an uncontested divorce, a criminal trial, an arbitration hearing, a session of arraignments, a sentencing session, a jury selection, a pre-trial conference, a civil jury trial, a Supreme Court argument (after a study of applicable briefs and a review of authorities relied on), a Sheriff's sale, a deposition, a real estate closing, and an administrative hearing.

39. *Id.* The clerk must also review the record of a case tried and appealed, investigate the facts of a pending case, help interview a client or litigant, participate in the administration of one estate, participate in a complete incorporation of a new company, and complete a title search under supervision.

40. Vt. Sup. Ct. Rules of Admission, § 6(i)(1).

41. Pennsylvania required candidates for admission to the bar to serve six-month clerkships in the office of any local attorney. BRENNER, SURVEY OF THE LEGAL PROFESSION, REPORTS OF CONSULTANTS AND THE ADVISORY AND EDITORIAL COMMITTEE ON BAR EXAMINATIONS AND REQUIREMENTS FOR ADMISSION TO THE BAR 107-108 (1952). Pennsylvania required that the attorney-mentor have five years' experience as well. In addition, Pennsylvania also required that at least four months of the clerkship be served after admission to the bar. Rhode Island required candidates for admission to the bar to serve six-month clerkships in the office of any local attorney.

fide service of such clerkship." The clerk was required to attend specified court proceedings, which amounted to approximately ten days of observation, and to attend the sessions of the legislature for one day.

The New Jersey program was discontinued for reasons which echoed criticisms of "reading for the bar" of an earlier age. The experiences of the New Jersey apprentices varied greatly, depending on the nature of the law firm in which they served. The quality of the experience could not easily be monitored.[42] The 1963 Report of Arden House II described some clerkships as "a form of near-peonage," and noted that a six to nine month clerkship, with little or no salary, could be a "serious economic burden" following three years of law school for graduates already in debt and with families to support.[43]

The apprenticeship systems currently retained in Vermont and Delaware may be subject to similar criticisms. Since the Vermont program does not specify the completion of any particular tasks or the observation of any particular proceedings, the Vermont intern, while introduced to practice in a supervised setting, has no assurance that he or she will spend time doing tasks that develop fundamental lawyering skills or even a superficial familiarity with the process of the judicial system in the state. All will depend on the attorneys with whom they serve. In Delaware, where greater direction is given to apprentices, the emphasis is largely on observation but not on the type of personal participation and interaction that is especially important to the development of lawyering skills. With respect to those tasks that are specified, there is no assurance that they are accomplished well. The program does not require the mentor to give the apprentice any particular degree of supervision or feedback, and does not establish any objective standard by which to evaluate the apprentice's work. Neither program provides adequate assurance that the mentor is qualified to train the new lawyer or will commit the time and effort to do so. Thus neither program emphasizes the three characteristics of effective skills instruction referred in Chapter 7.B, *supra*.

Programs of Transition Education

Some form of transition education program—commonly referred to as "bridge-the-gap program" and directed to new law graduates—

---

42. Fulton Haight, *Law Schools Are Still Training People to Be Associates in Major Firms*, THE BAR EXAMINER, Feb. 1990, at 24, 27.
43. ARDEN HOUSE II REPORT, *supra* note 32, at 23.

can be found in most states.[44] ALI-ABA's 1985 survey by Judge Kestin reported 45 programs, and noted that there were "relatively few significant differences of style or format."[45] This characterization remains accurate today. Approximately two-thirds of the states offer some kind of transition education. The programs range from a videotape available for rental in Arizona to an intensive, hands-on program that lasts a week and a half in the State of Washington. Some of the programs are in-depth, others are more cursory in nature and resemble bar review courses. About twelve states require specific training for the new attorney or as a prerequisite for admission.[46] Twenty to twenty-five states offer bridge-the-gap programs on a voluntary basis.[47] Some states have attempted to ensure competency by instituting minimum standards for specialties, such as trial advocacy.[48] As the Kestin Report noted, many of the programs offered outside of law school aimed at new practitioners are surprisingly uniform in program length, the topics covered, the class format, the identities of speakers and the type of program materials.

Topics covered. The most common type of bridge-the-gap course offers a series of lectures on substantive areas combined with

---

44. AMERICAN LAW INSTITUTE-AMERICAN BAR ASSOCIATION COMMITTEE ON CONTINUING PROFESSIONAL EDUCATION, REPORT ON THE SURVEY OF BRIDGE-THE-GAP PROGRAMS, (1985) at 2 [hereafter, "KESTIN REPORT"].

45. *Id.* at 9. Although some of the jurisdictions listed in the 1985 survey apparently no longer have state bar association-sponsored bridge-the-gap programs, others have since developed them.

46. States that require specific training for bar admission are Delaware, Georgia, Indiana, Maine, Michigan, New Hampshire, New Jersey, Oregon, Rhode Island, South Carolina, Utah, and Vermont.

47. These include Arizona, California, Connecticut, Florida, Iowa, Kentucky, Minnesota, Mississippi, Montana, Nevada, North Carolina, Pennsylvania, Virginia, Washington, and Wisconsin. *See* , *e.g.*, KESTIN REPORT, *supra* note 44, at 28-30.

48. South Carolina has set up a two-tier bar system. New attorneys cannot practice in the courts alone until they have completed eleven trial experiences, similar in nature to those required in the Delaware clerkship. *See* SC Rule 403. The Northern District of Illinois established a two-tier bar in 1982. *See* PROCEEDINGS OF THE 49TH JUDICIAL CONFERENCE OF THE DC CIRCUIT, 124 F.R.D. 241, 263-65. In the Northern District of Illinois, any attorney licensed by the State of Illinois can become a member of the general bar and practice in the courts after the payment of a one-time-only fee. (The only restriction is that he or she cannot appear alone during testimonial proceedings.) However, to qualify for admission to the trial bar, an attorney must pay an additional one-time-only fee and acquire four "qualifying units of experience." Two must be "participation units," which are prior trial experiences as lead or assistant to lead counsel in a state or federal trial proceeding. The remaining two may be "observation" or "simulation" units. The former is earned by observing a trial conducted by a member of the trial bar and consulting with the trial lawyer afterwards. The latter is earned by participation in a law school or CLE trial advocacy program.

detailed state-specific practice hints.[49] Typical areas include bankruptcy, civil litigation, corporations (small business), estate planning, wills and probate, criminal law, ethics, family law, real property, and workers' compensation.[50] Other topics often found in bridge-the-gap programs include taxation and insurance law. A less common topic is law office management.[51] Some courses introduce new lawyers to the procedures used in the local judicial system.[52] Few programs address lawyering skills,[53] and those that do typically utilize a static lecture format without interactive training. A handful of bridge-the-gap courses try to include an amalgam of substantive law, office management, procedure, and lawyering skills, and offer lectures on different topics in these four areas.[54]

---

49. For example, the New Jersey mandatory practical skills course has a first-year requirement where students take a core curriculum of five topics: professional responsibility (which includes fees, trust account accounting, IOLTA participation, and law office management), real estate, will drafting and probate practice, family law, and civil or criminal trial preparation. The Montana program differs in that it is offered through the University of Montana Law School and organized by the Montana Young Lawyers Division ("YLD"). The program occurs in the law school. Lectures are offered to all students in the evening (for no credit), with special attention paid to third-year students. The lectures are generally not substantive, but are rather aimed at the students' professional development. Occasionally, a substantive lecture is given to introduce the student to new developments in an area of law. The topics vary widely and are offered by guest attorneys.

50. KESTIN REPORT, *supra* note 44, at 7.

51. For example, the Kentucky program offers talks on topics that range from "Practical considerations of management, workloads, delegation and law office personnel" to client relations, and avoiding malpractice.

52. Many states offer procedural courses, such as trial preparation, civil and criminal. An example of this is found in the seminar portion of the Utah program. The first two days of the initial three-day seminar are devoted to procedural issues, such as Utah court rules. On the third day, the program attendees are brought to the courthouse in groups to meet the judges and the clerks and to be introduced to the process first-hand. Similarly, Maine offers a lecture entitled "A View from the Bench," to introduce new attorneys to the court system, and Indiana offers sections on civil trial, appellate, and criminal practice.

Another example is the Los Angeles County Walk Thru Program, which brings new attorneys into the courts. Trial judges recommended by local bar associations speak to the new lawyers and introduce them to procedural aspects of the court system. In addition, the judges walk the new lawyers through a civil jury trial with do's and don'ts, walk through a civil mandatory/voluntary settlement conference with do's and don'ts, and answer questions, as time permits. *See* Personal Viewpoint, *Judges Educate Inexperienced Trial Attorneys*, A.B.A.J., Jan 1981, at 10.

53. Several states offer aspects of skills training in addition to other topics. For example, Kentucky's program devotes time to different aspects of deposition taking.

54. For example, the California program, "Passport to Practice," offers client relations, business development, the art of lawyering, advocacy through writing, trial preparation, oral advocacy, and appellate practice, as well as a number of traditional subject matter practice areas. The Minnesota program offers individual lectures on standard topics as well as topics such as commercial practice, personal injury, and litigation. In addition, it offers a miscellaneous section that covers topics such as negotiation skills, how to survive a first job, and debtor/creditor relations.

The Wisconsin program offers lectures on few substantive topics, but covers areas such as office procedure, courthouse procedure, and stress management. The Nevada

The Washington Practice Skills Program is exceptional because it focuses exclusively on lawyering skills and attempts to teach them in a small-group, learning-by-doing context instead of the almost ubiquitous lecture. Its program covers interviewing, counseling, negotiation, drafting, motion practice, witness preparation, depositions, opening statements, direct and cross examinations, closing arguments, and organizational skills.

Program length. The standard bridge-the-gap program lasts two or three, generally consecutive, days. Most programs begin with a sign-in period and then a welcoming speech.[55] These are sometimes followed by an ethics or professionalism session. The day is most often split into at least two sessions, with lectures covering different substantive topics.

A few programs last longer than three days or less than two.[56] Again, a good example of the longer program is the Washington Practical Skills course, an intensive nine day, full-time program. A few programs are organized differently, and are spread out over several years in a tiered fashion.[57]

---

program offers lectures on conducting discovery and trials, and the Arizona videotape includes office management, motion practice, and taking and defending a deposition.

The Indiana course, entitled "Practical Skills— A Bridge-the-gap Seminar," includes dissolutions, negotiation skills, building a professional law practice, and counseling skills, among others. Florida offers lectures on interviewing, stress management, and court mechanics. South Carolina offers lectures on professional responsibility, "nuts and bolts" (i.e., practical hints plus procedural details), real estate, discovery, a presentation by the Young Lawyers Division of the South Carolina Bar Association, automobile negligence, product liability, probate, bankruptcy, and domestic relations, among others.

55. Many of the programs surveyed use the sign-in period as the only check on attendance. Occasionally, the student will also be asked to fill out an evaluation form that critiques either the speaker, the material, or both. Programs which fulfill CLE requirements often use sign-in sheets to verify actual attendance for CLE credit. Programs rarely provide for verification of attendance at individual lectures. The Virginia program does, however, require attendees to sign in and out at lectures, gives out homework assignments during the first year program and sets a deadline that attendees be no more than twenty minutes late.

56. For example, in the New Lawyer CLE program being developed in Utah, the new attorneys will attend a semiannual seminar, supplemented by a program of monthly evening workshops, each three or four hours long. The new lawyer will have to attend a sampling of ten to twelve programs, according to their interests. The Minnesota program lasts about fifty hours over nine days, and lets practitioners register for individual courses offered over that time span. The South Carolina bridge-the-gap program, required by SC Rule 402c9, is administered the week following the bar examination. At the shorter end of the spectrum, Arizona offers a 5 hour, 20 minute videotape.

57. For example, programs offered in New Jersey and Virginia are tiered. The New Jersey Skills Training Course, which is mandatory for New Jersey bar admission, is a three-year course. The first year is the "core" portion of the program. The second and third years comprise the "continuing education" components, in which different topics are offered and there are no practice exercise requirements. The Virginia program is also a three-year program, although the first year is the most intensive. It totals

Program format. The overwhelming majority of the programs offer information in a lecture format, which tends to be a passive method of learning requiring little interaction or participation by the new lawyers.[58] Some programs try to involve the new attorneys by supplementing the lectures with question and answer sessions or discussion periods at the end of the day. (Discussion periods are sometimes used to integrate matters of professional responsibility into the curricula.) Occasionally, the standard lecture fare is interrupted by a symposium or other more interactive type of learning.[59]

Thus, the American programs of transition education often suffer from a surfeit of substantive law and a concomitant lack of skills instruction. Despite their deficiencies, lectures are used for several reasons. Lectures are relatively cheap. The instructors are familiar with the lecture format, and are able to disseminate the substantive information in a digestible fashion, for which they need no additional training. Also, many new practitioners doubtless find it useful to be told where to find information they may require for the initial stages of their practice. (This may, in part, explain the generally positive reviews of most bridge-the-gap programs reported by ALI-ABA in the Kestin Report.)[60]

As we have noted, one state offers a significantly different program. Washington's Skills Practice Course is oriented to skills-training and offers "learning by doing" in small groups. It is one of the few programs that focuses primarily on the acquisition of lawyering skills. The Washington program uses extensive written materials specially developed for skills instruction, which include exercises, case problems and sample forms. The program is struc-

---

approximately thirty hours. The first year has homework requirements. The second and third years do not. The second year also has attendance required at two lectures, each of a half-day duration. The third year there are two lectures required, but the lawyer can choose two out of six topics, which include collection law, worker's compensation, bankruptcy, and landlord-tenant.

58. For example, the South Carolina program is administered in a lecture format the week after the bar exam—a time that may not be most conducive to additional training. The participants are not tested on their absorption of the material.

59. For example, Virginia's program has required homework assignments for the first-year course participants, as does the New Jersey practical skills course. The Minnesota program has a lecture/workshop format, Utah combines seminars and workshops, Mississippi has lectures and a panel discussion, Nevada has a series of lectures and offers two special extended panel formats, and Kentucky has a trial skills demonstration and critique using an auto crash fact pattern. The Los Angeles County Bar Association offers a Bridge-the-gap program in conjunction with the DAILY JOURNAL, and is in the process of revamping its program to include lectures and an information fair, with tables for those with something of interest to offer new lawyers. It will have panel discussions with question-and-answer sessions and handouts. Under discussion is the possibility of having from one to three tracks for specializations aimed specifically at certain types of legal practice, for example, litigation.

60. KESTIN REPORT, *supra* note 44, at 15-19.

tured to prompt student interaction, and the materials are supplemented with bibliographies for additional study. An important aspect of the Skills Practice Course is the small class size encouraging experimentation and providing students with feedback on their performance. The format of the Washington program is what separates it from other programs that deal with lawyering skills, but attempt to do so through a lecture method, not through "learning by doing."

Speakers. All of the programs of transition education rely principally on volunteer members of the local bar to give the lectures in their programs. Generally, they are local practitioners billed as experts in their respective fields. Sometimes they are local judges. Only the Washington program adds that their instructors are "specially trained to teach skills." This lack of training in skills teaching would be more troublesome if more programs had a skills component. Variation among speakers is reflected primarily in the nature of the accompanying written materials they prepare and in the quality of their lectures. Several of the programs have evaluation forms that the participants fill out, one aspect of which deals with the speaker's effectiveness and grasp of the information.[61]

Program materials. Often, the speakers themselves develop the material that is distributed to the program's participants.[62] The materials are generally directed at those going into solo or small firm practice and cover a wide range of topics typically encountered in a general practice. Many of the course outlines are similarly of an exhaustive nature.[63]

---

61. For example, the South Carolina attendees pick up the program information for the day at the registration desk in the morning, and hand in course evaluations. The course evaluations act as a type of attendance check, to make sure the students do not pick up the material in the morning and leave.

62. Program materials are generally collected in either a looseleaf binder, that lends itself well to updating, or a softbound series of books.

63. For example, the Indiana program makes an effort to supply everything the beginning attorney might need to start an Indiana practice. The program distributes a large amount of material: three loose-leaf binders of information totalling approximately 1500 pages. The information is substantive, practical, and process-related. For example, some of the information included in the section on guardianship and adoption are: general adoption forms, an overview of private adoption procedure, statutory information including "Highlights of the New Indiana Guardian Act" as well as termination of guardianship, avoidance of guardianship and estate planning with respect to guardianship. The New Hampshire Practice and Procedure Handbook chapter on corporations includes checklists, substantive information, forms and fees, and a bibliography. In contrast, the chapter on family law (which is very large) covers divorce and marriage, adoptions and more. It includes sections on drafting, settlements, statutes, cases, sample forms, checklists and rate tables.

The Washington course, with its emphasis on hands-on learning, provides new attorneys with a fairly brief outline, backed up by reading material that fleshes out the skeleton, as well as critiques, checklists, exercises and a course evaluation. Bibliographies are available for further study at the participant's option.

Most of the materials are in the form of lecture outlines supplemented by sample forms, which may be blank or completed. Some of the providers of the programs oversee the materials handed out, others do not. This is a potential problem because it leaves the possibility of wide variation in the quality of lectures and program materials within the same course. In addition, some materials are skeletal outlines of little use for future reference after the lecture is concluded.[64]

Assessing Transition Education in the U.S.

The inadequacy of the existing programs of transition education in this country becomes apparent when they are compared with comparable programs in Commonwealth jurisdictions. In Appendix E to the Report, we briefly describe six Commonwealth programs for instructing new lawyers in professional skills and values. Although these programs provide a range of different models, they have much in common with each other that sets them apart from their United States counterparts.

Unlike the typically cursory programs in the United States, the Commonwealth programs range in length from ten weeks to as many as seven months. And, rather than focusing on imparting additional substantive knowledge, as do many of the bridge-the-gap programs, the Commonwealth programs generally focus on developing lawyering skills such as legal research, drafting, negotiation, interviewing and counseling, and trial advocacy. Students work on developing these skills in the context of specific problems or transactions, such as a matrimonial, personal injury or criminal litigation, a real estate conveyancing, or an incorporation. While students may occasionally attend lectures or observe demonstrations, these programs center on students' active involvement in particular tasks, ranging from participation in simulations or role playing exercises to drafting various documents. Feedback is provided on an ongoing basis, often by professional instructors or by trained volunteers.

Unlike the Commonwealth programs, U.S. programs have not tested the attendees to determine how much of the material was absorbed. The New Jersey Practical Skills course, which is a requirement for admission to the state Bar, requires participants to complete homework exercises which are graded and are a condition of passing the course. The Virginia program also has required homework assignments during the first year. None of the programs otherwise

---

64. The Mississippi handout on family law is comprised of a list of twenty-three forms. It is unclear how useful all of these would be to the practitioner without any supporting text after the program is only a dim memory.

test participants with an eye towards assessing whether they attain a level of minimal competency.

In contrast to the Commonwealth programs, many American programs have not avoided the pitfalls warned against in the Kestin Report, and have become "overly analytical [and] too substantive."[65] Too many bridge-the-gap programs are like bar review courses, with a smorgasbord of substantive law force-fed in a relatively short period of time. Yet, at least three substantial practical problems confront those who seek to develop programs of practical skills instruction in the United States of comparable quality to those in Commonwealth jurisdictions.

The first problem is one of funding. Most of the Commonwealth programs receive at least some government funding. Others have access to funds not available in the United States, such as the income from lawyers' trust accounts. In this country the programs are often funded solely by tuition paid by the new attorney. It would be difficult to persuade new attorneys, many burdened with debt from seven years of graduate and undergraduate education, to defer practice while they pay for fairly expensive post-graduate training. This difficulty is enlarged when the additional training is of a kind that is of little relevance to the practice in which the new lawyer plans to engage.

A second problem is that many states admit a large number of new lawyers each year—far more than even the largest of the Commonwealth jurisdictions. Not surprisingly, the sole example of a meaningful post-graduate skills-training program in this country, the Washington Practical Skills Course, has limited enrollments and can handle only a fraction of the admittees to the Washington Bar.

Finally, there is the administrative problem. The Commonwealth programs are all administered in whole or part by central associations. For example, the Ontario program is administered by the Law Society of Upper Canada. In marked contrast, the programs in this country are offered by a myriad of providers even within a single jurisdiction. Some are subject to the approval of a local bar association, others are not. Many programs are run by independent CLE providers who must turn a profit to stay in business.

Despite these practical difficulties, there are elements present in legal education in the United States today that are more favorable than ever before to developing an effective integrated process to

---

65. Kestin Report, *supra* note 44, at 26.

assist new lawyers in acquiring their lawyering skills and professional values as they enter the profession.

We have reviewed in Chapter 7 the progress made in American law schools in developing effective instruction in professional skills and values. The law school programs are substantially more extensive than those offered in Commonwealth schools. Separate from the law schools, transition education has been developed in the United States, but primarily as an off-shoot of the earlier movement in the profession—dating from the 1920s—to establish programs of continuing legal education. Up to this time, transition education of this kind has been hit-or-miss in the 50 states.

However, there have been recent steps taken in some states by licensing authorities and the organized bar to strengthen their programs of transition education, and, in some states, to require specific training for new lawyers as a part of a mandatory continuing legal education system. At the same time, law firms, corporate law departments and government agencies have developed in-house programs of transition education; while ALI-ABA has sponsored a series of projects for the purpose of improving the quality of what have been referred to as "bridge-the-gap" programs.

In the concluding sections of this Chapter we review these several developments in transition education and suggest that the time is auspicious, with the help of the proposed national institute, for licensing authorities, the law schools and the organized bar to integrate the various programs of skills and values instruction into the continuum of professional development.

Mandating Transition Education

Seven states (Maryland, Michigan, Missouri, New Jersey, New Mexico, North Carolina, and Oregon) require specific training for new attorneys as a special part of their mandatory continuing legal education systems. In Maryland, a mandatory course on legal professionalism is imposed on successful bar applicants as a condition to admission.[66] In Michigan, the skills training requirement for new attorneys is the state's only mandatory CLE. There, new attorneys are required to take 36 hours of courses provided by the Michigan

---

66. There are twelve other states which require specific training as a prerequisite for admission but do not couch this requirement in terms of mandatory continuing legal education. See list of states in footnote 46, *supra*. Making such education mandatory was a subject of considerable debate at the Arden House III Conference, with the Conferees unable to reach a consensus. Proponents thought mandatory programs were an acceptable burden on new admittees, would introduce new attorneys to the importance of continuing legal education, and would show the profession was concerned about professional standards. See ARDEN HOUSE III REPORT, *supra* note 32, at 18.

State Bar Association. In Missouri, new admittees must take 3 hours of professionalism, legal/judicial ethics, or malpractice in their first 12 months of practice. In New Mexico, the requirement is 10 hours of practical skills in the first two years. North Carolina requires 9 hours of practical skills in each of the first 3 years of practice. Oregon mandates 15 hours of course work, including 10 in practical skills.

In New Jersey, the home state of Judge Kestin, the skills training course is quite complex and covers three years measured from the sitting for the bar examination. A "core" component of professional responsibility, real estate, will drafting and probate practice, family law, and a choice of either civil or criminal trial preparation must be completed either prior to admission or within the first year following the bar examination. In the second year, New Jersey admittees must take the remaining trial course (civil or criminal) and administrative law. In the third year, attorneys select two courses from the following: purchase, organization, and sale of a small business; bankruptcy practice; collection practice; municipal court practice; worker's compensation practice; and landlord/tenant practice.

A State Bar of California Commission on Lawyering Skills, co-chaired by Dean Paul Brest of Stanford and former member of the State Bar Board of Governors Robin Donoghue, recently recommended to the Board of Governors that the existing California MCLE obligation be altered so that newly admitted attorneys would discharge most of the first three years of their MCLE obligation (34 of 36 required hours) by taking courses in designated professional lawyering skills. The Commission described these areas as: law office management, interviewing, counseling, drafting, negotiation, mediation, arbitration, pre-trial, trial, and appellate practice. The Commission recommended that this lawyering skills training be provided through "classroom learning and practical exercises" and include four to eight hours of legal ethics involving the practice of the skills and up to four hours of law office management. The Commission also recommended that completion of this training could also occur between law school and admission to practice, which in California is typically four months after graduation if the candidate is successful on the first attempt at the bar examination.[67]

The California Commission on Lawyering Skills specifically rejected a proposal of the California Committee of Bar Examiners

---

67. State Bar of California, Report and Recommendations of the Commission on Lawyering Skills, October 11, 1991. The recommendations were accepted by the Board of Governors of the State Bar of California in April 1992, and referred for implementation to a Board committee.

which would have required all bar applicants to have completed a "professional skills training program" of at least sixty hours covering specific topics, and "preferably" taken in law school. The Commission reasoned that the "preference" would pressure law schools to offer a standardized package skills course rather than allow admittees to choose skills training that was most appropriate to their professional interests and employment.[68]

This element of choice is also an important part of the pre-admission proposal under discussion in New York, which would mandate at least 100 hours of practice skills courses drawn from at least three defined skills areas.[69] Although the New York proposed requirement would have to be satisfied prior to admission to the bar, New York has specifically left open for further study the important issues of what lawyering skills might appropriately be tested and what kinds of evaluation might be appropriate to different skills.[70]

The New York proposal highlights the inadequacies of all seven of the current mandated programs of transition education and of the California proposal. While each these jurisdictions recognizes the importance of skills and values instruction at the beginning of practice, the Task Force expresses grave concerns about the effectiveness of the small numbers of hours allocated for professional skills instruction. Surely 9 hours (North Carolina) or 10 hours (Oregon and New Mexico) are woefully inadequate. Even 27 hours (North Carolina), 34 hours (California proposal) or 36 hours (Michigan), spread out over three years, appear meager compared with a typical law school clinical course. Moreover, only New Jersey appears to have incorporated any evaluation of the performance of the new attorneys. In the balance of the jurisdictions, the skills training appears to miss an essential element of professional skills instruction: immediate feedback and evaluation.

In-House Programs for New Lawyers

For a growing number of new lawyers, a substantial portion of transition education occurs on-the-job in programs organized by their employers. Law firms, corporate legal departments, and government agencies have all begun to provide in-house training that is specifically geared to the newest attorneys in their legal organizations.[71] While comprehensive in-house programs for new lawyers seek to fit the specific needs of the particular law office, they are likely to

---

68. *Id.* at 8-10.
69. *See* CITY BAR REPORT, *supra* Chapter 8, note 11, at 22-26.
70. *See* the extensive discussion in CITY BAR REPORT, *id.* at 26-37.
71. *See* Richard D. Lee, "The Organization and Role of In-House Training," ARDEN HOUSE III REPORT, *supra* note 32, at 333-56.

contain many, if not most, of the following elements:

- *mentoring*—a system of continuing supervision by a senior lawyer who reviews significant portions of the junior's work product, assists in revising and improving the product, and is available for informal consultation and support;
- *orientation*—a systematic introduction to the practice areas of the organization, common transactions handled, and the structure, management, and procedures of the organization;
- *substantive presentations*—a series of presentations in different areas of practice by specialty units within the organization;
- *monitoring of work assignments*—efforts to expose new lawyers to a variety of assignments using a checklist of work experiences that should be covered;
- *placing work in transactional context*—training to assist lawyers to understand their own contributions to larger transactions by cross-department training in other areas;
- *training in lawyering skills and values*—programs which commonly include writing, document drafting, client interviewing and counseling, specialized research skills for specific areas of practice, negotiating, trial advocacy, and management of work.

The continuing development of in-house programs by many of the nation's law firms, corporate law offices, and government agencies, has significance for an evaluation of existing transition education for bar applicants and new lawyers. The in-house programs are comprehensive, detailed, and generally focused on the enhancement of lawyering skills and professional values. The existence of these programs suggests that many employers have concluded that these skills and values must be taught to new lawyers as they begin practice, in order to properly serve the needs of the firms and their clients. But if the recruits for these legal organizations are getting needed or highly useful training, what of the much larger number of new attorneys who begin practice by themselves or in offices that do not provide such training?

The scope and extent of the in-house programs suggest some measure of what effective transition education could provide for new lawyers. The Task Force remains concerned, however, that far too little of this education focuses on the development of professional skills and values, that the availability of this education is uneven and unpredictable, that the education often fails to provide adequate feedback and evaluation, and that the amount of this education is often inadequate to meet the professional development needs of many new attorneys. The Task Force recommends that *all* new lawyers be provided with the opportunity to pursue a core set of training in professional skills and values, offered either privately or by state and local bar organizations.

Programs for Strengthening Transition Education

The plight of new lawyers beginning a general practice by themselves or in offices that provide little or no on-the-job training have been at the center of the ALI-ABA projects to improve the quality of transition education. The Kestin Report identified the need for programs to help recent graduates and new members of the bar to "establish a basic foundation in certain skills, techniques and procedures which, although essential components of law practice, may not have been adequately addressed in the traditional law school curriculum."[72] The report concluded that such a program would ideally be skills-oriented and it would include "the rudiments of interviewing, counseling, drafting, negotiating, plea bargaining, tactics, strategy and techniques, client relations, filing procedures, local court house procedures, protocol, etiquette and everyday ethics."[73]

The Kestin Report recommended the development of a hybrid, bifurcated bridge-the-gap program.[74] In response, ALI-ABA engaged Professor Marilyn Yarbrough, then at the University of Kansas, who developed a concept for a Model Curriculum which would be divided into two parts. The first, described as a "minimal goal" curriculum (referred to as "Introduction to Practice"), would be directed to the neophyte practicing attorney and geared to the new lawyer studying and doing those things that a new lawyer would be likely to handle at the very beginning of a new general practice career. It would be a 40-hour component, given just after or in conjunction with the bar examination.[75]

It would be designed to convey a sense of "what constitutes professionally acceptable work" to help neophyte lawyers recognize their limits.[76] It would provide introductions to law practice organization and management and to eight transactional categories which

---

72. Kestin Report, *supra* note 44, at 27.
73. *Id.* at 26.
74. *Id.* at 25.
75. American Law Institute-American Bar Association Committee on Continuing Professional Education, A Model Curriculum for Bridge-the-Gap Programs, Discussion Draft (1988) at 9–11 [hereafter "Model Curriculum"].
76. *Id.* at 10.

a new lawyer in general practice would be likely to encounter.[77] It would also provide forms and materials that might be used throughout a lawyer's practice.

The second portion of the Model Curriculum would be a Basic Skills module,[78] but would wait until the new lawyer had some experience. As the Reporter for the project explained, this training module would build upon what the lawyer had acquired in law school, in the Introduction to Practice module and in some actual practice experience since the skills instruction segment would be within the first two years of practice.

The Reporter further explained that the Basic Skills module was "greatly influenced by reports and evaluations" of the Commonwealth programs, but sensitive to practical considerations of the American legal scene: "Jurisdictional differences, lack of precedent, lack of tolerance for extended periods of post-J.D. education and the existence of a number of specialized subject matter and traditional courses."[79]

In the Basic Skills modules the performance skills training would be in the context of the traditional short courses offered by CLE providers of 2 or 3 days duration. The following were identified in the Model Curriculum as the "sub-skills" to be acquired, akin to the Task Force's analysis in its Statement of Skills and Values:

- Listening and Observing
- Analyzing and Interpreting Behavior
- Creating Conditions for Effective Communication
- Responding and Reacting Skillfully to Others
- Using Acceptable Language and Grammar
- Organizing Information
- Speaking Effectively
- Questioning Effectively
- Identifying and Evaluating Relevant Facts
- Identifying and Evaluating Legal Issues

---

77. *Id*. at 9. The core components recommended by the MODEL CURRICULUM would include: administrative practice, civil trial preparation, criminal trial preparation, debtor/creditor proceedings, small business transactions, real estate transactions, family law transactions, and estates and wills. See *id*. at 10.

78. *Id*. at 9-10. Completion of the skills portion would be required of new attorneys, although they should be able to fulfill parts of this requirement by the successful completion of a skills-oriented class (perhaps a clinic) in law school. The MODEL CURRICULUM also suggests that the skills portion be available to established practitioners as a CLE offering. *Id*. The substantive aspects of the courses could be voluntary, perhaps part of an expanded CLE curriculum. If they were required, the new attorneys should be able to pick courses from a selection, to ensure the greatest relevance to their areas of practice.

79. *Id*. at 12-13.

- Analyzing and Selecting Appropriate Options
- Designing and Implementing a Plan of Action[80]

The short courses would be in specialized substantive areas, designed to integrate substantive knowledge, specific tasks and related skills.

The ALI-ABA Committee developed a pilot Bridge-the-Gap Real Estate Training Module (the "real estate training module") as an example of how Professor Yarbrough's recommendation might be implemented.[81] The real estate training module is a skills training program that uses "simulation learning" with role playing. It introduces new lawyers, including those with general practice experience, to the special problems associated with real estate acquisitions and sales. The participant solves problems within the context of an actual real estate transaction. The aim of the real estate training module is not to teach substantive law, but it does provide references to background material. The training module deals with negotiating different aspects of the transaction and drafting the contract of sale, and teaches the skills of interviewing, transaction planning, and drafting. The course materials include a fact pattern in the form of a memo from a partner to an associate, as well as sample contracts. It addresses relevant issues, including financing concerns and questions of professional responsibility.[82]

The ALI-ABA Committee has expressed the hope that the pilot real estate training module would "test the feasibility of creating a series of practice modules," and if the pilot module is successful, ALI-ABA believes the success will "encourage others to undertake some of the measures the Yarbrough report proposed."[83]

The successive ALI-ABA sponsored projects since 1963 directed to transition education, together with the development of mandated programs of skills training for new lawyers and the rapid expansion of in-house programs for new staff attorneys, lend direction today to the strengthening of transition education. They challenge licensing authorities, the law schools and the organized bar, with the aid of the proposed national institute, to develop an inclusive process, integrated with the law schools' expanded professional skills instruction, by which new lawyers may begin their professional

---

80. *Id.* at 13.

81. AMERICAN LAW INSTITUTE-AMERICAN BAR ASSOCIATION COMMITTEE ON CONTINUING PROFESSIONAL EDUCATION, BRIDGE THE GAP REAL ESTATE TRAINING MODULE, STUDENT MANUAL, DRAFT NO. 5, April 1, 1991 (submitted to the Advisory Committee April 19, 1991).

82. *Id.*

83. Paul Wolkin, ALI-ABA . . . XL! 174 (1988).

development by acquiring the skills and values requisite for competent and responsible practice.

The review of the diversity of existing programs for bar applicants and new lawyers—from apprenticeships to in-house training—points up the importance of transition education to the legal profession. However, while there are many different programs, the Task Force is concerned as to how few of the present programs focus on developing lawyering skills and professional values and on making the program an integral part of the lawyer's continuum of professional development. The Task Force believes that all new lawyers should have access, either in law school or during transition education, to effective skills and values instruction. To achieve this goal, transition education must be available that is not only of high quality but provided in sufficiently varied modes and with adequate flexibility to meet the differing needs of law students who have had markedly different instruction in law school and who enter practice in an extraordinary diversity of practice setting.

Chapter Nine
Professional Development After Law School

A. The Development of Continuing Legal Education

The history of continuing legal education in the United States is intertwined with the history of legal education. Legal education began as apprenticeships, then moved to free standing law schools, then to the academy as these law schools joined the university movement.[1] But this very movement to the academy, which promoted a common education program prior to entry into the profession, tended to neglect the further education and training of the attorney once in practice.

Programs of special instruction for new lawyers are primarily a development only of the last 30 years. They were an outgrowth, however, of the earlier movement to establish post-admission legal education for all lawyers. The first organized programs to provide supplementary legal education for lawyers after their admission to the bar were the courses for veterans returning from World War I. Some bar groups such as the Association of the Bar of the City of New York sponsored lecture series to provide update and refresher programs for the veterans to bring them back up to speed. The Depression and the resulting rash of New Deal legislation prompted a much larger number of sponsors around the country (including the University of Iowa College of Law, Stanford University, the Cleveland Bar) to sponsor more substantial continuing legal education programs.

The most lasting of these programs appears to be the courses organized in 1933 by Harold Seligson, with the encouragement of Dean Frank Sommer of New York University Law School, and called the "Practising Law Courses." The first series were held in July at

---

1. See Chapter 3, supra.

NYU's Law Review office, were free, consisted of fifteen two-hour evening lectures, and were attended by about sixty lawyers. The second series was held in October, this time with a charge of $25 for a series of 25 lectures. The fee did not discourage attendance. Seligson's series ultimately became in 1938 the Practising Law Institute (PLI).[2]

PLI's efforts spawned other programs. Seligson's presentation to the 1937 annual meeting of the ABA Section of Legal Education and Admissions to the Bar led to an ABA resolution to sponsor and encourage a nationwide program of continuing legal education, yet little happened at the national level for a number of years. By 1938 bar groups in Toledo, San Francisco, Los Angeles, Washington, Boston, Milwaukee, and Dallas had begun courses similar to the "Practising Law Courses" and which used the Seligson materials. Inspired by this interest, Seligson conducted a summer program in New York City to which he invited attorneys from across the country. This program is probably the first national CLE program.

The veterans returning from World War II stimulated the ABA Section of Legal Education and Admissions to the Bar to provide refresher courses around the country from 1944 through 1947. The success of these courses prompted the ABA House of Delegates, in 1946, to direct the Section, through its Committee on Continuing Education of the Bar, to initiate and foster a national program of continuing education of the bar. With the assistance of the Association of American Law Schools and the ABA Junior Bar Conference, the Section's Committee on Continuing Education, in August of 1947, presented its report to the ABA House recommending that the American Law Institute, with the cooperation of the ABA and PLI, develop the national program. The report was approved by the House of Delegates; however, the operating "Memorandum of Understanding" which followed was only between the ALI and the ABA. PLI was in effect relegated to conducting programs in New York, while the new group, a joint committee eventually called the American Law Institute-American Bar Association Committee on Continuing Professional Education (soon dubbed ALI-ABA), began its work.[3]

ALI-ABA quickly went about its mission. In the period from 1947 to 1958, ALI-ABA set about to encourage state and local bar associations to create sponsoring agencies which could put on CLE courses with ALI-ABA's help through co-sponsorship, supplying literature, and providing speakers. The first director was Harold Mulder, a law

---

2. For an account of these early years, as well as of the half century that followed, see Practising Law Institute, The First Fifty Years (1983).

3. The history of ALI-ABA is told by Paul Wolkin in ALI-ABA . . . XL! (1988).

professor at the University of Pennsylvania Law School. He was soon joined by a Director for the Western Area, Professor James Brenner of Stanford University Law School, and soon thereafter by Professor Charles Joiner, then of the University of Michigan School of Law, who became the Director for the Mid-Western Area. By 1958 ALI-ABA had participated in approximately 500 courses which drew an attendance exceeding 50,000 attorneys.

In 1958, the presidents of the ABA and the ALI convened the first Arden House National Conference on Continuing Education of the Bar. Arden House I recommended that permanent CLE organizations be formed in many states, modeled after existing organizations in California and Wisconsin. The conference recommended increased emphasis on education for professional responsibility. ALI-ABA was urged to stimulate lawyers to attend more CLE programs and to give special attention to meeting the needs of newly admitted lawyers. ALI-ABA was also asked to study the possibility of establishing standards for CLE programs.[4]

The Arden House recommendations quickly took root. In the next five years 22 additional states had established continuing legal education administrations. The state administrators had formed their own professional organization (now called ACLEA, the Association of Continuing Legal Education Administrators), with Felix Stumpf of California Continuing Education of the Bar as its first president and ALI-ABA Director Mulder as its secretary. ALI-ABA had begun to sponsor directly and independently national programs of continuing legal education. Success, however, bred its own problems as programs proliferated and private providers began offering CLE.

To deal with these problems, ALI-ABA sponsored a second Arden House conference, held in December 1963.[5] This conference dealt with four areas: (1) improvement of education literature, programs, and techniques; (2) meeting the education needs of the newly admitted lawyer; (3) implementing the concept of education for professional responsibility; and (4) the organization and financing of CLE.

For professional responsibility education, the conference concluded that while direct instruction was desirable, it was far more likely that issues of ethics and professional responsibility would be met if taught by a "pervasive" method of infusion into coursework

---

4. The text of the Final Statement of Arden House I can be found as Appendix A to the ARDEN HOUSE III REPORT (1988), at 579-82. See AMERICAN LAW INSTITUTE-AMERICAN BAR ASSOCIATION COMMITTEE ON CONTINUING PROFESSIONAL EDUCATION, CLE AND THE LAWYER'S RESPONSIBILITIES IN AN EVOLVING PROFESSION (1988). (Hereafter ARDEN HOUSE III REPORT.)

5. ARDEN HOUSE II REPORT, *supra* Chapter 8, note 32.

or by a "collateral" method where the problems were treated separately but as part of a substantive program. In response, ALI-ABA engaged Professor Vern Countryman of Harvard Law School to prepare professional responsibility materials for use by state CLE administrators.[6]

This same time period saw the emergence of the American Bar Association as a major provider of continuing legal education courses. The ABA Standing Committee on Continuing Education of the Bar had been established in 1958, perhaps to reestablish a separate role for the ABA in CLE apart from its joint participation in ALI-ABA. By 1966 the efforts of the ABA Standing Committee and the ABA Sections had begun to collide with the efforts of ALI-ABA. Attempts at reconciliation resulted in a standoff, with the ABA at its annual meeting authorizing the creation of an extensive program of National Institutes whose schedules were to be "coordinated" with ALI-ABA.[7] However the relationship is characterized, the ABA Standing Committee had become a major CLE player. In 1974, the ABA established, under the jurisdiction of the Standing Committee, the Division for Professional Education to assist sections and divisions in their CLE efforts and ultimately to develop CLE programs for the Association. In 1976 the ABA established the Consortium for Professional Education which has since become the leading producer of Video Law Seminars as an alternative to conventional CLE programming.

At about the same time the Practising Law Institute began to venture off Manhattan Island. During 1968-1969, PLI offered courses first in San Juan, Puerto Rico, then in St. Louis and Las Vegas. By 1970, PLI was offering 338 courses in 21 cities in 18 states. By the mid-1970s, PLI, ALI-ABA, and the ABA Division for Professional Education had all become major national providers.

In 1981, ALI-ABA began transmitting by satellite live programs which were produced by ALI-ABA or by the ABA. Today, the American Law Network (ALN), under ALI-ABA management, but working closely with both the ABA and PLI, operates a dedicated satellite broadcast network which delivers CLE programs of the three sponsors throughout the country to more than 75 downsites primarily at bar associations and law schools.

In response to the development during the 1980s of in-house

---

6. Professor Countryman's materials are published as AMERICAN LAW INSTITUTE-AMERICAN BAR ASSOCIATION COMMITTEE ON CONTINUING PROFESSIONAL EDUCATION, PROBLEMS OF PROFESSIONAL RESPONSIBILITY UNDER THE UNIFORM COMMERCIAL CODE, UNIFORM COMMERCIAL CODE PRACTICE HANDBOOK 7 (1969).

7. *See* Wolkin, *supra* note 3, at 77-93.

training programs, ALI-ABA, in cooperation with the ABA Standing Committee, established in 1984 the American Institute for Law Training within the Office (AILTO). By 1992 AILTO had 193 member law firms, corporate law departments, and government agencies sharing in its resource materials, workshops, special programs, and an extensive roster of consultants who deliver in-house programs in a wide variety of skills and substantive subjects.

Meanwhile ALI-ABA has continued an extensive program of research and development to enhance the quality of lawyering. In the recent past it has included projects relating to the quality of law practice, the quality of CLE, instructional models for newly-admitted lawyers, and methods for self-evaluation both as to the quality of law practice and as to subject competence in particular practice modules.[8]

The presidents of the ABA and the ALI have convened three Arden House National Conferences on Continuing Education of the Bar (in 1958, 1963, and 1987). Out of the recommendations from these conferences came permanent CLE organizations in many states; a professional organization for CLE administrators (ACLEA); concern for the organization, financing, and quality of CLE; and a continuing emphasis on the relationship between CLE and lawyer competence. The Final Statement of Arden House III urged the organized bar to encourage all efforts to enhance competence, stressed the role that law schools could continue to play in teaching skills, and encouraged CLE providers to conduct meaningul transition education programs and to offer a wide variety of skills programs. The report concluded that a central objective of CLE should continue to be the enhancement of lawyer competence.[9]

B. The Growth in Mandatory CLE

Concerns about lawyer competence were the impetus for Mandatory Continuing Legal Education (MCLE) which began in 1975 when Iowa and Minnesota adopted the first programs.[10] By the end of the seventies, these states had been joined by Colorado, Idaho, North Dakota, Washington, Wisconsin, and Wyoming.

In August 1986, the ABA House of Delegates, on the motion of

---

8. *See* AMERICAN LAW INSTITUTE-AMERICAN BAR ASSOCIATION COMMITTEE ON CONTINUING PROFESSIONAL EDUCATION, 1992 ANNUAL REPORTS, REPORT OF THE EXECUTIVE DIRECTOR 1-17.

9. ARDEN HOUSE III REPORT, *supra* note 4, at 4-5.

10. *See* Ralph G. Wellington, "MCLE: Does It Go Far Enough and What Are the Alternatives?" ARDEN HOUSE III REPORT, *supra* note 4, at 359-73.

the Young Lawyers Division and the State Bars of Colorado, Georgia, Mississippi and Wisconsin, adopted a resolution supporting the concept of mandatory continuing legal education for all active lawyers and urging the various states that had not yet adopted such a program to seriously consider doing so. The resolution was followed by additional states adopting MCLE.

In 1991 California became the thirty-seventh state to adopt MCLE (though in California the "M" stands for "Minimum" not "Mandatory"). Pennsylvania became the thirty-eighth state in mid-1992. Several other major states, including New York, are seriously considering joining these ranks.

The requirements in all of these states are strikingly similar.[11] Attorneys must complete a certain number of hours of coursework (ranging from 8 to 15 per year) and regularly report their compliance (every two or three years) to a state authority. Failure to comply leads ultimately to suspension from practice.

There are minor variations among state requirements. Many states grant exemptions for special groups, such as judges, elected officials, legislators, or non-residents. Some states grant credit for self-study; some for the preparation of teaching materials or attendance at bar meetings. Some states are hostile to in-house programs presented by law firms, while others grant full parity to such programs.[12]

A number of states specify substantive course requirements. Twenty states require hours in ethics or professionalism, eighteen in discrete course units, one (Minnesota) pervasively through regular course offerings. Pennsylvania, the twentieth, has as its only MCLE requirement five hours per year on the Pennsylvania Rules of Professional Conduct and "the subject of professionalism generally."

California has the largest number of special requirements. In California, of the 36 hours required in three years, at least eight

---

11. Many states have adopted requirements which are closely based on the AMERICAN BAR ASSOCIATION MODEL RULE FOR MINIMUM CONTINUING LEGAL EDUCATION, passed by the ABA House of Delegates in August 1988 (and slightly modified in February 1989) after development by the ABA Standing Committee on Continuing Education of the Bar. The Model Rule, in turn, was developed in response to a resolution adopted by the ABA House of Delegates in August 1986 supporting the concept of MCLE for all active members and urging the serious consideration of MCLE by the various states that had not yet adopted such a program. A chart summarizing the various state requirements can be found in the annual AMERICAN BAR ASSOCIATION, SECTION OF LEGAL EDUCATION AND ADMISSIONS TO THE BAR AND NATIONAL CONFERENCE OF BAR EXAMINERS, COMPREHENSIVE GUIDE TO BAR ADMISSIONS REQUIREMENTS.

12. *See* "MCLE Credit for In-House Activities," AILTO Update, THE AILTO INSIDER: A NEWSLETTER OF IN-HOUSE TRAINING DEVELOPMENTS, Vol. 5, No. 1 (Winter 1991).

must be in legal ethics and/or law practice management, with at least four of the eight hours in legal ethics. In addition, California requires at least one hour on the "prevention, detection, and treatment of substance abuse and emotional distress" and at least one additional hour on "elimination of bias in the legal profession based on any of, but not limited to the following characteristics: sex, color, race, religion, ancestry, national origin, blindness or other physical disability, age, and sexual orientation."

MCLE and Competence

MCLE has usually been justified as an effort to maintain the competence of the bar.[13] California, for example, describes the purpose of its continuing legal education requirement as "to assure that, throughout their careers, California attorneys remain current regarding the law, the obligations and standards of the profession, and the management of their practices."[14]

Not surprisingly, there is little evidence regarding mandatory CLE's effect on competence. Some writers focus on statistics that show that large numbers of attorneys do not participate in voluntary CLE and therefore need the inducement of a mandatory requirement in order to get appropriate education.[15] Efforts to compare attorneys in mandatory and non-mandatory states have not produced any useful results. An Arden House III recommendation that the ABA arrange for a study of MCLE to determine "whether it makes a significant contribution to lawyer competence" has not been followed.

While the debate over the effectiveness of mandating CLE continues,[16] the Task Force is concerned about the lack of focus on the development of lawyering skills and values. Despite the call at Arden House III for increased attention to professional skills instruction in CLE, there has been little progress to this time. For the new lawyer, only seven states require some instruction in

---

13. *See* the articles cited in Wellington, *supra* note 10. Indeed, the notion that all CLE, whether or not mandatory, is fundamental to enhancing competence was assumed by the Arden House III Conference. *See, e.g.*, the title of the Third Plenary Session: "CLE and the Responsibilities of the Lawyer: The Lawyer's Responsibility for Continuing Education to Enhance Competence." *See also* the Final Statement, ARDEN HOUSE III REPORT, *supra* note 4, at 4.

14. STATE BAR OF CALIFORNIA, MCLE RULES AND REGULATIONS, Section 1.0, adopted by the Board of Governors on December 8, 1990.

15. *See, e.g.*, the studies reported in Wellington, *supra* note 10, at footnote 8.

16. *See* Wellington, *supra* note 10, for a flavor of the debate. For recent negative commentary, see Chapter 5, "Mandatory CLE: An Incompetent Solution to the Competency Problem," in JOEL HENNING, HIRING, TRAINING AND DEVELOPING PRODUCTIVE LAWYERS (1992); and Victor Rubino, "MCLE: The Downside," THE CLE JOURNAL AND REGISTER, Vol. 38, No. 1 (January 1992), at 14-17.

professional lawyering skills.[17] For the established lawyer, none of the thirty-eight MCLE jurisdictions requires any instruction in lawyering skills. Only twenty states require any hours in ethics or professionalism.

The Task Force recommends that all states, including those that have yet to adopt an MCLE requirement, give serious consideration to imposing upon all attorneys subject to their jurisdiction a requirement for periodic instruction in fundamental lawyering skills and professional values. We would urge that such instruction be participatory in nature, be taught by instructors trained in teaching skills and values, and include concurrent feedback and evaluation.

C. The Extent and Diversity of Current CLE Programs

Today, continuing legal education is provided by an array of over 300 organizations. These range from the three national providers described above (PLI, ALI-ABA, and the ABA), to significant independent state organizations such as California's Continuing Education of the Bar (CEB) and Michigan's Institute for Continuing Legal Education (ICLE), to major local bar associations such as the Association of the Bar of the City of New York and the Bar Association of San Francisco, to joint ventures among various bar groups, to a number of law schools.[18]

The vast majority of CLE providers are not-for-profit organizations, although the last few years have seen a dramatic increase in the number of for-profit groups, such as The Rutter Group in California, and various publishers such as the Bureau of National Affairs (BNA), Federal Publications (FPI), the Law Journal Seminars-Press, Prentice-Hall, and Bancroft-Whitney. Other significant national for-profit groups include the Professional Education Group (PEG) and

---

17. See Chapter 8.E, *supra*.

18. *See* Austin Anderson, "Continuing Legal Education Organizations: Structure and Financing," ARDEN HOUSE III REPORT, *supra* note 4, at 81-99; and Kathleen H. Lawner, "Summary of Findings: CLE Structure and Finance Survey," *id.* at 101-57. For additional background *see* AMERICAN LAW INSTITUTE-AMERICAN BAR ASSOCIATION COMMITTEE ON CONTINUING PROFESSIONAL EDUCATION, A MODEL FOR CONTINUING LEGAL EDUCATION: STRUCTURE, METHODS, AND CURRICULUM, DISCUSSION DRAFT, ALI-ABA (1980); and AMERICAN LAW INSTITUTE-AMERICAN BAR ASSOCIATION COMMITTEE ON CONTINUING PROFESSIONAL EDUCATION, STUDY OF THE QUALITY OF CONTINUING LEGAL EDUCATION (1979). For a recent effort to establish standards for CLE organizations, *see* AMERICAN LAW INSTITUTE-AMERICAN BAR ASSOCIATION COMMITTEE ON CONTINUING PROFESSIONAL EDUCATION, ATTAINING EXCELLENCE IN CLE: STANDARDS FOR QUALITY AND METHODS FOR EVALUATION, OFFICIAL DRAFT (1991), [hereafter "CLE STANDARDS"] discussed in Chapter 9.D, *infra*.

Professional Education Systems, Inc. (PES). National not-for-profit groups include the Defense Research Institute (DRI), the Association of Trial Lawyers of America (ATLA), The National Institute for Trial Advocacy (NITA), and the American Arbitration Association.

The primary activity of most CLE providers is the furnishing of courses. However, the sales of course materials, hardbound books, audiotapes, video cassettes, periodicals, floppy diskettes, newsletters, special reports, and workshops, and in-house training have become increasingly important sources of revenue. The courses have usually fallen into three groups: intermediate and advanced courses for specialists; refresher courses for experienced practitioners; and courses stimulated by new court rules, new court decisions, new agency rulings, or new legislation. Fewer than 10 percent of the courses are introductory or so-called "bridge-the-gap" courses.

There do not appear to be any statistics on the proportion of CLE courses which deal with fundamental lawyering skills. The National Institute for Trial Advocacy (NITA) sponsors a large number of regional and national workshops in its field. Similarly intensive programs are offered by a few law schools, such as Hastings College of Law, University of California in San Francisco, and Temple University School of Law in Philadelphia. Shorter, less intensive programs are sponsored by specialty bar groups, some of the larger state CLE organizations, and by PLI, ABA, and ALI-ABA.

Fewer than half of the CLE organizations provide discrete courses on ethics and professional responsibility. Such discrete courses have not attracted large enrollments except when offered to satisfy specific ethics requirements in mandatory CLE jurisdictions. CLE providers claim that they have included ethics and professional responsibility issues in 90% of their substantive courses.

The 1980s saw a dramatic increase in the number and kinds of CLE providers within the following groups:

- National, state, and local bar associations;
- Special interest bar associations;
- Law schools and other private and public educational institutions;
- Individual lawyer entrepreneurs;
- For-profit organizations; and
- Law firms.

These new organizations provide the profession today with a wealth of opportunities to obtain CLE.

There are very few national statistics about the scope and

content of CLE course offerings. ALI-ABA publishes six times a year THE CLE JOURNAL AND REGISTER, which lists by date, state, and subject those courses which CLE providers have requested be listed. Regrettably, this is a self-selecting list that does not capture courses offered by many state CLE organizations and most local bar associations. It does, however, list most of the offerings of the major CLE providers.

These selected statistics are nonetheless impressive. A year of listings in THE CLE JOURNAL AND REGISTER (May 1991-March 1992) totals 3,734 courses. Of these, 1965 were provided by state sponsors, 390 by PLI, 116 by Federal Publications, 111 by ALI-ABA, 85 by the Bureau of National Affairs (BNA), and 76 by the ABA.[19] The largest number of courses offered by state CLE organizations were in Pennsylvania (321), California (312), Michigan (171), Texas (130), and New York (111). Even these incomplete statistics testify to the multitude of CLE courses available today to the legal profession.

D. On-the-Job and In-House Training

In the last decade, there has been dramatic growth of "in-house" (or on-site) training programs in law firms, corporate law departments, and government agencies.[20] Many of these legal organizations now have training committees, often assisted by part-time non-lawyer staff. A number have hired full-time professionals to develop and manage their training programs.[21] Others have made extensive use of outside training consultants for their in-office programs. The law training programs conducted within the office are perceived by these law organizations as an efficient way to deal with the expanded training needs for large legal staffs with special training requirements.

Today, many private law firms, corporate law departments, and government agencies rely on in-house training programs to handle a substantial portion of their training needs instead of CLE programs

---

19. AMERICAN LAW INSTITUTE-AMERICAN BAR ASSOCIATION COMMITTEE ON CONTINUING PROFESSIONAL EDUCATION, 1992 ANNUAL REPORTS, APPENDIX H/CLE PROGRAMS OFFERED 166-167.

20. *See* Richard D. Lee, "The Organization and Role of In-House Training," ARDEN HOUSE III REPORT, *supra* note 4, at 333-56.

21. There are now over seventy full-time professionals at some of the nation's larger firms, corporate law departments, and government agencies. These individuals have recently founded a professional organization, the Professional Development Consortium, which has formal meetings twice a year and regularly shares training and educational information. In a number of larger cities, such as San Francisco, Washington, New York, Atlanta, and Cleveland, full-time and part-time professional development managers have formed regional consortia which meet regularly.

outside the office. These programs (as in the case of in-house programs for new lawyers, *supra* Chapter 8.E) have many of the following formal elements:

- Orientation of new attorneys;
- Showcase presentations;
- Training in substantive areas;
- Training in lawyering skills and values;
- Senior attorneys trained as instructors;
- Outside experts used as presenters or consultants;
- Course materials developed from practice files; and
- Simulations, often taped and critiqued.

The programs are planned in advance, materials prepared, and participants informed as to specific content. Legal organizations, and particularly the larger law firms, have long engaged in less formal training efforts in the day-to-day supervision of work and discussion of assignments. It is the more formal programs that have recently been added.

The formal in-house programs have the advantage of being tailored to the specific needs of the lawyers in the particular office. The program may include forms and procedures that are unique to the office, and the attorneys can learn both the subject specialty and the related office practice. Moreover, the organization can use its own expertise. More senior attorneys can do the planning, develop teaching materials, and make actual presentations. Programs can be scheduled at the most convenient time. More attorneys can be exposed to more training opportunities. Travel to programs outside the office can be reduced and time away from the office.

Instruction and training in fundamental lawyering skills and professional values are a prominent part of many in-house programs. Many legal organizations regularly schedule training in research techniques, writing, drafting, client interviewing, client counseling, negotiating, trial preparation, and trial advocacy. Most of the skills training is done with simulations, with instruction by specially trained teachers, and with feedback and contemporaneous evaluation of lawyer performance.

An important element of many in-house programs is training senior attorneys to become more effective supervisors, to make better work assignments, to manage the efficient flow of work done under their direction, and to provide effective critiques of that work. A few firms have sought to improve supervisory skills by having associates regularly and systematically evaluate partner abilities to supervise effectively.[22]

Some legal organizations have developed regular, systematic training in-house in professional responsibility and in risk management topics, including conflicts of interest, confidentiality, new business intake procedures, and docket and calendaring procedures.

Austin G. Anderson, A PLAN FOR LAWYER DEVELOPMENT, prepared for the ABA Standing Committee on Continuing Education of the Bar, comprehensively treats the major phases involved in planning and implementing an in-office training program. *The AILTO Insider* is a newsletter of in-house training developments, published quarterly by AILTO, The American Institute for Law Training within the Office (a project of ALI-ABA in cooperation with the ABA Standing Committee). A third aid is the *Lawyer Hiring & Training Report* published monthly by Prentice-Hall, Inc. A useful new resource for law offices is the self-evaluation guide recently produced by ALI-ABA, A PRACTICAL GUIDE TO ACHIEVING EXCELLENCE IN THE PRACTICE OF LAW: STANDARDS, METHODS, AND SELF-EVALUATION (1992).[23]

E. The Continuing Quest for Excellence

The Arden House III Conference spent an entire plenary session addressing the quality of CLE. Attorneys expressed general satisfaction with the quality of the programs they attended, but professional educators expressed the view that programs could be substantially improved through better teaching methods adapted to the ways by which adults learn. Conferees identified other potential improvements, including innovative delivery systems, use of computer-assisted instruction, mandatory CLE, and the need for training of new CLE instructors. The Final Statement of the Conference included a recommendation that ALI-ABA "undertake a study to design methods to evaluate the quality of CLE programs and materials and the performance of CLE providers."

The ALI-ABA study, ATTAINING EXCELLENCE IN CLE: STANDARDS

---

22. *See* Richard D. Lee, "Associate Evaluations of Partners," In-House Applications, THE AILTO INSIDER: A NEWSLETTER OF IN-HOUSE TRAINING DEVELOPMENTS, Vol. 4, No. 4 (Fall 1990).

23. THE PRACTICAL GUIDE is divided in three parts: stages of client representation, managing the lawyer's practice, and skills to be employed in accomplishing the client's objectives. It includes "black letter" standards, followed by extensive Comments with suggested practice and ethical considerations, practical examples often drawn from actual cases, and a comprehensive series of self-evaluation questions which enable readers to evaluate their own practice.

FOR QUALITY AND METHODS FOR EVALUATION (Official Draft, 1991), is the product of the recommended study. The study was led by attorney Robert K. Emerson, who chaired the Arden House III conference, and Felix F. Stumpf (former head of the California Continuing Education of the Bar), who served as Reporter. The study stressed the importance of evaluating CLE providers to establish accountability and to ensure acceptable quality. The study concluded that CLE providers could effectively engage in self-evaluation if they rigorously tested themselves against a set of educational quality standards, but that it was "premature" to consider an independent accreditation system to ensure compliance with standards. The report noted that the standards could serve as guidelines in states with mandatory CLE in approving CLE programs and providers.

The standards are based on the PRINCIPLES OF GOOD PRACTICE IN CONTINUING EDUCATION, promulgated in 1984 by The International Association for Continuing Education and Training (formerly the Council on the Continuing Education Unit). The 1984 *Principles* have been lauded by some and criticized by others. The criticism has centered on what has been described as the "heavy emphasis on the ideology of technical competence" without addressing ethical concerns and values and the ends of education.[24]

The whole thrust of the Task Force effort is at odds with isolating "the ideology of technical competence" as expressed in the 1984 Principles of Good Practice. The Statement of Skills and Values emphasizes the essential linkage between lawyering skills and professional values. It is hoped that this holistic approach to lawyering will in the future help avoid the perpetuation of the notion that competence is simply a matter of attaining proficiency in specified skills.[25]

---

24. *See* critics cited in Introduction to CLE Standards, *supra* note 18, at 22.
25. *See* Chapter 4.D, *supra*, for a discussion of uses by practicing lawyers of the Statement of Skills and Values in self-evaluation and self-development.

Chapter Ten
The Need for a National Institute to Enhance the Process of Lawyers' Professional Development

In the preceding sections we have surveyed the extended process by which individual lawyers acquire and refine those lawyering skills and professional values, along with the learning, that are requisite for the lawyer's calling. Traditionally, this process has been considered in three discrete segments, commonly identified as "pre-law," "law school" and "post-admission legal education." This manner of viewing the process served to reinforce the separateness of the education of law students from the career and professional development of lawyers, adding to the perception of that "gap" between the two which this Task Force was created to address.

The issue of relating education in law school more closely to the practice of law has received recurring attention both before and after Jerome Frank posed the question: "Why Not a Clinical Lawyer-School?"[1] During the 1960s there was new interest in the question of what law schools could do to enhance the quality of lawyering and the sense of professional responsibility among members of the bar. Beginning in 1968 the Ford Foundation sponsored for the next ten years the Council on Legal Education for Professional Responsibility (CLEPR) with the declared mission "to incorporate clinical legal education as an integral and an esteemed part of the curriculum of the country's law schools; that is to say, to bring about a major reform of the entire system of legal education." While CLEPR may have fallen short of its ultimate goal, it is clear that the clinical education movement in the law schools grew significantly during the decade of the 1970s.

Meanwhile, in the separate sphere of post-admission legal education, ALI-ABA convened in 1968 a national conference to address the emerging issues of continuing legal education as it grew at the local, state and national level. The conference called upon ALI-ABA to initiate a comprehensive study of the entire structure of post-admission legal education. It was explicitly recognized that such a study of the profession's continuing education could not be isolated from education in law school, nor could it be separated from the practice of law and the lawyer's service to the public.

---

1. J. Frank, "Why Not a Clinical Lawyer-School?", 81 U. OF PA.L. REV. 907 (1933).

To conduct a preliminary feasibility study ALI-ABA secured the services of Willard Wirtz, who had recently served as Secretary of Labor. He proposed a project that would address the entire "educational continuum" of professional development from law school throughout the lawyer's professional life. ABA, ALI and AALS agreed jointly to sponsor such a project. Nevertheless, despite the great promise of the project it was abandoned for lack of funding and the idea of addressing the education of lawyers and their professional development as an integrated continuum remained dormant until revived by this Task Force.

The Task Force has undertaken to examine what law schools are doing to develop lawyers and to inquire to what end. This has led in turn to consideration of the changing nature and characteristics of the profession for which lawyers must prepare and what the profession itself is doing through post-admission legal education to further the professional development of its members. From all of this emerged the notion of a continuum of professional development as a unifying force to sustain and enhance the profession.

In Part I of this report we have provided an overview of the growth, change and diversity of the legal profession. We have noted how the profession, over the period 1947 to 1991, grew from less than 200,000 lawyers to just short of 800,000 and how, as the profession grew, it became ever more diverse and differentiated, but somehow more unified as a common calling.

Nevertheless, increasing concern has been expressed as to the competence of lawyers and as to their adherence to professional values. Despite the increased attention in the law schools to preparing lawyers for practice and wide-ranging efforts by the organized bar to enhance lawyer competence and professional responsibility, calls have persisted for a more comprehensive response focused upon the entire process, from before law school, during law school and throughout lawyers' professional lives, by which lawyers acquire and refine their lawyering skills and professional values.

We have concluded that the time has come to focus upon the interrelationships and the linkage between the several phases of lawyers' education and also upon the interdependence of law schools and the practicing bar. To that end, in developing this report we have sought to identify elements common to all three phases of the educational process which we believe should serve as the foundation for the lawyer's educational continuum. These are the elements that can help hold together an extraordinarily diverse profession and preserve its unity and identity as a public calling.

Thus in Part II of the report we have offered a vision of the lawyering skills and professional values which we suggest new lawyers should seek to acquire, helping to define for them what it means to be a lawyer. We have suggested uses in various phases of lawyers' development that could be made of a statement of skills and values: by law students, by law schools, by developers of CLE programs, by law offices designing in-house training programs and by individual lawyers in their self-evaluation and self-development. We look to an evolving statement of skills and values to provide the core elements for the lawyer's educational continuum.

This report itself can be only a beginning in overcoming the separateness in the several phases of lawyers' professional development and in eliminating gaps in the educational process. Something on-going and focused on enhancing the practice of law is needed to promote in the law schools and within the organized bar the concept of a continuum. To carry forward the project, we recommend that a new organization, a national institute, be established with the central purpose of promoting excellence in the practice of law. It would address on a continuing basis the entire process by which lawyers acquire and refine the lawyering skills and professional values which, together with the requisite learning, are required for competent and responsible practice.

We have earlier noted[2] how a national institute for the practice of law could stimulate discussion and refinement of thinking about lawyers' skills and values, could develop modes of instruction, course materials, problems, and methods of assessment to assist law schools to teach skills and values more effectively, and could serve as a clearinghouse of model curricula, instructional materials and teacher training for CLE and law office programs. In such ways, the national institute would help develop an educational continuum for all lawyers which could support their professional development throughout their careers in the law.

We would visualize the work and activities of the proposed institute falling in three principal areas:

- Serving as a resource center and forum for legal scholars, educators and practicing lawyers working to promote lawyers' professional development;
- Fostering research and development to enhance the profession's understanding of lawyering skills and professional values and the means and methods by which lawyers learn; and

---

2. See Chapter 4.D, *supra.*

- Developing a plan and organizational structure to promote and disseminate courses and programs of continuing legal education.[3]

Many of the individual activities to be included in the work of the institute would not be new. Existing organizations of the bar and of the academy since the 1930s and 40s have separately addressed different aspects of the work. What would be new would be a new interconnectedness and coordination of that work and the viewing of the educational process for lawyers as a continuing one, beginning before law school and stretching out through lawyers' professional lives.

In the preceding chapters we have traced the law school's role in the professional development of lawyers and assessed today's enhanced law school instruction in lawyering skills and professional values. We have noted the development of new methodologies of instruction and other advances, but we have stressed the need for a still greater focus upon preparing lawyers for practice and general professional development during the law school years.

We have also traced the development of post-admission legal education at the national, state and local level and the respective roles of PLI, ABA and ALI-ABA in initiation and great expansion of continuing legal education. We have marked the institution of a satellite broadcast network and other innovations in the delivery of educational programs and materials to lawyers, as well as the in-house movement to bring formal training programs into law offices. But we have called attention to the need for additional programs to help in the transition from law school to law practice and to address the special problems of those beginning practice without mentor or supervision.

It is clear that the geneses exist for creating an organization to promote excellence in the practice of law in the three national non-profit providers of continuing legal education. They offer the opportunity to build upon past accomplishment, experience and existing programs while bringing together what have been to this time separate and often duplicative efforts.

Since at least December 1980, the ABA and the ALI have given intermittent attention to the desirability of merging existing professional education activities into an independent 501(c)(3) education institution of the kind that the Task Force now proposes. The subject

---

3. Appendix F is a suggested Mission Statement for the proposed institute which enumerates in greater detail the activities visualized in each of the three principal areas.

was successively discussed early in 1981, again in 1982-83, and once again in 1985-86. To this time, such discussions have not borne fruit, but in the light of the Task Force report and the present circumstances and recent developments with respect to continuing legal education, we urge that the pooling of resources be reexamined and the additional possibility be explored of enlisting PLI and AALS as cosponsors of the merged organization.

In sum, we submit that the time has come to put the pieces together. We urge that a new corporation be organized that would qualify as a 501(c)(3) corporation. We suggest that the name of the corporation be "The American Institute for the Practice of Law" and that its mission and purpose be in accordance with those set forth above and in the Mission Statement set out in Appendix F.

Part IV.
Recommendations of the Task Force

Task Force Recommendations

A. Disseminating and Discussing the Statement of Skills and Values
B. Choosing a Career in Law and a Law School
C. Enhancing Professional Development During the Law School Years
D. Placing the Transition and Licensing Process in the Educational Continuum
E. Striving for Professional Excellence After Law School
F. Establishing an American Institute for the Practice of Law

This Report has provided a unique overview of the legal profession today for which new lawyers must prepare (Part I, *supra*). It has presented a vision of the skills and values that one aspiring to join that profession should seek to acquire before assuming responsibility for the handling of legal matters (Part II, *supra*). Against this backdrop, we have examined the process by which lawyering skills and professional values are acquired: before law school, during law school and after law school (Part III, *supra*).

Interspersed through these preceding chapters are recommendations for improving and integrating the process by which lawyers acquire their skills and values and for enhancing lawyers' professional development at all stages of their careers. In this final segment of the Report (Part IV), the recommendations of the Task Force are summarized with cross-references to the chapters where the recommendations are discussed. The recommendations are arranged by topic to emphasize the educational continuum which the report has sought to elucidate.

A. *Disseminating and Discussing the Statement of Skills and Values*
   1. The Statement of Skills and Values should be published by the American Bar Association and widely disseminated throughout the legal community and to other interested institutions and individuals. (Chapter 4.D and Chapter 5)
   2. The Statement of Skills and Values should be viewed as a work in process and the initial formulation of the Statement should be discussed, critically analyzed and progressively refined under the auspices of the proposed national institute. (Chapter 4.D, Chapter 5 and Chapter 10)
   3. The Statement should be used by law students as an aid

in preparing for practice and seeking out opportunities for professional development in their curricular planning and in their part-time or summertime employment. (Chapter 4.D, Chapter 5 and Chapter 7.D)

4. The Statement should be used by law schools in curricular development to help focus their consideration of proposals to modify their curricula to teach skills and values more extensively or differently than they do now. (Chapter 4.D and Chapter 5)

5. The Statement should be used by law schools in self-study when assessing the extent to which their curricula advance their students' professional development and prepare them for the practice of law. (Chapter 4.D and Chapter 5)

6. The Statement should be used by providers of continuing legal education both in the development of programs of transition education to assist new lawyers to acquire necessary skills and values and also in the development of other CLE programs to enrich generally the quality of instruction and enhance the process of professional development. (Chapter 4.D, Chapter 5 and Chapter 8.E)

7. Providers of continuing legal education should use the Statement as a vehicle for organizing their resources and for securing the requisite funding to implement the reforms suggested in this Report. (Chapter 4.D and Chapter 9.C)

8. The Statement should be used by individual lawyers in evaluating their own capabilities and to identify areas in which further study would be beneficial to their professional development as well as to aid them in reflecting upon and learning from their lawyering experiences. (Chapter 4.D, Chapter 5 and Chapter 9)

B. *Choosing a Career in the Law and a Law School*

1. Prelaw students contemplating a career in the law, as well as law students, should be advised that the foundation for professional development at each stage of a legal career is accurate self-assessment, the making of informed decisions and the setting of personal standards and goals. (Chapter 6.A)

2. Prelaw students contemplating a career in the law, when planning their undergraduate studies, should be advised to review the Statement on Prelegal Education of the Association of American Law Schools and that a broad

liberal education is a preferred, but not mandatory, preparation for law school. (Chapter 6.B)

3. Advisors of prelaw students should make use of the Statement of Skills and Values in their counseling as an aid in identifying what may be expected of one who seeks to make a career in the law. (Chapter 4.D and Chapter 5)

4. The organized bar through programs of law-related education should seek to inform students who contemplate a career in the law of the breadth, variety and differentiation of legal careers. (Chapter 2 and Chapter 6.B)

5. The ABA should consider producing a regularly updated volume of materials on careers in the law for use by prelaw students at an early stage in establishing their career goals. (Chapter 2 and Chapter 6.A)

6. The Section of Legal Education and Admissions to the Bar, in cooperation with the Law School Admission Council and the Association of American Law Schools, should seek to assure that prospective law students who are selecting a law school can obtain information about all law schools relating to:

   • admission statistics,
   • tuition, costs and financial aid,
   • enrollment and graduation statistics,
   • composition of faculty and administration,
   • curricular offerings and class sizes,
   • library resources,
   • physical plant,
   • housing availability,
   • financial resources available to support educational program, and
   • placement and bar passage statistics.
   (Chapter 6.B)

7. The current policy of absolute confidentiality for the information submitted annually by law schools to the Office of the ABA Consultant on Legal Education should be reconsidered to the extent such information is relevant, accurate and useful to applicants to law school in their decision-making. (Chapter 6.B)

8. Consideration should be given to providing all LSAT registrants with explanatory information (but not purported "rankings") explaining the differences among law schools and questions which they might ask law school

admissions personnel to elicit information upon which they might base their decisions. (Chapter 6.A and B)

C. *Enhancing Professional Development During the Law School Years*

  1. Law schools and the practicing bar should look upon the development of lawyers as a common enterprise, recognizing that legal educators and practicing lawyers have different capacities and opportunities to impart to future lawyers the skills and values required for the competent and responsible practice of law. (Introduction, Chapter 4.D, Chapter 5.C, Chapter 7.A, Chapter 7.B, Chapter 7.D, Chapter 8.E and Chapter 9)

  2. Standard 301(a) regarding a law school's educational program should be amended to clarify its reference to qualifying "graduates for admission to the bar" by adding: ". . . and to prepare them to participate effectively in the legal profession." This would affirm that education in lawyering skills and professional values is central to the mission of law schools and recognize the current stature of skills and values instruction. (Chapter 7.C and Chapter 7.B)

  3. It is time for the Section of Legal Education and Admissions to the Bar to revisit generally the treatment of skills and values instruction in the accreditation process in recognition of the skills and values identified in the Statement of Fundamental Lawyering Skills and Professional Values as those with which a lawyer should be familiar before assuming ultimate responsibility for a client. (Chapter 7.C, Chapter 4.D, Chapter 5.C, Chapter 7.A and Chapter 7.B)

  4. In light of developments in skills instruction and the Task Force's Statement of Skills and Values, the interaction between core subjects, treated in Standard 302(a)(i), and professional skills, treated in Standard 302(a)(iii), should be revisited and clarified. The interpretation of Standard 302(a)(iii) should expressly recognize that students who expect to enter practice in a relatively unsupervised practice setting have a special need for opportunities to obtain skills instruction. (Chapter 7.C, Chapter 7.A, Chapter 7.B, Chapter 4.D and Chapter 5.C)

  5. Each law school faculty should determine how its school can best help its students to begin the process of acquiring the skills and values that are important in the practice of law, keeping in mind not only the resources

presently available at the school, but the characteristics of effective skills instruction. (Chapter 7.B, Chapter 4.D and Chapter 5.C)

6. To be effective, the teaching of lawyering skills and professional values should ordinarily have the following characteristics:

   - development of concepts and theories underlying the skills and values being taught;
   - opportunity for students to perform lawyering tasks with appropriate feedback and self-evaluation;
   - reflective evaluation of the students' performance by a qualified assessor. (Chapter 7.B and Chapter 4.D)

7. The Interpretation to Standard 201(a) relating to the self-study process should require law schools to evaluate their programs in the light of Standard 301(a) and (c) and should refer to the Task Force's Statement of Skills and Values and the literature analyzing the roles and competencies of lawyers. (Chapter 7.C, Chapter 7.B and Chapter 4.D)

8. Each law school should undertake a study to determine which of the skills and values described in the Task Force's Statement of Skills and Values are presently being taught in its curriculum and develop a coherent agenda of skills instruction not limited to the skills of "legal analysis and reasoning," "legal research," "writing" and "litigation." (Chapter 7.B, Chapter 7.C and Chapter 4.D)

9. Law schools should identify and describe in their course catalogs the skills and values content of their courses and make this information available to students for use in selecting courses. (Chapter 7.B, Chapter 6.B and Chapter 4.D)

10. The Task Force's Statement of Skills and Values should be made available to all entering law students to inform them about the skills and values they will be expected to possess as lawyers and to help them seek appropriate educational opportunities in law school, in work experience and in continuing legal education. (Chapter 4.D, Chapter 5 and Chapter 6.B)

11. Law students should be advised with respect to course selection to consider what opportunities may or may not be available to them after law school to develop the skills and competencies they will need in practice. (Chapter 2, Chapter 6 and Chapter 7.B)

12. Law schools should continue to emphasize the teaching

of the skills of "legal analysis and reasoning" and "legal research," as described in the Statement of Skills and Values, through a wide variety of instructional modes, including well-structured clinical programs. (Chapter 7.B and Chapter 4.D)

13. Law schools should be encouraged to develop or expand instruction in such areas as "problem solving," "factual investigation," "communication," "counseling," "negotiation" and "litigation," recognizing that methods have been developed for teaching law students skills previously considered learnable only through post-graduation experience in practice. (Chapter 7.A, Chapter 7.B and Chapter 5.C)

14. In view of the widely held perception that new lawyers today are deficient in writing skills, further concerted effort should be made in law schools and in programs of transition education after law school to teach writing at a better level than is now generally done. (Chapter 7.B, Chapter 7.C, Chapter 8.E and Appendix B)

15. Law schools through well-structured clinical programs should help students understand the importance of the skill of "organization and management of legal work," although it will remain for the first employer or mentor to translate that awareness into a functioning reality through providing supervised practice experience. (Chapter 7.B, Chapter 7.D, Chapter 8.E and Chapter 5.C)

16. Law schools should play an important role in developing the skill of "recognizing and resolving ethical dilemmas" and in placing these issues in an organized conceptual framework, although the exposure in law school clinical programs or classrooms is necessarily very limited compared to the variety and complexity of the dilemmas presented in practice. (Chapter 7.B, Chapter 7.D, Chapter 8.E and Chapter 5.C)

17. Law schools should stress in their teaching that examination of the "fundamental values of the profession" is as important in preparing for professional practice as acquisition of substantive knowledge. (Chapter 7.A and Chapter 5.C)

18. The practicing bar should be assiduous in discharging its responsibilities for inculcating professional values through contact with students in part-time work and summer jobs and as colleagues or mentors in the early years of practice. (Chapter 7.A, Chapter 7.D and Chapter 5.C)

19. Law school deans, professors, administrators and staff should be concerned to convey to students that the professional value of the need to "promote justice, fairness and morality" is an essential ingredient of the legal profession; the practicing bar should be concerned to impress on students that success in the practice of law is not measured by financial rewards alone, but by a lawyer's commitment to a just, fair and moral society. (Chapter 7.A, Chapter 7.D and Chapter 5.C)

20. Law schools and the organized bar should work together to make law students aware of the full range of opportunity for professional development in the rich variety of private practice settings, in panels for prepaid and group legal services, in positions in the public sector, in staff counsel's offices in corporations and other organizations, and in the practice of public interest law in all its dimensions, as well as of the profession's expectation that all lawyers will fulfill their responsibilities to the public and support pro bono legal services for those who cannot afford a lawyer. (Chapter 2, Chapter 5 and Chapter 6.B)

21. Law schools and employers of law students should work together to inject educational value into any work experience during the law school years, developing models for strengthening the educational content of part-time employment and developing workshops offered at the beginning of the summer clerkship season to support the educational aspects of summer employment. (Chapter 7.D)

22. Since the employment marketplace is a crucial forum in which the practicing bar transmits its values to law students, members of the bar who recruit, interview, and hire should convey to students, both by words and by their decisions, the importance they place on a student's having had exposure to a broad range of skills and values instruction, including clinical courses. (Chapter 7.A, Chapter 7.D and Appendix B)

23. The National Association of Law Placement (NALP) should be asked by the Section of Legal Education and Admissions to the Bar to add to NALP's annual employer questionnaire questions designed to elicit information pertaining to the educational quality of law office summer programs. (Chapter 7.D)

24. Law schools should assign primary responsibility for instruction in professional skills and values to perma-

nent full-time faculty who can devote the time and expertise to teaching and developing new methods of teaching skills to law students. In addition, law schools should continue to make appropriate use of skilled and experienced practicing lawyers and judges in professional skills and values instruction with guidance, structure, supervision and evaluation of these adjunct faculty by full-time teachers. (Chapter 7.B)

25. There should be faculty involvement in the design, supervision and evaluation of every program of extern experience, and accreditation standards should emphasize the critical importance of faculty responsibility for overseeing extern programs. (Chapter 7.B and Chapter 8)

D. *Placing the Transition and Licensing Process in the Educational Continuum*

1. Licensing authorities should not set specific curriculum requirements for law schools but should look to the Council of the Section of Legal Education and Admissions to the Bar as the appropriate body for assuring through the accreditation process that adequate instruction in lawyering skills and professional values is provided to law students. (Chapter 8.B)

2. Licensing authorities should consider modifying bar examinations that do not give appropriate weight to the acquisition of lawyering skills and professional values to ensure that applicants for admission are ready to assume their responsibilities in practice. (Chapter 8.C and Chapter 4.D)

3. Licensing authorities, the law schools and the organized bar should engage in continuing dialogue to determine the optimum content, methods and mix of instruction in skills and values in law school, during the licensing process and after admission to practice. (Chapter 7, Chapter 8, Chapter 9 and Chapter 4.D)

4. The transition from law school into individual practice or relatively unsupervised positions in small law offices, both public and private, presents special problems of lawyer competence which the law schools, the organized bar and licensing authorities must address. (Chapter 8, Chapter 4.D and Chapter 7)

5. Apprenticeship programs, if retained, should be examined in the light of the Task Force's Statement of Lawyering Skills and Professional Values and consider-

ation should be given to revision of the programs to ensure that skills and values instruction is provided by practitioners in sufficient numbers and properly guided in their mentoring responsibilities to give adequate feedback to apprentices, holding them to an acceptable level of performance. (Chapter 8, Chapter 4.D and Chapter 7)

6. Sponsors of programs of transition education should examine their programs in the light of the Task Force's Statement of Lawyering Skills and Professional Values to ensure the inclusion of significant skills and values instruction. This instruction should include participatory exercises, trained instructors and concurrent feedback and evaluation. (Chapter 8.E, Chapter 4.D and Chapter 7)

7. The Task Force encourages sponsors of transition education programs to examine the State of Washington's Skills Practice Course for its "learn by doing" structure and small-group, problem-solving format. (Chapter 8.E)

8. The Task Force encourages sponsors of programs of transition education to study the programs in Commonwealth countries, described in Appendix E, for guidance on methods of funding, length of instruction, the focus on lawyering skills, the use of practitioners as instructors, and the assessment techniques used to determine competency levels. (Chapter 8.E and Appendix E)

9. The development, testing and evaluation of pilot programs of transition education, begun by ALI-ABA with the Real Estate Training Module, should be carried forward under the auspices of the proposed national institute. (Chapter 8.E and Chapter 10)

10. Jurisdictions that have mandated transition education programs should reexamine their programs in the light of the Task Force's Statement of Skills and Values to ensure that sufficient time is allocated for professional skills instruction, that there is sufficient flexibility to allow attorneys to choose the skills they wish to study, and that the programs incorporate the features set forth in Recommendation D.6. (Chapter 8.E and Chapter 4.D)

11. The Task Force encourages legal organizations with developed in-house programs of skills and values instruction for new lawyers to share their experience with local and state bar groups to improve bar-sponsored programs of transition education. (Chapter 8.E)

12. The organized bar, with the support of the proposed national institute, should strive to make available to all

new lawyers effective instruction in lawyering skills and professional values at a cost that new lawyers can afford with scholarship aid provided as needed. (Chapter 8.E, Chapter 4.D and Chapter 10)

E. *Striving for Professional Excellence After Law School*
1. Law schools should work with the organized bar to assure that the development of lawyering skills and values continues beyond law school and throughout lawyers' professional lives and that continuing legal education incorporates the characteristics of effective skills and values instruction. (Chapter 7, Chapter 8 and Chapter 9)
2. The Task Force urges that *all* states, including those states with an MCLE requirement and those who have yet to adopt MCLE, consider imposing upon all attorneys subject to their jurisdiction a requirement for periodic instruction in lawyering skills and professional values. This instruction should include participatory exercises, trained instructors and concurrent feedback and evaluation. (Chapter 9)
3. The Task Force urges the gathering of national data on the courses currently provided by CLE organizations to determine how many courses include significant instruction in lawyering skills and professional values. (Chapter 9)
4. The Task Force encourages law firms, corporate law departments and government agencies to examine their in-house training programs for lawyers in the light of the Task Force's Statement of Skills and Values to ensure that appropriate and effective instruction in skills and values is provided. Course materials and advice on skills and values instruction should be made available to sponsors of in-house programs by the proposed national institute. (Chapter 8.E, Chapter 9.D and E, Chapter 10 and Chapter 4.D)
5. The Task Force urges providers of continuing legal education to examine their programs in the light of the Statement of Skills and Values and the developments in effective teaching of skills and values described in this report, and strive to ensure that their courses provide for active participation by students, instruction by persons having special expertise and training in this sort of teaching, and a format that includes the immediate assessment of the students' participation. (Chapter 9, Chapter 7.B and Chapter 4.D)

6. The Task Force urges providers of continuing legal education in planning their programs and courses to focus upon the essential linkage between lawyering skills and professional values and to evaluate the quality and methods of their instruction mindful of this holistic approach to lawyering. (Chapter 9.E)

F. *Establishing an American Institute for the Practice of Law*
   1. A new national institute should be established that would qualify as a 501(c)(3) corporation and have the central purpose of promoting excellence in the practice of law; it would address on a continuing basis the entire process by which lawyers acquire and refine the lawyering skills and professional values requisite for competent and responsible practice. (Chapter 4, Chapter 5, Chapter 7, Chapter 9 and Chapter 10)
   2. The law schools and the organized bar should assume a shared responsibility for lawyers' professional development and support the proposed national institute as a means for working toward a more integrated process of education to assist the legal profession more adequately to meet the public's appropriate expectations with respect to lawyer competence and professional responsibility. (Chapter 10)
   3. The institute should play a central role in furthering the various uses of the Task Force's Statement of Skills and Values. It can facilitate critical analysis and progressive refinement of the Statement; develop modes of instruction, course materials and teaching aids to assist law schools to teach skills and values more effectively; create and serve as a clearinghouse for model curricula, instructional materials and teacher training for providers of continuing legal education and law office programs; and promote research and publication relevant to the understanding and enhancement of skills and values. (Chapter 4.D and Chapter 10)
   4. The work and activities of the institute should be in three principal areas:
      - Serving as a resource center and forum for those engaged in the professional development of lawyers in law schools and in continuing legal education;
      - Fostering research and development to enhance the profession's understanding of lawyering skills and professional values and the means and methods by which lawyers learn;

- Developing a plan and organizational structure to promote continuing legal education and the dissemination of courses and programs. (Chapter 10 and Appendix F)

5. The initiative for establishing the new institute should be taken by the American Bar Association and the American Law Institute. The educational resources of the ABA Division of Professional Education and of the ALI-ABA Joint Committee should be combined. The Practising Law Institute and the Association of American Law Schools should be invited to join ABA and ALI as joint sponsors of the new institute. (Chapter 10, Chapter 9 and Appendix F)

Appendices

339

Appendix A

Bibliography

Sources

ABEL, RICHARD L. 1989. AMERICAN LAWYERS. New York: Oxford University Press.

———. 1979. *Socializing the Legal Profession: Can Redistributing Lawyers' Services Achieve Social Justice?* 1 LAW & POLICY QUARTERLY 1.

Abrahams, R.D. 1964. *Twenty-Five Years of Service: Philadelphia's Neighborhood Law Office Plan.* 50 ABA JOUR. 728.

———. 1942. *The Neighborhood Law Office Experiment.* 9 U. CHI. L. REV. 406.

———. 1938. *Law Offices to Serve Householders in the Lower Income Groups.* 42 DICKINSON L. REV. 133.

ADMINISTRATIVE OFFICE OF THE UNITED STATES COURTS. 1990. ANNUAL REPORT OF THE DIRECTOR.

———. 1990. JUDICIAL FACTS AND FIGURES—MULTI-YEAR REPORTS THROUGH JUNE, 1990.

Alexander, Alice and Jeffrey Smith. 1989. *A Practical Guide to Cooperative Supervision for Law Students and Legal Employers.* 29 LAW OFFICE ECONOMICS AND MANAGEMENT 207

Allen, Francis A. 1983. *Legal Scholarship: Present Status and Future Prospects.* 33 J. LEGAL EDUC. 403.

Alpert, T.M. 1983. *The Inherent Power of the Courts to Regulate the Practice of the Law: An Historical Analysis.* 32 BUFFALO L. REV. 525.

ALTMAN, MARY ANN & ROBERT I. WEIL. 1990. HOW TO MANAGE YOUR LAW OFFICES. New York: Matthew Bender & Co.

THE AMERICAN ASSEMBLY, COLUMBIA UNIVERSITY. 1968. LAW IN A CHANGING AMERICA. Geoffrey Hazard ed. Englewood Cliffs, N.J.: Prentice-Hall, Inc.

AMERICAN BAR ASSOCIATION. 1988. MODEL RULE FOR MINIMUM CONTINUING LEGAL EDUCATION. Approved by the ABA House of Delegates, August 1988.

———. 1983. FINAL REPORT AND RECOMMENDATIONS OF THE TASK FORCE

ON PROFESSIONAL COMPETENCE. Chicago: ABA Press. (The Friday Report)

———. 1983. MODEL RULES OF PROFESSIONAL CONDUCT.

———. 1969. CODE OF PROFESSIONAL RESPONSIBILITY.

———. 1908. CANONS OF PROFESSIONAL ETHICS.

AMERICAN BAR ASSOCIATION COMMISSION ON ADVERTISING. 1992. YELLOW PAGES LAWYER ADVERTISING: AN ANALYSIS OF EFFECTIVE ELEMENTS. Chicago: American Bar Association.

AMERICAN BAR ASSOCIATION COMMISSION ON PROFESSIONALISM. 1986. IN THE SPIRIT OF PUBLIC SERVICE: A BLUEPRINT FOR THE REKINDLING OF LAWYER PROFESSIONALISM. Chicago: American Bar Association. (The Stanley Report)

AMERICAN BAR ASSOCIATION COMMISSION ON WOMEN IN THE PROFESSION. 1989. WOMEN AND THE ABA—A HISTORY OF WOMEN'S INVOLVEMENT IN THE AMERICAN BAR ASSOCIATION, 1965-1989. Research report on women's participation.

———. 1988. REPORT TO THE HOUSE OF DELEGATES. Approved by the ABA House of Delegates, August 1988.

AMERICAN BAR ASSOCIATION CONSORTIUM ON LEGAL SERVICES AND THE PUBLIC. 1989. REPORT OF THE AMERICAN BAR ASSOCIATION NATIONAL CONFERENCE ON ACCESS TO JUSTICE IN THE 1990s. Report on conference at Tulane Law School, June 9-11, 1989.

———. 1977. LEGAL SERVICES FOR THE AVERAGE CITIZEN. (Discussion paper reprinted 1978.) Chicago: ABA Press.

AMERICAN BAR ASSOCIATION COMMITTEE ON LEGAL EDUCATION AND ADMISSIONS TO THE BAR. 1879. REPORT OF THE COMMITTEE TO THE PRESIDENT AND MEMBERS OF THE AMERICAN BAR ASSOCIATION. Initial report of the Committee. YEARBOOK OF THE ASSOCIATION, 209-235.

AMERICAN BAR ASSOCIATION DIVISION FOR BAR SERVICES. 1991. DIRECTORY OF BAR ASSOCIATIONS.

AMERICAN BAR ASSOCIATION JOURNAL. September 1990. *The Making of a Professional—Law School in the Nineties.* 76: 43-73.

———. June 1988. *Women in Law—The Glass Ceiling.* 74:49.

———. October 1983. *Women In The Law.* 69: 1384-1419.

———. January 1981. *Judges Educate Inexperienced Trial Attorneys.*

AMERICAN BAR ASSOCIATION JUDICIAL ADMINISTRATION DIVISION APPELLATE JUDGES CONFERENCE. 1985. APPELLATE LITIGATION SKILLS

TRAINING: THE ROLE OF THE LAW SCHOOLS. REPORT AND
RECOMMENDATIONS OF THE COMMITTEE ON APPELLATE SKILLS
TRAINING. Chicago: American Bar Association. *Reprinted in*
54 CINN. L. REV. 129. (The Frank Report)

AMERICAN BAR ASSOCIATION OFFICE OF THE CONSULTANT ON LEGAL
EDUCATION. January 1992. STATUS OF PROFESSIONAL SKILLS
TEACHERS.
———. March 1988. A STUDY OF CONTEMPORARY LAW SCHOOL CURRIC-
ULA II.
———. January 1987. A STUDY OF CONTEMPORARY LAW SCHOOL
CURRICULA.
———. March 1985. STUDENT HOURS IN CLINICAL LEGAL EDUCATION.
———. June 1985. LEGAL WRITING SURVEY.
———. June 1985. PROFESSIONAL RESPONSIBILITY SURVEY.
———. August 1984. PROFESSIONAL RESPONSIBILITY STUDY.

AMERICAN BAR ASSOCIATION SECTION OF LAW PRACTICE MANAGEMENT.
1989. THE QUALITY PURSUIT—ASSURING STANDARDS IN THE
PRACTICE OF LAW. Chicago: American Bar Association.

AMERICAN BAR ASSOCIATION SECTION OF LEGAL EDUCATION AND ADMIS-
SIONS TO THE BAR. 1992. A REVIEW OF LEGAL EDUCATION IN THE
UNITED STATES FALL 1991.
———. October 1991. STANDARDS FOR APPROVAL OF LAW SCHOOLS AND
INTERPRETATIONS. Compiled and Distributed by Office of the
Consultant on Legal Education. Indianapolis, Indiana.
———. 1987. LONG RANGE PLANNING FOR LEGAL EDUCATION IN THE
UNITED STATES. (The McKay Report)
———. 1979. LAWYER COMPETENCY: THE ROLE OF THE LAW SCHOOLS.
REPORT AND RECOMMENDATIONS OF THE TASK FORCE ON LAWYER
COMPETENCY. (The Cramton Report)

AMERICAN BAR ASSOCIATION SECTION OF LEGAL EDUCATION AND ADMIS-
SIONS TO THE BAR AND THE NATIONAL CONFERENCE OF BAR
EXAMINERS. 1991 COMPREHENSIVE GUIDE TO BAR ADMISSION
REQUIREMENTS 1991-1992. ABA Press.
———. 1987. CODE OF RECOMMENDED STANDARDS FOR BAR EXAMINERS.
Reprinted in COMPREHENSIVE GUIDE TO BAR ADMISSION
REQUIREMENTS 1991-1992, vii-ix.

AMERICAN BAR ASSOCIATION SECTION OF LEGAL EDUCATION AND ADMIS-
SIONS TO THE BAR AND UNIVERSITY OF VIRGINIA. 1988. PROCEED-
INGS OF THE NATIONAL CONFERENCE ON LEGAL EDUCATION FOR
A CHANGING PROFESSION. Charlottesville, March 25-27, 1988.

AMERICAN BAR ASSOCIATION SPECIAL COMMITTEE ON PUBLIC INTEREST PRACTICE. 1975. RECOMMENDATION AND REPORT. Approved by the ABA House of Delegates, August 1975. (The Montreal Resolution).

AMERICAN BAR ASSOCIATION SPECIAL COMMITTEE FOR A STUDY OF LEGAL EDUCATION. 1980. LAW SCHOOLS AND PROFESSIONAL LEGAL EDUCATION. REPORT AND RECOMMENDATIONS OF THE SPECIAL COMMITTEE. (The Foulis Report)

AMERICAN BAR ASSOCIATION STANDING COMMITTEE ON DELIVERY OF LEGAL SERVICES. 1990. THE SURVEY OF LEGAL CLINICS & ADVERTISING LAW FIRMS. REPORT OF SPECIAL COMMITTEE. Project Director: Gerry Singsen.

AMERICAN BAR ASSOCIATION STANDING COMMITTEE ON LAWYER COMPETENCE. 1990. MAKING THE COMPETENT LAWYER: MODELS FOR LAW SCHOOL ACTION. (Reprint of course materials prepared for conference in St. Louis, Missouri, November 1-3, 1990.)

AMERICAN BAR ASSOCIATION STANDING COMMITTEE ON LAWYER REFERRAL AND INFORMATION SERVICES. 1991. CHARACTERISTICS OF LAWYER REFERRAL PROGRAMS. Chicago: American Bar Association.
———. 1989. REFERENCE HANDBOOK. Chicago: American Bar Association.

AMERICAN BAR ASSOCIATION STANDING COMMITTEE ON LAWYER REFERRAL SERVICES. 1951. REPORT OF THE STANDING COMMITTEE.

AMERICAN BAR ASSOCIATION STANDING COMMITTEE ON SPECIALIZATION. 1990. MODEL STANDARDS FOR SPECIALTY AREAS. Published by the Standing Committee in August 1990.
———. 1990. REPORT OF THE STANDING COMMITTEE. August 1990.

AMERICAN BAR ASSOCIATION TASK FORCE ON THE GENERAL PRACTI-TIONER AND THE ORGANIZED BAR. 1984. REPORT OF THE TASK FORCE ON THE GENERAL PRACTITIONER AND THE ORGANIZED BAR.

AMERICAN BAR ASSOCIATION TASK FORCE ON MINORITIES IN THE LEGAL PROFESSION. 1986. REPORT WITH RECOMMENDATIONS. Proposing a Goal 9 for the Association. Approved by the ABA House of Delegates, August 1986.

AMERICAN BAR ASSOCIATION TASK FORCE ON PROFESSIONAL COMPETENCE. 1983. FINAL REPORT AND RECOMMENDATIONS. (The Friday Report).

AMERICAN BAR ASSOCIATION TASK FORCE ON THE ROLE OF THE LAWYER IN THE 1980'S. 1981. REPORT OF THE TASK FORCE ON THE ROLE OF THE LAWYER IN THE 1980'S.

AMERICAN BAR ASSOCIATION TASK FORCE ON SOLO AND SMALL FIRM PRACTITIONERS. November 1991. REPORT AND RECOMMENDATIONS.

AMERICAN BAR ASSOCIATION YOUNG LAWYERS DIVISION. 1991. THE STATE OF THE LEGAL PROFESSION, REPORT # 2.
———. 1990. THE STATE OF THE LEGAL PROFESSION.
———. 1988. RECOMMENDATION AND REPORT. Approved by the ABA House of Delegates, August 1988. (The Toronto Resolution).

AMERICAN BAR FOUNDATION. 1988. PAPERS FOR THE CONFERENCE ON PROFESSIONALISM, ETHICS, AND ECONOMIC CHANGE. Evanston, Illinois, September 22-24, 1988.

AMERICAN LAW INSTITUTE-AMERICAN BAR ASSOCIATION COMMITTEE ON CONTINUING PROFESSIONAL EDUCATION. 1992. ANNUAL REPORTS. Philadelphia: ALI-ABA
———. 1992. A PRACTICAL GUIDE TO ACHIEVING EXCELLENCE IN THE PRACTICE OF LAW: STANDARDS, METHODS, AND SELF-EVALUATION. Philadelphia: ALI-ABA.
———. 1992. A CRISIS IN THE PROFESSION: THE FUTURE OF CONTINUING LEGAL EDUCATION AND PROFESSIONALISM. ALI-ABA conference papers. Dallas, Texas, February 2, 1992.
———. 1991. ATTAINING EXCELLENCE IN CLE: STANDARDS FOR QUALITY AND METHODS FOR EVALUATION, OFFICIAL DRAFT. Philadelphia: ALI-ABA.
———. 1991. BRIDGE THE GAP REAL ESTATE TRAINING MODULE, STUDENT MANUAL. DRAFT NO. 5. (Submitted to the Advisory Committee, April 19, 1991. Philadelphia: ALI-ABA.)
———. 1990. CLE QUALITY EVALUATION METHODS AND STANDARDS PROJECT. (Proposed final draft, October 22, 1990.)
———. 1988. A MODEL CURRICULUM FOR BRIDGE-THE-GAP PROGRAMS. Philadelphia: ALI-ABA. (The Yarbrough Report)
———. 1988. CLE AND THE LAWYER'S RESPONSIBILITIES IN AN EVOLVING PROFESSION. The Report on the Arden House III Conference, November 13th to 16th, 1987.
———. 1988. LAW PRACTICE QUALITY EVALUATION: AN APPRAISAL OF PEER REVIEW AND OTHER MEASURES TO ENHANCE PROFESSIONAL PERFORMANCE. Report on Williamsburg Peer Review Conference, September 10-12, 1987.
———. 1986. CLE AROUND THE COUNTRY: REPORTS ON ACTIVITIES OF

CLE ENTITIES IN THE UNITED STATES BY THEIR DIRECTORS AND GOVERNING BODIES. Philadelphia: ALI-ABA.

————. 1984 REPORT ON THE SURVEY OF BRIDGE-THE-GAP PROGRAMS. (Discussion Draft, November 1984.) Philadelphia: ALI-ABA. (The Kestin Report)

————. 1981. ENHANCING THE COMPETENCE OF LAWYERS: REPORT OF THE HOUSTON CONFERENCE. Philadelphia: ALI-ABA.

————. 1980. *A Model for Continuing Legal Education: Structure, Methods, and Curriculum.* (Discussion Draft, August 1, 1980.) Philadelphia: ALI-ABA.

————. 1980. *A Model Peer Review System.* (Discussion Draft.) Philadelphia: ALI-ABA.

————. 1979. STUDY OF THE QUALITY OF CONTINUING LEGAL EDUCATION. Philadelphia: ALI-ABA.

————. 1969. PROBLEMS OF PROFESSIONAL RESPONSIBILITY UNDER THE UNIFORM COMMERCIAL CODE. UNIFORM COMMERCIAL CODE PRACTICE HANDBOOK 7. (The Countryman Report)

————. 1967. MEETING THE EDUCATIONAL NEEDS OF THE NEWLY ADMITTED: A PROPOSAL FOR GENERAL PRACTICE COURSES. (Official Draft, Nov. 3, 1967.) Philadelphia: ALI-ABA.

————. 1964. ARDEN HOUSE II: TOWARD EXCELLENCE IN CONTINUING LEGAL EDUCATION. Report of the Second National Conference on the Continuing Education of the Bar.

AMERICAN PREPAID LEGAL SERVICES INSTITUTE. 1991. WHO'S WHO IN PREPAID LEGAL SERVICES. Chicago: APLSI.

————. 1989. NEWS BRIEFS. *Bar Foundation Study Yields Prepaid-Lawyer Use Data.* June 1989.

Amsterdam, Anthony G. 1984. *Clinical Legal Education—A 21st-Century Perspective.* 34 J. LEGAL EDUC. 612.

ANDREWS, LORI B. 1980. BIRTH OF A SALESMAN: LAWYER ADVERTISING AND SOLICITATION. American Bar Association.

Ansley, F.L. 1991. *Race and the Core Curricular in Legal Education.* 79 CALIF. L. REV. 1511.

Aron, Nan. 1989. *Non Traditional Models for Legal Services Delivery.* Conference on Access to Justice in the 1990s, Tulane Law School.

————. 1988. LIBERTY AND JUSTICE FOR ALL. Boulder, Colo: Westview Press.

ASSOCIATION OF AMERICAN LAW SCHOOLS. 1964. PROCEEDINGS PART ONE: REPORTS OF COMMITTEES.

_____. 1945. *The Place of Skills in Legal Education*. Report of the Committee on Curriculum of the Association of American Law Schools. 45 COLUM. L. REV. 345. (The Llewellyn Report).

ASSOCIATION OF AMERICAN LAW SCHOOLS-AMERICAN BAR ASSOCIATION. 1980. GUIDELINES FOR CLINICAL LEGAL EDUCATION. Report of the Association of American Law Schools-American Bar Association Committee on Guidelines for Clinical Legal Education.

ASSOCIATION OF THE BAR OF THE CITY OF NEW YORK COMMITTEE ON LEGAL EDUCATION AND ADMISSION TO THE BAR. 1992. DISCUSSION DRAFT REPORT ON ADMISSION TO THE BAR IN NEW YORK IN THE TWENTY FIRST CENTURY—A BLUEPRINT FOR REFORM. (City Bar Report).

AUCHINCLOSS, LOUIS. 1956. THE GREAT WORLD AND TIMOTHY COLT.

Bahls, Steven C. 1990. *General Practice Studies in Law School* in COMMITTEE UPDATE OF THE ABA GENERAL PRACTICE SECTION, Fall 1990.

Baird, Carlson, Reilly, & Powell. 1979. Defining Competence in Legal Practice: The Evaluation of Lawyers in Large Firms and Organizations (unpublished Research Paper of the Law School Admission Council). December 1979.

Baird, Leonard L. 1978. *A Survey of the Relevance of Legal Training to Law School Graduates*. 29 J. LEGAL EDUC. 264.

BALDWIN, J. AND M. MCCONVILLE. 1977. NEGOTIATED JUSTICE. London: Martin Robertson.

Balmford. April, 1988. *The Role of the Law School in Legal Education*. LAW INSTITUTE JOURNAL.

THE BAR EXAMINER. 1983. *Performance Testing: A Valuable New Dimension or a Waste of Time and Money*. November 1983. 52:21.

Bard & Bamford. 19____. *The Bar: Professional Association or Medieval Guild?* 19 CATHOLIC UNIV. L. REV. 393.

Barnhizer, David R. 1989. *Prophets, Priests, and Power Blockers: Three Fundamental Roles of Judges and Legal Scholars in America*. 50 UNIV. PITTSBURGH L. REV. 127.

————. 1989. *The Intellectual Contributions of Clinical Faculty: Facilitating Fundamental Change in the American Law Schools Through Aggressive Formulations of Models of Justice and Humanity.* (Written for the 1989 UCLA Clinical Symposium.)

————. 1979. *The Clinical Method of Legal Instruction: Its Theory and Implementation.* 30 J. LEGAL EDUC. 67.

————. 1977. *Clinical Legal Education at the Crossroads: The Need for Direction.* 1977 B.Y.U. L. REV. 1025.

BASTRESS, ROBERT M. AND JOSEPH D. HARBAUGH. 1990. INTERVIEWING, COUNSELING, AND NEGOTIATING: SKILLS FOR EFFECTIVE REPRESENTATION. Boston, Mass.: Little, Brown and Co.

BELL, SUSAN J. 1989. FULL DISCLOSURE: DO YOU REALLY WANT TO BE A LAWYER? ABA Young Lawyers Division.

Bell, Thomas R. 1969. Law Practice in a Small Town (in a rural Alabama county) (J.S.D. dissertation Howard University).

BELLOW, GARY AND BEA MOULTON. 1978. THE LAWYERING PROCESS: MATERIALS FOR CLINICAL INSTRUCTION IN ADVOCACY. Mineola, N.Y. Foundation Press.

Benthall-Nietzel. 1975. *An Empirical Investigation of the Relationship Between Lawyering Skills and Legal Education.* 63 KY. L. J. 373.

BERGER, CURTIS J., SHEILA H. AKABAS, AND CLAY HILES. 1978. FINAL REPORT TO THE FORD FOUNDATION ON MUNICIPAL EMPLOYEES LEGAL SERVICES PLAN. Submitted by District Council 37, AFSCME, Columbia School of Law and Columbia School of Social Work, September 1978.

Biehl, Kathy. 1989. *Things They Didn't Teach in Law School.* ABA JOURNAL, January 1989 52-55.

Bierbaum. 1983. *On the Frontiers of Public Interest Law: The New Jersey State Department of the Public Advocate—The Public Advocacy Division.* 13 SETON HALL L. REV. 475.

BINDER, DAVID A. AND PAUL BERGMAN. 1984. FACT INVESTIGATION: FROM HYPOTHESIS TO PROOF. St. Paul, Minn.: West Publishing Co.

BINDER, DAVID A., PAUL BERGMAN, AND SUSAN PRICE. 1991. LAWYERS

AS COUNSELORS: A CLIENT-CENTERED APPROACH. St. Paul, Minn.: West Publishing Co.

Blackman. 1986. *South Carolina Is Out of Line: A Response to Chief Justice Littlejohn.* 55 THE BAR EXAMINER 4 (Feb. 1986).

BLOCK, GERTRUDE. 1992. EFFECTIVE LEGAL WRITING.

Blodgett. *The Middle Man of Lawsuits.* 1986. A.B.A. J. 21.

Blunden, Audrey and Les Handler. June 1987. *A New Course at the New South Wales College of Law: The Introduction of the Full Time Course Strategy Plan.* J. PROF. L. EDUC. 42.

Boyer, Barry B. and Roger C. Cramton. 1974. *American Legal Education: An Agenda For Research and Reform.* 59 CORNELL L. REV. 221.

Bradlow, D. 1988. *The Changing Legal Environment, The 1980s and Beyond.* A.B.A. J., December 1988.

Brickman, Lester. 1973. *Legal Delivery Systems—A Bibliography.* 4 TOLEDO L. REV. 465.
_____. 1971. *Expansion of the Lawyering Process Through a New Delivery System: The Emergence and State of Legal Paraprofessionalism.* 71 COLUMBIA L. REV. 1153.

Brill, Steven. 1989. *The Law Business in the Year 2000.* AMERICAN LAWYER, Management Report, June 1989.

BROWN, E.L. 1948. LAWYERS, LAW SCHOOLS AND THE PUBLIC SERVICE.

Brown, L. and E. Dauer. 1982. *A Synopsis of the Theory and Practice of Preventive Law* in THE LAWYER'S HANDBOOK. ABA rev.ed.

Brown, L. 1967. *Corporate Counsel at the Forefront of Preventive Law.* CALIF. STATE BAR JOUR. Vol. 42, March-April 1967.

Buller, Paul F. and Caryn L. Beck-Dudley. 1990. *Performance, Policies and Personnel: How Does Your Firm Do It?* 76 A.B.A. J. 94-97. October 1990.

Burger, Warren R. 1980. *Some Further Reflections on the Problem of Adequacy of Trial Counsel.* 49 FORDHAM L. REV. 1.
_____. 1973. *The Special Skills of Advocacy: Are Specialized Training and Certification of Advocates Essential to Our System of Justice?* 42 FORDHAM L. REV. 227.

BYERS, MARK, DON SAMUELSON AND GORDON WILLIAMSON. 1988. LAWYERS IN TRANSITION, PLANNING A LIFE IN THE LAW. Natick, Mass.: Barkley.

CALIFORNIA STATE BAR ASSOCIATION. 1991. SURVEY RESULTS, SEPTEMBER, 1991 (preliminary results of a general survey of the State Bar).

CALIFORNIA STATE BAR JOURNAL. 1969. PRELIMINARY REPORT: RESULTS OF SURVEY ON CERTIFICATION OF SPECIALISTS. 44:140.

CAMPBELL & WILSON. 1972. PUBLIC ATTITUDES TO THE LEGAL PROFESSION IN SCOTLAND, RESEARCH REPORT OF THE LAW SOCIETY OF SCOTLAND.

CARLIN, JEROME. 1962. LAWYERS ON THEIR OWN: A STUDY OF INDIVIDUAL PRACTITIONERS IN CHICAGO. New Brunswick, N.J.: Rutgers Univ. Press.

Carlson, Robert L. 1976. *Measuring the Quality of Legal Services: An Idea Whose Time Has Not Come.* J. OF LAW AND SOCIETY 287.

Carrington, Paul D. 1992. *Butterfly Effects: The Possibilities of Law Teaching in a Democracy.* 41 DUKE L. JOUR. 741.

CARSON, G. 1978. A GOOD DAY AT SARATOGA. American Bar Association.

CERVERO, RONALD M. 1988. EFFECTIVE CONTINUING EDUCATION FOR PROFESSIONALS. San Francisco: Jossey-Bass Publishers.

CHADWICK, MICHAEL LOYD, ed. 1987. THE FEDERALIST. Washington, D.C.: Global Affairs Publishing Company.

Chase. 1986. *The Play's the Thing . . . .* 10 NOVA L. J. 425.

Chirelstein. 1989. Law Schools and Our Booming Profession (paper circulated at Columbia Law School.)

CHRISTENSEN, BARLOW F. 1970. LAWYERS FOR PEOPLE OF MODERATE MEANS, SOME PROBLEMS OF AVAILABILITY OF LEGAL SERVICES. American Bar Foundation.

Clark. 1987. *The Role of Legal Education In Defining Modern Legal Professions.* 1987 B.Y.U. L. REV. 595.

Clinical Legal Education: Reflections on the Past Fifteen Years and

Aspirations for the Future. 36 CATH. L. REV. 337.

Conference of Chief Justices. 1986. *Promoting Lawyer Competence.* 10 STATE COURT JOURNAL 15 (Fall 1986).

Conference of Chief Justices' Committee on Lawyer Competence. 1986. *Promoting Lawyer Competence.* 10 STATE CT. JOUR. 15.

Cort, H. Russell and Jack L. Sammons. 1980. *The Search for 'Good Lawyering': A Concept and Model of Lawyering Competencies.* 29 CLEVE. ST. L. REV. 397.

Costanzo, Margot. July 1983. *Leo Cussen Institute for Continuing Legal Education—Melbourne, Victoria. The Practical Training Course: Placing It in the Victorian Profession.* JOUR. PROF. LEGAL EDUC. 33.

COUNCIL OF STATE GOVERNMENTS. 1990. THE BOOK OF THE STATES 1990-91 Edition. Volume 28. Lexington, Kentucky.

COUNCIL ON LEGAL EDUCATION FOR PROFESSIONAL RESPONSIBILITY. 1979. PROCEEDINGS. REPORT OF THE PRESIDENT.
_____. 1973. Clinical Education for the Law Student (working papers prepared for the Council on Legal Education for Professional Responsibility National Conference Proceedings, Buck Hill Falls, Pa.)
COUNCIL ON LEGAL EDUCATION FOR PROFESSIONAL RESPONSIBILITY-INTERNATIONAL LEGAL CENTER. 1973. SELECTED READINGS IN CLINICAL LEGAL EDUCATION. Council on Legal Education for Professional Responsibility/International Legal Center.

COUNTRYMAN, V., T. FINMAN AND T.J. SCHNEYER. 1976. THE LAWYER IN MODERN SOCIETY. 2nd Ed.

Coyle, Marcia. 1992. *Indigent Defense System Is Voided.* NATIONAL LAW JOURNAL, February 24, 1992. 3.

Cramton, Roger C. 1986. *Demystifying Legal Scholarship.* 75 GEO. L. REV. 1.
_____. 1985. *The Trouble with Lawyers (and Law Schools).* 35 J. LEGAL EDUC. 359.
_____. 1982. *The Current State of the Law Curriculum.* 32 J. LEGAL EDUC. 321.
_____. 1981. *Lawyer Competence and the Law Schools.* 4 UNIV. ARK. LIT. ROCK L. J. 1.

Cruickshank, David A. 1985. *The Professional Legal Training Course in British Columbia, Canada.* December 1985 JOUR. PROF. LEGAL EDUC. 111.

CURRAN, BARBARA A. 1989. SURVEY OF THE PUBLIC'S USE OF LEGAL SERVICES IN AMERICAN BAR ASSOCIATION CONSORTIUM ON LEGAL SERVICES AND THE PUBLIC, TWO NATIONAL SURVEYS: 1989 PILOT ASSESSMENTS OF THE UNMET LEGAL NEEDS OF THE POOR AND THE PUBLIC GENERALLY. American Bar Foundation.
––––––. 1986. *The Legal Profession in the 1980s: A Profession in Transition.* 20 LAW & SOC'Y REV. 19.
––––––. 1977. *The Legal Needs of the Public.* American Bar Foundation.

CURRAN, BARBARA A. AND CLARA N. CARSON. 1991. SUPPLEMENT TO THE LAWYER STATISTICAL REPORT: THE U.S. LEGAL PROFESSION IN 1988. Chicago: American Bar Foundation.

CURRAN, BARBARA A., KATHERINE J. ROSICH, CLARA N. CARSON AND MARK C. PUCCETTI. 1986. SUPPLEMENT TO THE LAWYER STATISTICAL REPORT: THE U.S. LEGAL PROFESSION IN 1985.
––––––. 1985. THE LAWYER STATISTICAL REPORT: A STATISTICAL PROFILE OF THE U.S. LEGAL PROFESSION IN THE 1980S.

D'Alemberte, Talbot. 1991. *The Bar and Legal Education.* 65 FLORIDA BAR JOURNAL 27, July/August 1991.

Dart, Nancy C. 1988. *The First Five Years of Practice.* 21 CONN. L. REV. 81.

DEAN, ARTHUR H. 1957. WILLIAM NELSON CROMWELL, 1854-1948: AN AMERICAN PIONEER IN CORPORATION, COMPARATIVE AND INTERNATIONAL LAW.

DEL. SUPP. CT. RULES (revised June 30, 1989). R.52(a)(8), 52(c).

Dewitt, Edward J. 1978. *Improving Federal Trial Advocacy—II.* 78 FEDERAL RULES DECISIONS 251.
––––––. 1977. *Improving Federal Trial Advocacy* 72 FEDERAL RULES DECISION 471.

Distribution of African American Lawyers. NATIONAL BAR ASSOCIATION MAGAZINE. April 1991.

Doimberger & Sherr. 1989. *The Impact of Competition on Pricing and Quality of Legal Services.* 9 INTERNATIONAL REV. OF LAW AND ECON. 41.

_____. 1981. *Economic Efficiency in the Provision of Legal Services.* 1 INTERNATIONAL REV. OF LAW AND ECON. 29.

DONNELL, JOHN D. 1970. THE CORPORATE COUNSEL: A ROLE STUDY. Bloomington: Bureau of Business Research. Indiana University.

Dooley, John A. III. 1989. *Legal Services in the 1990's: Barriers to Access.* Conference on Access to Justice in the 1990s, Tulane Law School.

Edwards, Harry T. 1988. *The Role of Legal Education in Shaping the Profession.* 38 JOUR. LEGAL ED. 285.

EHRLICH, THOMAS & GEOFFREY C. HAZARD. 1975. GOING TO LAW SCHOOL? Boston: Little, Brown and Company.

EISENSTEIN, J. 1978. COUNSEL FOR THE UNITED STATES.

Elson, John S. 1989. *The Case Against Legal Scholarship or, If the Professor Must Publish, Must the Profession Perish?* 39 JOUR. LEGAL ED. 343.

ESAU. 1984. SPECIALIZATION REGULATION IN THE LEGAL PROFESSION. Report of the Law Society of British Columbia.

EVANS & NORWOOD. 1975. A COMPARISON OF THE QUALITY OF LEGAL REPRESENTATION PROVIDED BY LICENSED AND STUDENT ATTORNEYS. Law Enforcement Assistance Administration. Washington, DC.

FEDERAL TRADE COMMISSION STAFF REPORT. 1984. *Improving Consumer Access to Legal Services.*

FEFERMAN, RICHARD N. 1988. BUILDING YOUR FIRM WITH ASSOCIATES. ABA Section of Economics of Law Practice (now Law Practice Management).

Feinman & Feldman. 1985. *Pedagogy and Politics.* 73 GEO. L. REV. 875.

Feldman & MacNeille. 1983. *Certifying Profession Competence: The Alaska Experiment.* 52 THE BAR EXAMINER 1 (Feb. 1983).

Ferber, Paul S. 1992. *Vermont Law School's General Practice Program.* ABA GENERAL PRACTICE SECTION LAW SCHOOL CURRICULUM COMMITTEE UPDATE, March 1992.

Fiero, J. Newton. 1901. Albany Law School Semi-Centennial Remarks.

Finesilver. 1977. *The Tension Between Practical and Theoretical Legal Education: A Judge's View of the Gap*. B.Y.U. L. REV. 1061.

FISCHER, THOMAS C. 1990. LEGAL EDUCATION, LAW PRACTICE AND THE ECONOMY: A NEW ENGLAND STUDY. Littleton, Colo.: Rothman.

Fisher & Siegal. 1987. *Evaluating Negotiation Behavior and Results: Can We Identify What We Say We Know?* 36 CATH L. REV. 395.

FISHER, ROGER AND SCOTT BROWN. 1988. GETTING TOGETHER. Boston, Mass.: Houghton Mifflin.

FISHER, ROGER AND WILLIAM URY. 1981. GETTING TO YES. Boston, Mass.: Houghton Mifflin.

FOONBERG, JAY G. 1991. HOW TO START & BUILD A LAW PRACTICE. ABA Section of Law Practice Management, Career Series.

Fortin, Clement. Dec. 1985. *Preparing for the Practice of Law in Quebec*. JOUR. PROF. LEGAL EDUC. 101.

FORTUNE. March 13, 1992. *Free Lawyering for Employees*, 18.

Frankel. 1977. *Curing Lawyers' Incompetence: Primum Non Nocere*. 10 CREIGHTON L. REV. 613.

FRANKLIN, MARTIN AND DAVID FRANKLIN. 1984. INTRODUCTION TO QUEBEC LAW.

Fraser. 1984. *The Search for Competence: Implications for Academe*. 8 DALHOUSIE L.J. 70.

FREEMAN, ANNE HOBSON. 1989. THE STYLE OF A LAW FIRM: EIGHT GENTLEMEN FROM VIRGINIA.

FRIEDMAN, L.W. 1985. A HISTORY OF AMERICAN LAW. 2nd Ed. New York: Simon & Schuster.

GALANTER, MARC AND THOMAS PALAY. 1991. TOURNAMENT OF LAWYERS. Chicago: Univ. Chicago Press.
————. 1990. *Why the Big Get Bigger: The Promotion-to-Partner Tournament and the Growth of Large Law Firms*. 76 VIRGINIA L. REV. 747.

Galanter, Marc. 1974. *Why the "Haves" Come Out Ahead: Specula-tion on the Limits of Legal Change.* 9 LAW & SOC'Y REV. 95.

Gardiner, George K. 1934. *Why Not a Clinical Lawyer School?—Some Reflections.* 82 U. OF PA. L. REV. 785.

GARREAU, J. 1991. EDGE CITY, LIFE ON THE NEW FRONTIER. New York: Doubleday.

Garth, Bryant G. 1983. *Rethinking the Legal Profession's Approach to Collective Self-Improvement: Competence and the Consumer Perspective.* 1983 WISC. L.R. 639.

Gartles, B.G. 1989. *Legal Education and Large Law Firms: Deliv-ering Legality or Solving Problems.* 64 IND. LAW J. 433.

GAWALT, GERARD W. ed. 1984. THE NEW HIGH PRIESTS—LAWYERS IN POST-CIVIL WAR AMERICA. Westport, Conn. Greenwood Press.

Gee, E. Gordon and Donald W. Jackson. 1982. *Current Studies of Legal Education: Findings and Recommendations.* 32 JOUR. L. ED. 471.
_____. 1977. *Bridging the Gap: Legal Education and Lawyer Competency.* B.Y.U. L. REV. 695.
_____. 1975. FOLLOWING THE LEADER? THE UNEXAMINED CONSENSUS IN LAW SCHOOL CURRICULA AND BREAD AND BUTTER? ELECTIVES IN AMERICAN LEGAL EDUCATION. Results of study for the Coun-cil on Legal Education for Professional Responsibility.

Gewalt. 1973. *Massachusetts Legal Education in Transition.* 17 AM. JOUR. LEGAL HIST. 27.

GIFFORD, DONALD G. 1989. LEGAL NEGOTIATION: THEORY AND APPLI-CATIONS. St. Paul, Minn. West Publishing Co.

GILLIGAN, C. 1982. IN A DIFFERENT VOICE: PSYCHOLOGICAL THEORY AND WOMEN'S DEVELOPMENT.

Ginnane, John, Ainslie Lamb and Vin. Ryan. June 1986. *The Teach-ing of Advocacy at the Leo Cussen Institute, Melbourne.* J. PROF. L. EDUC. 81.

GOETSCH. _____ ESSAYS ON SIMEON E. BALDWIN.

Gold, Neil. May 1983. Pre-Admission Education and Training in Canada: Some Reflections and a Survey (paper for the Commonwealth Legal Education Association).

————. Dec. 1983. *The British Columbia Professional Legal Training Course: Training Towards Competence.* J. Prof. L. Educ. 1.

————. 1979-80. *Legal Education, Law and Justice: The Clinical Experience.* 44 Saskatchewan L. Rev. 97.

Goldring. *Academic and Practical Legal Education: Where Next? An Academic Lawyer's Response to Noel Jackling and Neil Gold.* J. of Professional Legal Education, Australia (cite unknown).

Gopen. 1987. *The State of Legal Writing: Res Ipsa Loquitur.* 86 Mich. L. Rev. 333.

Gorman. 1985. *Assessing and Reforming The Current Law School Curriculum.* 30 N.Y.L. Sch. Rev. 609.

Greenwood, Glenn. 1961. The 1961 Lawyer Statistical Report. Chicago: American Bar Foundation.

Greenwood, Glenn and Robert F. Frederickson. 1964. Specialization in the Medical and Legal Professions. Mundelein, Ill. Callaghan & Co.

Griswold, Erwin N. 1991. Ould Fields, New Corne. St. Paul: West Publishing.

Gullickson, Stuart G. 1988. *Bridge-the-Gap Training—A Comparative Study.* 34 The CLE Journal and Register, September 1988, 5.

Haight, Fulton. Feb. 1990. *Law Schools Are Still Training People to Be Associates in Major Firms.* —— The Bar Examiner ——.

Hamilton, Alexander, John Jay and James Madison, Jr. (M. L. Chadwick Ed.) 1987. The Federalist, Washington, D.C.: Global Affairs Publishing Co.

Halliday, Terence C. 1987. Beyond Monopoly: Lawyers, State Crises and Professional Empowerment. Chicago: Univ. Chicago Press.

Hanburger. 1974. *Private Suits in the Public Interest in the United States of America.* 33 Buffalo L. Rev. 343.

Handler, Hollingworth & Erlanger. 1978. Lawyers and the Pursuit of Legal Rights. New York Academic Press.

HANDLER, JOEL F. 1967. THE LAWYER AND HIS COMMUNITY: THE PRACTICING BAR IN A MIDDLE-SIZED CITY.

Handler, Les. July 1983. *The Practical Legal Training Course at the College of Law, Sydney, New South Wales.* J. PROF. L. EDUC. 9.

HANKIN, FAYE A. AND DUANE W. KROHNKE. 1965. THE AMERICAN LAWYER: 1964 STATISTICAL REPORT. Chicago: American Bar Foundation.

HARBAUGH, JOSEPH D. AND H. GRAHAM MCDONALD. 1977. TASK ANALYSIS OF THE CRIMINAL JUSTICE ATTORNEY: IMPLICATION FOR THE USE OF PARALEGALS.

HARNO. 1953. LEGAL EDUCATION IN THE UNITED STATES.

HARVARD LAW SCHOOL. 1982. REPORT OF THE COMMITTEE ON EDUCATIONAL PLANNING AND DEVELOPMENT. (The Michelman Report)

Hazard, Geoffrey C. 1991. *The Future of Legal Ethics.* 100 YALE L. J. 1239.
_____. 1985. *Curriculum Structure and Faculty Structure.* 35 J. LEGAL EDUC. 326.
_____. 1983. *Competing Aims of Legal Education.* 59 NO. DAKOTA L. REV. 533.
_____. 1978. ETHICS AND THE PRACTICE OF LAW.

Hazard, Pearce & Stimpel. 1983. *Why Lawyers Should be Allowed to Advertise: A Market Analysis of Legal Swiss.* 58 N.Y.U.L. REV. 1084.

HEINZ, JOHN P. AND EDWARD O. LAUMANN. 1982. CHICAGO LAWYERS. THE SOCIAL STRUCTURE OF THE BAR. New York: Russell Sage Foundation. Chicago: American Bar Foundation.
_____. 1978. *The Legal Profession: Client Interests, Professional Roles, and Social Hierarchies.* 76 MICH. L. REV. 1111.

HENNING, JOEL. 1992. HIRING, TRAINING AND DEVELOPING PRODUCTIVE LAWYERS. New York: Law Journal Seminars Press.

Hetzel. 1987. *Instilling Legislative Interpretation Skills in the Classroom and the Courtroom.* 48 U. PITT. L. REV. 663.

HEYMANN, PHILIP B. AND LANCE LIEBMAN. 1988 THE SOCIAL RESPONSIBILITY OF LAWYERS. Westbury, N.Y.: Foundation Press.

Hickerson, H.R. 1981. *Structural Change in Nebraska's Legal Profession and the Implications for Broad Based Efficacy in Representation.* 15 CREIGHTON LAW REV. 1.

Hirsch, Ronald L. 1985. *Are You on Target?* 12 BARRISTER, Winter, 1985. 17-20, 49-50.

Hobson, Wayne K. 1986. *The American Legal Profession and the Organizational Society 1890-1930. Printed in* AMERICAN LEGAL AND CONSTITUTIONAL HISTORY: A GARLAND SERIES OF OUTSTANDING DISSERTATIONS. Hyman & Bruckey eds. New York: Garland Publishing, Inc.
———. 1984. *Symbol of the New Profession: Emergence of the Large Law Firm 1870-1915. Reprinted in* THE NEW HIGH PRIESTS: LAWYERS IN POST-CIVIL WAR AMERICA. Gawalt ed.

HOFFMAN, DAVID. 1836. FIFTY RESOLUTIONS IN REGARD TO PROFESSIONAL DEPORTMENT. Baltimore, Md.

HOFFMAN, P. 1973. LIONS IN THE STREET.

HORSKY, CHARLES A. 1952. THE WASHINGTON LAWYER.

Houseman, A.W. 1990. *A Short Review of Past Poverty Law Advocacy.* April 1990. CLEARINGHOUSE REV. 1514.

Hurlburt. 1980. *Incompetent Service and Professional Responsibility.* 18 ALBERTA L. REV. 145.

HURST, JAMES W. 1950. THE GROWTH OF AMERICAN LAW: THE LAW MAKERS. Boston: Little, Brown and Company.

ILLINOIS STATE BAR JOURNAL. 1975. *Economics of Legal Services in Illinois—A 1975 Special Bar Survey.* 64:73.

Indiana Law Journal. 1989. *Symposium: The Growth of Large Law Firms and Its Effect on the Legal Profession and Legal Education.* 64 IND. LAW J. 433.

INTERNATIONAL ASSOCIATION FOR CONTINUING EDUCATION AND TRAINING (formerly the Council on the Continuing Education Unit). 1984. PRINCIPLES OF GOOD PRACTICE IN CONTINUING EDUCATION.

Israel. 1980. *Standards for the Performance of Lawyers and Legal Assistants.* 27 THE PRACTICAL LAWYER 79.

Janus, Eric S. 1990. *Clinics and "Contextual Integration": Helping*

Law Students Put the Pieces Back Together Again. 16 WM. MITCHELL L. REV. 463.

Johnson, Alex M. 1991. *Think Like a Lawyer, Work Like a Machine: The Dissonance Between Law School and Law Practice.* 64 S. CAL. L. REV. 1231.

Johnson, B. 1986. *Administration Grows Up.* NATIONAL LAW JOURNAL, April 28, 1986, 17.

JOHNSON, EARL JR. 1978. JUSTICE AND REFORM: THE FORMATIVE YEARS OF THE AMERICAN LEGAL SERVICES PROGRAM. Original Ed 1974. New York: Russell Sage Foundation. New Ed. 1978. New Brunswick, N.J. Transaction Books.

JOHNSTONE, QUINTON AND DAN HOPSON. 1967. LAWYERS AND THEIR WORK. Indianapolis: Bobbs-Merrill Co.

Jones, James W. 1988. *The Challenge of Change: The Practice of Law in the Year 2000.* 41 VANDERBILT L. REV. 683.

Jones, Phil. 1990. *A Skills-Based Approach to Professional Legal Education—An Exemplary Case.* 23 LAW TEACHER No. 2 173 (Spring 1989).

JONES, THOMAS GOODE. 1887. ALABAMA CODE OF ETHICS.

Jordan. 1988. *Counsel Competence: A Critical Concern.* 2 WASHINGTON LAWYER 6.

Judicial Conference of the District of Columbia Circuit. 1988. *Proceedings of the 49th Judicial Conference of the DC Circuit.* 124 F.R.D. 241.

Judicial Conference of the Second Circuit. 1975. *Final Report of the Advisory Committee on Proposed Rules for Admission to Practice.* 67 F.R.D. 159. (The Clare Report)

Judicial Conference of the United States. 1979. *Final Report of the Committee to Consider Standards for the Admission to Practice in the Federal Courts.* 83 F.R.D. 215. (The Devitt Report)

KATZ, JACK. 1982. POOR PEOPLE'S LAWYERS IN TRANSITION. New Brunswick, New York. Rutgers Univ. Press.
————. 1976. Routine and Reform: A Study of Personal and Collective Careers in Legal Aid (Ph. D. dissertation Northwestern University).

Karp, Marvin L. 1988. INTRODUCING THE CLEVELAND BAR ASSOCIATION'S MENTOR PROGRAM (brochure of the Cleveland Bar Association).

Kaufman. 1974. *The Court Needs a Friend in Court.* 60 A.B.A. J. 175.

Kaye, Judith S. 1988. *The Lawyer's Responsibility to Enhance Competence and Ethics.* AMERICAN LAW INSTITUTE-AMERICAN BAR ASSOCIATION COMMITTEE ON CONTINUING PROFESSIONAL EDUCATION, CLE AND THE LAWYER'S RESPONSIBILITIES IN AN EVOLVING PROFESSION: THE REPORT ON THE ARDEN HOUSE III CONFERENCE. Philadelphia, Pa. ALI-ABA. 55.
_____. 1988. Women Lawyers in Big Firms: *A Study in Progress Toward Gender Equality*, 57 FORDHAM L. REV. 111.

Kelly. 1982-1983. *Education for Lawyer Competency: A Proposal for Curricular Reform.* 18 NEW ENG. L. REV. 607.

Kelso & Kelso. *The Future of Legal Education for Practical Skills.* 1977 B.Y.U. L. REV. 1007.

Kennedy. 1982. *Legal Education and the Reproduction of a Hierarchy.* 32 J. LEGAL EDUC. 591.

Kimble, Joseph. 1992. *Plain English. A Charter for Clear Writing.* 9 T.M. COOLEY L. REV. 1.

Kissam. 1989. *Law School Examinations.* 42 VAND. L. REV. 433.
_____. 1986. *The Decline of Law School Professionalism.* 134 U. PA. L. REV. 251.

Klein & Bolus. 1982. An Analysis of the Relationship Between Clinical Legal Skills and Bar Examination Results (report prepared for the Committee of Bar Examiners of the State of California and the National Conference of Bar Examiners).

Korngold. 1985. *Legal Education for the Non-Litigators: The Role of the Law Schools and the Practicing Bar.* 30 N.Y.L. SCH. REV. 621.

Kovac, Susan D. 1990. Part-time Employment of Full-time Law Students: A Problem or an Opportunity (unpublished, University of Tennessee College of Law).

Kramer, John R. 1989. *Law Schools and the Delivery of Legal Ser-*

vices—First Do No Harm. Conference on Access to Justice in the 1990s, Tulane Law School.

———. 1989. *Who will Pay the Piper or Leave the Check on the Table for the Other Guy.* 39 JOUR. OF LEGAL ED. 655.

La Mothe, Snyder & West. 1991. *Women as Rainmakers*, 7 LITIG. No. 3, 29.

Lancaster. *If Your Legal Problems Are Complex.* WALL ST. J., July 31, 1980.

LANDON, DONALD D. 1990. COUNTY LAWYERS—THE IMPACT OF CONTEXT ON PROFESSIONAL PRACTICE. New York: Praeger.

Lasswell, Harold D. & Myres S. McDougal. 1943. *Legal Education and Public Policy: Professional Training in the Public Interest.* 52 YALE L. J. 203.

LAW AND BUSINESS DIRECTORY OF CORPORATE COUNSEL, 1991-92. Glasser & Glasser eds. Published annually.

LAW CENTRES FEDERATION. 1988. A FRAMEWORK FOR EVALUATION. LCF London.

LAW SCHOOL ADMISSION COUNCIL/LAW SCHOOL ADMISSION SERVICES IN COOPERATION WITH AMERICAN BAR ASSOCIATION AND ASSOCIATION OF AMERICAN LAW SCHOOLS. 1991. THE OFFICIAL GUIDE TO U.S. LAW SCHOOLS. Published annually.

LAW SCHOOL ADMISSIONS SERVICES. 1991. ANNUAL REPORT. Issued Annually.

LAW SOCIETY OF ENGLAND AND WALES. 1985. PROFESSIONAL STANDARDS.

LAW SOCIETY OF UPPER CANADA. 1990. 33RD BAR ADMISSION COURSE STUDENT HANDBOOK. Toronto: Osgoode Hall.

LAWYER'S ALMANAC 1992. Englewood Cliffs, N.J.: Prentice Hall Law & Business.

Lederman & Levenson. 1987. *Essay: Dealing with the Limits of Vision: The Planning Process and Education of Lawyers.* 62 N.Y.U. L. REV. 404.

Lee, Richard D. Fall. 1990. *Associate Evaluations of Partners.* THE AILTO INSIDER. NEWSLETTER OF IN-HOUSE TRAINING DEVELOPMENTS. Vol. 4, No. 4.

———. 1987. *The Organization and Role of In-House Training.* AMERICAN LAW INSTITUTE-AMERICAN BAR ASSOCIATION COMMITTEE ON CONTINUING PROFESSIONAL EDUCATION CONFERENCE ON CLE AND THE LAWYER'S RESPONSIBILITIES IN AN EVOLVING PROFESSION. REPORT ON THE ARDEN HOUSE III CONFERENCE.

LEGAL AID BOARD. 1988. SECOND STAGE CONSULTATION ON THE FUTURE OF THE GREEN FORM SCHEME.

Legal Education Issue. 5 AUST. J. OF L. & S. (1988-89) 1-168.

Legal Services Corporation. *1990 Annual Report.*

LEGAL SYSTEMS. 1978. Baltimore: John Hopkins University Press.

Lesnick. August 1989. *Infinity in a Grain of Sand: The World of Law and Lawyering as Portrayed in the Clinical Teaching Implicit in the Law School Curriculum.* Draft.

Levin. 1977. *Beyond Mere Competence.* B.Y.U. L. REV. 997.

Levinson. 1986. *Professing Law: Commitment of Faith or Detached Analysis?.* 31 ST. LOUIS U. L. REV. 3.

LEVY, B. 1961. CORPORATION LAWYER: SAINT OR SINNER.

LEWIS, ANTHONY. 1964. GIDEON'S TRUMPET.

LIEBENBERG, M. December 1956. INCOME OF LAWYERS IN THE POST-WAR PERIOD. U.S. Department of Commerce Survey of Current Business.

Lipsman, W.S. 1991. *American Corporate Counsel As In-House Advisers Overseas.* American Association of Corporate Counsel DOCKET, Spring 1991, 18.

Littlejohn, Bruce. 1985. *South Carolina's Rule 5 Works Well.* 54 THE BAR EXAMINER 19 (Aug. 1985).
———. 1987. Littlejohn's Half Century at the Bench and Bar (1936-1986), Columbia, S.C. The South Carolina Bar Foundation.

Llewellyn, Karl N. 1938. *The Bar's Trouble and Poultices—and Cures?* 5 LAW & CONTEMP PROB. 104
———. The Annals of the Academy of Political Science. 1933. *The Bar Specializes—With What Results?* May 1933. 176.

Macaulay. 1982. *Law Schools and the World Outside Their Doors II: Some Notes on Two Recent Studies of the Chicago Bar.* 32 J. LEGAL EDUC. 506.

MacCrate, Robert. 1989. *What Women Are Teaching a Male-Dominated Profession.* 55 FORDHAM L. REV. 989.

———. 1989. *Don't Squelch the Volunteers!* NEW YORK LAW JOURNAL September 29, 1989, 2.

———. 1988. "Perspectives on Professionalism," speech to the American Bar Foundation Conference on Professionalism, Ethics and Economic Change in the American Legal Profession. Evanston, Illinois. September 23, 1988.

———. 1988. *Paradigm Lost—or Revised and Regained?* 38 JOUR. LEGAL ED. 295.

———. 1988. "The Future of Professionalism," Jones Lecture, Emory University Law School, February 29, 1988.

———. 1988. *The Making of the American Lawyer.* 34 S.D.L. REV. 229.

———. 1987. *What Is the Purpose of Legal Education?* ABA Section of Legal Education and Admissions to the Bar National Conference of Professional Skills and Legal Education. Albuquerque, N.M. October 16-18, 1987. *Printed in* OCCASIONAL PAPERS OF THE SECTION, Number 1.

———. 1984. Legal Education and Preserving the Professional Paradox (paper presented at Conference Legal Education and the Profession, McGeorge School of Law, April 13, 1984).

Mackie. *Professional Legal Skills: Report of a Workshop.* Australia: J. OF PROFESSIONAL LEGAL EDUCATION (cite unknown).

MACKINNON, CATHERINE. 1987. FEMINISM UNMODIFIED.

Maddi. *Trial Advocacy Competence: The Judicial Perspective.* 1978. AMERICAN BAR FOUNDATION RES JOURNAL 105.

MAGUIRE, JOHN M. 1928. THE LANCE OF JUSTICE. Harvard University Press.

Maher, Stephen T. 1990. *The Praise of Folly: A Defense of Practice Supervision in Clinical Legal Education.* 69 NEBRASKA L. REV. 537.

Manning, Galanter, Hollinger & Priest. 1987. *Legal Education for a Changing Legal Profession.* (Symposium, Law School of the State University of New York at Buffalo). 37 BUFF. L. REV. 657.

Marshall, Thurgood. 1975. Financing Public Interest Law: The Role of the Organized Bar, address to the American Bar Association Bar Activities Section, August 10, 1975.

MARTIN, JOANNE WITH ROBERT M. TRAVIS. 1987. CORPORATE LAW DEPARTMENT TRENDS AND THE EFFECT OF THE CURRENT BAR ADMISSION SYSTEM: A SURVEY OF CORPORATE COUNSEL. Prepared by the American Bar Foundation. Washington, D.C.: American Corporate Council Institute.

Martyn, Susan R. 1989. *Peer Review and Quality Assurance for Lawyers.* 20 TOLEDO LAW REV. 295.

MAYER, MARTIN. 1967. THE LAWYERS. New York: Harper & Row.
———. 1956. *The Wall Street Lawyers, Part I: The Elite Corps of American Business; Part II: Keepers of the Business Conscience.* HARPER'S MAGAZINE.

McChesney & Muris. 1979. *The Effect of Advertising on the Quality of Legal Services.* 65 A.B.A.J. 1505.

McDiarmid, Marjorie Anne. 1990. *What's Going on Down there in the Basement: In-House Clinics Expand their Beachhead.* 35 N.Y.L. SCH. REV. 239.

McKay, Robert B. 1990. *The Rise of the Justice Industry and the Decline of Legal Ethics.* 68 WASH. UNIV. L. QUARTERLY 829.
———. 1987. *The Legal Profession: Some Compliments and Some Complaints.* 59 N.Y.S. BAR J. 516.
———. 1985. *What Law Schools Can and Should Do (and Sometimes Do).* 30 N.Y.L. SCH. REV. 491.
———. 1977. *Law Schools, Lawyers and Tightly Closed Circles.* B.Y.U. L. REV. 991.

MCLE Credit for In-House Activities. THE AILTO INSIDER: A NEWSLETTER OF IN-HOUSE TRAINING DEVELOPMENTS. Winter 1991. Vol. 5, No. 1.

McManis. 1981. *A History of First Century American Legal Education: A Revisionist Perspective.* 59 WASH. UNIV. L. QUARTERLY 597.

Menkel-Meadow, Carrie. 1984. *Toward Another View of Legal Negotiation: The Structure of Problem Solving.* 31 UCLA L. REV. 754.

Miner, Roger J. 1989. *Confronting the Communication Crisis in the Legal Profession.* 1989. 34 N.Y.L. SCH. REV. 1.

MINNESOTA STATE BAR ASSOCIATION. 1989. MINNESOTA RULES OF PROFESSIONAL CONDUCT. As amended Dec. 27, 1989.

Minow, Martha. 1987. *Foreword: Justice Engendered.* 101 HARV. L. REV. 10.

MISSOURI BAR. 1963. A MATRIMONIAL STUDY OF PUBLIC ATTITUDES AND LAW OFFICE MANAGEMENT.

Mixed Verdict: Prepaid Legal Services Draw Plenty of Customers and Criticism. WALL STREET JOURNAL, August 6, 1991. B1.

Moeser, Erica. 1992. *Some Reflections on Bar Admissions.* 23 SYLLA-BUS (Winter 1992) 8.

Morgan, Thomas D. 1991. *A Defense of Legal Education in the 1990s.* 48 WASH. & LEE L. REV. 1.

Mudd, John O. & John W. Latrielle. 1988. *Professional Competence: A Study of New Lawyers.* 49 MONTANA L. REV. 11.

THE MUNICIPAL YEARBOOK. 1991. Published annually by the International City and County Management Association. Washington, D.C.

Murphy, T.R. 1991. *Indigent Defense and the War on Drugs,* 6 CRIMINAL JUSTICE, No. 3, 14.

Murray, Florence K. 1990. *Women and the Law, Have We Really Come a Long Way?* JUDGES' JOURNAL Winter 1990, 19.

NATIONAL ASSOCIATION FOR LAW PLACEMENT. 1992. EMPLOYMENT REPORT AND SALARY DATA CLASS OF 1990. Issued annually.
————. 1991. DIRECTORY OF LEGAL EMPLOYERS.
————. 1990. Private Practice—Ten Year Comparison.

NATIONAL ASSOCIATION OF ATTORNEYS GENERAL. 1991. STATISTICS ON THE OFFICE OF ATTORNEY GENERAL.

NATIONAL CONSUMER COUNCIL. 1989. ORDINARY JUSTICE. HMSO.

NATIONAL CRIMINAL JUSTICE REFERENCE SERVICE. July 1990. BULLETIN BUREAU OF JUSTICE STATISTICS. U.S. Department of Justice.

NATIONAL DIRECTORY OF CRIMINAL LAWYERS. 1991. B. Tarlow ed. 3rd ed.

NATIONAL DIRECTORY OF NON-PROFIT ORGANIZATIONS. Published annually.

NATIONAL LAW JOURNAL. Feb. 24, 1992. *Public Defenders.* 3-4, 8.
_____. Dec. 30, 1991—Jan. 6, 1992. *Post-'Peel' Battles.* 1, 10-11.
_____. Sept. 9, 1991 corporate counsel supplement. Lyne, *The Pressure is On.* 51.
_____. July 8, 1991 supplement. *The NLJ Client List.* Published annually.
_____. June 10, 1991. *Mattox Chain of Storefront Law Offices.*
_____. April 22, 1991. MacLachlan, *Washington, D.C.'s Hidden Bar.* 1
_____. August 6, 1984. *The Myth—and Reality—of the Law.*
_____. Issued annually. *The NLJ 250.*

NATIONAL LEGAL AID AND DEFENDER ASSOCIATION. 1991. DIRECTORY, PROGRAMS FOR SPECIAL NEEDS 1991/92.
_____. 1991. *Legal Services of Northern California.* CORNERSTONE Summer 1991.
_____. 1986. STANDARDS FOR PROVIDERS OF LEGAL SERVICES TO THE POOR.
_____. 1973. THE OTHER FACE OF JUSTICE.

National Legal Services Policy Committee. Report to Board of Directors. January 4, 1965.

NATIONAL RESOURCE CENTER FOR CONSUMERS OF LEGAL SERVICES. 1991. *Legal Plan Letter, Special Census Issue.* August 30, 1991.

NELSON, ROBERT L. 1988. PARTNERS WITH POWER: SOCIAL TRANSFORMATION OF THE LARGE LAW FIRM.
_____. 1981. *Practice and Privilege: Social Change and the Structure of Large Law Firms.* 1981 AMERICAN BAR FOUND. RESEARCH JOUR. 95.

NELSON, ROBERT L., DAVID M. ZUBEK AND RAYMAN T. SOLOMON, eds. 1992. LAWYERS' IDEALS/LAWYERS' PRACTICE, TRANSFORMATIONS IN THE AMERICAN LEGAL PROFESSION. Ithaca, NY: Cornell University Press.

New Mexico School of Law. 1989. *Symposium 1989.* 19 N.M.L. REV. 1.

NEW SOUTH WALES LAW REFORM COMMISSION. 1982. REPORT OF ADVERTISING AND SPECIALIZATION.

NEW YORK LAW JOURNAL. November 1, 1991. *Minority Lawyers* 1-2.

New York Law School Symposium. 1990. *Women in the Lawyering Workplace: Feminists Considerations and Practical Solutions.* (Karen Gross, J. Williams, S. Caplow, S.A. Schneindlin, C. Fuchs Epstein.) 35 N.Y. LAW SCH. REV. 293.

NEW YORK STATE BAR ASSOCIATION. 1990. N.Y. LAWYER'S CODE OF PROFESSIONAL RESPONSIBILITY. As amended Sept. 1, 1990.

NYNEX YELLOW PAGES FOR MANHATTAN. 1990-1991. *Guide of Lawyers Arranged By Practice.*

O'Hara & Klein. 1981. *Is the Bar Examination an Adequate Measure of Lawyer Competence?* 50 BAR EXAM. 28.

Ogden. 1989. *Performance Testing in Colorado.* 58 THE BAR EXAMINER 19 (Nov. 1989).

ORGANIZATION OF ECONOMIC COOPERATION AND DEVELOPMENT. 1985. COMPETITION POLICY AND THE PROFESSIONS. Paris. OECD.

PARTRIDGE & BERMANT. 1978. THE QUALITY OF ADVOCACY IN THE FEDERAL COURTS. Federal Judicial Center.

Paterson. 1986. *Specialization and the Legal Profession.* 86 NEW LAW JOURNAL 687.

Peden. 1972. *Goals for Legal Education.* 24 J. LEGAL EDUC. 379.

Pennell, Jeffrey N. 1988. *Introduction: Whither Estate Planning.* 24 IDAHO L. REV. 339.

PENNSYLVANIA BAR ASSOCIATION YOUNG LAWYERS' DIVISION. 1984. PRACTICUM: BASIC SKILLS TRAINING COURSE PROJECT MATERIALS MANUAL.

Peterson, Andrews, Spain & Greenberg. 1956. *An Analytical Study of North Carolina General Practice. 1953-54.* 31 J. OF MED. EDUC. 1.

Philadelphia Bar Association Special Committee on Pennsylvania Bar Admissions Procedures. 1971. *Racial Discrimination of Pennsylvania Bar Examinations.* 44 TEMPLE LAW QUARTERLY 141.

PINCUS, WILLIAM. 1980. CLINICAL EDUCATION FOR LAW STUDENTS.

Pirie. 1987. *Objectives in Legal Education: The Case for Systematic Instruction Design*. 37 J. LEGAL EDUC. 576.

Polak, Werner L. & Stephen V. Armstrong. 1987. *Why Law Firms Should Adopt In-House CLE and What They Can Expect It To Do*. AMERICAN LAW INSTITUTE-AMERICAN BAR ASSOCIATION COMMITTEE ON CONTINUING PROFESSIONAL EDUCATION. CLE AND THE LAWYER'S RESPONSIBILITIES IN AN EVOLVING PROFESSION, THE REPORT ON THE ARDEN HOUSE III CONFERENCE.

Pollock, E.J. 1991. *Big Firms Learn that They, Too, Are a Cyclical Business*. WALL STREET JOURNAL, August 15, 1991, 1.

POUND, ROSCOE. 1953. THE LAWYER FROM ANTIQUITY TO MODERN TIMES. St. Paul, Minn.: West Publishing Co.

POWELL, MICHAEL. 1989. FROM PATRICIAN TO PROFESSIONAL ELITE: THE TRANSFORMATION OF THE NEW YORK CITY BAR ASSOCIATION. New York: Russell Sage Foundation.

POWERS, WILLIAM. 1986. A STUDY OF CONTEMPORARY LAW SCHOOL CURRICULA. Office of the American Bar Association Consultant on Legal Education.
_____. 1987. A STUDY OF CONTEMPORARY LAW SCHOOL CURRICULA II: PROFESSIONAL SKILLS COURSES. Office of the American Bar Association Consultant on Legal Education.

PRACTISING LAW INSTITUTE. 1983. THE FIRST FIFTY YEARS.

PRENTICE-HALL. 1991. THE OF COUNSEL 500. Issued annually. May 6, 1991.

PROFESSIONAL LEGAL EDUCATION FOR TOMORROW'S LAWYERS. 25 Jan. 1991. PROPOSAL FOR THE POSTGRADUATE CERTIFICATE IN LAWS. COURSE STRUCTURE AND STAFF DETAILS. No. 1 (Hong Kong Proposal).

Pye, A. Kenneth. 1987. *Legal Education in an Era of Change: The Challenge*. 1987 DUKE L. J. 191.
_____. 1973. *On Teaching the Teachers: Some Preliminary Reflections on Clinical Education as Methodology*. Working Papers for Council on Legal Education for Professional Responsibility Conference, June 1973. 21.

RAIFFA, HOWARD. 1982. THE ART AND SCIENCE OF NEGOTIATION. Cambridge, Mass. Harvard U. Press.

REED, ALFRED Z. 1921. TRAINING FOR THE PUBLIC PROFESSION OF THE LAW. Carnegie Foundation.

Rehnquist, William H. Oct. 1987. *The State of the Legal Profession.* 59 N.Y. ST. BAR J. 18.

Reichert, I.F. 1968. *The Future of Continuing Legal Education* in LAW IN A CHANGING SOCIETY. Geoffrey Hazard ed., 167-182.

Rhode, D.L. 1988. *Prospectives on Professional Women.* 40 STANFORD L. REV. 1163.

Richards, Carol. 1981. *Legal Clinics: Merely Advertising Law Firms?* ABA SPECIAL COMMITTEE ON THE DELIVERY OF LEGAL SERVICES, November 1981.

Rosenthal, Douglas E. 1976. *Evaluating the Competence of Lawyers.* 11 LAW & SOCIETY 256.
———. 1974. LAWYER AND CLIENT: WHO'S IN CHARGE? New York: Russell Sage Foundation.

ROSENTHAL, KAGAN & QUATRONE. 1971. VOLUNTEER ATTORNEYS AND LEGAL SERVICES FOR THE POOR: NEW YORK'S CLO PROGRAM. New York: Russell Sage Foundation.

ROUCH. 1974. COMPETENT MINISTRY. Nashville.

Rowan, Meltsner & Givelber. August 2, 1989. *Moving Beyond Nuts and Bolts.* LEGAL TIMES.

ROYAL COMMISSION ON LEGAL SERVICES IN SCOTLAND (the Hughes Commission). 1980. HMSO, London, Cmnd 7846.

ROYAL COMMISSION ON LEGAL SERVICES (the Benson Commission). 1979. HMSO, London, Cmnd 7846.

Rubin, Alvin B. 1975. *A Causerie on Lawyers' Ethics in Negotiation.* 35 LA. L. REV. 577.

RUBIN, JEFFREY Z. AND BERT R. BROWN. 1975. THE SOCIAL PSYCHOLOGY OF BARGAINING AND NEGOTIATION. New York, NY: Academic Press.

Rubino, Victor. January 1992. *MCLE: The Downside.* THE CLE JOURNAL AND REGISTER. Vol. 38, No. 1.

Rutter. 1968. *Designing and Teaching the First Degree Law Curriculum.* 37 U. CINN. L. REV. 9.
_____. 1961. *A Jurisprudence of Lawyers' Operations.* 13 J. LEGAL EDUC. 301.

St. John's Law Review. 1976. *Symposium on Current Trends in Legal Education and the Legal Profession.* 50 ST. JOHN'S L. REV. 431.

Sandalow. 1984. *The Moral Responsibility of Law Schools.* 34 J. LEGAL EDUC. 163.

Sander, R.H. and E.D. Williams. 1989. *Why Are There So Many Lawyers? Perspectives on a Turbulent Market.* 14 LAW & SOC. INQUIRY 478.

Sarat, Austin and William I.F. Felstiner. 1986. *Law and Strategy in the Divorce Lawyers Office.* 20 LAW AND SOC'Y. REV. 93-134.

Schafran, Lynn H. 1989. *Lawyers' Lives, Clients' Lives: Can Women Liberate the Profession?* 34 VILLANOVA L. REV. 1105.

Schmidt, S. 1986. *Firm Development Mobilized by a "New Breed" of Resource.* NATIONAL LAW JOURNAL, August 25, 1986, 15.

SCHON, DONALD A. 1987. EDUCATING THE REFLECTIVE PRACTITIONER. San Francisco: Jossey-Bass Publishers.
_____. 1983. THE REFLECTIVE PRACTITIONER. New York: Basic Books, Inc.

Schwartz, Murray L. 1968. *Changing Patterns of Legal Services* in LAW IN A CHANGING SOCIETY. Geoffrey Hazard ed. 109-124.

Schwartz, Robert A. 1973. *The Relative Importance of Skills Used by Attorneys.* 3 GOLDEN GATE L. REV. 321.

SCOTTISH CONSUMER COUNCIL. 1987. REPORT OF A SURVEY ON THE USE OF SOLICITORS.

Seavey, W.A. 1950. *The Association of American Law Schools in Retrospect.* 3 JOUR. LEGAL ED. 153.

SEGAL, GERALDINE. 1983. BLACKS IN THE LAW, PHILADELPHIA AND THE NATION.

SERON, CARROLL. 1992. MANAGING ENTREPRENEURIAL LEGAL SERVICES: THE TRANSFORMATION OF SMALL FIRM PRACTICE IN LAWYERS'

IDEALS/LAWYERS' PRACTICES: TRANSFORMATION IN THE AMERICAN LEGAL PROFESSION. Nelson, Trubek & Solomon eds., 63-92.

————. 1988. *Managing Legal Services* (unpublished research paper C.U.N.Y.).

Sharswood, George. circa 1855. The Aims and Duties of the Profession of the Law. Lectures, Univ. of Pennsylvania.

SHERR, A. 1986. CLIENT INTERVIEWING FOR LAWYERS. London. Sweet Maxwell.

————. 1986. *Lawyers and Clients: The First Meeting.* 49 MODERN LAW REVIEW 3.

Shreve, 1983. Book Review. 97 HARV. L. REV. 597 (reviewing R. STEVENS, LAW SCHOOL: LEGAL EDUCATION IN AMERICA FROM THE 1850S TO THE 1980S, (1983)).

SINGSEN, G. August 1990. REPORT ON THE SURVEY OF LEGAL CLINICS. ABA Special Committee on the Delivery of Legal Services.

SKOLER, D.L. 1982. THE ADMINISTRATIVE LAW JUDICIARY: CHANGE, CHALLENGE AND CHOICES.

SMIGEL, E. 1969. THE WALL STREET LAWYER'S PROFESSIONAL ORGANIZATION MAN? New York: The Free Press of Glencoe.

Smith, J.C. 1982. *Black Bar Associations in Civil Rights.* 15 CREIGHTON L. REV. 3, 651.

Smith, Reginald H. 1947. *Legal Services Offices for Persons of Moderate Means.* 31 AM. JUDICATURE SOCIETY JOUR. 37.

————. 1919. JUSTICE AND THE POOR. Reprint edition 1971, New York: Arno Press.

Smith. 1989. *Performance Testing in California, 1983-1989.* 58 THE BAR EXAMINER 17 (Aug. 1989).

Smith. 1984. *Preparing and Grading the California Performance Test.* 54 THE BAR EXAMINER 1 (Feb. 1984).

Smith. 1931. *Progress in Education for Admission to the Bar.* 7 AMERICAN LAW SCHOOL REV. 267.

Spaeth. 1988. *To What Extent Can a Disciplinary Code Assure the Competence of Lawyers?.* 61 TEMPLE L. REV. 1211.

Spangenberg, Davis & Smith. Fall 1982. *Contract Defense Systems Under Attack: Balancing Cost and Quality.* 39(1) NLADA BRIEFCASE 5.

SPANGLER, EVE. 1986. LAWYERS FOR HIRE, SALARIED PROFESSIONALS AT WORK. New Haven, CT: Yale University Press.

Spence, James M. Dec. 1988. *The Teaching Term of the Ontario Bar Admission Course: A Critical Assessment and Proposal for Change.* J. PROF. L. EDUC. 163.

Spiegel. 1987. *Theory and Practice in Legal Education: An Essay on Clinical Education.* 34 UCLA L. REV. 577.

Stanford Law Review. 1988. *Gender, Legal Education, and the Legal Profession: An Empirical Study of Stanford Law Students and Graduates.* 40 STAN. L. REV. 1209.

STATE BAR OF CALIFORNIA. October 11, 1991. REPORT AND RECOMMENDATIONS OF THE COMMISSION ON LAWYERING SKILLS.
————. December 8, 1990. MCLE RULES AND REGULATIONS.

STATE BAR OF CALIFORNIA COMMITTEE OF BAR EXAMINERS. 1988. INFORMATION REGARDING PERFORMANCE TESTS.

Stanton, Michael. 1991. *Stepping Up To The Bar.* OCCUPATIONAL OUTLOOK QUARTERLY. Spring 1991. 3.

Stehlow, Nancy A. 1981. *Evaluating "Competency" Criteria: Toward a Uniform Standard of Lawyer Performance.* 59 WASH. UNIV. L. Q. 1091.

Stein, Robert A. 1991. *The Future of Legal Education.* 75 MINN. L. REV. 945.

STEVENS, GEORGE NEFF. 1970. A.A.L.S. BAR EXAMINATION STUDY PROJECT, BAR EXAMINATION COVERAGE, LAW SCHOOL CURRICULA AND THE APPLICANT. April 10, 1970.

STEVENS, M. 1986. POWER OF ATTORNEY: THE RISE OF THE GIANT LAW FIRMS.

STEVENS, ROBERT B. 1983. LAW SCHOOL: LEGAL EDUCATION IN AMERICA FROM THE 1850S TO THE 1980S. Chapel Hill: Univ. North Carolina.

Strong, Frank R. 1973. *The Pedagogic Training of a Law Faculty*. 25 J. LEGAL EDUC. 226.

Stuckey, Roy T. 1990. *Preparing Lawyers for Law Practice: New Roles for the NCBE and the ABA*. 59 THE BAR EXAMINER 12 (May 1990)

Studley, Jamienne S. 1991. *Building on the Assets of Midsize Firms*. MANHATTAN LAWYER, November 1991, 45.

Susman, T. 1992. *A Perspective on the Washington Lawyer Today and Charles Horsky's Washington Lawyer of 1992*. 44 ADMINISTRATIVE LAW REV. 1.

Sussman, Fern S. 1989. *The Large Law Firm Structure—An Historic Opportunity*. 57 FORDHAM L. REVIEW 701.

SUTHERLAND, ARTHUR E. 1967. THE LAW AT HARVARD. Belknap.

SWAINE, R.T. 1948. THE CRAVATH FIRM AND ITS PREDECESSORS. Volume 2.
———. 1946. THE CRAVATH FIRM AND ITS PREDECESSORS. Volume 1.

Taylor, G. 1991. *Party's Over in Insurance*. NATIONAL LAW JOURNAL, Sept. 23, 1991, 1.

Teaching Legal Ethics: A Symposium. 1991. 41 JOUR. LEGAL ED. (No. 1 1991)

Thorner, Abbie Willard. 1987. *Legal Education in the Recruitment Marketplace: Decades of Change*. 1987 DUKE LAW J. 276.

Tomain, Joseph P. and Michael E. Solimine. 1990. *Skills Skepticism in the Postclinic World*. 40 JOUR. L. ED. 307.

TOMASIC. 1978. LAWYERS AND THE COMMUNITY. Law Foundation of New South Wales.

Trakman. 1982. *Competence and the Law*. 11 CAPITAL UNIVERSITY LAW REV. 401.

Trubek, Sarat, Felstiner, Kritzer & Grossman. *The Costs of Ordinary Litigation*. 31 UCLA L. REV. 72.

Tushnet. 1981. *Legal Scholarship: Its Causes and Cure*. 90 YALE L. REV. 1205.

TWEED, HARRISON. 1955. THE CHANGING PRACTICE OF LAW. Association of the Bar of the City of New York.

U.S. CENSUS BUREAU. 1990 CENSUS: Washington, D.C. U.S. Government Printing Office.

U.S. DEPARTMENT OF COMMERCE. May 1944. SURVEY OF CURRENT BUSINESS.

U.S. DEPT. OF COMMERCE INTERNATIONAL TRADE ADMINISTRATION. 1991. U.S. INDUSTRIAL OUTLOOK. PROFESSIONAL SERVICES: LEGAL SERVICES (SIC81).

University of Arizona Law School. 1971. *Symposium—The Practice of Law in the Public Interest.* 13 ARIZ. L REV. 797.

UTLEY, F. & G.A. MUNNECKE. 1984. FROM LAW STUDENT TO LAWYER. ABA Career Series.

Vermont Supreme Court Rules of Admission.

Vogt, Leona M. May 1986. *From Law School to Career: Where Do Graduates Go and What Do They Do?* Harvard Law School Program on the Legal Profession.

VOGT, SILVERMAN, WHITE & SCANLON. 1976. FIELD TEST RESULTS OF THE PEER REVIEW QUALITY ASSESSMENT OF LEGAL SERVICES FOR THE LEGAL SERVICES CORPORATION.

Wahl, Rosalie E. 1987. *The Linking of Skills and Values in Legal Education.* ABA Section of Legal Education and Admissions to the Bar National Conference of Professional Skills and Legal Education. Albuquerque, N.M. October 16-18, 1987. *Printed in* OCCASIONAL PAPERS OF THE SECTION, Number 1.

Wangerin, Paul T. 1988. *Objectives, Multiplistic and Relative Truth in Developmental Psychology and Legal Education.* 62 IND. L. REV. 1237.

WARREN. 1911. A HISTORY OF THE AMERICAN BAR.

Watson, 1968. *The Quest for Professional Competence: Psychological Aspects of Legal Education,* 37 CINN. L. REV. 93.

WEINFELD, W. August 1949. INCOME OF LAWYERS, 1929-48. U.S. Department of Commerce Survey of Current Business.

Weiss, C. & Louise Melling. 1988. *The Legal Education of Twenty Women.* 40 STANFORD L. REV. 1299.

Wellington, Ralph G. 1987. *MCLE: Does It Go Far Enough and What Are the Alternatives? in* AMERICAN LAW INSTITUTE-AMERICAN BAR ASSOCIATION COMMITTEE ON CONTINUING PROFESSIONAL EDUCATION. CLE AND THE LAWYER'S RESPONSIBILITIES IN AN EVOLVING PROFESSION, THE REPORT ON THE ARDEN HOUSE III CONFERENCE. Philadelphia, Pa. ALI-ABA.

Wells, Richard S. 1963. The Legal Profession and Political Ideology: The Case of the Carr Law Firm of Manchester, Iowa (Ph.D. dissertation State University of Iowa).

White, James P. 1984 *Lawyer Competency and the Law School Curriculum: An Opportunity for Cooperation.* 53 THE BAR EXAMINER 4 (Feb. 1984).

White, James P. 1987. *Legal Education in the Era of Change: Law School Autonomy.* 1987 DUKE L. JOUR. 292.

WILLIAMS, G. 1983. LEGAL NEGOTIATION AND SETTLEMENT.

Windeler, Ruth. June 1986. *Administration of a Professional Legal Training Course: The British Columbia Professional Legal Training Course.* J. PROF. L. EDUC. 69.

Wirtz, Willard. 1971. *A Proposal for a Study of Legal Education and Professional Development and for Implementing Its Recommendations.* On behalf of the Association of American Law Schools, the American Bar Association and the American Law Institute.

WISE, P.B. 1973. THE ENDANGERED SPECIES: AMERICA'S PRIVATE CRIMINAL LAWYERS.

WOLFRAM, CHARLES. 1986. MODERN LEGAL ETHICS.

Wolkin, Paul. 1988. ALI-ABA...XL! Philadelphia: ALI-ABA.
————. 1976. *On Improving the Quality of Lawyering.* 50 ST. JOHN'S L. REV. 523.

Yudof, Mark G. 1989. *Law School Curriculum: The Immovable Object.* MANHATTAN LAWYER. June 27, 1988. Commentary p. 11.

Zander, Michael 1978. *Research as a Way to Improve the Quality of Legal Work.* 1978 NEW LAW JOURNAL 576.

ZEMANS, FRANCES KAHN AND VICTOR G. ROSENBLUM. 1981. THE MAKING OF A PUBLIC PROFESSION. Chicago, Ill. American Bar Foundation.

Zillman, Donald N. and Vickie R. Gregory. 1987. *The New Apprenticeships: An Empirical Study of Student Employment and Legal Education.* 12 JOUR. CONTEMP. LAW 203.

Cases

Argersinger v. *Hamlin*, 407 U.S. 25 (1972).

Bates & O'Steen v. *State Bar of Arizona*, 433 U.S. 350 (1977).

Brotherhood of Railroad Trainees v. *Virginia*, 377 U.S. 1 (1964).

Brown v. *Board of Education*, 347 U.S. 483 (1954).

Ex parte Secombe, 19 How. 9, 60 U.S. 9 (U.S. Minn., Dec. Term 1856).

Ex rel. Thacher, 22 Ohio Decisions 116 (1912)

Gideon v. *Wainwright*, 372 U.S. 355 (1963).

Goldfarb v. *Virginia State Bar*, 421 U.S. 773 (1975).

Illinois State Bar Association v. *People's Stock Yards State Bank*, 344 Ill. 462 (1931).

In re Cooper, 22 N.Y. 67 (1960).

In re Day, 181 Ill. 73 (1899).

In re Saddler, 55 Okla. 510 (1913).

Johnson v. *Zerbst*, 304 U.S. 458 (1938).

Missouri ex rel. Gaines v. *Canada*, 305 U.S. 337 (1938.

NAACP Legal Defense Fund v. *Button*, 371 U.S. 415 (1963).

Pearson v. *Murray*, 168 Md. 478, 187 A. 590 (1936).

Peel v. *Illinois Attorney Registration and Disciplinary Commission*, 110 Sup. Ct. 2281 (1990).

People ex rel. Karlin v. *Culkin*, 248 N.Y. 465 (1928).

Powell v. *Alabama*, 287 U.S. 45 (1932).

Schware v. *Board of Examiners.* 1957. 353 U.S. 232, 247-51. (concurring opinion of Justice Frankfurter).

United Mine Workers of America v. *Illinois State Bar Association*, 389 U.S. 217 (1967).

United Transportation Union v. *State Bar of Michigan*, 401 U.S. 576 (1971).

Worth v. *Seldin*, 422 U.S. 490 (1975).

Appendix B

The American Bar Foundation Study
Learning Lawyering: Where Do Lawyers
Acquire Practice Skills?
Bryant G. Garth, Donald D. Landon, Joanne Martin

Teachers of law and practicing lawyers often seem to inhabit different worlds. To many observers, law schools, steeped in the traditions of academia and legal scholarship, appear far removed from the realities of law practice. A study is currently underway at the ABF that identifies the knowledge and skills which lawyers now consider important to the practice of law; where they acquired the skills; and their view of the role that law school did, or should, play in transmitting knowledge, skills, and values. While data analysis is still in progress, some interesting preliminary findings have emerged from this research.

The study is being conducted by ABF Director and Research Fellow Bryant Garth, ABF Assistant Director Joanne Martin, and Professor Donald Landon of Southwest Missouri State University. Three surveys, designed to tap the perceptions of both urban and rural lawyers, were fielded. Those surveyed include:

- Partners in Chicago law firms who have responsibility for hiring new lawyers;
- Lawyers currently practicing in the Chicago area who have been admitted to the practice of law since 1986;
- Lawyers practicing in rural and mid-sized towns in the state of Missouri who have been practicing for ten or fewer years.

The Urban Bar

The survey of hiring partners, conducted by telephone, was directed to a representative sample of all firms in Chicago that have at least five partners. One hundred and seventeen hiring partners, representing a 50 percent response rate, completed interviews which elicited their views on the importance of various skills during the hiring process.

At the resume review stage, law school, class rank, and participation in law review were identified by two-thirds of the hiring partners as the most important considerations. At the interview stage, the criteria change. Here, over 70% of the partners considered oral communication skills, general appearance and demeanor, and class rank to be most important. These three factors, joined by law school, remained of prime importance at the point at which the ultimate hiring decision is made.

Hiring partners indicated that they expect new associates to bring with them oral and written communication skills, ability in legal analysis and reasoning, computer and library research skills, and sensitivity to ethical concerns. Among the skills which hiring partners believe will be developed on the job are drafting skills, negotiation and counseling, litigation skills and the ability to obtain and keep clients. These perceptions held true for hiring partners generally, regardless of firm size and the number of years of experience in a hiring capacity. The hiring partners surveyed have not seen much change recently in the level of skills brought by new associates, with a couple exceptions. They do see a decrease in written communication skills and an increase in both computer research skills and sensitivity to ethical concerns. Again, there were no significant differences among the hiring partners based on firm size or the number of years of hiring experience.

The mail survey of recent law school graduates was sent to about 1,500 lawyers, a random sample of those admitted to the bar since 1986 in the Chicago area. One of the striking characteristics of this group is a disproportionate representation of large law firm lawyers. About three-fourths of the Chicago group practice in law firms, and most of these firms are relatively large. The respondent pool is not a picture of the bar in Chicago, but rather a very accurate picture of the career distributions of individuals recently admitted to the practice of law in the Chicago area.

The new lawyers were asked to indicate the importance to them of each item in a list of 17 skills and where they acquired the skills:

- Oral and written communication skills, the ability to instill others' confidence, and legal reasoning skills were considered most important; knowledge of substantive and procedural law fell in the middle; research skills, litigation skills and ability to obtain and keep clients were considered least important. The latter finding is in part a result of legal aid, government, and corporate counsel, who rate client development understandably quite low.
- Mirroring the perceptions of the hiring partners about which skills are brought and which are learned, new lawyers state that the all-important communication skills were acquired from their own experience, not from the law school or their firm experience. Law schools are viewed as responsible for developing knowledge of substantive and procedural law, ability in legal analysis and legal reasoning, research skills,

and sensitivity to ethical concerns. Skills such as those involved in litigation, counseling and negotiation as well as client skills are learned primarily in the firm setting.

One major thrust of the study is an attempt to identify teaching gaps in law school training, that is, those areas which law school graduates think can be taught in law school but which, in their view, did not receive sufficient attention in the law school setting. The data, indeed, do disclose some significant gaps. Among them:

- Over three-fourths of those surveyed think oral communication skills can be taught; only 39% felt such skills received sufficient attention.
- Written communication skills can be taught in the view of 91% of the respondents, yet only 55% say they received sufficient attention. Seventy-nine percent of the respondents feel that legal drafting skills can be taught, but only 24% perceive that sufficient attention was given to development of these skills.

Gaps: Then and Now

With Chicago as the site of data gathering for the urban component of the study, the research team is able to use the Zemans and Rosenblum data, also collected in Chicago in the '70s, as a baseline to measure change. At first glance, it does not appear that many gaps have been closed since the late 1970s. Despite all the recent attention to clinical education, gaps still exist, for example, in the areas of negotiation and counseling. But there have been changes that provide some grounds for optimism:

- While there is still a gap, many more lawyers now think that negotiation can be taught effectively (up from 35% to 68%) and that it received sufficient attention in law school (up from 15% to 29%).
- A very dramatic change has occurred in the area of professional responsibility. In the Zemans and Rosenblum study the basic attitude was that ethical concerns can't be taught, are not all that important, and are something that evolve in practice. In a sharp reversal, 87% of the current respondents say sensitivity to ethical concerns can be taught effectively and 68% say sufficient attention was paid to this area. Professional responsibility has arrived as a substantive concern in the law schools.

The data also indicate that some skills have declined in relative important in the past decade, notably, fact gathering and legal research. This decline may stem from a general shift in emphasis from adversarial fact intensive litigation to negotiated settlements. Another change in the last decade is the elevation of general business skills. This is reflected in the decided increase in importance assigned by new graduates and hiring partners to oral communication skills and ability to instill others' confidence.

The Rural Bar

In contrast to the large-firm Chicago bar, the rural lawyers surveyed by Professor Donald Landon reside at the opposite end of the legal practice spectrum. The rural lawyers are less likely to have an area of concentration (78% in Chicago; 32% in the rural sample, mainly in the criminal area), tend to serve individuals rather than businesses (three-fourths of rural beginners serve individuals for more than half their caseload, 85% in Chicago serve businesses in three-fourths of their cases or more), and appear in court more often earlier. These lawyers are working in towns of 20,000 or less with some as small as 250 residents. Nationally, lawyers working in nonmetropolitan areas represent about 13% of the Bar. But the small percentage is deceptive in that:

- There are about as many lawyers practicing in rural settings as there are lawyers practicing in firms with 50 or more lawyers.
- The rural bar is far more representative of all practicing lawyers. Nearly two out of three practicing lawyers nationally are doing exactly what rural lawyers do—practicing solo or in firms of under five lawyers or less and representing primarily individual and small business clients.

The entrepreneurial nature of rural law practice and its emphasis on personal plight legal matters shape evaluations of lawyering skills.

Despite the significant practice differences outlined above, lawyers from all settings were in agreement that the three most important skills for the practicing attorney were self-presentational skills, not technical legal skills. Oral communication, written communication, and ability to instill others' confidence achieved the highest importance scores of the entire list of 17 skills and knowledge areas.

The rural bar tended to give higher importance rankings overall to all of the skill areas than did the more institutionally situated Chicago lawyers. This is not an unanticipated finding. As general practitioners, they are likely to draw on a broader range of skills and knowledge than the urban specialists.

Significant differences between Chicago and rural beginners' ranking of skill and knowledge areas occurred in three predictable areas. Knowledge of procedural law and understanding and conducting litigation were ranked significantly higher in importance by the rural practitioners than the Chicago practitioners. This finding is understandable given that at least 25% of the beginning rural practitioners are prosecuting attorneys or public defenders. The new rural lawyers as a whole are twice as likely to appear in court as even their Springfield colleagues from the mid-size sample. The beginning Chicago practitioner is far less likely to appear regularly in court even though he or she may work on litigation matters.

Finally, and perhaps unexpectedly, rural lawyers ranked sensitivity to professional ethical concerns significantly higher than their Chicago counterparts. Possible interpretations of this finding include the relative immunity of associates in law firm settings from ethical exposure and temptation as compared with rural practitioners who have full responsibility for clients, the majority of whom are individuals. A second interpretation suggests that the high levels of personal accountability typical of small communities makes ethical sensitivity particularly salient. Lawyers in small settings live by their reputations.

As might be expected, the rural beginning practitioners were generally more confident that most of the skill and knowledge areas could be effectively taught in law school. With their options for mentoring somewhat less than their urban counterparts, it is understandable that they would feel that the skills necessary to practice law would be available through law school. But once they affirmed law schools' ability to teach the requisite skills, they went on to indicate that in only 7 of the 17 areas did they actually learn the skill essentially through law school.

Rural lawyers gave law schools the strongest endorsement for the teaching of ethics, substantive law, library legal research, ability in legal analysis and legal reasoning and knowledge of procedural law. They felt sufficient attention was given to each of these skill areas.

Sources for Developing Practice Skills

When asked to identify one of ten listed sources as "most important for developing a particular legal skill," lawyers from each setting agreed that for most skills, including oral and written communication, "your own repeated experience" was the most valuable source. That is both unremarkable and predictable, although it is often neglected in assessment of skills and education. Both sets of practitioners also agreed that law school was the most valuable source for learning substantive law, legal research skills, legal analysis and legal reasoning, and sensitivity to professional ethical concerns.

There were, nevertheless, some differences. For example, rural lawyers designated "your own repeated experience" more regularly than did Chicago lawyers, not a remarkable finding considering the rural attorney's tendency to practice solo or in a small firm. Rural lawyers also identified the "general law school curriculum" as the second ranked source for developing legal skills. Chicago lawyers cited "observation of or advice from other lawyers in your office" more frequently than they cited the "general law school curriculum," especially for the development of technical skills such as legal drafting, diagnosing and planning legal solutions, litigation, counseling and negotiation. Again, this difference in perception is consistent with the differences in practice experience. Rural lawyers are less likely to have the benefit of firm mentors, colleagues or partners who can systematically share their accumulated knowledge. Their reliance on law school preparation is contextually determined. By contrast, the urban associates enter firm practice with the understanding that they will learn practice skills under the tutoring of experienced mentors.

Appendix C

Report of the Subcommittee
on Hearings and Conferences of the
Task Force on Law Schools and the Profession:
Narrowing The Gap

Robert B. McKay, Chair to
July 1990 [Deceased]
Roy T. Stuckey, Chair
Cory M. Amron
Joseph D. Harbaugh
Harold L. Rock

October 1991

Introduction

The Task Force on Law Schools and the Profession: Narrowing the Gap ("Task Force") determined that it was very important to its work to hear from the legal profession on the issue of the preparation of lawyers for law practice. This report summarizes testimony presented to the Task Force at four hearings conducted between February, 1990 and January, 1991.

Representatives of the ABA Young Lawyers Division appeared before the Subcommittee at the first hearing, held in February, 1990, in Los Angeles. In the second hearing, conducted in June, 1990, in Ann Arbor, Michigan, clinical law teachers presented testimony. The third hearing was held during the 1990 ABA Annual Meeting in Chicago and a wide range of representatives of the profession expressed their views to the Subcommittee. The final hearing, conducted during the AALS annual meeting in Washington, D.C. in January, 1991 focused on the presentations of deans and other representatives of law schools. Annex A is a list of participants in the four hearing sessions.

The Subcommittee was struck with the rich variety of carefully prepared remarks which were presented at these hearings. There were many constructive ideas about how to improve the preparation of lawyers for law practice. Perhaps the only consensus among the groups and people who appeared was that they are eager for the Task Force to provide direction, guidance, advice, encouragement and leadership. There seems to be significant agreement that change is needed in the manner in which lawyers are prepared for practice, although not everyone who testified saw this need or agreed what the changes should be.

There was also general agreement that law school graduates are not prepared to practice law without supervision. Certain participants pointed out that the current role of the law schools is the same as it was historically: to bring students to a point where they are prepared to become competent practitioners under the supervision of experienced lawyers. There was less consensus, but certainly a fair amount of support for the proposition that law school graduates are not adequately prepared for their first jobs in law practice and that the gulf is widening as the practice of law becomes more complex and the range of skills more diverse.

It should be noted that the summary that follows (which is organized around the questions presented to the participants, see Annex B) represents neither the thinking of the Task Force, nor the consensus of all speakers. Rather, it is an attempt to capture the diversity and common ground of the comments made by the hearing participants.

Summary

1.   What should law schools be teaching (or teaching better or more of) to improve their graduates for practice?

It was generally agreed by those testifying that law schools should be teaching about the knowledge, skills and values of law practice. There was also a consensus that law schools should be focusing on the basics. That is, they should provide an introduction or orientation to law practice. There was a fairly long list of suggestions about what law schools should be teaching better or more of including:

> **Practical Skills**, such as negotiation; settlement techniques; discovery techniques; drafting of documents and pleadings; non-academic prose; reaching a conclusion; statutory construction; traditional research skills; finding the issues in a fact situation and what to do about them; developing the theory of the case; advocacy on behalf of a client; dry, technical analysis; and proofreading and detail oriented skills;

> **People Skills** such as communication, social skills, counseling clients, working through emotional and psychological issues, handling opposing counsel, working with colleagues, and dealing with the overlap of business and legal advice;

> **Economic and Management Issues**, such as spending the

appropriate amount of time on a matter; "sticker shock" (i.e., high bills and how to negotiate them); time sheets; billing and collection; time, case and office management; delegation; and supervision;

Life Style Issues, such as what it is really like in a particular practice setting, career choices and "trade offs," balancing work and professional life and billable hours; and

Professionalism, Ethics and Other Value Issues, such as the minimization of the effects of bias, ignorance, fear and the promotion of tolerance, fairness and justice.

There was some agreement that law schools should be increasing their emphasis on teaching non-litigation skills, interpersonal skills, writing skills; professional responsibility; law practice techniques; case management, and knowledge about court systems, procedures and administrative practices. A number of speakers in each group recommended providing more opportunities for students to obtain experience through student practice, observation and role play. Providing a practical component to law school courses was suggested as a method of integrating theory with practice.

There were as many suggestions about increases or augmentations in curricula as there were participants.

Although not asked directly, some participants volunteered ideas about what law schools should be doing less of. Some speakers commented that law schools spend too much time reviewing substantive law, but they noted that it is difficult to avoid doing so given the current emphasis of the bar exams. Other speakers believed the law schools should be less focused on litigation skills, although some went on to comment that they did not think litigation skills are being taught effectively.

2. How should additional training be accomplished?

A common recommendation was to provide progressive, integrated courses or programs which begin in the first year of law school and continue through graduation and into (or throughout) law practice. These additional training programs should involve academics, bar examiners, practitioners and judges.

Speakers stated that law schools should set clear objectives, and tailor their curriculums, to prepare their students for their first law practice jobs. Specialty tracks were mentioned by some as a way to accomplish this. Overall, the program should emphasize progression and integration. Three law schools were mentioned as potential models: Montana, Northeastern and CUNY-Queens. [One should note that D.C. Law School and Mercer have also implemented creative curriculum proposals.]

Quite a few speakers urged the law schools to use more practitioners and to use them more effectively. They want law schools to integrate practitioners into their courses, including in-house clinics and field placement clinics. Some speakers saw the use of practitioners as being a hopeless endeavor. And even the clinical law professors conceded that it was too optimistic to believe that sufficient resources could be obtained to enable every student to participate in a good in-house clinical experience.

There was some mention that law schools should hire faculty with practice backgrounds and interests or to improve the quality of law faculty in other ways. Others disagreed, pointing out that hiring people with an emphasis on their practice backgrounds would be inconsistent with the basic mission of research institutions. Some speakers urged that the case study method of instruction should be dropped and law schools should move toward more problem-solving oriented courses. A large number of speakers urged the law schools to provide more experiential learning opportunities such as in-house and field placement clinics and simulation courses. A few encouraged the adoption of a "teaching law office" for legal education similar to the medical model of teaching hospitals.

One speaker stated that the problems with law schools would take care of themselves if law schools provided an appropriate set of values. He believes these would control the students' future conduct as lawyers. Another pointed out that if the law schools would teach students to be self-educators, they would be effectively training lawyers for the practice of law ten to thirty years from graduation.

Possibly because of the format and context of this question, most respondents addressed the issue of additional training within the law schools. However, a number of participants did focus on education and training outside the law school setting, whether after graduation or before, post or pre-admission to the Bar.

For example, part-time clerking during the school year was praised by some speakers and condemned by other speakers. Those who condemned it pointed out that clerkships often provide little training and sometimes provide a skewed view of law practice. Summer clerking positions were somewhat less condemned because they did not interfere with the school year. However, the educational value and consistency of the experience was questioned.

Many of the same people who recommended the use of more practitioners in the law schools also encouraged finding ways to make clerking jobs more valuable as an educational experience, for example, by monitoring or guidance by the law schools. Other speakers, however, warned the Task Force about the dangers of viewing clerking jobs as substitutes for well run clinical courses.

The bar admissions process was also viewed as having a role in accompanying additional training. Not many people spoke to this issue, but many of those who did opined that the present system of bar admissions does more harm than good. It encourages the law school to load up with broad, substantive law courses. They would urge that the bar exam and the bar admissions process be revamped, primarily to become more supportive of law school practice orientation. Some speakers suggested that the resources currently devoted to bar review courses would be better used either by law schools or for an intensive skills training course between law school and bar admission.

There was a significant dispute over the role of skills training requirements and performance testing for bar admission. However, those who questioned the value of performance testing seemed to do so primarily on a belief that it could not be done well. Others suggested that even if it can be done well, it would be better to postpone performance testing until sometime after bar admission. One speaker suggested using skills based criteria in hiring decisions.

There were a number of suggestions for additional training following admission to the bar. Most frequently cited of course were bridge-the-gap programs and CLE programs (particularly if they focus on skills and specialty practice training.) Others suggested that competency testing and evaluation should continue throughout law practice. Some recommended mandatory CLE; others argued that it was not a solution to the problem.

One of the most frequently spoken words in response to this question was that of "mentor." Many speakers said they believed that finding a good mentor was the best way to obtain the additional training one needs to become a good lawyer. Some speakers urged that mentoring programs should be mandatory, formal and operated by bar associations. A few pointed out that many graduates, particularly at larger law firms received adequate supervision in their early years. Others stated that small firms cannot afford in-house training. Some commented, in general, that the bar had abdicated its responsibility to train new lawyers.

3.   What obstacles hinder a law school's ability to improve the preparation of its graduates for the practice of law?

The primary obstacles mentioned to innovations in this area were cost and the high student-faculty ratios. Staffing was also found to be a problem. Law faculties lack interest and the qualifications to do more practice-oriented instruction, claimed many speakers. In addition, these speakers observed that practitioner-adjuncts when utilized by law schools lack the time and the priorities and, perhaps, the teaching skills needed to do a good job.

Speakers also noted that law faculties are resistant to change. Some stated that many of the traditional members of law school faculties lack appreciation of the values of clinical education and professional skills instruction. As a result, they say they are either apathetic or hostile toward it.

Speakers pointed out another problem: law school incentives now reward and encourage scholarship while detracting from teaching. One speaker believes it would take a paradigm shift to accomplish meaningful reform and does not believe that "tinkering" will do enough.

A major problem discussed is that there is disagreement on the issue of what a modern law school should be trying to accomplish. Even with respect to specifically stated goals, there is insufficient knowledge about the most effective ways to accomplish them. The speakers contend that there are unresolved issues about content, methodology, staffing, sequencing, coordination and progression.

Last, participants pointed to the current three year curriculum as being filled with courses involving legal analysis and surveying substantive law. Although driven in large part by student demand which is created by the bar exam requirements, those substantive courses nonetheless prevent law schools from developing more practice-oriented courses.

4.   What recommendations should the Task Force make in order to improve legal education for competent practice?

Speakers recommended that the Task Force help educate law schools about setting goals, why it is important to set goals, how to do it, what the goals should be, and where to focus. There is a need to develop a consensus about common and individual goals among law schools and about shared and independent goals between law schools and the profession.

Others suggested that the Task Force should:

- Describe model courses and programs and promote experimentation and model pilot projects;
- Encourage a lower student-faculty ratio (in the range of 10 to 1);
- Support the development of more experiential programs;
- Recommend that state bars disseminate pre-law curriculum pamphlets;
- Help make the case for clinical legal education;
- Help develop a strategy for moving toward a live client clinical experience for all students;
- Describe how to train and use adjuncts;
- Encourage more problem supplements to text books;
- Recommend that each school decide for itself what training to provide, but urge adherence to certain principles;
- Sponsor conferences and research projects;
- Help identify sources of new funding for law schools;
- Encourage the ABA to provide financial support;
- Encourage an incentive system that rewards innovative curriculum work and teaching; and
- Assess which core elements and values can be addressed effectively in law schools, and which are the product of experience, application and responsibility and are better addressed after graduation.

A number of speakers suggested modifications to the American Bar Association's Standards for Approval of Law Schools. One participant suggested requiring schools to adopt the recommendations listed in the Cramton report. Others said law schools ought to encourage improved self-study programs and be more critical of shortcomings.

The Task Force, it was recommended, should continue to encourage increased cooperation between the profession and law schools. A suggestion was made that a separate entity should be created to pull together the bench, the bar and the academy to address these issues.

Annex A to Report on Hearings and Conferences
List of Participants at the Hearings
and Written Submissions

This is a list of the people who made appearances at one of the hearings or who submitted written comments to the Task Force.

1. *February 9, 1990, Los Angeles (Young Lawyers Division)*

Appearances

*Pamela Barker, Milwaukee, Wisconsin
*Hillarie Bass, Miami, Florida
*Ira Bodenstein, Chicago, Illinois
*William Crenshaw, Miami, Florida
*David Delpierre, Norfolk, Virginia
*Patricia Garcia, New Orleans, Louisiana
*Robert Goepel, Racine, Wisconsin
*Marcia Gonzales, Los Angeles, California
*Christopher Griffin, Tampa, Florida
Carroll Robinson, Houston, Texas
*Marc Scheineson, Washington, D.C.
John Tarpley, Tennessee

2. *June 7, 1990, Ann Arbor, Michigan (Clinical Teachers)*

Appearances

Mark Heyrman, Clinical Professor, Chicago
*Robert Dinerstein, Professor, American
*David Barnhizer, Professor, Cleveland State
Graham Strong, Visiting Professor, UCLA
Alan Kirtley, Professor, Washington
Peter Hoffman, Professor, Nebraska
Suellen Scarnecchia, Professor, Michigan

In addition, a round table discussion was conducted with approximately twenty-five clinical teachers.

Written Submissions

Lisle Baker, Professor, Suffolk
Frank Bloch, Professor, Vanderbilt
Stacy Caplow, Professor, Brooklyn
John Elson, Professor, Northwestern
Marty Guggenheim, Professor, NYU
Jack Sammons, Professor, Mercer

3. **August 5, 1991, Chicago, Illinois (ABA Representatives)**

Appearances

*Luther Avery, San Francisco, California
Richard Bartlett, Glen Falls, New York
*Gail McKnight Beckman, Professor, Georgia State
Frank Kaufman, Judge, Baltimore, Maryland
*Leary Davis, Professor, Campbell
*William Ide, Atlanta, Georgia
William Lawless, Reno, Nevada
Alice O'Donnell, Washington, D.C.
Leonard Ring, Chicago, Illinois
David Robinson, Pasadena, California
*James St. Clair Huntington, West Virginia
*Antone Singsen, III, Professor, Harvard
*Carroll Stevens, Associate Dean, Yale
*Jamienne Studley, Executive Director, NALP, Washington, D.C.
*Robert O. Sullivan, President, NALP, Washington, D.C.
*Shepard Tate, Memphis, Tennessee
Francis Zemans, Chicago, Illinois

Written Submissions

Paul Brest, Dean, Stanford
M. Carr Ferguson, New York, New York
Geoffrey Hazard, Professor, Yale
Sharon Funcheon Murphy, Indianapolis, Indiana
James Neuhard, Detroit, Michigan
Jeffrey Pennell, Professor, Emory
Don Samuelson, former Dean, Chicago
Larry Sipes, Williamsburg, Virginia
William Weston, Baltimore, Maryland
Charles Wolfram, Professor, Cornell

4. **January 4, 1991, Washington, D.C. (Law School Representatives)**

Appearances

Thomas A. Arthur, Associate Dean, Emory
Sylvia Bacon, Judge, Washington, D.C.
Michael P. Cox, Dean, Thomas M. Cooley Law School
Victor M. Goode, Associate Dean, CUNY at Queens College
Harry J. Haynesworth, IV, Dean, Southern Illinois University
*Howard I. Kalodner, Dean, Western New England College
Homer LaRue, Professor, University of Maryland

Norman Lefstein, Dean, Indiana University—Indianapolis
*Michael P. Malloy, Professor, Fordham University
James E. Moliterno, Professor, College of William and Mary
Arthur W. Murphy, Vice Dean, Columbia University
Anne-Marie Rhodes, Professor, Loyola University—Chicago
Gail Richmond, Associate Dean, Nova University
Katherine Vaughns, Professor, University of Maryland

Written Submissions

Steven C. Bahls, Professor, University of Montana
Robert Batey, Professor and former Associate Dean, Stetson
    University
Ralph Cagle, Professor, Wisconsin
David Dittfurth, Associate Dean, St. Mary's University
H. Reese Hansen, Dean, Brigham Young University
John Kramer, Dean, Tulane
Richard Morgan, Dean, Arizona State
Steven R. Smith, Dean, Cleveland State University
Gerald F. Uelman, Dean, Santa Clara University

*denotes oral testimony was supplemented by written submissions

Annex B to Report on Hearings and Conferences
Questions Presented to Hearing Participants

1. In your opinion, are newly admitted lawyers prepared to practice law without supervision?
2. What should law schools be teaching (or teaching better or more of) to improve their graduates for practice?
3. What obstacles hinder your school's ability to improve the preparation of its graduates for the practice of law?
4. If you believe additional training is desirable, specifically how would you suggest this be accomplished?
5. Do you favor a skills training requirement and/or performance testing for bar admission? If so, specifically what would you recommend?
6. What recommendations should the Task Force make in order to improve legal education for competent practice?

Appendix D

Survey on Professional Skills Instruction[*]
April 1990

SEND COMPLETED SURVEY TO:
Consultant's Office
American Bar Association
Indiana University School of Law
735 West New York Street, Suite 002
Indianapolis, IN 46202

The survey is in three parts.

Part I involves identifying and describing certain aspects of your program. In Part I, please fill out a sheet for each course identified, using additional sheets if necessary. (Be sure to identify each course with the letter and number which you will specially assign for this survey.)

Part II seeks your responses to a few additional questions.

Part III is designed to provide a snapshot of the reach and depth of professional skills instruction, using the 1990 graduating class as the survey sample. This will give us an important data base which the Task Force can then use to describe the 1989-90 state of professional skills instruction in ABA approved law schools.

Part I—Courses

(Please complete Part I by June 30, 1990.)

Completion of this part should be addressed by a person thoroughly familiar with the entire academic program, *e.g.*, an Associate Dean for Academic Affairs. That person should identify the courses to be reported in this survey and send a copy of the two page information form to each faculty member who teaches a course on the list. A separate form should be filled out for each course the faculty member teaches which is to be reported in this survey.

Be sure to make sufficient photocopies of the two page survey form, so that you will have one for each course to be reported.

If the courses you are reporting have changed in this period, please report the current content, but note on the form that the course has changed from when members of the class of 1990 may have taken

---

[*]Please address questions concerning how to answer to Dean James White (317-274-8071) or Dean Susan Prager (213-825-8202).

the class. Please note only significant changes. If there were courses taught during the previous two years which are not being taught this year but were available to members of the 1990 graduating class, please fill out the two page sheet for that course, indicating on the sheet that the course has not been offered in 89-90. If not offered in 89-90, indicate whether you plan to offer the course again.

On the attached sheets please provide the requested information about your introduction to lawyering and advanced lawyering courses, including all professional skills courses offered during 1989-90. List only programs offered for unit credit; *do not* list any course in more than one category. The category "other" should be used for all other courses you believe should be included in the survey.

Please include all courses which fit within the following categories:

A.   First year "introduction to lawyering."
B.   First year research, writing, or drafting.
C.   Advanced research, writing, or drafting, (*e.g.*, business planning). (Do not include supervised independent research, traditional seminars, or law review work).
D.   Interviewing and/or counselling.
E.   Negotiation and/or alternative dispute resolution.
F.   Trial practice/trial advocacy.
G.   Pretrial litigation practice.
H.   Appellate advocacy, including moot court.
I.   Lawyering courses set in specific substantive contexts with non-litigation focus (*e.g.*, business planning*).
J.   Combination of two or more topics listed in D, E, F, G, H or I (e.g., "interviewing, counselling and negotiation" or "trial and appellate practice" or "general lawyering skills").
K.   Externships/internships. (If possible, please list judicial as K/J, non-judicial as K/N. If it is not possible to break out judicial from non-judicial, list all internships under K/JN.)
L.   Clinics.
M.   Other

Within each category, assign each course a number and place the letter and number on the sheet in the space provided. If you have one "introduction to lawyering" course in the first year, it would be identified in Part II as Al; the course listed third in category H would be H3. Example:

Course Title	*Survey Code*
Trial Advocacy	F1

---

*Some schools may choose to list this course under C and some under I depending on the nature of the course. Do *not* list any course under both.

Course Information Form (page one of two)

School #   Course Title _____
                            [Assign a letter and number
                            corresponding to the list in Part I]
                            Survey Code assigned for this
                            survey _____

Course Description:

Principal Competencies
Developed in Course:

Instruction Methods:

Course Information Form (page two of two)

Sections Offered in 1989-90 or in Most Recent Years in
Which Course was Taught

School #

| | Number of Teachers full-time | | | | | | Were any Students Closed Out |
	full-time (permanent or visiting)	part time (not permanent)	Number of Students Enrolled	Student/ Faculty Ratio	Credit Awarded	Enrollment Limit	(yes/no) (unknown)
Section 1							
Section 2							
Section 3							
Section 4							
Section 5							
Section 6							
Section 7							
Total							
Averages							

---

*(For this page, section means any single offering of the course during the year. Thus if the sheet reports the course on negotiation, and you offered 1 negotiation class in the fall and 2 in the spring, you would report 3 sections on this sheet even though the course in the fall was not "sectioned".)

Part II—Additional Questions Relating to Professional Skills Instruction

SEND COMPLETED SURVEY TO:
Consultant's Office
American Bar Association
Indiana University School of Law
735 West New York Street, Suite 002
Indianapolis, IN 46202

(Please complete Part II by June 30, 1990.)

A. If you have programs or sequences which combine two or more professional skills courses, please describe them.

B. If you have begun integrating professional skills instruction into traditional courses, indicate the courses and briefly describe the nature of the integration of professional skills instruction in them. Estimate the number of students who take the course each year.

C. If you think any of your professional skills courses or programs should be highlighted by the Task Force as models, please list them below and describe their special features. You may also want to attach further information about these courses such as the syllabus.

D. If your school has recently evaluated its efforts to provide professional skills instruction, please attach a copy of those portions of any reports which are not confidential. (If you are currently engaged in an evaluation of the professional skills curriculum or expect to be in the near future, please indicate the anticipated completion date: _____.)

E. What are the obstacles which hinder your school's ability to improve the preparation of your graduates for the practice of law?

Part III—Snapshot of 1990 Class

(Please complete Part III by August 1, 1990.)

In Part I you have identified your professional skills courses and given them a letter and number (the survey code). To complete Part III:

1) Compile a summary list of the courses covered in the Part I charts. Example:

Course Name	Code Assigned for this Survey
Legal Research (1st Year)	B1
Trial Advocacy	F1
Negotiation	E1
Judicial Externship	K/J1

(This becomes the tool a staff person can use during the required records search.)

2) Assign each student in the 1990 graduating class a number. (We suggest that mechanically you do steps 2 & 3 together to save time.) Please include Winter 1989 and Spring 1990 grads. Please be certain to retain your school's record of student names and numbers. Forward a copy of the list of students and their assigned numbers to your placement director to be used in connection with Question III 4.

3) Search the transcript or record for each student in the 1990 class to determine which of the courses identified in Part I were taken by the particular student and for what number of units. Record after the student number the course code (letter and number) with the number of units in parenthesis after the survey course code. Example:

Student #	Courses Taken & Units Awarded for Each Course
1	A1(5), B1(4), F1(8)
2	B1(4)

DETACH THIS PAGE AND ROUTE IT TO YOUR PLACEMENT DIRECTOR

4) Please review your employment data for the 1990 class (including winter and spring graduates) and correlate that data with respect to the employment categories using your school's record of student names and numbers used in this survey. These names and numbers are to be supplied to you by your records staff.* Using the same number to identify the student, indicate the type of employment which each student has chosen.

For example, if John Arena is number 1 on the list used by your records office and he has accepted a position in a five person private law firm and Sally Barker is number 2 on the list and has accepted a judicial clerkship, record the information using the appropriate NALP Survey categories as:

Student #	Type of Employment
1	Very Small Firm (2-10)
2	Judicial Clerkship

If the student is known to you to be unemployed, indicate "unemployed/seeking work" or "unemployed/not seeking work." If the student's status is not known, you indicate "unknown."

We would like to have your response as soon as feasible and no later than *January 31, 1991*. Mail this correlated list and any internal compilation of the employment data which is not confidential to:

Consultant's Office
American Bar Association
Indiana University School of Law
735 West New York Street, Suite 002
Indianapolis, IN 46202

---

*If the numbers are not forwarded to you, you should ask your records office for the names and numbers used to complete Part III 1-3 of this survey.

Appendix E

Practical Skills Training in Commonwealth Jurisdictions

Over the past thirty-five years, various Commonwealth jurisdictions have developed programs for instructing new lawyers in
professional skills and values. These programs are generally intended
to supplement both the new lawyers' formal legal education and the
practical learning they receive through articling. Although these
programs develop out of a tradition of legal practice somewhat
different from our own, they are nevertheless designed to accomplish an educational function comparable to that of so-called "bridge-
the-gap" programs in the United States.

However, the Commonwealth programs are perceived to be far
more effective than our existing bridge-the-gap programs. They may
therefore provide useful models for the development of programs in
this country to instruct new lawyers in lawyering skills and values.
With that possibility in mind, this Appendix briefly describes the
following six Commonwealth programs:

- *Ontario*: Started in 1957 by the Law Society of Upper Canada,
  the Bar Admission Course ("BAC") at Osgoode Hall in Ontario
  is the oldest of the skills training programs.[1]
- *Quebec*: The civil law jurisdiction of Quebec[2] instituted the
  Professional Training Program ("PTP") in 1974, as a manda-
  tory part of new lawyers' training.[3]
- *British Columbia*: The British Columbia Professional Legal
  Training Course ("PLTC"), another mandatory program, was
  started in 1981.[4]
- *New South Wales*: A practical training program has been in

---

1. LAW SOCIETY OF UPPER CANADA, 33RD BAR ADMISSION COURSE STUDENT HANDBOOK,
Osgoode Hall, Toronto, 1990 at § 1-4 [hereafter "BAC HANDBOOK"]. The original program
existed in substantially the same form for almost thirty years, consisting of a twelve-
month articling period, followed by six months of practical instruction. *Id.* The BAC
format was revised in 1990, and the new program began with the 1991 administration.
Id.
2. *See, e.g.*, MARTIN FRANKLIN & DAVID FRANKLIN, INTRODUCTION TO QUEBEC LAW
(1984). Quebec is the only one of the jurisdictions examined in this Section that does
not share with the United States a heritage of English common law. The Province of
Quebec is a civil law jurisdiction. *Id.* at 3-9.
3. Clement Fortin, *Preparing for the Practice of Law in Quebec*, J. PROF. L. EDUC.,
Dec. 1985, at 101. In 1968, the Bar Association of the Province of Quebec assumed
responsibility for the practical training of new lawyers and established a Professional
Training School, which is run by the Professional Training Committee. *Id.* The Professional Training Program was revised in the mid-1980s. *Id.*
4. Neil Gold, *The British Columbia Professional Legal Training Course: Training
Towards Competence*, J. PROF. L. EDUC., Dec. 1983, at 1.

place at the College of Law in Sydney, New South Wales, since 1973 (the "NSW program").[5]

- *Victoria*: The Leo Cussen Institute in Melbourne, Victoria, offers the Practical Training Course, a non-mandatory practical skills program, as an alternative to articling (the "Leo Cussen program").[6]

- *Hong Kong*: In Hong Kong, the Postgraduate Certificate in Laws ("PCLL"), a professional training program,[7] was made a mandatory part of the curriculum at the City Polytechnique in 1991.[8]

Topics covered. The Commonwealth programs aim to prepare prospective lawyers for the practice of law through a combination of theoretical and practical skills training.[9] These programs teach skills training with a "learning by doing" emphasis. Most of the programs focus on a number of skills needed by new lawyers, and the programs approach their acquisition in a transactional context.

The Quebec PTP is aimed at developing six skills: legal research, drafting legal documents, negotiation, acting as counsel, communicating with clients, and managing a law office.[10] These skills are developed within the context of various legal transactions. For example, the student develops negotiation skills in the context of matrimonial litigation and a commercial transaction.[11]

Similar in intent, the Hong Kong PCLL comprises three sections: (1) Business and Personal Planning, (2) Dispute Settlement, and (3) Practice Management.[12] In addition to teaching some substantive law,

---

5. Les Handler, *The Practical Legal Training Course at the College of Law, Sydney, New South Wales*, J. PROF. L. EDUC., July 1983, at 9-10. The majority of the New South Wales program participants opt for the six-month practice course.

6. Margot Costanzo, *Leo Cussen Institute for Continuing Legal Education—Melbourne, Victoria. The Practical Training Course: Placing It in the Victorian Profession*, J. PROF. L. EDUC., July 1983, at 33.

7. 1 PROFESSIONAL LEGAL EDUCATION FOR TOMORROW'S LAWYERS. PROPOSAL FOR THE POSTGRADUATE CERTIFICATE IN LAWS. COURSE STRUCTURE AND STAFF DETAILS (Jan. 25, 1991) [hereafter "HONG KONG PROPOSAL"]. This program was designed for students who already had an LL.B. degree, to prepare them to be trainee solicitors and pupil barristers during their articling period. *Id.*

8. *Id.* at 2.

9. Fortin, *supra* note 3, at 104 (*quoting* Professional Training Committee statement of principles issued in 1984).

10. *Id.* at 105.

11. *Id.*

12. HONG KONG PROPOSAL, *supra* note 7, at 73-74. The largest of the three segments, Business and Personal Planning, covers business law and practice, conveyancing and probate, and revenue law. *Id.* The Dispute Settlement area spans civil and criminal procedure, family and public law. *Id.* Practice Management includes accounts, professional ethics, office systems and computer technologies, and personal management systems. *Id.*

the program focuses on five areas: research skills, interpersonal skills, problem-solving ability, initiative and judgment, and language skills.[13]

The Ontario BAC attempts to develop a minimum level of lawyer competency to ensure that new lawyers "are equipped with the skills, knowledge, and sense of professional responsibility and purpose" sufficient to "assure not only appropriate service of their clients' interests but also a steady constructive growth of their own professional character and lawyering capacity."[14] The seminars are split into mandatory morning sessions and optional afternoon sessions. The morning classes, which are devoted primarily to skills training and "learning by doing," cover topics such as professional responsibility and practice management, interviewing and client counselling, legal research, legal writing and drafting, negotiation, and basic advocacy.[15] The afternoon sessions, designed to equip the student to manage the articling period successfully, cover topics such as stress management, time management, and various court appearances and include demonstrations on aspects of practice such as French language motions, discovery, and real estate closings.[16]

The British Columbia Professional Legal Training Course[17] combines intensive skills training with procedural and substantive law, practice methods, and instruction on professional responsibility.[18] The student develops lawyering skills in the context of nine transactions: a real estate conveyance, an incorporation, a lien action, negotiation of a personal injury case, a criminal trial, drawing a will, drawing a separation agreement, buying and selling a business, and conducting a foreclosure proceeding.[19] For example, interviewing and counselling are taught via transactions in divorce, incorporation, and conveyancing, whereas legal research is taught through a personal injury action.

---

13. *Id.* at 10. The program is intended to enable the students "to learn from experience and instruction so that they may adapt to the professional and social responsibilities they will be expected or required to undertake." *Id.* at 19.

14. James M. Spence, Q.C., *The Teaching Term of the Ontario Bar Admission Course: A Critical Assessment and Proposal for Change*, J. Prof. L. Educ., Dec. 1988, 163, 164 (defining competency as a combination of knowledge, skills, and attitudes); *see also* Gold, *supra* note 4, at 1-5.

15. BAC Handbook, *supra* note 1, at 37-38.

16. *Id.*

17. *See* Gold, *supra* note 4, at 3. The British Columbia program, like the Ontario program, aims to develop new lawyer competency by "promot[ing] the acquisition of sufficient knowledge, skill and appropriate attitudes for competent practice." *Id.*

18. *See* Ruth Windeler, *Administration of a Professional Legal Training Course: The British Columbia Professional Legal Training Course*, J. Prof. L. Educ., June 1986, at 69. The Law Society of British Columbia created the program in 1981. David A. Cruickshank, *The Professional Legal Training Course in British Columbia, Canada*, J. Prof. L. Educ., Dec. 1985, at 111. The program was revised in 1983. *Id.*

19. Cruickshank, *supra* note 18, at 122.

At the Leo Cussen Institute, in Melbourne, Victoria, as in other Commonwealth courses, the students learn legal skills within a specific legal context.[20] They receive instruction in many different topics, ranging from civil and criminal procedure to conveyancing and family law to consumer and credit law, insolvency, trusts, and partnerships, among others.

The NSW course is taught in two sections called practice modules, one dealing with litigation and the other dealing with property and commercial practice.[21] The NSW program integrates legal skills into the program's substantive and procedural sections.[22] Skills taught throughout the course in the two major practice modules include: legal practice, accounts, professional responsibility, office management, computer skills, interviewing, advising, research, drafting, and negotiation.[23]

Program length. All of the Commonwealth practical skills programs are considerably longer than their American counterparts. Programs range from the British Columbia PLTC's ten weeks to seven months or more.[24] The Ontario BAC program is a fifteen-month "sandwich" program. It is divided into three phases: Phase One, a month-long skills training session; Phase Two, the eleven-month articling term; and Phase Three, a three-month teaching term.[25] The NSW program is offered both on a part-time basis and on a full-time basis. The full-time program is a six-month (twenty-three-week) program.[26] The part-time program spans eighteen months (sixty-six weeks).[27]

Program format. Unlike most of their American counterparts, the Commonwealth programs emphasize "learning by doing." In addition to being mandatory, most of the Commonwealth programs employ some sort of assessment system. The Quebec PTP emphasizes practical exercises, but also includes role playing, supervised

---

20. Costanzo, *supra* note 6, at 33, 34-35.
21. Audrey Blunden & Les Handler, *A New Course at the New South Wales College of Law: The Introduction of the Full Time Course Strategy Plan,* J. Prof. L. Educ., June 1987, 42, 45-49.
22. *Id.* at 42-45.
23. *Id.* at 49.
24. The Hong Kong PCLL program spans thirty weeks over three semesters. The Quebec PTP program is a seven-month program, and the Melbourne Leo Cussen program lasts six months.
25. BAC Handbook, *supra* note 1, at § 3-1. In Phase Three, the students receive further instruction in general principles in a broad range of substantive and procedural subjects, while further honing their skills and continuing to develop their sense of professional responsibility. *Id.* at 6. Students are required to complete a transaction in each practice area. They are assigned to small seminar groups, because active participation is an important element in the learning process. *Id.*
26. Handler, *supra* note 5, at 9-10.
27. *Id.*

projects, workshops, and simulations.[28] Written examinations are the primary means of assessing student absorption of the substantive information and skills acquisition.

The Hong Kong PCLL uses lectures, individual and group projects, consultations, field trips, skills seminars, simulations, role playing, work on "live" case files, mentor meetings, and "homebase" meetings (informal, small group debriefing sessions).[29] The students are assessed according to examination performance and course work.[30] Skills instruction is interwoven into all three segments of the PCLL; the program's unifying theme is "problem solving."[31] Some skills appear more than once throughout the PCLL, given the different contexts of the segments.

The skills portion of the Ontario BAC teaches a skill in several steps. First, the skill is broken down to its essential elements and is demonstrated for the students. Second, the students practice it and are given feedback on their work, and third, the students practice it again, incorporating the comments they received.[32] In the first phase of the course, students are assessed with respect to their level of competency.[33] They are graded based on class participation, the development of their project during the course, and their successful completion of assignments. Failure is based on commission of a serious academic offence (*e.g.*, plagiarism), non-attendance, or non-participation.[34] In the third section of the course, student assessments are also made via formal examinations.[35] Students can be examined on civil procedure, business law, criminal procedure, family law, real estate, and public law.[36]

The British Columbia PLTC relies on a certain amount of in-office training via articles to supplement the course.[37] Lecturing is limited to between one and three hours any one day, with "active learning,

---

28. Fortin, *supra* note 3, at 105-06.
29. Hong Kong Proposal, *supra* note 7, at 86-92. Most of the instruction time (*e.g.*, 60% of the business and personal planning segment) is spent on group and individual supervised practice work; the remaining 40% is divided between lectures, skills seminars, observation, casework, and other activities. *Id.* at 72-74.
30. *Id.*
31. *Id.* at 23, 76.
32. Spence, *supra* note 14, at 165.
33. *Id.* at 171.
34. BAC Handbook, *supra* note 1, at § 1-2 - § 1-3.
35. *Id.* at § 3-1.
36. *Id.*
37. Cruickshank, *supra* note 18, at 116-17. The student can take the program at the beginning, in the middle, or at the conclusion of his or her thirteen-month articling period. *Id.* A student will not be admitted to the PLTC without an articling position. *Id.* The PLTC is not an alternative method for admission to the bar for students who are unable to find articling positions. *Id.*

rather than passive information absorption . . . the hallmark of the teaching units."[38] Learning methods include role playing, simulations, demonstrations, problem exercises, and videotape feedback.[39] To complete the PLTC, a student must pass both skills assessments in writing, drafting, advocacy, interviewing, and counselling, and a two-hour short answer PLTC Examination covering reading in eight subjects, and obtain a satisfactory written appraisal on class and assignment performance from a PLTC instructor.[40] Assessment is conducted on an on-going basis throughout the course. Students do not sit for formal examinations.[41]

In the NSW program, skills are taught through group meetings, video viewings, or role playing.[42] The students learn by working through a series of "case studies," or "new matters," which are simulated files that the students work through, as would a new solicitor. They process the cases from the initial telephone call from the client, through to the final billing and closing the file. Other "learning by doing" exercises include advocacy and interviewing.[43]

In Melbourne, Victoria, the law student has the option of completing the Leo Cussen course[44] or completing a period of articles. In addition, each student is assessed as to progress of skills assimilation on an on-going basis by his or her instructors. The students are assessed based on both their work in simulated cases and on subjects on which they received formal instruction.[45]

Speakers. Several of the Commonwealth programs rely on volunteer practitioners to teach the material, as do most of the American programs. Some supplement the volunteer staff with professionals, train the volunteers, or utilize a wholly professional staff.

In the Quebec PTP, the course designers, instructors, and examiners are all practitioners, and there is no impetus to replace them

---

38. *Id.* at 118.

39. *Id.* at 119-21.

40. *Id.* The skills assessments are pass-fail decisions based on an evaluation of a student's videotaped performance. They are conducted in specific substantive areas (*e.g.*, advocacy in a foreclosure proceeding). *Id.* at 123. The students extensively evaluate the program, the instructors, the administrators, and their own assessments. *Id.* at 116.

41. Handler, *supra* note 5, at 13.

42. Blunden & Handler, *supra* note 21, at 52.

43. *Id.*; *see also* Handler, *supra* note 5, at 12.

44. Following the completion of the Leo Cussen course, the student must complete six months of restricted practice with a solicitor before embarking on a solo practice. Costanzo, *supra* note 6, at 33.

45. Costanzo, *supra* note 6, at 35. Students have conferences with the instructors to discuss the assessments. *Id.* If a minimum level of competency is not attained, remedial work is given. *Id.*

with a full-time teaching staff.[46] In the Melbourne, Victoria, Leo Cussen program, teaching methods include instruction from practicing attorneys, lectures from judges and practitioners billed as experts, use of videotapes, observation during court visits, exercises in advocacy, and current matters.[47] The Hong Kong PCLL employs a full-time academic staff as instructors and uses practitioners as guest lecturers and as mentors. The staff is trained in skills teaching.[48] In the Ontario BAC, the teachers are volunteer practitioners, with full-time faculty as support. The faculty are experienced in skills training and can aid the practitioners.[49] In the British Columbia program, the faculty is composed of seven full-time instructors with practical skills experience.[50] They are supplemented with guest lecturers.[51] At the NSW course, the instructors are drawn primarily from the faculty of the College of Law.[52] Guest instructors are recruited from the profession. The instructors are trained in skills training by the Legal Practice Section.[53]

Program materials. Unlike most American bridge-the-gap programs, lectures in the Hong Kong PCLL are not given on substantive law, although the students are provided with summaries of relevant substantive law for each section, to facilitate the completion of the practical exercises.[54] Like many of the American programs, the British Columbia PLTC gives practice manuals to the students.[55] In addition, the students are given the Law Society Acts and Rules, the Canadian Bar Association Code of Professional Conduct, and the Law Society Practice Checklist Manual.[56]

---

46. *See, e.g.*, Spence, *supra* note 14, at 175 (noting that Quebec used contract lawyers as instructors); Fortin, *supra* note 3, at 101 (discussing Quebec program designers). The instructors were offered courses to help them teach the revised, skills-oriented program. *Id.* at 108.
47. John Ginnane, Ainslie Lamb & Vin. Ryan, *The Teaching of Advocacy at the Leo Cussen Institute, Melbourne*, J. PROF. L. EDUC., June 1986, at 81.
48. HONG KONG PROPOSAL, *supra* note 7, at 121-22.
49. BAC HANDBOOK, *supra* note 1, at 10-16.
50. Cruickshank, *supra* note 18, at 118.
51. Windeler, *supra* note 18, at 72-73.
52. Blunden & Handler, *supra* note 21, at 48.
53. *Id.* at 52-54. There are plans for the instructors to specialize in either one of the two practice modules or the skills training. *Id.*
54. HONG KONG PROPOSAL, *supra* note 7, at 106.
55. Cruickshank, *supra* note 18, at 119. The binders contain an overview of law and procedure, short papers on specialty fields of practice, precedents of litigation documents and agreements, and relevant statutes. They cover twelve substantive areas of law and total over 3600 pages. *Id.*
56. Windeler, *supra* note 18, at 71.

Appendix F

A Mission Statement for
an American Institute for the
Practice of Law

To promote excellence in the practice of law, addressing the entire process by which lawyers acquire and refine the lawyering skills and professional values required for competent and responsible practice in a changing profession of increasing diversity:

(1) *To serve as a resource center and forum*
  - convening educational conferences bringing together legal scholars, educators and practicing lawyers to promote lawyers' professional development as an educational continuum, beginning in law school and extending throughout lawyers' professional lives;
  - stimulating continuing discussion and critical analysis of the lawyering skills and professional values that lawyers should seek to acquire for competent and responsible practice;
  - acting as a clearinghouse, available to law schools, the organized bar and regional, state and local providers of continuing legal education, for model curricula and instructional materials on professional development;
  - serving as a link between the law school community and providers of CLE at the local, state and national level on matters relating to professional development;

(2) *To foster research and development*
  - enhancing the profession's understanding of lawyering skills and professional values and how they are acquired;
  - developing methods and instruments for assessing and evaluating the acquisition of skills and values;
  - developing models and methodologies of instruction;
  - furthering knowledge about adult learning and the role of performance, experience and self-evaluation;
  - utilizing new technologies for information processing and communication;
  - exploring simulation and other learning methodology which includes the opportunity for feedback and reinforcement;

(3) *To develop and disseminate courses and programs of continuing legal education*
  - developing a plan and organizational structure together

413

with an effective strategy to promote continuing legal education throughout the profession and to keep abreast of the educational needs of lawyers in all settings of public and private practice;

- sponsoring and cosponsoring with others courses and programs of CLE;
- lending assistance, upon request, to sections and committees of the American Bar Association in providing courses and programs;
- publishing audio-visual materials, texts, handbooks, study outlines and other material for CLE;
- conducting the American Law Network (ALN) for CLE programming;
- sponsoring the American Institute for Law Training within the Office (AILTO);
- providing administrative support for the Association of Continuing Legal Education Administrators (ACLEA) and assisting in the coordination of CLE courses and programs to promote cooperation among CLE providers.